Education and Middle-Class Society in Imperial Austria

1848–1918

Education and Middle-Class Society in Imperial Austria

1848–1918

Gary B. Cohen

Purdue University Press
West Lafayette, Indiana

00 99 98 97 96 5 4 3 2 1

♾ The paper used in this book meets the minimum requirements of American National Standard for Information Sciences—Permanence of Paper for Printed Library Materials, ANSI Z39.48-1992.

Printed in the United States of America

Design by Anita Noble
Maps by J. Mahlke

Library of Congress Cataloging-in-Publication Data

Cohen, Gary B., 1948–

Education and middle-class society in imperial Austria, 1848–1918 / Gary B. Cohen.

p. cm.

Includes bibliographical references and index.

ISBN 1-55753-087-4 (cloth : alk. paper)

1. Middle class—Education—Austria—History—19th century.
2. Middle class—Education—Austria—History—20th century.
3. Education—Social aspects—Austria—History—19th century.
4. Education—Social aspects—Austria—History—20th century. I. Title.

LC4975.A9C65 1996

370'.9436'09034—dc 20 95-51646

CIP

The TransSlavic font used to print this work is available from Linguist's Software, Inc., PO Box 580, Edmonds, WA 98020-0580 tel (206) 775-1130.

for

CARL E. SCHORSKE

and

JAN HAVRÁNEK

teachers

CONTENTS

xi **FIGURES AND TABLES**

xiii **ACKNOWLEDGMENTS**

xv **A NOTE ON PLACE NAMES**

xvii **ABBREVIATIONS**

xviii **MAPS**

Crown Lands and Provinces of the Habsburg Monarchy *xviii* Principal Ethnic/National Groups in the Austrian Half of the Habsburg Monarchy *xx*

INTRODUCTION
Social Development and Austria's Modern Educated Elites

1

CHAPTER 1
Education and the Modernization of Austria in the Mid-nineteenth Century

11

Stagnation and Crisis, 1790–1848 *11* The Counterrevolution in Education *23* Political Modernization and the Consolidation of the Educational System *36*

CHAPTER 2
Opening the Gates

Expansion of the Educational Network

55

Institutional Development and the Growth of Secondary Education *63* The Expansion of Higher Education *75*

CHAPTER 3
Guarding the Gates

The Social Politics of Education after 1880

95

The Conservative Search for Social Balance *97* Deluge at the Turn of the Century *108* Debates over Secondary School Reform *119*

CHAPTER 4
The Changing Ethnic and Religious Recruitment of Students

127

The Early Modern Heritage *128* Measuring the Representation of the Major Ethnic and Religious Groups *134* The Major Ethnic and Religious Groups in Secondary Education *140* The Recruitment of University and Technical College Students *147* Expanding Access to Education and the Question of Social Privilege *168*

CHAPTER 5
The Limits of Opportunity

Students' Occupational and Class Origins

170

Secondary School Students *170* Students in Higher Education *175* Social Class, Group Culture, and the Demand for Advanced Education *194* Access to Advanced Education and the Limits of Social Change *202*

CHAPTER 6
The Social Experience of Students

The Many Paths of Academic Education

212

The Many Purposes of Academic Secondary Education *215* The Everyday Realities of Higher Education *224* Student Organizations and Social Bonds in Higher Education *233* Advanced Education and Nation-Building: The Case of the Czechs *240*

CONCLUSION
Education, Society, and the State in the Late Nineteenth Century

249

A
APPENDIX
Supplementary Tables

271

B
APPENDIX
Statistical Methods

293

301 **NOTES**

347 **SOURCES**

379 **INDEX**

FIGURES TABLES

Figures

62 1. Enrollments in Austrian Secondary Schools
62 2. Matriculated Students in Austrian Higher Education
181 3. Social Origins of Matriculated Vienna University Students
182 4. Social Origins of Matriculated University Students, Prague
182 5. Social Origins of Matriculated University Students, Vienna and Prague
191 6. Social Origins of University Students in Prussia and Vienna-Prague
191 7. Social Origins of Matriculated Students in the Vienna Technical College
192 8. Social Origins of Matriculated Technical College Students in Prague
193 9. Social Origins of Matriculated Technical College Students in Vienna and Prague

Tables

56 2/1. Enrollments in Austrian Secondary and Higher Education
57 2/2. Enrollments in Austrian Secondary and Higher Education Relative to Age Cohorts
59 2/3. Enrollments in Austrian and German Universities and Technical Colleges Relative to Population
65 2/4. Growth of Austrian Volksschulen Relative to Population
69 2/5. Numbers of Austrian Gymnasien and Realschulen Relative to Territory and Population
78 2/6. Austrian University and Technical College Enrollments by Province of Birth Relative to Population
141 4/1. Mother Tongue of All Students in Austrian Academic Secondary Schools
146 4/2. Religion of All Students in Austrian Academic Secondary Schools
148 4/3. Religion and Mother Tongue of Austrian University Students

149 4/4. Religion and Mother Tongue of Austrian Technical College Students
160 4/5. Distribution of Ethnic Groups by Faculties in All Austrian Universities
167 4/6. Distribution of Religious Groups by Faculties in All Austrian Universities
178 5/1. Frequency of Tuition Exemptions in Austrian Universities and Technical Colleges
180 5/2. Scheme of Occupational Stratification

Supplementary Tables
(Appendix A)

272 1. Enrollments in Austrian Secondary Schools
273 2. Matriculated Students in Austrian Universities and Technical Colleges
274 3. Mother Tongue of All Students in Austrian Academic Secondary Schools
276 4. Religion of All Students in Austrian Academic Secondary Schools
278 5. Religion and Mother Tongue of Austrian University Students
279 6. Religion and Mother Tongue of Austrian Technical College Students
280 7. Social Origins of Matriculated University Students in Vienna and Prague
281 8. Distribution by University Faculty in Vienna and Prague of Matriculated Students from Various Social Origins
286 9. Social Origins of Matriculated German Christian, Czech Christian, Jewish, and Women Students in the Vienna and Prague Universities
289 10. Occupational Stratification of the Austrian Population
290 11. Social Origins of Matriculated Technical College Students in Vienna and Prague
291 12. Social Origins of Matriculated German Christian, Czech Christian, and Jewish Students in the Vienna and Prague Technical Colleges

ACKNOWLEDGMENTS

The generous assistance of a number of institutions and individuals enabled me to complete this study. The American Council of Learned Societies, the American Philosophical Society, the Fulbright-Hays Program of the United States Department of Education, the International Research and Exchanges Board (IREX), the National Endowment for the Humanities, and the College of Arts and Sciences and Research Council of the University of Oklahoma, Norman Campus, supported research in Austria and the Czech Republic as well as analysis and writing at home. The Summer Research Laboratory in Slavic and East European Studies at the University of Illinois made possible two weeks of research in Champaign-Urbana. The staffs of the State Library, Prague; the Vienna University Library; the University of Oklahoma Libraries; the Population Research Center at the University of Texas, Austin; the General Administrative Archive of the Austrian State Archives; and the archives of the Charles University, the Czech Technical College (Prague), the Vienna University, and the Vienna Technical University responded to my research requests with patience and care. In the General Administrative Archive in Vienna, Dr. Lorenz Mikoletzky provided critical assistance in locating important ministerial documents.

Many friends and colleagues provided valued advice and support during the research and writing. In Prague, Miroslav Hroch, Jiří Kořalka, Robert Kvaček, and Otto Urban guided me to sources and offered diverse perspectives on the development of Czech and Austrian society during the late nineteenth century. In Vienna, Horst Haselsteiner, Waltraud Heindl, Richard Georg Plaschka, Gerald Stourzh, Arnold Suppan, and Peter Urbanitsch shared with me their deep knowledge of Austrian history and helped to find ways through some of the Austrian Republic's bureaucratic mazes. Dr. Helmut Engelbrecht in Krems an der Donau generously shared his knowledge of Austrian educational history and pointed me to valuable sources. In the early stages Péter Hanák in Budapest and Victor Karady in Paris offered important suggestions for framing the project.

It is hard to find adequate words to express my gratitude to the several families in Prague and Vienna who provided friendship and hospitality during my repeated stays in their cities. During a grim period of recent Czech history that is happily now past, Anna and the late Antonín Hybš and the late Jan Heřman and his family did their best to make my visits to Prague easier. In Vienna, Werner and Ruth Meron and Bernard and Kitty Snower made me part of their families.

A number of friends and colleagues on this side of the Atlantic contributed much to the latter stages of the project. Myron Gutmann and Konrad Jarausch provided advice on various methodological points, and Alan Nicewander and Joe Rodgers helped with statistical problems. Willard Blanton and Angelika Tietz undertook some of the tedious work of transcribing student registration records from microfilm. John Mahlke drew the maps that appear here. As the efforts required for the research and analysis of data grew to exceed my original expectations, István Deák, Konrad Jarausch, and Robert and Mary Jo Nye encouraged me to persevere. Mary Jo Nye generously took time from her own work to give the whole manuscript a close and thoughtful reading. James Albisetti and Daniel Snell also offered helpful suggestions for revising the manuscript.

In studying the history of modern Central Europe, I have been fortunate in having many gifted teachers. In the pursuit of analytic rigor, some present-day historians tend to underestimate the importance of a deeper insight into the circumstances and outlooks of historical actors for interpreting the past soundly and convincingly. The historian's work, though, is as much synthetic as it is analytic; and it requires a multilayered understanding of the people, events, and conditions in question. Though the two dedicatees of this book come from different personal backgrounds and distinct academic traditions, both have exemplified over long careers how important to historical interpretation is that deeper appreciation of the perspectives, thought, and experience of people in a particular age. It has been my privilege to be among the several generations of students of modern Central Europe who have learned from the precepts and models of Carl E. Schorske and Jan Havránek. I can only acknowledge here the debts that I owe to each of them and all the others who have helped me along the way. There is no way they can ever be adequately repaid.

A NOTE ON PLACE NAMES

Where there are commonly recognized English designations for places discussed here, such as Vienna, Prague, or Bohemia, they will be used. Otherwise, the place names that are currently recognized by the various states of Central and East-Central Europe will be employed so that readers can find these places in present-day atlases and other reference works. For readers more accustomed to the German or Hungarian place names that were used before 1918, those will be given in parentheses the first time a place is mentioned.

ABBREVIATIONS

AČVUT	Archiv českého vysokého učení technického (Archive of the Czech Technical College), Prague
AUK	Archiv Univerzity Karlovy (Archive of the Charles University), Prague
AVA Wien	Allgemeines Verwaltungsarchiv (General Administrative Archive, Austrian State Archives), Vienna
fl.	florin (Gulden; Austrian currency to 1892)
kr.	Krone (Austrian currency after 1892)
KUM	Ministerium für Kultus und Unterricht
MVB	*Ministerial-Verordnungsblatt*
RGB	*Reichsgesetzblatt*

Crown Lands and Provinces of the Habsburg Monarchy

RUSSIA
KRAKOW
L'VIV
GALICIA
CHERNIVTSI
BUKOVINA
BUDAPEST
HUNGARY
TRANSYLVANIA
ROMANIA
SERBIA
JEVO
GOVINA
0 50 100 200 MILES
0 50 100 200 300 KILOMETERS

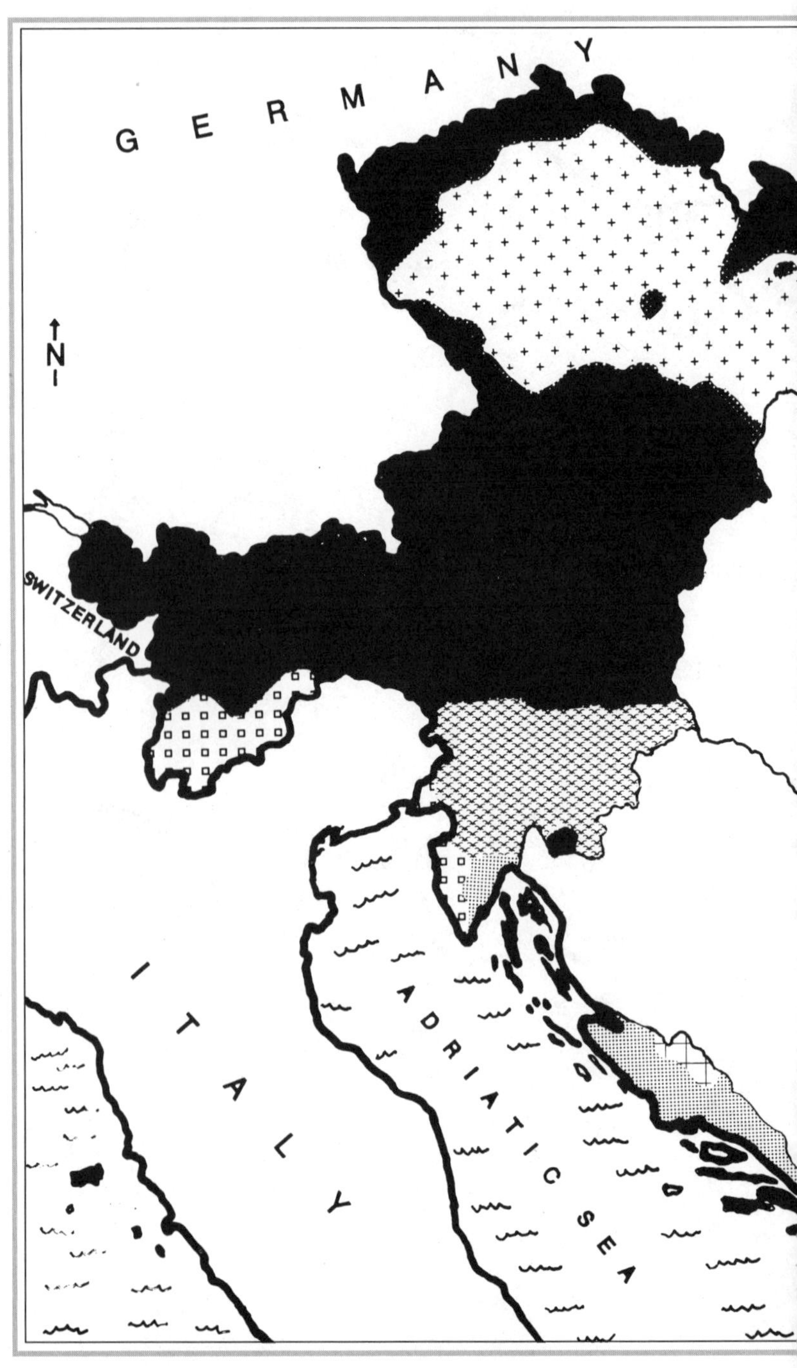

Principal Ethnic/National Groups in
the Austrian Half of the Habsburg Monarchy

Ethnic or national groups that constituted more than 50 percent of the population in each of the shaded regions

INTRODUCTION

Social Development and Austria's Modern Educated Elites

Standard historical accounts offer unflattering views of Austria's middle classes in the nineteenth century. In Austria, as in much of Germany, slower economic and political development than in Western Europe caused the modern middle classes to develop more gradually and achieve less social and political power before 1914. Even after the 1860s, when Austria finally inaugurated constitutional government and representative bodies, the historic forces of the Habsburg dynasty, its officialdom, the aristocracy, and the Catholic Church all retained great power. According to conventional views, the continuing role of the historic elites prevented the modern entrepreneurial and professional middle classes from achieving the political dominance that their Western European counterparts enjoyed by the late nineteenth century; and there has been considerable agreement in this across the interpretive spectrum from conservative scholars to liberals to Marxists.

Conventional historical accounts also argue that the Austrian middle classes' own ideological beliefs and political performance contributed to their political failure. Middle-class political movements in Austria proved at least as susceptible to division and competition among themselves as were their counterparts in Germany and Western Europe, and the widening fissures along ethnic and religious lines in nineteenth-century Austria caused even greater fragmentation of middle-class politics there than in Germany. Austria's middle-class liberals in the mid-nineteenth century proved even less willing to accept the risks of a genuine revolution against the imperial regime and more prone to compromise with the ruling dynasty, great landowners, and bureaucrats than were many of the liberal forces in the German states.[1] During the late 1860s and the 1870s, when Austria's German middle-class liberals won some share of power, they, like the liberals in Germany who allied with Bismarck, pursued policies of rapid commercial and economic development and the rationalization of state administration that alienated craft producers, small farmers, and many landed noblemen. The German liberals in Austria also indulged in anticlerical campaigns against the Catholic Church, which proved even more self-defeating in strongly Catholic Austria than was the *Kulturkampf* in

Germany. In the meantime, the German Liberal Party's preferment of German ethnic interests antagonized middle-class politicians among Austria's other ethnic groups, who might otherwise have made common cause with German liberals on behalf of constitutional rule and a free economy.

Austria's middle classes during the late nineteenth century were unable, in the standard view, to sweep away all the survivals of the preindustrial social hierarchy or to consolidate their own political and social order. The Austrian middle classes became divided politically into competing ethnic camps, and by the late 1880s or the 1890s the middle classes of each major ethnic group also faced revolts against their claims to leadership from industrial labor and the lower middle classes, social formations that matured with the economic development championed by middle-class liberals. Not surprisingly, given this historiographical framework, scholars in the last several decades have produced sophisticated studies of Austrian Social Democracy, the Christian Social movement, agrarian politics, and radical nationalist formations, while leaving liberal politics and ideology in relative neglect until quite recently.[2]

The conventional view of nineteenth-century Austrian politics rests, in fact, on assumptions similar to those of many historians of modern Germany about the triumph in Western Europe of liberal, parliamentary government and its middle-class champions and the failure of all this in Central Europe. Unfortunately, historians of imperial Austria have generally been more reticent about questioning their fundamental assumptions than have recent students of modern German history or, indeed, many specialists on the Austrian Republic. For example, few scholars other than John Boyer have taken up seriously the implications for understanding nineteenth-century Austria of David Blackbourn and Geoff Eley's challenges to the widely held belief in Germany's distinctive course of modern development, its *Sonderweg*.[3]

The traditionally strong emphasis on politics, diplomacy, and high culture by historians in the Habsburg Monarchy and its successor states has caused the study of social and economic development to evolve more slowly in those lands than in Western Europe and North America.[4] Since the 1970s, however, study of the social and economic history of modern Austria and East-Central Europe has begun to catch up with the richer literature on Germany and Western Europe. The Marxist-Leninist historiography that developed in the communist states during the 1950s and 1960s had already increased research there on economic and social development. Under East-Central Europe's more rigid communist governments, however, the academic authorities prescribed an emphasis on laborers and poor peasants and their exploitation by noble landowners and the capitalist bourgeoisie that skewed perspectives and narrowed the attention given to the middle classes.[5] Surviving nationalist traditions in East-Central Europe still required some treatment of the national revivals and middle-class nationalist politics, but orthodox communist historiography gave the most thorough treatment to the lower classes. The perspectives of historians in East-Central Europe began to broaden noticeably, though, with the weakening of cultural controls in Hungary and Poland during the 1970s and 1980s and more slowly in Czechoslovakia after the early 1980s.[6] Even with increasing research on social and economic development, most general accounts of nineteenth-century Austrian society still emphasize the slow and uneven emergence of a modern economy and convey the image of a bourgeoisie *manquée*. The persistence of traditional corporate social structures and of restrictions on trade and manufacture through the early nineteenth century retarded the development of modern entrepreneurial elements and the associated service sector. Since the middle and late 1970s, economic historians have begun to argue that the older scholarship underestimated the actual degree of economic development in nineteenth-century Austria and Hungary; but the still common emphasis on the slow and uneven evolution of modern capitalist relations in the monarchy has perpetuated the image of a backward and feeble modern middle class.[7]

Those intellectual historians who have shown any concern for the social and political context of thought and the arts in nineteenth-century Austria have had to give some attention to the development of the modern middle classes. As elsewhere in Europe, economic pressures and broadening audiences caused aristocratic patronage to fade during the early and middle nineteenth century, and few from the nobility figured among the most influential Austrian scholars, writers, or artists after the 1840s. Until the very end of the century, Hungary and Galicia experienced less economic development and urbanization than did the western portions of the monarchy; and landowning nobility were relatively more numerous and more powerful in Hungarian and Galician society than in the western Habsburg territories. In Austria's Alpine and Bohemian lands, though, as in Western Europe, the great majority of writers and artists during the late nineteenth century worked in urban middle-class circumstances for largely middle-class audiences; and they spent much effort in expressing and criticizing bourgeois values. Nonetheless, intellectual and cultural historians of Austria, like so many political historians, have tended to stress the failings of the middle class and its values, which helped fuel a modernist cultural revolt at the turn of the century. In these arguments, many of the urban entrepreneurs and professionals in the Alpine and Bohemian lands between the 1840s and the 1890s, whether ethnic Germans, Czechs, or Jews, espoused a self-consciously "European" liberal rationalism. Those values found only weak social and political bases in Austria, though; and they never fully uprooted the conflicting values of the Catholic baroque. In Carl E. Schorske's widely respected interpretation, the political and social weaknesses of Austrian liberals helped to precipitate the modernist rejection of liberal rationalist values in a broad range of artistic and intellectual pursuits.[8]

While since the 1960s scholars have shown great interest in the intellectual revolt *against* liberal middle-class culture in late-nineteenth-century Austria, less research has been devoted to the rise of that class culture and the supporting social structures. Carried to its logical extreme, the dramaturgy of much previous writing on Austrian political and intellectual history would treat the propertied and educated middle classes in the late nineteenth century as little more than a necessary foil, required to explain the slow demise of the old dynastic regime and the explosive emergence of conflict-laden twentieth-century society, but deserving of much less intensive study in their own right. Economic historians did study Austrian entrepreneurship and business structures, but through the early 1980s middle-class social structures and popular culture did not receive the attention in studies of nineteenth-century Austria that those topics attracted in work on Western Europe and Germany.[9]

Since the early 1980s, historians of imperial Austria and the successor states have been making up for the previously superficial treatment of the modern middle classes with increasingly sophisticated studies of social structures, popular culture, and everyday life.[10] Still, much remains to be done on the emergence and development of the various segments of the modern middle classes in the nineteenth century. But for several studies of the state officialdom, there are still hardly any studies of major middle-class and lower-middle-class occupational groups.[11] The bourgeois property owners, professionals, white-collar employees, and purveyors of services all deserve careful analysis with respect to their growth, geographical distribution, social and ethnic recruitment, economic bases, group values, and political behavior. This represents a large research agenda that will produce many specialized studies. A broader study of access to academic secondary and higher education and the social functions of such education, however, can advance that agenda for the educated and semieducated segments of the middle classes at large.

Access to advanced education has become a critical factor for social mobility in modern societies. Even with significant growth after the mid-nineteenth century, academic secondary and higher education in Austria and nearly all Western societies before World War II served no more than a few percent of the school-aged population at any one time. As the numbers of students in secondary and higher education and those engaged in educated or semieducated professions increased after the 1850s and 1860s, the public in most of Europe and North America became acutely aware that the social dynamics of advanced education determined access to the powers and privileges of the professions. By the early twentieth century, public opinion in the industrial societies widely held that access to the advanced education that provided certification for professional careers was a crucial test of chances for upward social mobility. As the German historian Peter Lundgreen observes, the popular belief in the possibility of free, open competition for occupational positions based on educational accomplishment became "fundamental (*konstitutiv*) for many modern industrial societies and provides legitimacy."[12] With such popular views came also increasing and ultimately irresistible pressures on governments to make secondary and higher education more widely available to the public than ever before and to assure that educational advancement would depend on merit, not simply on birth or wealth.

Of course, those in nineteenth-century Austria, or anywhere else, who managed to pass through academic secondary schools and perhaps went on to universities or specialized colleges formed only the pool of the semieducated and educated who might eventually enter various professions. Academic credentials did not guarantee finding positions or career success. Any full study of the social formation and recruitment patterns for the modern professions needs to trace over time the social origins of the membership for each group. For multiple professions in any large country, such a project could easily occupy teams of researchers for years. A more tractable task is to analyze the changing social recruitment of students in academic secondary and higher education and the experience within the educational system of youth from various social origins as they prepared for entry into the range of semieducated and educated professions. Such a project can examine not only the social origins and formation of the educated elites as a whole but also the overall social functions of advanced education.

Since the late 1960s, the social functions and dynamics of education have become a significant field of historical and sociological research for modern Britain, France, the United States, and Germany, to mention only the major Western countries. The resulting studies of education and society have yielded much about the impact of educational institutions on the evolution of modern social structures.[13] So far, though, such research has developed only slowly for old Austria and its successor states. Around 1900 historians began to produce institutional and political studies of Austrian education, and such research has continued since. Changes in literacy rates and popular access to primary schools have been studied in connection with governmental efforts to extend compulsory basic education. Research on the social functions of secondary and higher education and on social access to such advanced education, however, has been limited to occasional studies of one or another institution and often lacked methodological sophistication. Though good in many ways, the standard histories of Austrian education in the nineteenth century have treated only superficially questions of the social functions of secondary and higher education.[14] As a consequence, relatively little is known about the recruitment and formation of the educated elites in late-nineteenth-century Austria or in the successor states during the interwar period.

Scholars have done much to define analytic questions and to refine research methods as they have studied the changing social recruitment of educated elites elsewhere in modern Europe and North America.[15] One needs, first of all, to assess and explain the trends in total enrollments in academic secondary and higher education relative to the total population to establish just how *inclusive,* in Fritz Ringer's terminology, was education at those levels.[16] The critical issue regarding social access to advanced education is change in the representation of various segments of society relative to those groups' respective shares of the total population. Since birth rates and age stratification may vary among different social groups, each group's representation in the educational system should be gauged, wherever possible, against the size of its own school-aged population to measure precisely its relative educational opportunities.[17] Changes in the social composition of the enrolled students or the new graduates for various segments of an educational system may mean little if they are not measured against the changing composition of the school-aged population.

A number of causal factors must be assessed in explaining changes in the overall inclusiveness of secondary and higher education and in the opportunities afforded particular segments of society. How have population growth, economic development, changing popular aspirations for education, political contention over schooling, and the needs of government itself affected access and educational opportunities for particular social groups? It is usually difficult, if not impossible, to isolate the effects of individual causes for such complex social and political phenomena; but one can at least try to depict the relationship and interaction of the various factors.[18] It is necessary to achieve some statistical precision in analyzing the recruitment of students and social-mobility patterns in advanced education, and there will be some close statistical analysis of these factors in chapters 4 and 5. Still, the limits of available historical sources must be recognized. Historians, after all, often cannot answer all the empirical questions sociologists would like to ask.

The statistical facts about students' social origins are important, but they can only tell us part of the story of the recruitment and formation of the educated elites in any society. The processes of selecting and training new recruits for the professions and the public and private officialdoms also involve developing social relationships and forming group values. The social experience of such youth as they pass through the educational system and the formal and informal content of their schooling must also be examined, for these also play important roles in molding new recruits to the educated ranks.[19]

In studying the social dynamics of advanced education in late-imperial Austria, some questions must be posed specific to the emergence during the nineteenth century of a free-market industrial economy, a class-based society, and a constitutional government. As Austria's early modern corporate society dissolved during the early nineteenth century, to what extent did advanced education before 1848 function primarily to perpetuate existing educated and propertied elites? After the midcentury did the reproduction of existing privileged elites in the schools increase or decrease with the rise of a modern class society and a new educational system? Did various formerly underrepresented or excluded social strata gain increased access to advanced education? How and to what extent did population growth and the economic forces of developing modern capitalist agriculture, industry, and commerce affect the provision of secondary and higher education and the demand for it among various segments of the population? Did popular values and customs, the state educational authorities, or the educational institutions themselves work to mediate or even resist the effects of demographic and economic forces on advanced education? How were students affected by the selection processes involved in Austrian secondary and higher education and by their social experience in the schools? Given Austria's ethnic and religious diversity, changes in access to education must be measured not only for various social classes or occupational groups but also for the various ethnic groups and religious denominations. In this connection, one must also ask how the rise of the contending nationalist political movements during the late nineteenth century affected the development of secondary and higher education and how the growth of educational opportunities may have contributed to national identification and nation-building among the various peoples.

In analyzing the social functions of advanced education and the recruitment of the educated elites during the second half of the nineteenth century, there are good reasons to treat the Austrian half of the Habsburg Monarchy separately from Hungary and, within Austria, to focus primarily on the Alpine and Bohemian lands.[20] The sheer magnitude and diversity of the monarchy's territories makes it impossible to study the whole realm at once with the degree of precision that is needed. Educational developments in the Austrian and Hungarian halves of the monarchy during the late nineteenth century must be studied separately in any case, since Hungary's social structures and economic development differed significantly from Austria's, and Hungarian educational institutions followed their own path after the Austro-Hungarian Compromise of 1867. The monarchy's Alpine lands are now contained in the Austrian Republic, Slovenia, and northeastern Italy; and the Bohemian lands of Bohemia, Moravia, and Silesia today constitute the Czech Republic (see map 1). Historically, the Alpine and Bohemian lands represented the political and economic core of the Habsburgs' western territories. From the sixteenth century onward, Austria's most advanced economic development and densest educational networks were to be found in Vienna, the surrounding province of Lower Austria, the Bohemian lands, and in smaller centers in and around Graz in Styria, Innsbruck in Tirol, Trieste on the Adriatic, and the small province of Vorarlberg bordering Switzerland and Lake Constance. During the nineteenth century, the Alpine and Bohemian lands experienced the highest degree of urbanization and the strongest development of modern middle-class society of any parts of the monarchy; and the Alpine and Bohemian lands in many ways functioned as an economic and social unit. The educational institutions of Lower Austria and the Bohemian lands also played a disproportionate role in the formation of the modern educated elites for the whole Austrian half of the monarchy. As will be seen, Vienna and the Bohemian capital, Prague, by themselves had more than half of all Austrian university and technical college enrollments throughout the second half of the nineteenth century.

Dalmatia on the Adriatic coast and the Carpathian lands of Galicia and Bukovina had a different experience from the Alpine and Bohemian lands during the late nineteenth century. The Adriatic and Carpathian lands had considerable population increase but only limited economic development in this era. Up to World War I, per capita income and literacy rates in these provinces remained among the lowest in the whole monarchy; and social development here was hardly comparable to the experience of much of Western and Central Europe during the nineteenth century.

As will be seen, secondary and higher education in late-nineteenth-century Austria experienced a great process of growth. The share of the nineteen- to twenty-two-year-old population that was able to enroll as matriculated students in the Austrian universities and technical colleges more than doubled between the late 1860s and 1910. During the same period, publicly supported secondary and higher education in Czech and Polish expanded greatly, and eventually secondary instruction in Ukrainian, Romanian, Slovene, and Serbo-Croatian also increased. The existing propertied and educated elites retained their representation among the students, but growing numbers came from the families of small businessmen, craft producers, and peasant farmers. The expanding ranks of white-collar employees generated by modern industry, commerce, and government also sent increasing numbers of students to the academic secondary schools, universities, and technical colleges. Formerly disadvantaged ethnic groups such as the Czechs or religious minorities such as Jews and Protestants greatly increased their representation in secondary and higher education. Before the mid-nineteenth century, families in smaller towns and villages who lacked privilege, wealth, or advanced education had been able to send only a few of their sons to *Gymnasien,* universities, and technical institutes. At the end of the century, much larger numbers of youth from humble circumstances were able to study even though as late as 1910 the academic secondary schools still enrolled only around 3 percent of all eleven- to eighteen-year-olds and the universities and technical colleges, less than 2 percent of all nineteen- to twenty-two-year-olds as matriculated students. Tomáš G. Masaryk, Gustav Mahler, Karl Renner, and Ignaz Seipel are only four of the most famous among the many from modest backgrounds who managed to join Austria's academic, artistic, professional, and political elites before World War I. The growth in enrollments and the accompanying changes in the social and ethnic recruitment of students during the six decades after the 1850s involved major transformations in popular attitudes regarding advanced education and the social functions of the educational institutions that need to be examined. In Austria during the 1840s and 1850s, the institutions of secondary and higher education already faced strong pressures to change to meet the needs of a growing population, emerging new economic and social structures, and changes in government. The discussion must take up first the radical reform and modernization of advanced education carried out between the 1840s and the early 1870s.

CHAPTER 1

Education and the Modernization of Austria in the Mid-nineteenth Century

Between the 1790s and the early 1840s, Austria's social and political structures changed slowly compared with Western Europe. In the early 1780s Emperor Joseph II abolished the legal status of serfdom, but the great majority of Austrian peasants still had to render labor services or other feudal payments to manorial lords. In the early nineteenth century, modern textile manufacture and metallurgy found footholds in Lower Austria, Bohemia, Moravia, and Vorarlberg, with some additional activity in Styria and Carinthia; but restrictive economic regulations and guild structures persisted in most towns. Traumatized by rebellions in the late 1780s and then by the French Revolution and the Napoleonic Wars, the imperial authorities tried to maintain a centralized absolutist government. Empress Maria Theresa (ruled 1740–80) and her son Joseph II (1780–90) had already reformed and streamlined the secondary schools and universities to meet the practical needs of government and society as they understood them. As will be seen, their successors continued nearly all the same basic regulations and policies for advanced education into the 1840s despite rising calls for reforms to meet the needs of a changing society. Only in response to the deep economic, social, and political crisis of the 1840s did the Austrian government begin to create a new system of advanced education comparable to those in neighboring Central European states.

Stagnation and Crisis, 1790–1848

Judged by any reasonable standard, Austrian secondary and higher education tended to stagnate between the 1790s and the 1840s. Enrollments and the numbers of institutions showed little or no growth, and by the 1830s and 1840s observers complained about paralysis in many sectors of the educational establishment. Population and the economy were growing in Austria, although not as rapidly as in parts of Western Europe during this era. The Austrian population increased by an average of 1.0 percent annually for the period between 1817 and 1845. The British population, in contrast, grew by an average 1.3 percent annually between 1800 and 1850. Between 1830 and 1845,

Austria's industrial production expanded at an average per capita rate between 1.8 percent and 2.6 percent per annum, depending on which index is used.[1] Austria's systems of secondary and higher education, however, showed no clear tendency to expand or develop. The Habsburgs' non-Hungarian crown lands had 79 *Gymnasien* in 1817 and only 80 in 1847. The provinces with the most advanced economic development and the most important administrative centers had the highest density of *Gymnasien* per territory: in order, Silesia, Bohemia, Lower Austria, and Moravia. Total enrollments in the Austrian *Gymnasien* fluctuated, with only a marginal increase between the late 1820s and the mid-1840s: 19,389 in 1828, down to 18,251 in 1838, and 21,246 in 1847.[2]

Realschulen made only a minor contribution to Austrian secondary education before the mid-nineteenth century. Austria's first such institution was founded in Vienna in 1809 to give greater emphasis than did the *Gymnasien* to mathematics, physics, chemistry, and modern languages and help prepare future engineers, technicians, and businessmen. Others followed in Brno (Brünn) in 1811, Prague in 1833, and Graz in 1845. Over time, the *Realschulen* came to focus on preparing students for the technical institutes in those cities and in several cases were attached to those institutes.[3]

The Austrian universities showed a stasis similar to that of the *Gymnasien* during the first half of the nineteenth century. Emperor Joseph II reduced the universities in Graz and Innsbruck to *Lyzeen* as part of efforts to achieve greater efficiency in state services, and no new universities were opened during the succeeding half century. When Salzburg passed to Austrian control at the end of the Napoleonic Wars, the Habsburg government retained only a small lyceum there; and it allowed the University of Olomouc (Olmütz) to decline during the early nineteenth century.[4] The universities of Vienna and Prague then were the only fully articulated universities of significance in the Alpine and Bohemian lands between 1815 and 1848.

The Vienna and Prague universities experienced almost none of the curricular reforms and raising of scholarly standards that invigorated university education in northern Germany during the early nineteenth century. Between 1815 and 1848 the Austrian government made few reforms in any of the university curricula but medicine. Most of the medical faculties offered only a two-year program focusing on basic surgery and obstetrics, and only the Vienna medical faculty had a four-year program in medicine and advanced surgery. The government agreed to augment the program of the Vienna medical faculty in 1810 and 1833, and by the 1840s that faculty, with professors such as Joseph Skoda, Karl Rokitansky, and Joseph Hyrtl, was poised for the international eminence that it achieved during the next four decades.[5] Between 1820 and the early 1840s the Vienna University's total enrollments fluctuated between four and five thousand. Among the various faculties, the numbers of students in the law faculty grew sharply during the 1830s and 1840s at the expense of the others.[6] In the Prague University, enrollments in the philosophical faculty, which in this era served primarily to prepare students for the other faculties, reached a peak of just over one thousand students in the early 1820s just after the end of the wars. In 1824 the Austrian government reformed the philosophical faculties to dispense with what it considered superfluous, impractical subjects and reduced their program of study from three years to two. Fearing a potential excess of new graduates, the state authorities took other steps at the same time to reduce enrollments. As a result, the number of students in the Prague philosophical faculty fell within two years to less than eight hundred and remained between seven and eight hundred until the 1848 revolution.[7]

Supplementing university education, a number of smaller, more specialized academies arose during the eighteenth century to train military officers and state officials and provide noblemen with advanced general education. Beginning in Kremsmünster, Upper Austria, in the late 1730s, various monasteries and the central government founded academies for young noblemen, *Ritterakademien,* following the model of institutions in the German states. These academies were to prepare noblemen for the military, diplomacy, and other state service or for management of estates. Their curricula combined advanced secondary education with introductory philosophy, law, public administration, history, mathematics, natural history, modern languages, practical economics, and the noble *Exerzitien*—dancing, fencing, and riding. Under Maria Theresa the imperial government worked to improve the education of noblemen for state service, and the empress authorized the Jesuits in 1746 to found what became the most famous and durable of these academies in Austria, the Collegium Theresianum in Vienna. The government opened a training institution for the diplomatic service in 1754, the Academy of Oriental Languages, later called the Consular Academy. In 1751 Maria Theresa founded a military academy in Wiener Neustadt to train young noblemen from needy families and the sons of distinguished army officers. An engineering academy had already started in Vienna in 1717; under military direction after 1760, that institution focused on the training of officers for artillery, sapper, and engineering units. In the mid-1780s Emperor Joseph II added a "medical-surgical military academy" in Vienna to train army field surgeons, the so-called Josephs-Akademie.[8]

Most of these academies were initially small, and they developed slowly in their early decades. In 1783–84 the Austrian government interrupted the development of all those not specifically engaged in military training when Joseph II ordered their closure for budgetary reasons. Many of these reopened after the emperor's death in 1790, but few of the academies except the Theresianum and the military academy in Wiener Neustadt played any major role in Austrian government and society during the second half of the nineteenth century.

During the early nineteenth century, a number of Austrian entrepreneurs, engineers, and educators advocated the development of higher technical institutes to help advance technology and industry. Nonetheless, higher technical education progressed slowly and made only a limited contribution to the formation of Austria's educated elites before the 1850s. Maria Theresa's government in 1763 founded a mining school (*Montanlehranstalt,* later *Bergakademie*) in Banská Štiavnica (Schemnitz), northern Hungary, today Slovakia. The first Austrian "polytechnic institute" opened in Prague in 1806, modeled in part after the famed Parisian school. A polytechnic institute followed in Vienna in 1815. By the time of the 1848 upheavals, the Habsburg Monarchy had polytechnic institutes in Vienna, Prague, and Graz in the Alpine and Bohemian lands; in Krakow and L'viv (Lwow, Lemberg) in Galicia; in Pest in Hungary; in Milan and Venice in northern Italy; and a special nautical institute in Trieste. Although many of these institutes had serious academic weaknesses, higher technical education with respect to numbers of institutions and students relative to total population was actually more advanced in Austria in the 1840s than in many of the German states. The Austrian institutes differed fundamentally from the Parisian Ecole polytechnique in that most were essentially civilian institutions, not devoted primarily to training military officers. All these schools suffered from poor funding and limited facilities. Austria had no state certification process for civilian engineers in the early nineteenth century, and the technical institutes granted no degrees or titles and administered no comprehensive examinations.[9] Few of the students in the first decades stayed for more than a semester or two. Austria generated limited demand for technically and scientifically trained individuals during the first half of the nineteenth century. Even in Bohemia, one of the centers of early industrial development, more than half of all who studied in the Prague technical institute between 1806 and 1856 left for other crown lands after their studies.[10]

During the eighteenth century Maria Theresa and Joseph II reformed the educational system in pursuit of pragmatic goals for the state. In 1781 Joseph II established the principle of mandatory primary education for all children from ages six to twelve, although in practice it took decades to realize this in many crown lands. In the late eighteenth century the government modernized somewhat the curricula for academic secondary and higher education, making them more rational and practical and reducing control by the Catholic clergy. The reforming absolutist state made no effort, however, to expand the network of *Gymnasien* and universities or to increase significantly the portion of the population that enrolled. Indeed, the government radically reduced the numbers of *Gymnasien* and Latin schools in the 1770s when it closed many small schools of low quality and banned the Jesuit order, which previously had controlled many of the *Gymnasien* and most of the philosophical and theological faculties in the universities. In Bohemia, the number of *Gymnasien* shrank from 44 in 1773 to 13 in 1777, and in Moravia from 15 to 8. Even in these two provinces, with their relatively prosperous agriculture and nascent industrialization, the number of secondary schools increased only modestly between the era of Maria Theresa and the 1840s: in 1847 Bohemia had 21 *Gymnasien* and Moravia still only 8.[11]

As in other areas of public policy, the Austrian state followed the utilitarian ideals of the eighteenth-century cameralist thinkers in the reforms of secondary and higher education. The *Gymnasien* and universities were to serve the practical purposes of training state servants, clergy, physicians, and some notaries and lawyers. The state undertook no obligation to provide secondary or higher education to the public more generally nor to assist the pursuit of broad learning for its own sake.[12] It fit logically into the policies of Maria Theresa and Joseph II to close many secondary schools deemed superfluous and to reduce instruction in the universities of Graz and Innsbruck.

The eighteenth-century reformers expected only able youth to be admitted to the *Gymnasien* and universities and took steps to prevent any excessive influx of students. The central government was particularly concerned that secondary and higher education not cause any loss of labor from agriculture or any destabilizing social change by taking in significant numbers from the poorer strata. In May 1761 the government prohibited the admission of burghers' and peasants' sons to *Gymnasien* unless they possessed "extraordinary talents," and other decrees followed in July 1766 and May 1767 allowing the higher Latin schools and *Gymnasien* to admit from the lower classes only those youth who possessed extraordinary abilities and the financial wherewithal.[13] When run by religious orders, the secondary schools and universities had generally charged no tuition; but Joseph II's government introduced fees to help meet operating costs and discourage the poorest youth from attending.[14]

The eighteenth-century reformers' policies for secondary and higher education tended to harden into an immobile system under Emperor Francis I (ruled 1792–1835) and Ferdinand I (1835–48). Whatever the pressures of population increase and economic development during the early nineteenth century, the Austrian government adhered to rigidly conservative policies regarding advanced education. Secondary education expanded somewhat at the end of the Napoleonic Wars in response to needs for more clergy and state employees, but that trend soon dissipated in the face of tight budgets and the government's enveloping conservatism.[15] Due to limited funds and shortages of lay teachers during the reign of Francis I, a number of formerly secularized *Gymnasien* returned to the control of religious orders—the Benedictines, Piarists, Cistercians, and Premonstratensians. Many clergy continued to teach in the university faculties of philosophy as well as theology. In the meantime state regulation of instruction tightened. State officials approved the textbooks and course syllabi for all university professors, and lecture content had to conform to the officially sanctioned syllabi.[16]

Beyond the ever-present desires to economize expenditures and combat any subversive political tendencies in the educational system, the governments of Francis I and Ferdinand I feared the production of any more aspirants to the state bureaucracy or the learned professions than were needed. The highest state commission for educational matters, the Studienhofkommission, followed up on the efforts of the mid-1820s to reduce enrollments in the philosophical faculties with steps to cut enrollments in the *Gymnasien* and to exclude those social elements it deemed unsuitable. In 1826 the commission reintroduced the admissions examinations that had been dropped in 1804, imposed a limit of eighty students per class in the lower forms, and encouraged a more rigorous weeding out of weaker students. The state authorities also tried to make enrollment more difficult for students from the poorer strata who might only want advanced education for social and economic advancement. Tuition fees went up, and anyone over fourteen years old who wished to begin *Gymnasium* studies now had to pass a special admissions examination. In practice, the *Gymnasien* continued, as before, to grant liberal exemptions from tuition, but enrollments declined significantly in the years after 1826–27. Cholera epidemics that raged in many parts of the monarchy in 1831–32 and the economic difficulties and labor unrest that hit the centers of textile production in 1831 contributed, no doubt, to the decrease. Enrollments in the *Gymnasien* of Lower Austria outside of Vienna fell by about one-third in the late 1820s before beginning slowly to climb again during the 1830s.[17] Despite the government's vigilance, the supply of educated young men coming out of the *Gymnasien* and the university faculties began to exceed the number of positions available to them later in the 1830s and 1840s. During the crisis years of the 1840s, Austria's Alpine and Bohemian lands, like much of Western and Central Europe, heard complaints of an excess of educated applicants relative to employment opportunities, particularly in law and state service.[18]

During the first half of the nineteenth century, the Austrian government clearly expected its *Gymnasien* and universities to serve the interests of the state in training future government officials, clergy, and professionals. The state authorities resisted any reforms, such as those introduced in some of the German states, that pointed toward a broader concept of advanced education and freer intellectual inquiry in the *Gymnasien* and universities. The curriculum adopted for Austrian law faculties in 1810 emphasized the teaching of Austria's newly codified statute law and natural law. This approach resembled in some ways that for legal studies in France under Napoleon Bonaparte and differed from the stress on common law and legal history that became the hallmark of legal education in the University of Berlin founded that same year.[19] Indeed, the basically utilitarian purposes and rigid curricular controls in Austria precluded the broad humanistic learning and free scholarly inquiry by students and professors that Wilhelm von Humboldt and Johann Gottlieb Fichte championed in organizing the Berlin University.[20] Accurately or not, the following statement was widely attributed to Emperor Francis I: "I need no learned men; I need only good officials."[21]

In practice, of course, all the German universities that accepted the Humboldtian model had to balance the pursuit of broad intellectual development and scholarly inquiry with the needs of professional training and to compromise somewhat their vaunted principles of freedom of teaching and of study (*Lehr- und Lernfreiheit*). There could be no mistaking, though, the very different organization, curriculum, and atmosphere in the Austrian universities during the early nineteenth century. The Austrian police suppressed virtually all efforts to establish *Burschenschaften* and other student associations between 1815 and the early 1840s, and foreign travelers noted that Austrian university students were generally much less given to brawling and nocturnal mayhem than were their counterparts in the German states.[22]

Those who studied in the Austrian *Gymnasien* and universities during the 1830s and 1840s later painted grim pictures of their experience. Even though colored by knowledge of conditions elsewhere and the subsequent changes in Austria, those recollections suggest some of the realities of how Austria formed its educated elites before 1848. Leopold von Hasner (1818–91)—law professor, state official, and German liberal minister of religion and instruction from 1867 to 1870—was born in Prague, the son of a government official. He entered the Old Town *Gymnasium* in 1826 and studied in the Prague law faculty between 1836 and 1842. Looking back, Hasner recalled how strong were the efforts to regulate academic studies, even to the point of stifling scholarly inquiry, in order to stop the spread of dangerous liberal ideas.[23] The Jewish poet Ludwig August Frankl (1810–94) came to the Vienna medical faculty in 1828 after finishing studies in the lyceum of Litomyšl, Bohemia. Nearly all his professors in Vienna were engaged in research and writing, but he complained that their teaching consisted of imparting information and drilling the students without stimulating any independent inquiry.[24] Adolf Pichler began studies in the Innsbruck philosophical faculty in 1838, going on to the Vienna medical faculty in 1842. He noted in his memoirs that the introductory studies in the philosophical faculty were little more advanced than the *Gymnasium* courses and suffered from lack of academic freedom and the obvious professional orientation of university education. While university students had to be addressed as "Herr," in practice they were treated as little more than school boys.[25]

Eduard Hanslick (1825–1904), the famed late-nineteenth-century Viennese musicologist and critic, attended a Prague *Gymnasium* and then began studies in the Prague law faculty before going to the Vienna University in late 1846. He stated in his memoirs what were common complaints about the Austrian *Gymnasien* in the early and late nineteenth century: world history was presented according to a conservative official Austrian outlook, and the study of Latin and Greek so emphasized grammar that it lost the spirit of the ancient civilizations. Hanslick claimed never to have heard a word about Gotthold Lessing, Friedrich Schiller, and Johann Wolfgang von Goethe in the *Gymnasium* instruction on German literature. Since as a youth Hanslick did not want to become a musician, physician, or priest, "what else remained for me at that time but to study law? The official career was by far the pre-eminent one among the educated *Mittelstand*."[26] A life of scholarship was out of the question for most youth of his generation who went to the universities.[27] Hanslick completed the doctorate of law and began work in 1849, serving first in an imperial treasury office and then a tax office in Klagenfurt before he become a docent for music history and esthetics in the Vienna University later in the 1850s.

By the time Eduard Hanslick completed his legal studies, however, Austrian education and the state itself faced a deep crisis. The tendencies of Austrian government policies and institutions toward immobility during the 1830s hardened into virtual paralysis in the 1840s. A state that was responding poorly to long-term social changes proved utterly unable to deal with the economic emergency of the "Hungry Forties."[28] By the mid-1840s, the imperial government faced growing university enrollments, particularly in the law faculties, despite limited employment opportunities in the public and private sectors. The authorities properly feared that the increasing numbers of educated young men who were frustrated in their career aspirations would join the growing ranks of dissidents. In the 1840s the government again tried to stiffen admissions standards for the *Gymnasien* and considered banning impoverished youth from higher studies altogether, but it could not easily stem the rising tide of students in the law faculties. As an expedient, the government increased the hiring of new law graduates for the lowest bureaucratic positions, whether paid or unpaid; but this only added to the problems in various state agencies.[29]

Despite the government efforts to control education and prevent the spread of subversive ideas in the population, criticisms of state policies rose in many parts of Austrian society during the 1840s. Austrian censorship stopped the printing of liberal and radical ideas inside the monarchy, but the emperor's subjects could still read them in newspapers and books brought in from some of the German states. In fact, the Austrian government had less control over society than is often assumed. As John Boyer has pointed out, the Austrian administration under Emperors Francis I and Ferdinand I combated opposition with negative police measures but was neither willing nor equipped to undertake the broad intervention in society attempted by the Prussian government in the same period.[30] The Austrian authorities could not stifle the calls for liberal reforms that emanated from students, professionals, some entrepreneurs, and even some state officials and university professors during the 1840s.[31] The demands for change in state policies and institutions included public education.

A debate had already begun in the late 1830s among school directors, university professors, and members of the Studienhofkommission over possible reforms in the Austrian *Gymnasien* and the philosophical faculties. Some wanted to raise the academic standards of the *Gymnasien* and augment their curriculum by taking the two-year preparatory "philosophical studies" (*philosophische Jahrgänge*) out of the universities and adding them to the existing six-year program of most *Gymnasien*.[32] This would make Austrian *Gymnasium* education more like that in many of the German states, although the various Austrian plans for eight-year programs still differed from Prussia's nine-year model.[33]

Professors in several of the Austrian philosophical faculties had already begun in 1826 and 1827 to discuss proposals to expand the curricula of their faculties, give up much of their former preparatory functions, and gain equal status with the other university faculties.[34] Such changes would only follow those made by a number of German universities after the late eighteenth century. Advocates of reform in the Austrian philosophical faculties now urged adopting the same principles of broad cultivation of the intellect and character and free inquiry that the Austrian educators credited with the great advance of many German universities during the preceding decades. In 1838 the Studienhofkommission agreed to consider changes in the philosophical faculties and the *Gymnasien* and ordered various studies over the next four years. Nonetheless, Austria's central authorities proved unwilling to enact any of the new plans that came forward before 1848.

The greatest impediments to educational reform disappeared with the fall of Prince Klemens von Metternich and the old government in March 1848 and the appointment of a new cabinet committed to change. As early as 30 March 1848, the new minister of public instruction, Franz Freiherr von Sommaruga, promised to make freedom of study and of teaching the foundation for a revitalized system of higher education and praised the flourishing institutions of Germany "that we honor as models of thorough scholarly education."[35] The Austrian university faculties won the basic right to govern their own intellectual and academic life at the beginning of April, and on 10 May 1848, the government decreed that the two years of "philosophical studies" be shifted from the philosophical faculties to the *Gymnasien*. The philosophical faculties could now assume a status fully equal to the other university faculties. Following the model of many German institutions, the Austrian universities in 1848 adopted the practice of *Habilitierung* to enable young scholars to begin teaching as *Privat-Dozenten*. To help streamline medical education, the central government in August 1848 authorized the medical faculties to drop their doctoral dissertations and accompanying disputations, which were no more than formalities in any case.

The new Ministry of Public Instruction also began to prepare a comprehensive reform of secondary and higher education. This effort was led by Franz Seraphin Exner (1802–53), a professor of philosophy in Prague who had begun to advocate reform of the universities during the 1840s. The resulting "Proposal of the Basic Features of Public Education in Austria" summed up the views of the liberal educational reformers of 1848.[36] The document proposed to follow the model of the "non-Austrian German universities" in transforming the Austrian institutions because the German universities offered the best example and "because the future mutual interaction between them and the Austrian universities required it." The Austrian universities would remain primarily teaching institutions, but the level of scholarly accomplishment was to be raised among both the professors and the students. In the interests of learning, the basic academic governance of the universities must be placed in the hands of the professors, who would be responsible to qualified state officials and public opinion.

The "Proposal" invoked the goals and spirit of the Humboldtian reforms in Berlin by stipulating that the basic purpose of educating youth in the Austrian universities must be "to effect, through freedom of teaching and study, the vigorous development and, through scholarship and appropriate discipline, the ennoblement of the character."[37] The secondary schools, universities, and technical institutes were all expected to offer a broad education that would develop the students' analytic and synthetic abilities and stimulate independent inquiry. Before 1848 Austria had no comprehensive examinations to certify graduates of the *Gymnasien*. According to the "Proposal," young men would henceforth qualify for admission to the universities by completing a broad course of humanistic studies in the *Gymnasien* and passing a general examination of intellectual maturity (*Maturitätsprüfung* or *Reifeprüfung*), equivalent to the *Abitur* that was required for admission to the Prussian universities after 1834.

Three-year *Bürgerschulen* and three-year *Realschulen* would offer other modes of secondary education as alternatives to the *Gymnasien*. The *Realschulen* would prepare students for the technical institutes with an emphasis on modern languages and literature, mathematics, and natural science. Graduation from a *Realschule* and passing an appropriate general examination of maturity would entitle a young man to enter a technical institute. In addition, the *Bürgerschulen* and *Realschulen* would also provide more practical, nonacademic education for youth headed into the crafts. Austria's liberal educational reformers in 1848, like their contemporaries elsewhere in Central Europe, did not consider the question of advanced academic education for women.

In the turmoil of 1848, Franz von Sommaruga had already been replaced by another minister by the time the final sections of the "Proposal" were published in late July. With the revival of the imperial court's military and political fortunes in the Alpine and Bohemian lands by summer 1848, it moved to suppress radical tendencies. A new emperor, Francis Joseph, established a constitution by decree in March 1849; but he suspended even that document at the end of December 1851 and reinstituted absolutist rule. In the meantime, the Habsburg authorities began rebuilding all the state institutions, having learned bitter lessons from the decay of the government apparatus in the late 1830s and the 1840s. Even if they opposed the revolutionaries' political goals, however, the new ministers could not ignore the need for change in secondary and higher education or efface the steps for restructuring that were initiated in 1848. Indeed, the neo-absolutist regime of Emperor Francis Joseph and ministers such as Prince Felix zu Schwarzenberg, Alexander Bach, and Count Leo Thun-Hohenstein did not try to stop, let alone reverse, the educational reforms.

The Counterrevolution in Education

Austria's neo-absolutist government of the 1850s accepted most of the educational reforms begun in 1848 and carried out a broad transformation. Late-nineteenth-century liberal commentators saw essentially reactionary purposes and methods in the government's domestic policies during the decade after 1848. In fact, Prince Schwarzenberg, the prime minister from November 1848 until his death in April 1852, worked aggressively to modernize the government's apparatus and policies so that a revitalized state could address effectively the social and economic challenges of the era.[38] As minister of interior, Bach, himself a liberal in spring 1848, undertook a massive renovation of the state officialdom. The new imperial authorities now gained a more unified and centralized control over all the crown lands than they had enjoyed at any previous time in the monarchy's history. In the meantime, Karl Ludwig von Bruck, minister of commerce and then of finance, championed the reform of trade regulations and development of the economy. The Schwarzenberg cabinet was aware of the advances in industry, transportation, and commerce elsewhere in Western and Central Europe. The ministers wanted to speed the monarchy's recovery from the crisis of the 1840s and overcome its obvious economic backwardness, and they supported the private construction of railroads and development of metallurgy during the 1850s. The neo-absolutist regime believed that the monarchy must be restored as the pre-eminent force in Central Europe and that it must continue to lead the German Confederation. Impressed by the pace of Prussian development, the new Austrian leaders proved willing to accept parts of the Prussian model as they charted new policies for state administration, economic development, and education.[39]

Many of the innovative policies and new administrative structures evoked opposition from reactionaries among the aristocracy and some of the Catholic hierarchy, but the trauma of 1848 and the ensuing war with Hungary convinced the new emperor and his advisors that they must carry out broad reforms. Their policies of bureaucratic, economic, and social modernization amounted to a counterrevolution under neo-absolutist direction. Count Leo Thun-Hohenstein (1811–88), member of a great Bohemian aristocratic family, took charge of education as minister of public instruction in late July 1849; and his ministry also took responsibility for religious affairs in August 1849.

A firm conservative and committed Catholic believer, Leo Thun stoutly opposed liberal revolution. He was drawn to the Catholic romantic ideology of Joseph Görres and his circle in Munich, and in Vienna the prominent conservative Catholic thinker, Karl Ernst Jarcke, also influenced Thun. Between 1827 and 1831, Count Thun studied in the Prague law faculty; and he later traveled in France and Britain, including a visit to Oxford.[40] Thun knew of developments in the German universities and recognized the comparative backwardness of Austrian education. Interested in the cause of Czech cultural rights, he was also sensitive to a degree to the diversity of the monarchy's population and the various ethnic groups' claims to independent cultural development.

As minister of religion and instruction from 1849 until 1860, Leo Thun believed that the Austrian state must raise academic standards and transform curricula throughout the educational system. It was essential to the welfare of the state and its peoples that Austria achieve educational standards comparable to those of other European nations.[41] In this view, Austria had to follow the model of Prussia and other German states in fostering free scholarly inquiry in higher education in order to raise levels of accomplishment and better serve the needs of a stable, orderly Christian society.

Leo Thun and his advisors opposed the secularizing, etatist methods of the policies passed down from the era of Joseph II. As Count Thun and his colleagues saw it, the Josephinist bureaucratic methods had stifled scientific progress while weakening the influence of Catholicism on popular morality and failing to stop radicalism. Thun insisted that students and teachers respect established state and religious authority, and he supported prohibitions of political agitation in the schools and universities. Like the regime of Francis I and Metternich, the neo-absolutist government banned student organizations. Under Leo Thun, the ministry was willing to appoint Protestants, Jews, or non-observant Catholics as professors in the universities; but there must be respect for the teachings of the Catholic Church. To assure the safety of religion and public morals, Count Thun argued that the Church must have an important role in public primary schools and control the education of future clergy in the university theological faculties.[42]

Otherwise, Leo Thun rejected heavy-handed surveillance of advanced education. His ministry invoked the principles of academic autonomy and far-reaching, but not complete, freedom of teaching and study to revitalize Austrian higher education.[43] He walked a tightrope trying to find a workable compromise between free inquiry and respect for conservative political and religious principles. In the universities, Count Thun argued for some supervision of teaching and for judging its soundness by the standard of Catholic doctrine. As he put it, the purpose of the universities must "lie in the cultivation of as thorough a scholarliness as possible, inspired by genuine religiosity."[44] Nonetheless, he and his colleagues believed that true enlightenment, rather than repression, was the best means to develop the intellect and ennoble the individual character.[45] Under Count Thun, the Ministry of Religion and Instruction implemented nearly all the basic reforms of secondary and higher education that were proposed in 1848. In the process, the ministry established institutional foundations for advanced education in Austria that lasted to the end of the monarchy.

The ministerial authorities began in late 1848 and early 1849 to put into effect the provisions of the July 1848 "Proposal of the Basic Features of Public Education" dealing with *Gymnasium* and university education, and they continued along those lines under Leo Thun. Mindful of the distinct educational traditions of northern Italy and of Poland, the ministry pursued somewhat different policies for the universities of Pavia and Padua and for Krakow and L'viv than those for the institutions in the Alpine and Bohemian lands. The first major step for the latter was a Provisional Law on the Organization of Academic Authorities, drafted by Exner, which went into effect in late September 1849. This law promised freedom of teaching to the university professors as well as broad freedom for students in selecting courses and instructors, subject to some specific curricular requirements. The ministry drew up a new code of discipline and new curricula for the faculties of law, medicine, and philosophy. The new university regulations effectively abolished the control over the faculties by the old directors of studies (*Studiendirektoren*) and, following the German model, gave considerable powers of self-government to the full professors (*Ordinarien*) in each faculty. In the Vienna and Prague universities, however, a vestige of the old corporate structure survived for another two decades in the "doctors' colleges" (*Doktorenkollegien*), corporate associations of each faculty's graduated doctors, which had rights to participate in doctoral examinations and elections of rectors.[46]

The government now saw the universities and technical institutes as centers of scholarly research as well as teaching, following the Humboldtian principle that true cultivation of the intellect and character required a broad education and scholarly inquiry by both professors and students. Preparation for entry into learned professions, of course, must continue; but such training was to be carried out with a stronger scholarly spirit than before and with more attention to research. Inevitably, of course, the Ministry of Religion and Instruction under Count Thun and his successors had to face the sometimes conflicting claims of professional training and scholarly inquiry.

Whatever the promises of self-government to the universities, the ministry frequently had to dictate many of the reforms and the appointment of new professors over opposition, both inside the institutions and out. Traditionalists among the professors and in the doctors' colleges opposed many of the changes. The reform of the philosophical faculties was particularly difficult, since those faculties had to be greatly expanded and many new academic specialties had to be added. The faculties forwarded to the ministry short lists of candidates for professorships, but the ministerial officials in Vienna made the final selections and the emperor sanctioned the appointments. During the early 1850s Leo Thun used virtually dictatorial authority to name talented new professors to the philosophical faculties as well as in medicine and law. Catholic conservatives objected to the non-Catholics and some of the foreigners who were now appointed, and liberals and radicals were suspicious of almost anyone named by Count Thun and the neo-absolutist regime.[47]

The educational authorities in the 1850s also expected to improve the technical institutes, but reforms proceeded more slowly there than in the universities. The ministry initially was most concerned with transforming the universities and the *Gymnasien,* and the various technical institutes remained fiscally and administratively under the provincial governments. Before 1848 most of these institutions had offered broad curricula, ranging from engineering and surveying to modern languages and bookkeeping. Such traditions and the lack of adequate, uniform preparation among the students continued to hamper the technical institutes in the 1850s.[48] Before 1848 several of the technical institutes had offered their own *Realschule* classes, and all of them had provided "preparatory" or remedial classes for new students.

After 1849 the Ministry of Religion and Instruction ostensibly committed itself to developing a system of independent *Realschulen* to prepare students for the technical institutes and transforming the latter into genuine institutions of higher learning. Nonetheless, Austria's *Realschulen* did not grow fast enough during the early 1850s to take over all the preparatory functions. With the ministry's failure to establish a comprehensive examination to certify graduates of the upper *Realschule* forms in the 1850s, the technical institutes had to continue offering their own preparatory classes.

Only after the late 1850s did the Austrian technical institutes develop into modern institutions of higher education. In the late 1850s and the early 1860s, the Ministry of Religion and Instruction made various studies of higher technical education in the German states, Switzerland, France, Belgium, and Britain. After extended deliberations, the ministerial authorities and the emperor approved new charters (*Statuten*) for the technical institutes in Prague in 1863, Graz in 1864, and Vienna in 1865 although these institutes remained under the administrative control of the provincial governments. The charters established separate schools (*Fachschulen*) within each institute for the principal engineering and technical disciplines, somewhat along the lines of the university faculties. At the end of studies in each such school, students would be able to take comprehensive examinations and earn a diploma. The technical institutes in Vienna and Prague both dropped their preparatory classes in 1863.[49]

Great efforts were needed to carry out the changes in *Gymnasium* education begun in 1848. The *Gymnasien* had to extend their former six-year program of studies by two years in order to absorb the universities' old introductory philosophic courses, and they would now administer to graduating students a general examination of intellectual maturity. The ministry also worked to broaden the *Gymnasium* curriculum in mathematics and the natural sciences. In designing the new program of studies, Count Thun followed the recommendations of Exner and a young Prussian classicist, Hermann Bonitz, who was called from a *Gymnasium* in Szczecin (Stettin) in February 1849 to a chair in classical philology at the Vienna University. Exner and Bonitz drafted a "Proposal for the Organization of *Gymnasien* and *Realschulen* in Austria," which the emperor approved provisionally on 15 September 1849. This document provided the basic framework for academic secondary education in Austria for most of the late nineteenth century.[50]

The increased attention to mathematics and the natural sciences in the *Gymnasien* meant a reduction in the hours devoted to Latin grammar and literature and, thereby, some compromise in the classical humanistic curriculum. In the new eight-year curriculum, instruction in Latin grammar and literature accounted for only one-quarter of all the hours, compared with more than half in the old six-year curriculum. The eight-year course of studies was divided between a four-year *Untergymnasium* and a four-year *Obergymnasium*. Many topics were to be introduced in the early years and then taken up again with greater sophistication in the *Obergymnasium*. In place of the "class teachers" who taught a range of subjects before 1848, the new arrangements provided for expert teachers for each subject. The new regulations required *Gymnasium* teachers to have studied in a university and to have passed examinations there for certification in their specialties.[51]

The regulations of 1849 established a *Maturitätsprüfung* to verify each student's fulfillment of the goals of *Gymnasium* education and grant admission to the universities. This examination soon came to be known popularly as the *Matura,* a term still used in nearly all the former lands of the monarchy. It was to be a general examination testing not so much detailed knowledge but the general level of intellectual ability achieved by the student. To take the *Matura,* a student must have reached eighteen years of age and completed the eight-year curriculum of the *Gymnasium,* either as an enrolled student or as an external or "private" student who had passed all the course examinations. The oral portions of the *Matura* were administered by panels of *Gymnasium* professors chaired by the provincial *Gymnasium* inspector or some other official designated by the higher educational authorities. Students who failed might take the *Matura* again after six or twelve months, but only in exceptional cases could a student attempt it a third time.[52] In principle, completing *Gymnasium* studies and passing a *Matura* administered by an accredited *Gymnasium* granted the student admission to any Austrian university; and the *Matura* soon became a qualification for many civil service positions.

Creating a new plan of studies for the *Realschulen* proved much more difficult than for the *Gymnasien*. Previously, Austria's few *Realschulen* had offered mainly two-year programs in technical and commercial subjects without any broader academic secondary education. Now, according to Exner and Bonitz's "Organizational Proposal," the *Realschulen* were to serve multiple purposes: offer a general academic secondary education without any classical languages, prepare students for the technical institutes, and provide an intermediate stage of schooling for youth headed to crafts and manufacturing pursuits. The "Organizational Proposal" promised to make the *Realschulen* a parallel track to the *Gymnasien* with a six-year course of study giving increased attention to modern languages, mathematics, and sciences. This would help democratize Austrian secondary education by making a "higher general education" (*höhere allgemeine Bildung*) available to the "majority of the citizenry who were excluded [previously] by the organization of the schools."[53] Nonetheless, various interests, particularly manufacturers, insisted on continued emphasis of vocational and technical education in the *Realschulen,* and the ministry had to compromise. The regulations for the "Organization of Manufacturing Instruction in General and the Establishment of *Realschulen* in Particular," approved by the emperor in March 1851, provided for only limited hours of general education in a largely vocationally oriented curriculum. The new plan of studies did not require study of modern foreign languages nor did it provide for any *Maturitätsprüfung*.[54] Only at the end of the 1850s and in the 1860s did *Realschule* teachers and various local communities again raise the question of giving the *Realschulen* greater parity with the *Gymnasien*.

The reforms for the *Gymnasien* and *Realschulen* drafted by Exner and Bonitz, in fact, aroused considerable opposition among Austrian educators and in the wider society. That Bonitz was a Protestant from Prussia raised hackles. Even though considerable organizational and curricular differences still remained between the Austrian and Prussian secondary schools, conservative Austrian Catholic interests and, later, some Czech nationalists accused Count Thun's ministry of slavishly copying Prussian models.[55] Traditionalists among the university professors and the state officialdom defended the old practices, and some in the bureaucracy and the general public worried about the financial cost of the reforms. Also, some educators complained about the speed with which the changes were introduced.

The latter concerns among teachers and school directors revealed characteristic features of the reform process during the 1850s and, indeed, of the regulation of Austrian secondary education for the rest of the century. Under Leo Thun, the ministry undertook only limited consultations with selected educators in drawing up the new regulations and did not submit drafts to any representative bodies. The new laws and regulations granted considerable powers over the schools to state bureaucrats, and ministerial officials retained much of that authority even after 1867, when constitutional government emerged and more public debate arose about educational policies.[56] Helmut Engelbrecht, the most eminent recent student of the institutional and political history of Austrian education, has concluded that the Austrian state laid down foundations for the direction of secondary schools that were essentially "authoritarian and directive" (*obrigkeitlich und dirigistisch*) although more democratic features were later added at the lower administrative levels.[57]

Throughout the second half of the nineteenth century, the central government in Vienna had the authority to establish standards and basic procedures for all levels of public education throughout the Austrian crown lands. The same regulations were binding on all institutions that wanted public accreditation even though community and provincial governments had financial and operating responsibilities for the primary schools and many secondary schools. Even during the constitutional era, the ministry issued most of the regulations for public education as ordinances and decrees without going through any legislative process in the provincial diets or the Austrian parliament, the Reichsrat. In Engelbrecht's view, these authoritarian tendencies were only strengthened by the circumstance that officials who were trained in law and public administration and spent their careers in the bureaucracy generally had greater influence in the Ministry of Religion and Instruction than did individuals with professional educational expertise.[58] The principles of academic freedom and faculty self-governance in the universities and technical institutes gave their professors somewhat greater influence over higher education, but there, too, the central state bureaucracy exercised considerable power.

The Ministry of Religion and Instruction under Leo Thun took a pragmatically conservative line with regard to the extent of public access to advanced education. Apparently, the ministry contemplated a widening of access only in connection with the plans for expanding the *Realschulen*. In practice, however, the Austrian *Realschulen* operated largely as enhanced vocational secondary schools during the 1850s and early 1860s and made little contribution to advanced academic education. The 1848 "Proposal of the Basic Features of Public Education in Austria" stipulated mandatory primary education for all children from ages six to twelve with additional Sunday classes through the fifteenth year. Under the Exner-Bonitz reforms of the secondary schools, boys could enter a *Gymnasium* at age ten after completing the fourth year of an elementary school with adequate marks, without having to take any admissions examination. Nonetheless, the educational authorities could safely assume that, as before, many students would quit the *Gymnasium* after several years in the lower forms to pursue careers in commerce or the crafts. The old hurdles of Latin and Greek, along with the rigors of the newly added subjects and the *Matura,* would cause further attrition and restrict the total number of *Gymnasium* graduates eligible to go on to the universities. In the 1850s the ministry neither intended nor encouraged any significant democratization of *Gymnasium* education. The reformed *Gymnasien* charged tuition, although provisions were made for exemptions; and the numbers of schools offering the full eight-year course of studies grew little during the 1850s.[59]

Regarding enrollments in higher education, the educational authorities showed similar caution during the 1850s, apparently hoping to keep a balance between supply and demand for graduates. The ministry expected a serious commitment to study from the youth who enrolled, and it used fees to help discourage those who might lack the proper motivation. The Austrian government had replaced hourly tuition with flat fees earlier in the century, but in July 1850 the ministry introduced a charge per weekly instructional hour, the *Kollegiengeld,* which the universities turned over to the lecturing professors and docents. This fee would support the unsalaried docents and give the professors additional income, but the ministry also defended it as a means to encourage greater responsibility among students regarding their academic work.[60] Of course, even with the possibility of scholarships and exemptions from the fees, the instructional fees would also help discourage the poorest youth from enrolling in the universities.

Regarding the institutional expansion of higher education, the ministry appointed additional professors during the 1850s, most obviously in the philosophical faculties. Nonetheless, the ministry founded no new universities in this period; and it terminated all university-level instruction in Salzburg and Olomouc except for theology. For higher technical education, the central government authorized in 1849–50 the development of schools for mining and metallurgy (*Montan-Lehranstalten*) in Leoben, Styria, and Příbram, Bohemia, and the opening of a new technical institute in Brno, Moravia. All these new institutions, however, remained modest for some time. Enrollments in the philosophical faculties were still small during the 1850s, and the medical faculties were unable to produce enough graduates to meet current governmental and public needs. In 1849 the government dissolved the program for training military physicians and surgeons at the Josephs-Akademie in Vienna as part of efforts to unify medical education within the universities, but in 1851 it ordered that the program be reopened because of overcrowding in the Vienna medical faculty and the inability to meet current demand for practitioners.[61]

As the neo-absolutist regime rebuilt the state bureaucracy after the crisis of 1848 and centralized control from Vienna, it needed larger numbers of graduates from the university faculties of law and public administration. In 1853 when Jarcke and others voiced concern about apparent overcrowding in the law faculties, Leo Thun explained to the ministerial conference that the state itself was to blame because it stipulated higher legal education for so many officials. It was also the state's fault, he added, if many of the young men crowding into the law faculties were more interested in passing examinations than in gaining a scholarly education.[62] It is hard to track the precise balance between the supply of graduates from the law faculties and the demand for educated state officials during the 1850s, but it is known that during the economic boom of the 1860s and early 1870s, a shortage of educated recruits developed for many bureaucratic positions in the provinces despite increases in the numbers of law students.[63]

Count Thun's discussion of enrollments in the law faculties in 1853 also touched on the relationship in the universities between professional training and the pursuit of scholarship and a general humanistic education. Here, too, the ministry pursued a pragmatically conservative course in raising scholarly standards while still expecting the preparation of competent state officials, lawyers, notaries, educators, and other professionals. Following the model of the earlier reforms in many German universities, the ministry worked to make the Austrian philosophical faculties, in particular, important centers of scholarly research as well as teaching. The Vienna University offered its first seminars in fall 1848 in the philosophical faculty.[64] Throughout the universities, research and teaching were expected to complement each other. Graduates were now expected to bring to their professional careers greater intellectual command of their fields as well as higher levels of general education than was possible under the old plans of study.[65]

Leo Thun saw professional training as an essential part of the work of universities and technical institutes, compatible with scholarly inquiry. He rejected, for instance, the arguments of Jarcke that the government reduce or drop the requirement of university legal studies for various state offices so that the law faculties might have more freedom to pursue the advanced study of law.[66] On the other hand, Count Thun also opposed proposals on the professional side to divide the law curriculum into various tracks leading to particular sectors of government service. In the end the ministry ordained a unified course of studies that combined elements of scholarly inquiry with a broad professional preparation. Resistance to changes in the curriculum and examinations for the law faculties proved so great, however, that the new examination system of 1855 was never fully implemented. Only in 1872 were new requirements established for the doctorate in law.[67]

Like the governments of France and other continental countries after the crises of the late 1840s, Austria's neo-absolutist regime accorded an important role to religious authorities in its reformed public educational system. In 1850 the government recognized the Protestant theological institute in Vienna as an independent faculty in a demonstration of tolerance for religious minorities, but in 1855 the state signed a concordat with the Vatican that gave the Catholic Church broad powers over Austrian education and marriage law while reducing government intervention in the internal administration of the Church. Leo Thun considered the primary function of the Catholic theological faculties in the universities to be the training of prospective clergy, and the ministry left those faculties under the bishops' control. As a result, there was little concerted effort during the 1850s to raise their academic standards.[68] Count Thun supported the 1855 Concordat and Church supervision of public primary and secondary education to free the Church from the old Josephinist bureaucratic controls and to strengthen its moral influence over the public.[69]

In secondary education, a ministerial ordinance of January 1854 and the Concordat of 1855 established episcopal oversight over the *Gymnasien* to assure the Christian moral content of the education. Non-Catholics might enroll in the *Gymnasien* and other secondary schools, but only Catholics could be appointed professors except in the handful of specifically Protestant or Eastern Orthodox institutions.[70] The neo-absolutist government was eager to have members of religious orders teaching in the secondary schools for both ideological and budgetary reasons, and it exempted a number of regular clergy, including all Jesuits, from the new educational requirements for secondary school teachers. At the end of the 1850s, Catholic clergy directed the great majority of *Gymnasien* in the Alpine and Bohemian lands and accounted for a majority of the teachers.[71]

While granting the Catholic Church great sway over primary and secondary education, the neo-absolutist government put some limits on clerical influence in higher education. In October 1853 Leo Thun assured the other ministers that no teaching contradictory to Christian revelation would be tolerated in the universities.[72] The Catholic Church controlled the theological faculties, and Jesuits operated the new theological faculty that opened in 1857 in Innsbruck. Nonetheless, the Ministry of Religion and Instruction held out against putting the universities fully under Church control. As one student of Count Thun's reforms has noted, the clear delineation of the Church's powers in public education in the 1855 Concordat made it easier, in fact, to appoint Protestants as university professors when no qualified Catholic was available.[73] Nonetheless, the educational provisions of the Concordat gave Austrian liberals a major target for political attack when they got the opportunity during the next decade.

Revolutionaries in 1848 had raised the question of the language of instruction in public education as part of their advocacy of equality for Austria's various peoples, and this remained an issue during the 1850s. Public secondary schools, universities, and technical institutes in the Alpine and Bohemian lands had all taught in German before 1848, although individual university courses were offered on various Slavic languages and literatures. In 1848 Czech nationalists demanded public education in their mother tongue at all levels, and that year Czech became the language of instruction for some courses of the Prague University and several Bohemian secondary schools.[74] After

1849 Leo Thun and some of his aids believed it to be in the best interests of the state and society to provide primary education in the students' mother tongues for all major ethnic groups. The ministry under Count Thun also initially supported instruction in students' mother tongues in secondary and higher education wherever it was practicable, while still recognizing the central role of German in government and commerce. In addition, during the early 1850s Count Thun approved the appointment of some distinguished Czech scholars as professors in the Prague University.

Others in the neo-absolutist regime, however, were committed to a unified state and to the dominance of the German language in administration and commerce. They argued against giving equal status to the other languages in advanced education. The ministerial conference decided in July 1853 to cut back instruction in the other languages and to reaffirm the primacy of German in the secondary schools and the higher classes of the primary schools.[75] As a result, instruction in Czech declined sharply in Bohemian secondary schools between 1853 and 1860, and pressures developed in the central government against the appointment of any more Czech professors in the Prague University.[76]

Leo Thun and his colleagues in the Ministry of Religion and Instruction completed most of their work in reforming secondary and higher education by the time of the signing of the Concordat in 1855. After that, Thun increasingly found his efforts blocked by more rigid Catholic conservatives like Cardinal Rauscher of Vienna, who questioned whether there was sufficient clerical influence in higher education. Other high state officials and some educators also balked at some of his policies. The doctors' colleges of the Vienna and Prague universities, for instance, helped prevent the adoption of new doctoral examinations in the faculties of law and philosophy.

Leo Thun remained as minister of religion and instruction until October 1860. By the end of the 1850s the neo-absolutist regime faced growing criticism from the nobility, particularly in Hungary; from liberal Austrian German bankers, entrepreneurs and professionals; and from Czech nationalists. A general business downturn between 1857 and 1859 and a severe fiscal crisis in 1858 and early 1859 weakened the government. Then, in June 1859 defeat in the war with Piedmont-Sardinia and France humiliated the regime. In August 1859 Emperor

Francis Joseph dismissed Bach and the chief of state police and began a series of constitutional experiments. The emperor approved the introduction of representative institutions, first in a federal arrangement under the so-called October Diploma of 1860 and then in a more centralized system under the February Patent of 1861.[77] Deferring to provincial interests, the emperor dissolved the Ministry of Religion and Instruction when he issued the October Diploma, leaving some of its policy functions to the Ministry of State and giving many of the administrative duties to the individual crown lands.[78] Austria then had no central authority for educational affairs at the ministerial level until the Austro-Hungarian Compromise of 1867, when Austria and Hungary each received its own cabinet of ministers for internal affairs.

Political Modernization and the Consolidation of the Educational System

In the period of emerging constitutional government between 1860 and 1867 and the succeeding era of German liberal dominance through the 1870s, Austria consolidated the modern system of advanced education begun between 1848 and 1855. Central and provincial authorities expanded greatly the institutional network. They also completed some of the unfinished initiatives of the neo-absolutist era such as establishing a full seven-year curriculum and a *Matura* for the *Realschulen,* defining new requirements for doctoral degrees in the universities, and transforming the technical institutes into full-fledged institutions of higher learning. Nearly all these actions followed the general policies enunciated by Thun and his colleagues in 1849 and the early 1850s.

Liberal German political forces gained strength in the Alpine and Bohemian crown lands during the mid-1860s. With the 1867 Compromise with Hungary and the adoption of new constitutional laws for each half of the monarchy, the German liberals and their allies won dominance in Austrian politics. Still, the emperor retained important powers over the military and foreign policy, and his ministers were not formally responsible to a parliamentary majority. Nonetheless, the German liberals, with support from entrepreneurs, professionals, and some of the noble landowners, were dedicated to establishing centralized parliamentary government in Austria. The state bureaucracy continued to wield considerable authority, but the officials were now expected to respect constitutional principles and uphold equal individual rights for all citizens, regardless of birth, property, religion, or mother tongue. The new constitutional laws also explicitly recognized the principles of freedom in "scholarship and its teaching."[79]

Liberal politicians and journalists had already showered criticism on the Concordat with the Vatican for years before 1867. Now the German liberals wanted to abolish Catholic Church control over state services and responsibilities, particularly education and marriage regulations. The Catholic Church was to remain an important public corporation, though; and representatives of all major religious denominations would continue to offer religious instruction as a required subject in the public primary and secondary schools. That instruction, however, like the rest, must be under state supervision. The enactment in March 1862 of a law increasing the powers of elected community councils had already sparked calls by German and Czech liberals for giving local governments greater authority over primary schools.[80] After the so-called bourgeois ministry (*Bürgerministerium*) led by the German liberals came into office in late 1867, the Austrian Reichsrat acted on 25 May 1868 to abolish the supervision of public primary and secondary schools by the Catholic Church. In August 1870, a few weeks after the first Vatican Council accepted the doctrine of papal infallibility, the Austrian government revoked the 1855 Concordat altogether, despite the opposition of many Catholic clergy and conservative laymen.[81]

These political changes, along with financial pressures on the Catholic Church and the various religious orders, caused a sharp decline in the role of clergy in secondary education. Many of the orders during the 1860s faced increasing difficulty in providing teachers and meeting expenses for their schools, problems made worse after 1867 by new state requirements that all teachers be properly educated and certified. After 1867 any secondary school run by a religious corporation had to meet all the curricular requirements of the state and accept state inspection and regulation if it wanted public accreditation and the right to administer a *Matura*. In 1861, 62 percent of the teachers in Austrian *Gymnasien* were in Catholic religious orders; but only 36 percent of the teachers were in 1871. In 1870 religious orders still operated thirty-six *Gymnasien* in Austria, but in the following three years more than half of these were secularized. The central state authorities took over thirteen, a provincial government took on one, and five passed to local community administration.[82] In later decades other monastic *Gymnasien* were secularized or closed.

The free, modern civic order envisioned by the German liberal forces required an up-to-date, comprehensive system of public education. The Austrian cabinets of the late 1860s and the 1870s assiduously improved and expanded education at all levels. That this wave of expansion began in a period of significant economic growth and development was no accident. As elsewhere in Western and Central Europe, the great economic boom of the 1860s and early 1870s aided the development of the educational system by increasing popular demand for professional services and the need for educated employees in public and private bureaucracy.[83] Economic growth during this period also provided additional financial resources for education while putting wind in the political sails of liberal forces more generally. Whatever impact the economic trends had on the development of the educational system, however, they worked through the prisms of political mechanisms and changing popular attitudes about education.

New laws and administrative arrangements for public education emerged almost immediately with the establishment of a full-fledged constitutional system in 1867–68. The emperor reinstituted the Ministry of Religion and Instruction in March 1867, just as the negotiations for the Austro-Hungarian Compromise were being concluded in Budapest. The 1868 legislation that abolished Catholic Church control over primary and secondary education established a system of school boards at the provincial, district, and local levels to administer and supervise public schools (the *Landes-*, *Bezirks-*, and *Ortsschulräte*).[84]

Regarding primary education, the German liberals won enactment of a landmark general primary school law (*Reichsvolksschulgesetz*) in May 1869. This act provided for mandatory free primary education under secular state control for boys and girls from ages six to fourteen. Fulfillment of this goal during the following years was good but not perfect. Many peasants and factory workers feared the loss of labor and income of their teenage children that would result from extended primary schooling, and exemptions were allowed from the last two years of school in the poorest Carpathian and Adriatic coastal regions.[85] The new regulations obliged the local authorities to operate general *Volksschulen* with an eight-year program or, alternatively, five-year *Volksschulen* with separate three-year *Bürgerschulen*.[86] The law of 1869 advanced secular primary education significantly; thereafter religious corporations could operate only private schools in Austria.

The liberal legislation after 1867 obliged the Austrian public schools to serve equally children from all major language groups and all religious denominations.[87] Article 19 of the December 1867 constitutional laws guaranteed the full "equality of all the languages customarily spoken in each crown land [*aller landesüblichen Sprachen*] in school, state offices, and public life." Following this, the primary school law of 1869 stipulated the practical requirements for operating schools or parallel classes for pupils of each mother tongue in each local district.[88]

The liberal educational policies of the late 1860s and the 1870s guaranteed free government-sponsored primary schooling to the general population while maintaining a segmented and selective system of public secondary education. Able pupils who wished to pursue advanced academic or technical education were to leave the *Volksschule* after four years to attend a *Gymnasium* or *Realschule*. Independent three-year *Bürgerschulen* developed as general public middle schools with instruction in reading, writing, arithmetic, geography, history, religion, geometry, natural history, and basic science, but no physics, foreign languages, or advanced literature courses.

To provide competent teachers for the *Volksschulen* and *Bürgerschulen,* the new school regulations provided for establishing four-year teacher training schools, with separate institutions for men and women. Austria's teacher training schools were initially modeled after those in Saxony, although with a course of study two years shorter; and they functioned during the late nineteenth century as a distinct track of advanced secondary education, alongside the upper forms of the *Gymnasien* and *Realschulen*. Admissions requirements for the teacher training schools changed several times in the succeeding decades, but generally the students had to be at least fifteen years old and to have completed a *Bürgerschule* and, until 1883, the lower forms of a *Gymnasium* or *Realschule* as well.[89] Insofar as Austrian primary school teachers, like their counterparts in Germany, were not required to complete an academic secondary school or study in an institution of higher learning, they did not belong to an educated profession.

In the *Gymnasien* and *Realschulen,* the liberal ministerial authorities after 1867 generally followed the purposes and plans originally outlined by Exner and Bonitz. The *Realschulen* remained under the direct administrative control of the provincial diets until the Ministry of Religion and Instruction strengthened its power over those schools in the late 1870s. Nonetheless, in 1868 the ministry presented to the Reichsrat a proposal to make the *Realschulen* full seven-year secondary schools that would emphasize mathematics, natural sciences, and modern foreign languages and provide appropriate preparation for the technical institutes. *Realschule* teachers had been calling for greater equality of status with the *Gymnasien* for some years, and reorganization of Austria's technical institutes in the mid-1860s required expansion of the *Realschulen* and additions to their curriculum to prepare students adequately. The provincial diets responded positively to the ministry's initiative of 1868 with measures to reform their *Realschulen* and to establish general examinations to certify graduates for admission to the technical institutes. The number of *Realschulen* grew rapidly during the early 1870s, and the rise of government-operated craft schools (*Gewerbeschulen*) made it easier for the *Realschulen* to dispense with their former vocational instruction.[90] The extension of the program of studies for the *Realschulen* and the introduction of their own *Matura* greatly enhanced their status as academic secondary schools, but the public continued to view them as inferior to the classical *Gymnasien*. One of the most obvious signs of this was the requirement for graduates of the upper forms of the *Realschulen* to take supplementary courses and special examinations in *Gymnasium* subjects if they wanted admission to a university.

Still, the grassroots pressures to raise the status of the *Realschulen* that surfaced in the 1860s reflected a desire among some local educators and parts of the public to broaden access to the privileges of academic secondary education by creating alternatives to the classical *Gymnasien*. The social and economic benefits of academic secondary education grew substantially in Austria and throughout Western and Central Europe between the 1850s and the 1870s. Expanding public and private bureaucracies in Austria increasingly required the *Matura* or at least some secondary education for intermediate and lower-level positions.[91] When the Reichsrat adopted a general military obligation of three years' service in 1848, the Austrian state ratified and reinforced the popular belief in the social value of secondary education by granting to any graduate of the upper forms of a *Gymnasium* or *Realschule* the privilege of "one-year, volunteer service" as an officer candidate to be followed by a period in the reserves. Here, again, Austria followed a German model. Prussia had begun to grant such a privilege in the early nineteenth century, and the North German Confederation adopted it in 1867. Later, the Austrian government extended the privilege to graduates of commercial schools and some other nonacademic secondary schools as well.[92]

Popular pressure for greater access to academic secondary education motivated an experiment in a number of Austrian localities during the 1860s and 1870s of combining the initial forms of the *Gymnasium* and *Realschule* in a single four-year curriculum after which students could proceed to either conventional *Gymnasium* or *Realschule* studies. For any smaller community that was trying to expand secondary education and had to pay most or all the costs until the provincial or central government agreed to assume the fiscal burdens, such a *Real-Gymnasium* had the advantage of offering the lower forms of both a *Gymnasium* and a *Realschule* under one roof. After the first four forms, these schools typically offered the upper forms of either a *Gymnasium* or a *Realschule,* but seldom both. The Czech city of Tábor in Bohemia started the first such *Real-Gymnasium,* or *reálné gymnasium* in Czech, in 1862. Additional *Real-Gymnasien* soon followed in Bohemia, Moravia, Galicia, and Lower Austria, but fewer developed in the other Alpine lands.

The *Real-Gymnasien* faded in Austria after the 1870s. The reform of the *Realschule* curriculum at the beginning of that decade made it more difficult to find a compromise between the *Realschule* and *Gymnasium* programs in the first four forms, and, not surprisingly, the *Gymnasium* curriculum tended to win out. Moreover, officials in the Ministry of Religion and Instruction had taken a dim view of this locally initiated innovation. For the ministry, it was simpler and more logical to have a distinct *Gymnasium* education and a separate *Realschule* curriculum with its own requirements.[93] Also, the possibility of the *Real-Gymnasien* offering the public broader access to secondary education had little attraction to ministerial officials, who considered such education appropriate only for a limited segment of youth. The ministry could make its preferences felt in these matters even when a particular local school was not in the central state budget.

After the 1870s, Austrian secondary education was slow to develop any alternative to the classical *Gymnasium* that would have equal status in the preparation of university students. As will be discussed later, Austrian educators around the turn of the century began to call for new variants to the classical *Gymnasium* curriculum. Only in 1908, though, did the Ministry of Religion and Instruction authorize an eight-year *Realgymnasium* with a different curriculum from the *Real-Gymnasium* of the 1860s and 1870s, whose graduates might go on to university study. Modeled after the like-named Prussian schools, this institution would offer less Latin, no Greek, but more mathematics and science than the classical *Gymnasium*.[94]

As part of the educational initiatives in the late 1860s, the ministry reviewed the functioning of the *Gymnasien* to determine whether they were fulfilling the basic goals laid down in the early 1850s. The officials wanted to know whether they needed to increase scientific instruction, teach modern languages, or take steps to insure that the *Matura* was testing general intellectual accomplishment and not simply specific knowledge.[95] Increases in the numbers of schools and students during the 1860s raised fears that too many youth were entering without adequate preparation or a real commitment to advanced learning. The *Gymnasien* could administer admissions examinations, but the great majority of schools simply accepted students on the basis of their grades in primary school. Some ministerial officials and local educators believed that the *Gymnasien* only encouraged the entry of many unqualified students by offering year-long "preparatory" or remedial classes.

In March 1870 the Ministry of Religion and Instruction issued a new ordinance on admissions for all state-recognized *Gymnasien, Real-Gymnasien,* and *Realschulen*. Henceforth all applicants for the first year of any secondary school would have to pass oral and written examinations on reading, writing, spelling, and grammar in the language of instruction; basic arithmetic skills; and religion.[96] Whatever else may have motivated the ordinance, the officials clearly wanted to tighten admissions and assure a more uniform level of accomplishment among new secondary school students.[97]

In late September 1870, the minister of religion and instruction, Dr. Karl von Stremayr, followed up on the new admissions procedures by calling for an advisory commission to conduct a broad review, an *Enquête,* of the Austrian *Gymnasien*. A month after the revocation of the 1855 Concordat, Stremayr was signaling the government's desire to restore the uniform, centralized regulation of secondary education that had been weakened earlier in the 1860s; and he promised a new general law for the *Gymnasien*.[98] The commission was to consider whether to continue the preparatory classes, increase instruction in the natural sciences, require modern foreign languages, change religious instruction in the upper forms, or alter the structure of the *Matura*.[99]

The *Gymnasium* professors, provincial school inspectors, and ministerial officials who participated in the 1870 *Enquête* generally supported raising the curricular standards and voiced no objections to the admissions examination. Some participants noted that accepting students simply on the basis of *Volksschule* grades and offering preparatory classes had opened the *Gymnasien* to youth of weak ability and poor preparation. Students in ethnically mixed areas often had particular need for remedial work in the language of instruction. The commission agreed that recent improvements in the primary schools made the preparatory classes less necessary than before. It also agreed that the *Gymnasien* should stop admitting nine-year-olds, who might not yet be ready for more advanced studies. Not wanting too radical a change overnight, though, the commission recommended continuing the preparatory classes wherever needed, but now to be independent of the *Gymnasien*.[100]

No member of the commission voiced any concern about how the admissions examination and the stricter age requirement might affect various social strata, but the participants in the *Enquête* demonstrated their awareness of social realities during the deliberations on curricular issues. In recommending increased attention to the natural sciences, Dr. Mathias Wretschko, the provincial school inspector for Styria, Carinthia, and Carniola, reminded his colleagues of the persisting differences between Austria's *Gymnasien* and their counterparts in Germany. He noted that even among the various German states, the teaching of the sciences in the *Gymnasien* differed according to local social and economic circumstances. Wretschko urged his colleagues as they looked for ways to improve the curriculum to consider the real motives of many youth who enrolled in the Austrian *Gymnasien*.[101]

> In Austria currently a much smaller portion of the students goes on to the university. Due to the lack of other kinds of schools, poor economic circumstances, and in many cases because of traditional views, youth seek out the higher schools mainly for the purposes of achieving a better, more lucrative career. Therefore,

> the *Gymnasium* here will continue in the future, as in the past, to be the most attractive and most highly attended secondary school.

Wretschko advocated no additional efforts to weed out students who lacked appropriate academic goals, but he called for more effective pedagogy in the natural sciences.

After considerable debate on the curricular issues, the commission endorsed increased instruction in the natural sciences in both the lower and upper forms of the *Gymnasien* and the addition of required gymnastics exercise and freehand drawing in the lower forms. Taking a conservative stand on language instruction, they rejected requiring modern foreign languages. The commission recommended continuing religious instruction in all eight years, although religion would no longer be included in the *Matura*.[102] After the *Enquête* the ministry adopted most, but not all, the curricular reforms recommended by the commission.[103]

The *Gymnasium* professors, school inspectors, and ministerial officials in the 1870 commission apparently held common assumptions about the fundamentally elitist character of *Gymnasium* education. It was clear that growth in the number of schools during the preceding decade and increased instruction in languages other than German or Italian were expanding access to secondary education. Overcrowding in many schools demonstrated the growing public appetite for advanced education. Professors and administrators knew, however, that many of the youth who were pushing into the *Gymnasien* were not staying beyond the third or fourth year. A full eight years of Latin vocabulary, grammar, and reading and six years of Greek, not to mention the sciences and mathematics, were clearly not for all teenage youth; nor by the same token were passing the *Matura* and going on to a university to be expected for more than a small minority.

Even while the Austrian state was expanding advanced education, the new admissions examinations and reforms in the *Gymnasium* curriculum introduced after 1870 reaffirmed the elitist character of academic secondary education.[104] The admissions requirements provoked no significant debate about access to the secondary schools among the general public or politicians, and the coming to office of more conservative ministers between March 1870 and October 1871 made no difference regarding this area of educational policy.[105] Perhaps the admissions examinations might have elicited an outcry if they had actually caused a noticeable reduction in student numbers. In fact, first-year enrollments in Austria's *Gymnasien* and *Real-Gymnasien* continued to grow through the 1870s without interruption. In 1870–71, the first year for the examinations, the *Gymnasien* and *Real-Gymnasien* throughout Austria had 7,310 first-year students, compared with 6,864 the previous year. A number of the poorer and more rural crown lands, such as Styria, Carinthia, and Carniola, experienced declines in first-year enrollments that year, but this may have resulted from various factors. In contrast, the schools in Lower Austria and Bohemia showed increases in 1870–71.[106] In 1874–75, all state-recognized *Gymnasien* and *Real-Gymnasien* in Austria had a total of 34,137 students compared with 30,497 in 1869–70, while the *Realschulen* had increased from 13,237 students in 1869–70 to 21,552 in 1874–75 (see table 1 in the appendix).[107] It should be remembered that local *Gymnasium* professors and directors administered the admissions examinations. Those educators lived in the communities and had to face the prospective students and their parents. The ministerial officials could ordain higher standards, but local social environments affected their implementation.

Decisions by the central and provincial governments during the late 1860s and the 1870s about providing advanced education in the languages of Austria's various peoples provoked much more public debate than did the introduction of admissions examinations for the secondary schools. The constitutional laws of 1867 promised equal status in public education for all the principal languages spoken in each crown land, but parliamentary and cabinet politics conditioned implementation of those provisions. In the Bohemian lands Czech politicians demanded more instruction in Czech at all educational levels. Slovene nationalists came into conflict with German interests when they pressed for Slovene instruction in Carniola, southern Styria, and southern Carinthia. As Polish propertied interests took over much of the administration of Galicia during the constitutional era, their efforts to consolidate a full system of Polish-language education collided with Ukrainian cultural aspirations in the eastern part of the province.

Instruction in languages other than German or the Italian used in parts of the southern provinces had already advanced with the shift to the crown lands of administrative authority over many educational matters in 1860. During the early 1860s some German-language secondary schools initiated parallel classes taught in other languages, but after 1865 separate institutions developed increasingly. In 1860, the Bohemian Diet moved to have Czech taught as a second language in the German secondary schools of the province. Soon, in the Czech regions of Bohemia and Moravia, many formerly German-language *Gymnasien* and *Realschulen* switched to Czech; and new Czech institutions opened. In the 1870s Czech political leaders could still point, though, to the inadequate supply of Czech-language instruction relative to the Czech share of the population in the Bohemian lands.[108] In 1860 the Poles quickly established Polish as the language of instruction in the secondary schools of western Galicia although some German-language schools remained in eastern Galicia, where the Jewish population was denser. Slovene nationalists campaigned from the early 1860s onward for Slovene instruction in the secondary schools of southern Styria and Carniola, but German interests there put up strong resistance. By 1875 three state *Gymnasien* in Carniola were teaching in German and Slovene; but in that same year no *Realschule* in Carniola and no public *Gymnasium* or *Realschule* in Styria used Slovene as the language of instruction. By the mid-1870s several Dalmatian towns had secondary schools that taught in Serbo-Croatian, but in the Carpathian lands the Ukrainians, or Rusins/Ruthenians as they were often called there, still had little secondary education in their mother tongue.[109]

Czech-language instruction grew rapidly during the early 1860s in Prague's Bohemian Polytechnic Institute. The Bohemian Diet approved new regulations for the Polytechnic Institute in 1863 that included full equality of Czech and German in instruction and administrative dealings.[110] By 1865–66 German professors found themselves in the minority in the institute and began to call for dividing the school into separate Czech and German institutions. Czech politicians and educators questioned the motives for such action and feared an unjust division of institutional resources, but the Bohemian Diet approved the split in August 1868, when the Czech deputies were boycotting the sessions.

It took longer for Czech instruction to achieve parity with German in the Prague University. In October 1864 the central government promised Czech political leaders that in appointing professors in Prague henceforth it would give preference among equally qualified candidates to those who could lecture in Czech.[111] The Bohemian Diet followed up in 1866 with measures to add Czech lecturers in all examination fields and to accept the Czech language for all major examinations in the Prague University. During the 1860s and 1870s, Czech scholars first achieved effective parity with their German counterparts in the philosophical faculty, reflecting the vigorous Czech scholarship in the humanities and the need to train teachers for the growing number of Czech secondary schools. In this period Czechs also enjoyed a strong presence among the professors of theology and the students in that faculty. The numbers of Czech professors grew more slowly in the law faculty with its ties to the conservative, still largely German state bureaucracy; and in the medical faculty nationalist political loyalties and a sense of ethnic competition developed later than in other parts of the Prague University.[112]

The influential Polish noble landowners in Galicia worked during the 1860s and 1870s to establish Polish as the language of instruction in the universities of Krakow and L'viv. In the 1850s German instruction had predominated in L'viv and even in Krakow, which had only Latin and Polish lectures before 1846; but the Galician Diet won the gradual conversion of both universities to Polish-language instruction after 1860. Polish was the basic language of instruction in both universities by 1871.[113]

When German liberals and their allies dominated the Austrian cabinets between 1867 and 1870 and then again between 1871 and 1879, they sponsored a considerable expansion of primary and secondary education that benefited nearly all of Austria's major ethnic groups in varying degrees. Still, the German liberals were anxious to defend German ethnic interests and a privileged position for German-language instruction in advanced education. In 1868, for instance, German liberals in the cabinet nullified the 1863 act of the Bohemian Diet that required all students in Bohemia's secondary schools to study the second language of that crown land, whether German or Czech.[114]

The reaction of conservative and Slavic interests to some of the German liberals' educational policies was clear when the Czech educator Josef Jireček served as minister of religion and instruction in the short-lived Hohenwart cabinet in 1871. Jireček approved the introduction of Slovene as a language of instruction in the *Gymnasien* of Carniola, except for the German district of Gottschee. In higher education, he supported increased Czech instruction in the Prague University and the conversion of the University of L'viv to Polish-language instruction. Jireček also encouraged enhanced roles for the provincial diets and school boards in policy-making for primary education in order to weaken central authority and German liberal centralizing tendencies.[115]

After the German liberals regained control of the cabinet in November 1871, Czech and Slovene nationalists could again complain of bias in favor of German-language education by the Ministry of Religion and Instruction. With Stremayr again in charge, the ministry insisted that the law faculties in Krakow and L'viv offer their courses on German law in German. With community, provincial, and state support, Czech secondary education had experienced considerable growth during the 1860s in parts of Bohemia and Moravia. After 1871 Czech secondary schools continued to expand, but during the 1870s the ministry also sponsored many new German secondary schools in the Bohemian lands. The ministerial authorities aided German interests in the expansion of state-sponsored vocational education as well.[116] To assure that teachers in the non-German *Volksschulen* and *Bürgerschulen* would still have at least some German-language education, the ministry ordered in April 1878 that the requirements for teacher certification include passing an examination in German and evidence of having read German books after graduation from a teacher training school.[117]

To compensate in part for the loss of German-language university education in Galicia, the central government founded in 1875 a new German-language university in remote Bukovina, the Francis Joseph University of Chernivtsi (Czernowitz, Cernauti). The 1880 census reported that only 19 percent of the population in Bukovina was German-speaking, 42 percent Ukrainian, and 33 percent Romanian.[118] Nonetheless, Stremayr later made no secret of his motives in pushing for the new university in Chernivtsi: "I made great efforts to persuade first the crown and then parliament to establish a new university—in Chernivtsi—as a beachhead of German education in the eastern part of the monarchy."[119]

In favoring German-language education, Austria's German liberal ministers and parliamentary leaders affirmed their beliefs in the superior value of German for scholarship, administration, and commerce; the need for some uniformity in government and cultural affairs; and the continuing role of the German-speaking population as a progressive, unifying force in Austria. The German liberal leaders did not deny access to secondary and higher education to members of the non-German ethnic groups, although they hoped that many would be willing to pursue such education in German. But for the stiffening of the admissions requirements for the secondary schools in 1870, the Austrian government under German liberal leadership did far more to expand popular access to education at all levels than to limit it. In contrast, the conservative forces who came to power after 1879 proved more interested in limiting access to advanced academic education and trying to reduce enrollments.

In higher education, the central government after 1867 completed the university reforms begun in 1848–49 and the early 1850s. In 1865 with the liberal political forces gaining strength, professors in the Vienna University began to call openly for an end to special privileges in university governance for the doctors' colleges and the Catholic Church. The doctors' colleges in Vienna and Prague stoutly defended themselves, and conservatives insisted on preserving the special Catholic character of the Austrian universities, particularly in Vienna and Prague, where the archbishops carried the title of university chancellor. Nonetheless, in December 1870 Emperor Francis Joseph accepted the recommendations of Stremayr to remove the doctors' colleges from the Vienna and Prague universities, restrict to the theological faculties the roles of the Vienna and Prague archbishops as chancellors, and make the universities otherwise neutral with regard to religion. In 1873 the Reichsrat formalized these changes in a new law on the organization of the universities.[120] The new regulations also permitted non-Catholics to be elected as deans of faculties or university rectors.

The removal of the doctors' colleges from university governance enabled the professors and the Ministry of Religion and Instruction to complete changes in the requirements for doctoral degrees in philosophy, law, and medicine that were first proposed in the late 1840s and the 1850s. The ministry approved new regulations for those degrees in 1872. In the philosophical faculties the doctorate would now require a scholarly dissertation to demonstrate the student's ability to carry out research and develop an original theory or synthesis. The new doctoral examination or *Rigorosum,* taken after at least three years of study, was expected to test in-depth knowledge and analytic ability in specified subjects rather than encyclopedic breadth. The new requirements for the doctorate in law stipulated the completion of at least eight semesters and the passing of three examinations in place of the previous four. The doctorate in law would no longer require a dissertation or written disputation, which had turned into a trivial exercise over the years.[121]

The new requirements for the medical doctorate adopted in 1872 were part of an ongoing professionalization of medicine and efforts by the government and university-trained physicians and surgeons to reduce the role of practitioners with lesser education. The 1872 regulations required that medical students complete at least ten semesters of study. Following proposals first made in the Vienna medical faculty in 1846, the 1872 code introduced a new degree, the "doctorate of all medical science" (*Doktorat der gesamten Heilkunde,* or *Doctor universae medicinae,* in Latin), in place of the former more specialized diplomas in medicine, surgery, obstetrics, and ophthalmology. This only replicated the efforts to establish a unified medical doctorate begun in various German states from the 1820s onward.[122] The new Austrian doctoral examinations were divided into three segments, and students and observers of Austrian education agreed that the new rules made the examinations more difficult than before 1872. The changes helped reduce the numbers of medical students during the 1870s.[123] Over the longer term, however, the medical students' increased latitude in selecting and attending lecture courses under the principle of freedom of study only encouraged larger enrollments.[124]

After the mid-1870s the university medical faculties established a monopoly in the training and certification of Austrian physicians and surgeons. Already in 1848–49 and the early 1850s, the Austrian government, like some of the smaller German states, had begun to close down the surgeons' schools that had operated on the level of advanced vocational schools. The Vienna authorities terminated the last such programs in 1871 in L'viv, Olomouc, and Salzburg.[125] In the meantime, an imperial decree of 1868 ordered the final closing of the Josephs-Akademie; and its last students finished in 1874.

Any increases in the academic requirements for the medical doctorate and measures to terminate alternative paths to professional certification restricted public access to medical careers. The professors and ministerial officials who sponsored the changes spoke about improving the scientific quality of the training and raising the standards for professional practice. Such discourse helped them to avoid addressing explicitly the potentially controversial questions of access to the profession for various segments of the population. This was all part of a social politics of advanced education, however, which began to emerge under Austria's constitutional government after the 1860s.[126]

The Catholic theological faculties changed more slowly during the late 1860s and the 1870s than did the other university faculties. The bishops continued to dominate the theological faculties, and the comprehensive examinations and doctoral requirements changed in only minor ways. A four-part doctoral examination was still required, and the bishops were able to name up to half the members of the examining committees. A more substantial doctoral dissertation replaced the old disputation in 1873. Students in the other faculties had long looked down on their counterparts in theology as being, on average, economically poorer and academically weaker; but the bishops and the professors of theology worried about the declining attraction of the priesthood for contemporary youth and were willing to accept students with somewhat lesser qualifications.[127] A ministerial order in January 1869 allowed the theological faculties to admit students simply on the basis of passing the *Gymnasium Matura,* while medicine and law at that time required, in addition, grades of first-class "good" in certain *Gymnasium* subjects.

The new wave of educational reform at the beginning of Austria's constitutional era and the need for improved technical education generated by the economic boom of the 1860s enabled the technical institutes to expand and improve their academic status. The constitutional laws of 1867 guaranteed freedom of teaching and study in the technical institutes. New organizational statutes and ordinances for the institutes in Vienna (1872), Graz (1872), and Prague (1874) abolished their admissions examinations and provided for admission to be based simply on a *Realschule Matura* or a *Gymnasium Matura* with supplementary examinations in geometry and freehand drawing. The institute in Graz was already officially titled a *Technische Hochschule* (technical college). The institute in Vienna received that designation in 1872 and the two in Prague in 1879. The new regulations provided for the *Habilitierung* of young scholars as docents in the technical colleges just as in the universities, and the enhanced status of these institutions forced the government authorities to raise the professors' salary levels closer to those of university professors.[128]

Most of these changes in higher technical education signified only the belated fulfillment of goals enunciated in Franz Exner's "Proposal of the Basic Features of Public Education in Austria" of 1848.

Under the new constitutional government after 1867, liberals in the cabinet of ministers and the Reichsrat pursued further rationalization and uniformity in the regulation of universities and technical colleges alike. Those policies, along with the growing scope and costs of higher technical education, led the Ministry of Religion and Instruction in the early and mid-1870s to take over from the provincial governments the operation of the technical colleges one by one.[129]

One sticking point in raising the status of higher technical education was the question of state certification, diplomas, and titles for the graduates. With the institutional changes of the early and mid-1860s, it became possible for the Austrian technical institutes to administer comprehensive examinations and award diplomas; but those examinations lacked the official status of the state examinations administered by university faculties, and technical college diplomas brought no legal or professional privileges. Even under reform-minded German liberals in the late 1860s and the 1870s, the Ministry of Religion and Instruction resisted calls from professors and students in the technical colleges to establish state examinations in engineering and applied sciences. The ministry's footdragging, in part, only reflected the less-developed state of engineering and other technological professions, their weaker political influence, and their lesser social status compared with the older professions. By 1876 associations of engineers were joining in the agitation for more formal certification of technical college graduates, and in January 1877 the ministry declared its willingness to introduce state examinations. In July 1878, the ministry finally approved a system of state examinations for technical college students. Students had to pass the first state examination, covering multiple subjects, at the end of the fourth semester of studies or during the fifth semester. The second state examination, again covering an array of fields, was to be taken after either four or six additional semesters, depending on which school the student chose within a technical college.

Government approval for the technical colleges to award a formal degree comparable to the university doctorate came only after another two decades. In April 1901, two years after the Prussian technical colleges won the right to grant doctoral degrees, the Austrian government approved a doctorate of technical sciences requiring comprehensive doctoral examinations and a scholarly treatise. Not until

1917, however, did the Austrian government establish legal standards and protections for the title of *Ingenieur*.[130]

The extent to which the changes in Austrian secondary and higher education during the late 1860s and the 1870s only completed initiatives begun in the early 1850s suggests how much the later liberal reformers shared with their neo-absolutist predecessors in their goals for state education. Count Thun and his colleagues as well as their liberal successors were convinced of the backwardness of Austrian secondary and higher education compared with the best education elsewhere in Western and Central Europe. They were prepared to look to Switzerland, occasionally France, and, above all, to some of the German states for models of how Austria's educational institutions might be better operated. The deep social, economic, and political crisis of the 1840s and then the humiliating military defeats of 1859 and 1866 taught the Habsburg dynasty and leading elements in society painful lessons about weaknesses in the economy, government, and military defenses that made broad reform efforts imperative.

Both the neo-absolutist reformers of the 1850s and the liberal politicians of the 1860s and 1870s could agree on the necessity of greatly enhanced systems of secondary and higher education, patterned generally, but not totally, after the successful earlier reforms in Prussia and other German states. Networks of modern *Gymnasien, Realschulen,* universities, and technical colleges producing well-educated graduates would support more effective state administration and defense, assist in economic development, and improve the general welfare. The neo-absolutist regime expected improved advanced education to help strengthen government authority and produce leadership elements who would assure the loyalty of the population to established state laws and religious precepts. The later liberal reformers, on the other hand, aimed to build a stable but freer political and social order based on equal civil rights and just laws that the citizenry, churches, and state authorities themselves would all be obliged to respect. The liberal reformers considered it essential to enhance secondary and higher education to produce the able, well-prepared public and private officials, professionals, and educators needed to lead a modern state and society. A system of universal primary education in the *Volksschulen* and *Bürgerschulen* would teach the basic knowledge, skills, and civic responsibilities needed among the general population; and specialized secondary schools would provide the vocational instruction needed in various parts of the economy.

Even though committed to principles of broad general education and the cultivation of intellect and character, academic secondary and higher education were also expected by conservative and liberal reformers alike in Austria to serve the practical purposes of preparing professionals and higher officials. Enhancing academic secondary and higher education to meet the needs of a reforming state, developing economy, and growing population inevitably meant expanding the state educational institutions and their enrollments; but neither conservatives nor liberals initially intended those institutions to serve any large portion of the school-aged population. By the early 1870s, however, growth trends were apparent that threatened to go far beyond the early expectations. The discussion must now turn to the processes of expansion.

CHAPTER 2

Opening the Gates

Expansion of the Educational Network

In the 1850s and 1860s Austria's educational authorities launched an ambitious program of institutional development. They wanted a modern educational system comparable to the best in the neighboring European states. Austria's secondary schools, universities, and technical colleges were expected to develop as distinguished centers of learning. In more utilitarian terms, these institutions were to produce the professionals, technical personnel, and educated employees required to assure order and prosperity in a modern society. The reformers of the 1850s and 1860s expected the educational system to grow in numbers of institutions and people served, but they could hardly have expected the expansion in student enrollments and the resulting pool of the educated and semieducated that occurred during the late nineteenth century. Compared with its school-aged population, Austria's enrollments in secondary and higher education at the beginning of the twentieth century were among the highest in Europe.

After the 1850s Austria experienced unprecedented growth in its academic secondary schools, universities, and technical colleges. The number of students in the *Gymnasien* and *Realschulen* increased from 25,630 in 1851 to 140,545 in 1910 (see table 2/1).[1] In roughly the same period, the number of matriculated university students in Austria increased sixfold, expanding from 3,709 in winter 1856–57 to 23,068 in winter 1909–10, while the number of matriculated students in the technical colleges nearly quintupled from 2,235 to 10,110.[2] Enrollments in secondary and higher education grew significantly faster than did the total population, so that relative access, or the inclusiveness of academic education, increased as well. In 1851, there were only 1.46 *Gymnasium* and *Realschule* students per thousand in the total population (male and female); but by 1910, the number had grown to 5.03 per thousand. Between 1857 and 1910, the matriculated university enrollments expanded from 0.20 per thousand in the total population to 0.82 per thousand (see table 2/1).[3]

A more telling measure of educational opportunities is a comparison of the enrollments at each level to the population in the appropriate

TABLE 2/1
Enrollments in Austrian Secondary and Higher Education, 1851–1910

Gymnasien, Realgymnasien, & Realschulen

At end of acad. year	Total enrolled (matr. & priv.)	Per 1,000 in total pop.
1850–51*	25,630	1.46
1860–61*†	36,262	1.99
1869–70*	43,734	2.15
1879–80	65,935	3.03
1889–90	71,295	3.04
1899–1900	95,914	3.74
1909–10	140,545	5.03

Universities and Technical Colleges

At end of winter sem.	Total matr. in univ.	Per 1,000 in total pop.	Total matr. in tech. col.	Per 1,000 in tot. pop.
1856–57*	3,709	0.20	2,235	0.12
1869–70*	7,904	0.39	1,841	0.09
1879–80	8,114	0.37	2,988	0.14
1889–90	12,421	0.53	1,608	0.069
1899–1900	14,331	0.56	4,843	0.19
1909–10	23,068	0.82	10,110	0.36

Sources: Schimmer 1858; Schimmer 1877; *Statistisches Jahrbuch für das Jahr 1869; Statistisches Jahrbuch für das Jahr 1879; Öster. Statistik* 28, no. 4 (1892); 68, no. 3 (1903); n.s., 7, no. 3 (1913); Mitchell 1978, 3; Urbanitsch 1980, 3, pt. 1: 38, table l.

* *Statistics on the total numbers of matriculated university and technical college students for 1850–51 and 1860–61 are not available in these sources. The 1857 and 1869 censuses included only the civil population in the statistics on total population.*

† *Total population statistics taken from the 1857 Austrian census.*

age bracket.[4] The Austrian government published the first general statistics on age stratification with the December 1869 census returns. In 1870 Austria had 14.09 *Gymnasium* and *Realschule* students per thousand in the eleven- to eighteen-year-old population, male and female. The expansion of academic secondary education had more than doubled that number by 1910 to 30.57 per thousand people in the age group (see table 2/2).[5] In the male and female population aged nineteen to twenty-two, the prime age group for university study, enrollments in the Austrian universities also more than doubled from 5.53 matriculated students per thousand in winter 1869–70 to 12.08 in winter 1909–10. The matriculated students in the Austrian technical colleges increased even faster than in the universities, quadrupling from 1.02 students per thousand people aged eighteen to twenty-two in winter 1869–70 to 4.19 per thousand in 1909–10 (see table 2/2).[6]

TABLE 2/2
Enrollments in Austrian Secondary and Higher Education Relative to Age Cohorts, 1870–1910

Gymnasien, Realgymnasien, & Realschulen

At end of of acad. year	Total enrolled (matr. & priv.)	Per 1,000 in 11–18 yr. coh.
1869–70	43,734	14.09
1879–80	65,935	19.52
1889–90	71,295	19.04
1899–1900	95,914	23.41
1909–10	140,545	30.57

Universities and Technical Colleges

At end of winter sem.	Total matr. in univ.	Per 1,000 in 19–22 yr. coh.	Total matr. in tech. col.	Per 1,000 in 18–22 yr. coh.	Per 1,000 in 19–22 coh.
1869–70	7,904	5.53	1,841	1.02	1.29
1879–80	8,114	5.15	2,988	1.53	1.90
1889–90	12,421	7.59	1,608	0.79	0.98
1899–1900	14,331	7.81	4,843	2.16	2.64
1909–10	23,068	12.08	10,110	4.19	5.30

Sources: Schimmer 1877; *Statistisches Jahrbuch für das Jahr 1869; Statistisches Jahrbuch für das Jahr 1879; Bevölkerung und Viehstand* 1871, no. 3; *Öster. Statistik* 2, no. 1 (1882); 28, no. 4 (1892); 32, no. 1 (1892); 63, no. 3 (1903); 68, no. 3 (1903); n.s., 1, no. 3 (1914); n.s., 7, no. 3 (1913).

One can debate whether Austria's secondary schools and higher education actually achieved the standards of quality that obtained in the finest of Germany's institutions during the late nineteenth century.

Austrian educational authorities and parliamentary representatives proudly pointed to the accomplishments of the most renowned Austrian scholars, scientists, and physicians, but who or what was responsible for the accomplishments of these eminent few is far from clear. There could be little doubt, though, that Austria overcame much of its backwardness and reached Germany's standards in terms of the percentage of its school-aged population that was enrolled and the degree of access for school-aged youth. In 1870 in Prussia, for instance, enrollments in academic secondary schools—23 students per thousand in the prime age group of eleven to nineteen years—surpassed Austria's by 60 percent. Over the succeeding four decades, access to secondary schools grew substantially in both Prussia and Austria; but the Austrian rate of growth actually outpaced the Prussian, so that Austria's rate of enrollment caught up. In 1911 the Prussian rate of 32 secondary school students per thousand males and females in the prime age group only marginally exceeded Austria's 1910 figure of 30.6 per thousand in its prime age group.[7]

This level of secondary school attendance was more than respectable by European standards. Hartmut Kaelble has calculated that among European countries in 1910, Switzerland led by a clear margin in the number of students in academic secondary schools compared with the ten- to nineteen-year-old population, with a rate of enrollment three times that of Germany. After Switzerland, though, only Germany and Norway surpassed Austria, and that by small margins. Austria's rate of enrollment, in turn, slightly exceeded the rates of France, Denmark, Belgium, Italy, and England.[8] One must keep in mind, however, that beyond the strong similarities in the curricula and organization of German, Swiss, and Austrian academic secondary education, the character of secondary education varied greatly across the rest of Europe.

Austria's enrollment per capita in higher education caught up with Germany's even more quickly than did the secondary school enrollment, although some allowances must be made for institutional differences between the two countries. In 1856–57, all the German states had an average of 0.34 matriculated university students per thousand in the total population compared with Austria's 0.20. Thanks to the rapid growth in the number of Austrian university students during the late 1850s and 1860s, the Austrian rate slightly surpassed the German in 1870 (see table 2/3). Growth in the rate of university attendance in Germany outpaced Austria's increases from the 1870s to the 1890s, but the differences between them were marginal in 1900 and 1910.[9] Comparisons of university enrollments in Austria and Germany relative to the populations in the prime age groups between 1870 and 1910 show the same patterns (see table 2/3).[10]

TABLE 2/3
Enrollments in Austrian and German Universities and Technical Colleges Relative to Population, 1870–1910/11

Universities	**No. of matr. students per 1,000 total pop.**		**No. of matr. students per 1,000 in total age group**	
	AUSTRIA	GERMANY	AUSTRIA	GERMANY*
1870†	0.39	0.35	5.5	5.1
1880	0.37	0.47	5.2	6.8
1890	0.53	0.59	7.6	8.4
1900	0.56	0.60	7.8	8.2
1910	0.82	0.85	12.1	12.4
Technical Colleges	**No. of matr. students per 1,000 total pop.**		**No. of matr. students per 1,000 in total age group**	
	AUSTRIA	GERMANY	AUSTRIA	GERMANY‡
1870	0.09	0.067	1.02	0.76
1880	0.14	0.11	1.53	1.24
1890	0.069	0.067	0.79	0.79
1900	0.19	0.18	2.16	2.04
1910	0.36	0.17	4.19	1.97

Sources: For Austria, *Statistisches Jahrbuch für das Jahr 1869*; *Statistisches Jahrbuch für das Jahr 1879*; *Bevölkerung und Viehstand* 1871, no. 3; *Öster. Statistik* 2, no. 1 (1882); 28, no. 4 (1892); 32, no. 1 (1892); 63, no. 3 (1903); 68, no. 3 (1903); n.s., 1, no. 3 (1914); n.s., 7, no. 3 (1913); Mitchell 1978, 3; and Urbanitsch 1980, 3, pt. 1: 38, table 1. For Germany, Ringer 1979, 291–92 (universities); and Titze 1987, 28–29, 70–73 (technical colleges).

* *The prime age group for the German universities here is the 20- to 23-year-olds, following Ringer; that for the Austrian universities is the 19- to 22-year-olds, since the Austrian Gymnasium curriculum was one year shorter.*

† *Austrian enrollment statistics represent the number of matriculated students for the winter semester of the academic year in question; the German statistics are from the spring semesters, which were typically marginally lower than in the winter semesters.*

‡ *The prime age group for the Austrian technical colleges here is the 18- to 22-year-olds; that for the German technical colleges is 19- to 23-year-olds, following Jarausch and Titze.*

Austrian enrollments in higher technical education exceeded the statistics for Germany when compared with both the total population and the school-aged segment throughout the second half of the nineteenth century. Advanced technical education developed more slowly in the German states than in Austria during the first half of the nineteenth century, so that enrollment in technical institutes compared with total population in Austria in 1856–57 was three times larger than for the German states overall. The German institutions grew rapidly between the 1850s and 1870s, but the enrollment rates for the total population and for the prime age group never caught up with the corresponding rates for Austria except in the 1880s, when the depressed economic conditions caused significant declines in the Austrian institutions (see table 2/3).[11] After 1900 the number of matriculated students in the Austrian technical colleges grew explosively, roughly doubling between 1900 and 1910 compared with the total population and with those in the prime age group, while the rate of technical college enrollment in Germany actually declined. As a result of the strong growth in the Austrian technical colleges, the number of students in Austrian higher education compared with the total population and with the prime age group exceeded the figures for Germany in the last years before World War I.

The growth of Austrian higher education was so strong after the mid-1890s that Austria had one of the highest rates of enrollment throughout Europe in the last two decades before World War I. According to Kaelble's calculations, 1.06 percent of all Austrians twenty to twenty-four years old were enrolled in institutions of higher education in 1900, compared with 1.40 percent in Switzerland, 1.02 percent in Italy, 0.93 percent in France, 0.89 percent in Germany, and 0.79 percent in the United Kingdom.[12] An older study of enrollments compared with total population in 1910–11 showed that Austria had a rate of enrollment in all higher education 11 percent higher than Germany's, 30 percent higher than France's, 75 percent higher than England's, nearly twice Italy's, more than double Hungary's, and more than triple Russia's.[13]

Austria's educational reformers in the 1850s and 1860s could hardly have anticipated such strong growth in enrollments. Expansion was so rapid at times during the succeeding decades that more conservative politicians and officials considered it out of control. It is difficult to establish precisely the causes for the increases during the second half of the nineteenth century. Many factors contributed: population growth, economic development and new employment opportunities, urbanization, government policies, and changing public attitudes about the utility of advanced education. In most regions the school-aged population was clearly larger than in previous eras, but it was not simply that there were more students but also that larger proportions of the school-aged youth pursued secondary and higher education than ever before. State officials and educators talked much of the increasing requirements of commerce and industry as well as of state bureaucracy for educated and semieducated functionaries, engineers, lawyers, and physicians. Economic conditions, of course, affected what parents thought they could afford in educational expenses and the loss of labor or income incurred by keeping their offspring in school longer. In periods of economic growth, private entrepreneurs and various organized local interests might take the initiative in endowing scholarships and supporting new private schools. Beyond this, however, one must ask what combination of circumstances influenced the decisions of local or central authorities to open, expand, or close various public educational institutions, of parents to enroll their children in these schools, and of youth to attend schools and aspire to enter learned occupations. In this connection, economic trends and conditions may have had indirect as well as direct effects.

There was no simple relation between economic growth and prosperity on the one hand and increasing enrollments in advanced education on the other or, at other times, between depressed economic conditions and enrollment decline. Attendance in secondary schools, for instance, grew rapidly during the boom years of the late 1860s and early 1870s. In that period the increasing numbers of *Gymnasien* and *Realschulen* competed for enrollments, with the more "modern" *Realschulen* and *Real-Gymnasien* proving more attractive than the *Gymnasien*.[14] During the depression years between 1875 and 1880, however, total secondary enrollments still increased by 14 percent; but now the classical *Gymnasien* gained more than sixteen thousand students, while *Realschule* enrollments fell by nearly thirty-six hundred (see figure 1 and table 1 in the appendix).[15] Similarly, increases in university enrollments during the 1880s more than made up for the sharp declines in the technical colleges caused by poorer job opportunities for engineers and industrial scientists (see figure 2 and table 2 in the appendix).

FIGURE 1
Enrollments in Austrian Secondary Schools, 1851–1910

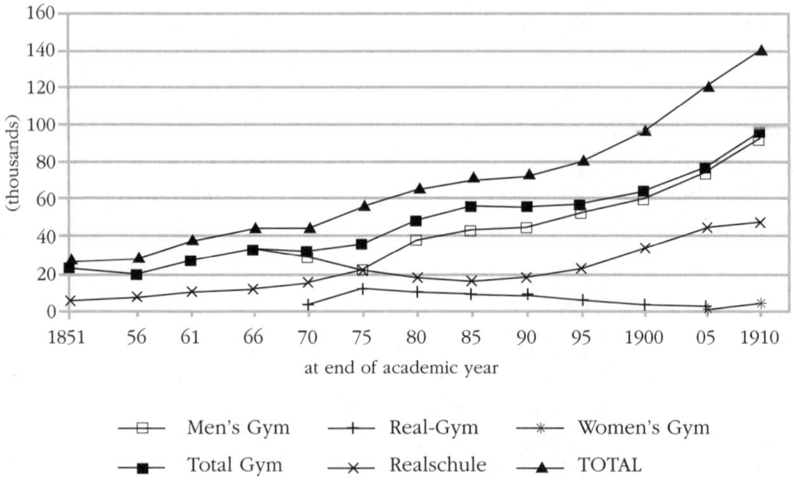

160
140
120
100
80
60
40
20
0
(thousands)
1851
56
61
66
70
75
80
85
90
95
1900
05
1910
at end of academic year
Men's Gym
Real-Gym
Women's Gym
Total Gym
Realschule
TOTAL

Sources: Schimmer 1858; Schimmer 1877; *Statistisches Jahrbuch für das Jahr 1874; Statistisches Jahrbuch für das Jahr 1879; Öster. Statistik* 2, no. 1 (1882); 16, no. 2 (1887); 28, no. 4 (1892); 61, no. 1 (1898); 68, no. 3 (1903); 79, no. 3 (1908); n.s., 7, no. 3 (1913).

FIGURE 2
Matriculated Students in Austrian Higher Education, 1857–1910

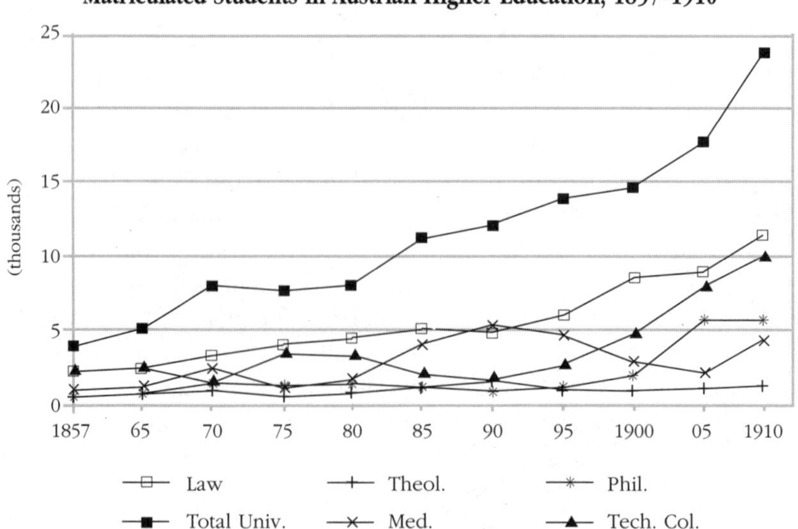

25
20
15
10
5
0
(thousands)
1857
65
70
75
80
85
90
95
1900
05
1910
Law
Theol.
Phil.
Total Univ.
Med.
Tech. Col.

Sources: Schimmer 1858; *Statistisches Jahrbuch der öster. Monarchie für das Jahr 1865; Statistisches Jahrbuch für das Jahr 1869; Statistisches Jahrbuch für das Jahr 1874; Statistisches Jahrbuch für das Jahr 1879; Öster. Statistik* 2, no. 1 (1882); 16, no. 2 (1887); 28, no. 4 (1892); 61, no. 1 (1898); 68, no. 3 (1903); 79, no. 3 (1908); n.s., 7, no. 3 (1913).

To contemporaries the most obvious proximate cause for growth in the number of students in advanced education was the substantial increase in the number of institutions, particularly secondary schools. Counting all accredited public and private institutions, the numbers of *Gymnasien* and *Realschulen* in Austria rose from 101 in 1851 to 432 in 1909–10.[16] The technical institute opened in Brno, Moravia, in 1850 and the new university begun in Chernivtsi in 1875 were the only completely new institutions of higher education established after the mid-nineteenth century. Still, during the second half of the century, the Austrian government added to existing institutions many new professorial chairs, institutes, laboratories, and several new faculties of medicine and theology. Government statisticians viewed the increasing numbers of primary and secondary schools compared with the population and with spatial area as important measures of the growing public access to advanced education.[17] Nationalist politicians pointed to the number of advanced schools that taught in languages other than German as a measure of each nationality's cultural achievements and general standing.[18]

Expansion of the educational infrastructure, of course, was only one factor that worked to increase enrollments. The overcrowding that afflicted many secondary schools and some university and technical college programs during periods of peak growth suggests the strength of other forces. The institutional development resulted from the interaction of the central bureaucracy, provincial officials, community governments, elected representatives, religious orders, pressure groups, and voluntary associations, all responding in varying degrees to popular pressures and economic conditions. The patterns and dynamics of institutional growth can reveal much about what caused the numbers of students and graduates to increase so powerfully.

Institutional Development and the Growth of Secondary Education

The growth of Austrian secondary and higher education rested, of course, on the base of primary schooling. At midcentury the level of basic popular education in Austria stood at roughly the European average.[19] Compared with some of the German states at that time, the availability of primary education in Austria was at best moderately good. One Austrian historian around 1900 argued that as late as the early 1880s, popular educational levels in the most advanced regions of the Alpine and Bohemian lands equaled those in the parts of Prussia where primary education was least developed.[20] School attendance had been low in eighteenth-century Austria until Empress Maria Theresa's government established the principle of mandatory attendance for six- to twelve-year-olds and began to expand the network of primary schools. In 1780 even in Lower Austria, at least 64 percent of the children of primary school age did not attend school. Progress was clear by the 1830s in Lower and Upper Austria, Vorarlberg, and the Bohemian lands, where most six- to twelve-year-olds were attending school. As many as 96 percent of the school-aged children were attending in Lower Austria in 1828.[21] During the middle decades of the nineteenth century, attendance remained somewhat lower, however, in less-developed Carinthia and parts of Styria.[22]

Through much of the nineteenth century, levels of popular education in Austria's poorest crown lands in the northeast and along the Adriatic coast lagged far behind the Alpine and Bohemian lands. In the 1870s and 1880s the majority of school-aged children in Galicia, Bukovina, Istria, and Dalmatia did not attend the *Volksschulen,* girls much less than boys. In 1880 only 23 percent of the population six years or older in Galicia could read, and only 12 or 13 percent in Dalmatia and Bukovina, compared with over 90 percent in Vorarlberg, Lower and Upper Austria, and Bohemia.[23] The overall literacy rate for the Austrian population six years or older in 1880 stood at 65.6 percent, compared with Prussia's 87.8 percent (for those eleven years or older) and England's 83 percent (eleven years or older).[24] In 1910, 83.5 percent of Austria's total population eleven years or older was literate; but even then only 58 percent of the population eleven or older in Galicia and Bukovina could read and 67 percent of those eleven or older in Carniola, Görz, Istria, and Dalmatia.[25]

Over the half-century after 1848, growth in the total number of Austrian primary schools, the *Volksschulen,* approximately kept pace with the increase in the total population (see table 2/4). With respect to the male and female school-aged population, six through thirteen years of age, there were 241.6 school-aged children per public school in 1880 and 237.5 per school in 1900.[26] After midcentury, the primary school network grew fastest in the 1850s, particularly between 1851 and 1856, when the number of schools increased by nearly 7 percent, and again after 1880, with an 18.4 percent increase in the number of institutions between 1880 and 1900.[27] Formally, the initiative for opening new *Volksschulen* after the 1850s fell to the community councils, which operated the primary schools. Nonetheless, the central educational authorities established the general regulations and set the requirements for new schools with regard to the minimum number of students and permissible distances. Provincial governments often had to subsidize school budgets for the poorest communities, particularly as educational expenses increased.[28]

TABLE 2/4
Growth of Austrian Volksschulen Relative to Population, 1850–1900

Year	No. of Volksschulen	Total Austrian Pop.	Schools/Pop.
1850–51	12,784	17,535,000	1 per 1,372
1860–61	14,130	18,225,000	1 per 1,290
1870–71	14,769	20,345,000	1 per 1,378
1880–81	15,567	21,794,000	1 per 1,400
1899–1900	18,431	25,633,000	1 per 1,391

Sources: Schimmer 1877; *Statistisches Jahrbuch für das Jahr 1880; Öster. Statistik* 68, no. 3 (1903); Mitchell 1978, 3; Urbanitsch 1980, 3, 1: 38, table 1.

In instrumental terms, the spectacular growth in the numbers of *Gymnasien* and *Realschulen* throughout Austria between the mid-nineteenth century and World War I was perhaps the critical factor in expanding the ranks of the educated. Even without going on to higher education, any graduate of the upper forms of a *Gymnasium* or *Realschule* was considered to belong in some sense to the educated elites and, after 1868, gained the privilege of "one-year, volunteer" military service. Even without higher education, secondary school graduates might qualify for positions in the growing lower and intermediate levels of state service.[29] Increases in the number of secondary school graduates led inescapably to rising enrollments in higher education. The universities and technical colleges had to admit anyone who had acceptable *Gymnasium* or *Realschule* grades and passed the appropriate *Matura* unless severe overcrowding forced taking emergency measures.[30]

Austria inherited only a modest complement of secondary schools from the late eighteenth and early nineteenth centuries. In 1851 Austria, with a population of 17.5 million people, had only eighty-two accredited *Gymnasien,* many not offering the full eight-year course of study, and only nineteen *Realschulen,* most offering only two or three years of instruction.[31] *Gymnasien* were generally located only in provincial capitals; in some of the oldest or largest secondary provincial cities such as Jičín and Plzeň in Bohemia, Krems and Wiener Neustadt in Lower Austria, or Maribor (Marburg) in Styria; or at some of the largest monasteries in the countryside, such as Melk in Lower Austria, Kremsmünster in Upper Austria, and Broumov (Braunau) in Bohemia. Compared with their territory, Silesia, Bukovina, the maritime lands (Trieste, Istria, Görz), Moravia, Lower Austria (with Vienna), and Bohemia had the largest complements of *Gymnasien* at the beginning of the 1850s. In contrast, Upper Austria had only two such schools—in Linz and Kremsmünster. Carinthia had only two—in Klagenfurt and St. Paul—and Carniola only two—in Ljubljana (Laibach) and Tržič (Neustadtl). Galicia had thirteen *Gymnasien,* but they had to serve a large territory.[32] At the beginning of the 1850s, *Realschulen* could only be found in provincial capitals and a few lesser cities.

Although the numbers of secondary schools increased enormously over the succeeding six decades, the growth came in waves and benefited some crown lands earlier and to a greater extent than others. Economic conditions were clearly an important factor in the growth periods, but the opening of new schools depended in practice on initiatives from the central government, provincial authorities, or town councils, which were influenced by public opinion and special interests as well as fiscal considerations.

The network of secondary schools grew only to a limited extent during the 1850s and early 1860s. After the economic crisis of the 1840s, the period of recovery between 1850 and 1857 saw a rapid increase in *Unterrealschulen,* offering only the first three or four forms. Most of these schools were begun by town councils and provincial governments that wanted to expand the more practically oriented sector of secondary education. The number of *Gymnasien* stagnated throughout most of the 1850s; the Ministry of Religion and Instruction was more interested during these years in improving the quality of academic secondary education and preparation for university studies than in increasing popular access. Tight state finances also made it difficult to expand the number of state-supported *Gymnasien.*[33] At the end of the 1850s, economic crisis, war with Piedmont-Sardinia, and near state bankruptcy made it even harder for the central authorities or the provincial governments to assume costs for new secondary schools. Still, substantial increases in enrollments for the *Gymnasien* and the *Realschulen* during the late 1850s indicated growing popular demand for secondary education (see figure 1 above and table 1 in the appendix).

The number of secondary schools grew rapidly during the middle and late 1860s and the early 1870s, particularly during the boom period after 1867. The popular appetite for advanced education was clearly increasing. State finances permitted greater institutional expansion, and many critics of the Austrian government thought that military defeat by Prussia in 1866 called for further improvements in popular education.[34] The now dominant German liberal politicians were eager to consolidate the educational reforms begun in 1848–49 and to increase somewhat access to secondary education. The central government was willing to bear the costs of new schools, enforcing higher educational requirements for *Gymnasium* and *Realschule* teachers, replacing unqualified monks as teachers in state schools, and taking over a number of formerly church-run *Gymnasien*.[35] Between 1866 and 1871 the total number of state-accredited *Gymnasien* and *Real-Gymnasien* in Austria increased by nearly 16 percent; between 1871 and 1876 the number increased again by 30 percent. The *Realschulen* were administered by the crown lands during this period and showed somewhat different growth patterns. Their numbers grew by only 8 percent between 1866 and 1871, perhaps a result of public debate and legislative activity regarding their curriculum in those years; but the total number of *Realschulen* increased by 38 percent between 1870 and 1875.[36]

Community councils and the provincial governments often shared the initiative with the central authorities in founding new secondary schools or expanding older institutions during the late 1860s and 1870s. For example, the southern Bohemian town of Český Krumlov (Krumau), dominated by a great Schwarzenberg castle, had had no *Gymnasium* since the closing of a Jesuit school in 1777. The town council opened the first class of a new *Real-Gymnasium* in 1871.[37] In Lower Austria at the beginning of the 1860s, the cities of Wiener Neustadt and Krems established full *Realschulen* with provincial assistance.[38] In Prague's Malá strana (Kleinseite) district, a new Czech *nižší reálné gymnasium* (*Unter-Real-Gymnasium*) opened in 1865 as a private institution. Within a few years the Prague city council decided to take over the school and add the higher *Gymnasium* forms.[39] The Vienna city council opened two communal *Unter-Real-Gymnasien* in 1865 and then decided in June 1867 to expand them into full eight-year institutions.[40] In establishing new secondary schools in the 1860s and 1870s, the local governments apparently responded to popular tastes and generally preferred the more modern and more practically oriented curricula of the *Realschule* or the *Real-Gymnasium* over that of the classical *Gymnasium*.[41] Often the town councils began with only the first three or four forms and then waited to see if enrollments proved sufficient and subsidies could be obtained from higher authorities to expand the school into a full seven- or eight-year institution. Eventually, a town council or provincial government might succeed in having a locally founded secondary school put on the central state budget.[42]

The *Gymnasien, Real-Gymnasien,* and *Realschulen* showed diverse trends in enrollments during the 1860s and early 1870s. The *Real-Gymnasien* and *Realschulen* were hard-pressed to keep up with the flood of additional students: between 1865 and 1875 the numbers attending *Real-Gymnasien* increased more than ten times, and *Realschule* enrollments nearly doubled.[43] In this period of great commercial and industrial growth, such schools had greater attraction for the public than did the *Gymnasien* with their emphasis on Latin and Greek. Total enrollments in the classical *Gymnasien* fell by one-quarter (a loss of 7,628) between 1865 and 1875.[44] Even with the decline in attendance for the *Gymnasien,* the increase in total secondary school enrollments of nearly 31 percent between 1865 and 1875 exceeded by a significant margin the growth rate for the school-aged population, showing that academic secondary education was reaching broader segments of the population than before. Not all the students who came to these schools, however, had the intention of going on to the universities and technical colleges. Throughout the period between the 1850s and World War I, enrollments in the lower forms of Austria's *Gymnasien, Real-Gymnasien,* and *Realschulen* exceeded by a wide margin the numbers of students in the upper forms.[45]

The secondary educational network grew unevenly during the 1860s and early 1870s in geographical terms. Lower Austria (including Vienna) and Bohemia, followed by Moravia, gained by far the greatest number of new *Gymnasien, Real-Gymnasien,* and *Realschulen*. These were relatively populous and prosperous lands, and they had the strongest new commercial and industrial growth. Additionally, their local governments showed great initiative in opening new schools; and the Reichsrat and central ministries often gave their greatest attention to these lands in matters of social and cultural development.

Because of this uneven development, both before the 1850s and during the 1860s and 1870s, the density of academic secondary schools relative to territory varied greatly among the various crown lands. In 1874, small Silesia had the highest density of any crown land, followed closely by Lower Austria, Moravia, the maritime lands, and Bohemia (see table 2/5).[46] In the mid-1870s, *Gymnasien* and *Realschulen* were still much rarer in the less-developed regions of the Alpine lands: each secondary school in Tirol, Styria, Carinthia, and Vorarlberg, for example, served an average territory four times as large

TABLE 2/5
Numbers of Austrian Gymnasien and Realschulen Relative to Territory and Population in 1874 and Enrollments Relative to Population in 1880

Prov.	Sq. km./school (1874)	Tot. pop./school (1874)	Stud./tot. pop. (1880)	Stud./11–18 yr. pop. (1880)
Silesia	570.9	60,500	4.11 per 1,000	24.7 per 1,000
Lower Austria	619.4	65,250	4.92	30.8
Moravia	673.3	62,300	4.30	28.8
Maritime Lands	756.6	55,540	3.21	21.8
Bohemia	850.6	86,680	3.70	24.6
Dalmatia	1,421	51,150	1.62	10.6
Carniola	1,997	93,600	2.20	15.1
Upper Austria	1,999	123,650	1.92	15.1
Bukovina	2,090	107,560	2.87	17.6
Tirol	2,429	71,590	2.92	21.1
Styria	2,495	129,390	1.78	12.2
Carinthia	2,593	84,500	2.02	13.9
Vorarlberg	2,602	103,340	1.56	10.4
Galicia	2,997	224,150	1.83	10.7
Salzburg	3,582	76,690	3.23	24.1

Sources: Ficker 1875; *Öster. Statistik* 2, no. 1 (1882); *Statistisches Jahrbuch für das Jahr 1879*; Urbanitsch 1980, 3, 1: 38, table l.

as the area served by the average school in Lower Austria. In poor, far-flung Galicia, the average territory for a secondary school was nearly five times that in Lower Austria.

The level of secondary-school enrollments compared with total population showed similar differences among the various lands. In 1880 Lower Austria (including Vienna), Moravia, Silesia, and Bohemia had the highest rates of enrollment relative to their populations (see table 2/5). The enrollments for Lower Austria were inflated somewhat by migration of students from other crown lands to secondary schools in Vienna. Still, compared with any of the educationally most advanced provinces, the populations of Upper Austria, Carinthia, Styria, and Galicia, for example, were sending students to *Gymnasien* and *Realschulen* at significantly lower rates. In 1880, for instance, attendance compared with the school-aged population in the latter crown lands ranged from 52 to 37 percent of Moravia's rate (see table 2/5).[47]

The opening of new secondary schools continued after the financial crash of 1873 into the early 1880s, although at a slower pace than before. In the 1880s, the conservative coalition cabinet led by Count Eduard Taaffe took a reserved stance toward the expansion of advanced education. Depressed economic conditions in agriculture, the crafts, and some industries; fiscal stringency; conservative desires to protect more traditional economic pursuits; and fears of a surplus of the educated led the central authorities to restrict the growth of academic secondary education. As will be seen, the Taaffe government opposed the opening of new institutions, cut subsidies to existing schools, and even tried to close some of the smallest of them.[48]

Relative to the total school-aged population, attendance in Austria's academic secondary schools actually declined marginally during the 1880s; and significant shifts occurred in enrollments among the various segments of secondary education (see tables 2/1 and 2/2 above and table 1 in the appendix). The German liberal educational authorities began in the mid-1870s to develop state-supported advanced craft schools (*Gewerbeschulen*) as the *Realschulen* increasingly emphasized preparation for the technical colleges. In the difficult economic conditions of the 1880s, popular confidence diminished in the *Realschulen* as avenues to rewarding careers; their total enrollments fell while attendance rose in the craft schools.[49] At the same time, enrollments in classical *Gymnasien* increased in absolute terms. For those students who considered secondary school as a way-station to higher education, preferences for *Gymnasien* over the *Realschulen* only increased as prospects for successful careers in engineering and applied sciences declined after the mid-1870s and aspiring youth looked more to medicine, law, state service, or secondary school teaching.[50] As will be seen, university enrollments, particularly in the medical faculties, grew during the 1880s as attendance fell in the technical colleges. The *Gymnasien* benefited to some degree from weakening interest in the *Realschulen* and to an even greater extent from the decline of the *Real-Gymnasien* after the mid-1870s. Many erstwhile *Real-Gymnasien* dropped the *Realschule* option during the late 1870s and 1880s and became *Gymnasien* with only slightly augmented curricula.[51]

Total secondary school enrollments began to grow more rapidly again after 1890, and the opening of new *Gymnasien* and *Realschulen* accelerated after the mid-1890s. Between 1895 and 1910, the total number of *Gymnasien* in Austria increased by more than half, and the number of *Realschulen* by three-quarters. That increase in numbers of institutions, however, failed to keep pace with enrollments. Between 1895 and 1910 *Gymnasium* enrollments grew by two-thirds, and *Realschule* enrollments nearly doubled (see table 1 in the appendix). The *Realschulen* were aided by further enhancements of their curriculum and rising public regard as criticism grew of the many hours devoted to the classical languages in the *Gymnasien.* The Austrian Ministry of Religion and Instruction nonetheless resisted changing the relationship between the *Gymnasien* and *Realschulen* or making the status of *Realschule* graduates equal to that of *Gymnasium* graduates.[52]

Popular demand for academic secondary education increased rapidly at the turn of the century. Growth in enrollments significantly exceeded the increases in the school-aged population and in the total population (see tables 2/1 and 2/2). Indeed, enrollments expanded compared with the school-aged population and with the total population at significantly faster rates between 1900 and 1910 than during the decade of the 1870s. The increased popular demand doubtless was fueled by the new economic boom after 1896 and particularly during the decade before World War I and by structural economic changes that increased the need for the educated and semieducated. Just as in the 1860s and 1870s, economic growth also helped provide the governmental authorities with financial resources to open new schools and expand existing institutions.[53] The Ministry of Religion and Instruction was barely able to meet the rising demands for additional expenditures, but the central government managed to increase its commitment to education from 2.5 percent of the Austrian state budget in the 1870s to 3.6 percent in 1908.[54]

Nearly all the Austrian crown lands shared in the expansion of the secondary school network after the mid-1890s. As in the 1860s and 1870s, Lower Austria, Bohemia, and Moravia experienced significant growth. Between 1890 and 1909–10 Lower Austria doubled the number of its public and private *Gymnasien* from 18 to 36 (including one private women's school), although the number of *Realschulen* there increased by only six to a total of 23. Bohemia and Moravia were already relatively well provided with *Gymnasien* and *Real-Gymnasien* in 1890, but the numbers grew by nearly 40 percent there in the next twenty years. Advanced industrial development and the technical colleges in Prague and Brno helped make *Realschulen* more popular in the Bohemian lands than in Lower Austria. The number of *Realschulen* in Bohemia and Moravia more than doubled in the two decades, reaching 76 in 1910, compared with 103 *Gymnasien* and *Real-Gymnasien*. In contrast, Carinthia had only 3 *Gymnasien* and 1 *Realschule* in 1910, just as it had had in 1890, although each of these now had a full complement of forms.[55]

In 1910 the less advanced Alpine lands—Upper Austria, Styria, Tirol, and Carinthia—still lagged behind Lower Austria, Moravia, and Bohemia in secondary school attendance compared with school-aged population, but they had narrowed the gap. In spring 1910 Upper Austria was sending to *Gymnasien* and *Realschulen* 23.31 students per thousand of its eleven- to eighteen-year-olds, male and female, a rate more than 50 percent higher than that of 1880. By comparison, in 1909–10 Lower Austria (including Vienna) and Moravia each had slightly more than 40 secondary school students per thousand in the prime age group, while Bohemia enrolled just over 30 per thousand.[56]

The most rapid growth in secondary education during the last decades before 1914 occurred in some of the historically poorest and least-developed regions. Dalmatia experienced little advance after 1890 in numbers of institutions or in relative enrollments, but Bukovina had ten *Gymnasien* in 1910, compared with only three in 1890. Galicia nearly tripled the number of its *Gymnasien* and *Real-Gymnasien* while more than doubling its *Realschulen*. Enrollments grew spectacularly in Galicia and Bukovina. Compared with its total population, Galicia increased the rate of secondary school attendance by two and one-half times between 1880 and 1910, so that it surpassed Carinthia, Upper Austria, and Styria in the last years before World War I.[57] Bukovina had such a small territory that, with the opening of additional schools, its enrollments relative to total population in 1910 were slightly higher than even Lower Austria's.

In Galicia and Bukovina the provincial governments and the ministerial authorities were responding to strong popular and political pressures to expand the secondary schools and to open advanced education to children from poorer social strata who had never had access before. So strong were those pressures that in 1909 the prominent sociologist at the University of Chernivtsi, Eugen Ehrlich, openly criticized the local Ukrainian and Romanian politicians for showing so much zeal for expanding secondary education while neglecting other popular needs. Ehrlich worried that opening more *Gymnasien* was only leading to impractical demands for more bureaucratic jobs: "*Hofräte* (court councilors) are good, but first there must be farmers."[58]

The spreading popular demand for academic secondary education at the turn of the century affected women as well as men and led to heightened efforts to expand education for women. Until this time, public secondary education for Austrian women had been limited almost exclusively to training schools for elementary school teachers (*Lehrerinnenbildungsanstalten*). In the 1860s and 1870s various private associations began to take the initiative to develop vocational schools for women, but publicly supported *Gymnasien* and *Realschulen,* like the universities and technical colleges, would not admit them as regular students. The liberal ministerial authorities in the late 1860s and 1870s as well as their more conservative successors in the 1880s and early 1890s opposed opening academic secondary education to women. As long as legal practice, intermediate and higher state service, medicine, theology, engineering, architecture, and teaching in the *Gymnasien* and *Realschulen* offered women no employment opportunities, the officials saw no need to provide them with academic secondary education, particularly when the state's resources were strained by other demands. After 1872 Austrian women could take a *Gymnasium Matura* examination as special external students (*Hospitantinnen*), but until the late 1890s the Ministry of Religion and Instruction denied women the right to matriculate in a university.[59] After the early 1880s, the Austrian universities accepted women as auditors but only began to admit them as matriculated students in the philosophical faculties in 1897–98. Women first matriculated in the Austrian medical faculties at the end of 1900, nearly a decade before Prussia took final action to accept women as matriculated university students in fall 1908. Austria's faculties of law and Catholic theology never matriculated women under the monarchy, and the technical colleges were almost equally slow to change. The Vienna Technical College first accepted women as auditors in the 1902–3 academic year but did not matriculate them until 1919–20.[60] As late as winter 1909–10, only four women were matriculated in Austrian technical colleges with only five more auditors, all of these at the German and Czech colleges in Brno.[61]

The breakthroughs in the philosophical and medical faculties at the turn of the century increased the pressure on men's secondary schools in many communities to accept more women as external students so that they could take the *Matura.* Still, the ministerial officials opposed coeducational schools, citing overcrowding of the men's *Gymnasien* and *Realschulen* and the "natural inequality" of the sexes. Even after the Ministry of Religion and Instruction began to permit women to earn degrees in the philosophical and medical faculties, women still faced impediments to taking the *Matura* examination; and the central government provided no funds for women's *Gymnasien.* The ministry granted some concessions on women's secondary education under Minister Gustav Marchet between 1906 and 1908, but in 1910, under Count Karl Stürgkh, it made new efforts to stem the increase of women students by restricting sharply their enrollment as external students in men's secondary schools.[62]

Private associations, supported by some of the more progressive middle-class elements in the larger cities, initiated the first academic secondary schools for Austrian women, beginning in the 1870s. At first most of these schools took the form of a six-year girls' lyceum, with a curriculum more like that of the *Realschule* than the *Gymnasium,* emphasizing modern languages, literature, and mathematics. A Czech private school, Minerva, founded in Prague in 1890, and the *gymnasiale Mädchenschule* opened in Vienna by the Society for Expanded Women's Education in 1892 were the first schools in Central Europe that approximated women's *Gymnasien.*[63] Other private initiatives followed in various cities, but until 1906 their graduates could only take the *Gymnasium Matura* at accredited men's secondary schools after completing supplementary studies. In December 1900 a ministerial ordinance formally recognized the six-year curriculum of the girls' lyceum with its own special final general examination, but up to World War I the ministry refused to accept state financial responsibility or to approve definitively a full eight-year curriculum for a woman's *Gymnasium.* After 1910 a trend began to develop for women's *Lyzeen* to add the seventh and eighth forms on the model of a Prussian-style *Realgymnasium* and to style themselves *Gymnasien,* but they did so as private institutions without central government funding.

By spring 1910 there were thirteen private women's *Gymnasien* in all of Austria. Only eight of these had a full eight-year program. Altogether, the thirteen schools enrolled only 2,639 regular students and 93 external students that spring. In the Alpine and Bohemian lands, only Vienna and Prague had such institutions. Even in the more-developed crown lands, people in the smaller towns and countryside showed little interest in advanced education for women. Remarkably, Galicia had nine women's *Gymnasien* that year; but there, too, these schools still appealed to an exceptional constituency. All but two of the Galician women's *Gymnasien* were located in Krakow and L'viv, and 41 percent of their students were Jewish.[64] For women of any strata anywhere in Europe to seek advanced education still required a willingness to display considerable nonconformity with established social values. Not surprisingly, women from historically disadvantaged minority groups like the Jews or from the families of educated professionals and officials accounted for a large share of the pioneering female students in Austria's secondary schools and higher education.[65]

The Expansion of Higher Education

As elsewhere in Europe during the late nineteenth century, aspirations spread among broader segments of the Austrian population than before for careers in public service, medical and legal practice, and business management. Those ambitions fueled a growth in university and technical college enrollments between the 1850s and 1910 that was more than three times the increase in total population (see table 2/1). Not surprisingly, the growth in higher education came in waves that corresponded roughly to those in secondary school enrollments, allowing a lag for the time it took students to graduate from the secondary schools (see tables 1 and 2 in the appendix).[66]

Although functionally differentiated, the universities and technical colleges competed to some extent for the same students, much like the *Gymnasien* and *Realschulen*. One should not try to draw too sharp a distinction between the social appeals of university and technical college education, for at times total enrollments in the two tracks showed a clear reciprocal relationship.[67] Total attendance in the universities and technical colleges declined between 1851 and 1856 because of the aftereffects of economic crisis and political upheaval in the late 1840s, the introduction of the *Matura* for the universities, and the curricular reforms in secondary and higher education.[68] Once secondary school enrollments began to expand in the late 1850s and 1860s, the numbers of students in the universities and, to a lesser extent, the technical colleges began to increase rapidly. During the slight recession of the middle 1860s and the wars of German unification, Austria's technical colleges lost enrollments, while the universities gained. At the peak of the economic boom in the early 1870s, attendance in the technical colleges ballooned, while the numbers of university students declined somewhat.

The trends reversed during the next decade. Just as *Gymnasium* enrollments grew strongly at the expense of the *Realschulen* during the depression years of the 1880s, university attendance increased by half while the technical colleges lost nearly half their enrollments. Well into the late nineteenth century, the Austrian state continued to prefer university education, particularly in law, over technical studies for its higher functionaries.[69] In the 1880s, with straitened conditions in industry and commerce, greater numbers of Austrian youth than before chose university studies, apparently in preparation for state employment or careers in law, medicine, and secondary school teaching, as opposed to advanced technical education. Technical college enrollments also suffered in these years from the growing competition of industrial and trade schools and from the introduction in 1889–90 of more rigorous state examinations in the technical fields.[70]

Enrollments in the technical colleges recovered after 1890 as economic growth quickened. Indeed, while all higher education experienced unprecedented expansion during the next twenty-five years, technical college enrollments increased more rapidly in relative terms during each five-year period than did the number of university students. Besides the growing employment opportunities in industry after the mid-1890s, the rising formal status of the technical colleges helped make them more attractive to students than before. At the turn of the century, the Austrian educational authorities, like the German, recognized the growing importance of research in advanced technical and engineering fields and, after two decades of agitation by professors and alumni, approved doctoral degrees for the technical colleges. The more than doubling of technical college students between 1900 and 1910 caused critical overcrowding in many of the institutions in the Alpine and Bohemian lands.[71]

Enrollments in the Austrian technical colleges increased so strongly compared with the universities around 1900 that Austria had a much higher ratio of technical college students to university students in the last years before World War I than did Germany. It is commonly assumed that Germany, with its larger population, stronger economy, more-developed chemical and electrical industries, and eminent scientific institutes, had a stronger commitment to modern science and technology than did Austria. In fact, Austria had considerable accomplishments in the applied sciences and technology, and one comparative study of academic physics around 1900 has found that the Habsburg Monarchy as a whole had a smaller number of physicists in its universities and technical colleges than did Germany but spent almost twice as much on their work relative to national income as did Germany.[72] Larger percentages of the students in Austrian higher education, particularly in the Alpine and Bohemian lands, chose to attend technical colleges than was the case in Germany. In 1870, 18.9 percent of the matriculated students in Austrian higher education attended technical colleges, compared with 16.5 percent in Germany. In 1911, 30.6 percent of the matriculated students in Austrian higher education attended technical colleges, but only 17.5 percent in Germany.[73]

The rates of enrollment in higher education during the late nineteenth century showed many of the same inequalities among the various Austrian crown lands as did attendance in the academic secondary schools (see table 2/6). If the differences among the various lands were somewhat narrower for higher education than for secondary education, that was due largely to the more arduous screening, intellectual and social, that had to be endured in order to reach a university or technical college, regardless of a student's geographical origin. As in secondary education, Lower Austria and the Bohemian lands produced larger numbers of university and technical college students with respect to their populations than did any of the other larger crown lands for most of the period between the 1850s and 1914. In winter 1879-80, compared with total population, youth born in Lower Austria were enrolled in Austrian universities as matriculated and nonmatriculated students at a rate nearly twice as high as for Upper Austrians and nearly 60 percent higher than for natives of Carniola or Dalmatia.[74] Obviously, natives of crown lands without universities or technical colleges and ethnic groups that lacked higher education in their mother tongue suffered serious disadvantages, but local economic conditions, social mores, and popular culture also mattered. Silesia, like Upper Austria, had no institutions of higher education within its borders in 1880; its youth had to travel to Vienna, Prague, or perhaps Krakow to study in a university. Nonetheless, Silesia, with its significant mining

TABLE 2/6

Austrian University and Technical College Enrollments by Province of Birth Relative to Population, Winter 1879–80 and Winter 1909–10

Winter Semester 1879–80

Province of birth	**Matr. & non-matr. univ. students per 1,000 pop. &**	***per 1,000 19–22 yrs.***	**Matr. & non-matr. tech. col. students per 1,000 pop. &**	***per 1,000 18–22 yrs.***
Lower Austra	0.451	*5.23*	0.154	*1.450*
Upper Austria	0.238	*3.74*	0.101	*1.272*
Salzburg	0.263	*3.96*	0.088	*1.067*
Vorarlberg	0.467	*7.10*	0.029	*0.352*
Tirol	0.496	*7.18*	0.378	*0.441*
Carinthia	0.296	*4.14*	0.073	*0.818*
Styria	0.303	*4.34*	0.095	*1.096*
Carniola	0.283	*4.38*	0.071	*0.871*
Bohemia	0.369	*5.41*	0.206	*2.431*
Moravia	0.407	*5.41*	0.193	*2.282*
Silesia	0.307	*4.33*	0.118	*1.331*
Galicia	0.348	*4.73*	0.066	*0.720*
Bukovina	0.403	*5.32*	0.060	*0.630*
Maritime Lands	0.264	*3.15*	0.077	*0.750*
Dalmatia	0.286	*3.68*	0.064	*0.671*

Winter Semester 1909–10

Province of birth	**Matr. & non-matr. univ. students per 1,000 pop. &**	***per 1,000 19–22 yrs.***	**Matr. & non-matr. tech. col. students per 1,000 pop. &**	***per 1,000 18–22 yrs.***
Lower Austra	1.080	*13.12*	0.471	*4.57*
Upper Austria	0.547	*8.74*	0.134	*1.70*
Salzburg	0.662	*9.77*	0.144	*1.70*
Vorarlberg	0.767	*10.10*	0.196	*2.03*
Tirol	0.787	*10.04*	0.120	*1.26*
Carinthia	0.597	*8.12*	0.212	*2.33*
Styria	0.783	*11.61*	0.220	*2.59*
Carniola	0.669	*11.22*	0.212	*2.62*
Bohemia	0.813	*12.42*	0.536	*6.42*
Moravia	0.853	*13.78*	0.574	*7.24*
Silesia	0.651	*9.64*	0.371	*4.30*
Galicia	1.010	*15.65*	0.190	*2.31*
Bukovina	1.323	*19.44*	0.114	*1.33*
Maritime Lands	0.679	*7.68*	0.243	*2.25*
Dalmatia	0.591	*8.32*	0.169	*1.91*

Sources: *Statistisches Jahrbuch für das Jahr 1879; Öster. Statistik* 2, no. 1 (1882); n.s., 7, no. 3 (1913); Urbanitsch 1980, 3, 1: 38, table l.

and industry, had a rate of university attendance relative to total population nearly 30 percent higher than Upper Austria's. Whatever the distances to the institutions, the less urbanized and less industrialized character of Upper Austria, Styria, and Carinthia and the continuing strength of the traditional culture of village, farm, and forest in those crown lands limited aspirations for higher education among their populations throughout most of the late nineteenth century.[75] Tirol shared many of the same characteristics, of course, but the size and vigor of the Catholic theological faculty in Innsbruck helped boost university attendance by Tiroleans above the norm for the more rural Alpine lands. In 1879–80 enrollment in technical colleges with respect to population was also significantly weaker for natives of the less-developed Alpine lands and Dalmatia than for Lower Austria, Bohemia, and Moravia.

By 1910 some of the gaps in rates of university and technical college attendance had narrowed between the less advanced Alpine lands and Lower Austria or the Bohemian lands, but there were still great differences among the crown lands. Between 1880 and 1910, Carniola, for example, with a population 94 percent Slovene, more than doubled the rate at which its natives were attending Austrian universities despite the fact that none of the institutions used Slovene as the language of instruction. Nonetheless, Carniola's 1910 rate of university enrollment for its nineteen- to twenty-two-year-olds was 81 percent that of Moravia. Upper Austria's rate of enrollment in universities that year was less than two-thirds the rate for Moravian-born youth (see table 2/6).

The appetite for higher education proved noticeably stronger among the populations of Moravia and Bohemia, both Czech- and German-speaking, than in the less-developed and more rural Alpine lands. In 1880, Moravia and Bohemia each had relatively more of their nineteen- to twenty-two-year-olds attending universities than did even Lower Austria. This was partly a matter of the historically strong development of secondary and higher education in the Bohemian lands before the nineteenth century. Beyond that, the rise of modern market-oriented agriculture, the slow decline of a rich craft tradition, and the development of a diverse modern industrial sector during the nineteenth century encouraged growing popular demand for advanced education in all forms. Czech educators during the 1860s introduced in Austria the concept of the *Real-Gymnasium* as a unitary secondary school, and *Realschulen* also enjoyed strong growth in Bohemia and Moravia after the 1850s. In higher education the populations of these two crown lands developed a particularly strong interest in engineering and the applied sciences. During much of the late nineteenth century, enrollments of Bohemian- and Moravian-born students in technical colleges with respect to total population or to the population in the prime age group far surpassed the rates for the other populous crown lands, even Lower Austria. In winter 1909–10, Moravia and Bohemia ranked just behind little Bukovina, Lower Austria, and Galicia in the numbers of their natives enrolled in universities compared with their total populations; and they still led all the Austrian crown lands in technical college attendance by their natives relative to total population or to eighteen- to twenty-two-year-olds (see table 2/6).

Besides economic development, political mobilization and popular commitments to social change also helped increase demand for higher education. In 1880, Galicia ranked just below Lower Austria and above Carniola, Styria, and Silesia in the number of Austrian university students born in the province compared with the province's nineteen- to twenty-year-old population. Galicia at that time had next to no modern industry, and its per capita income was among the lowest in Austria. Nonetheless, it had two universities, which, thanks to the political influence of Polish landowners, taught primarily in Polish after the 1860s.[76] In addition to the Galician-born students in the universities of Krakow and L'viv, significant numbers also attended the Vienna University, most of these Jewish. After 1875 some Galician students went to Chernivtsi as well. In the last decades of the century the offspring of Polish noblemen, some of the Polish and Ukrainian peasants and craftsmen, and Galicia's Jewish craftsmen and small business owners pressed into universities to prepare for careers in law, state or private administration, and secondary school teaching.[77] Compared with the nineteen- to twenty-two-year-old population, attendance in Austrian universities by the Galician-born more than tripled between 1880 and winter 1909–10. In the winter 1909–10 semester, Galicia's rate of university attendance actually exceeded the levels for Moravia and Lower Austria. Over those three decades the enrollment of the Galician-born in technical colleges compared with the eighteen- to twenty-two-year-old population also tripled, but Galician demand for higher technical education still lagged significantly behind that of the Moravian, Bohemian, and Lower Austrian populations.

Bukovina, like Galicia, also had a remarkably high rate of university attendance at the beginning of the twentieth century. Economically, Bukovina remained far less developed than the Alpine and Bohemian lands, and much of its population was extremely poor; but by 1900 this fairly compact territory was relatively well provided with secondary schools and a university. Jews and Romanians there took particular advantage of the educational opportunities, the Ukrainian inhabitants to a lesser extent. In 1909–10, Bukovina had the highest rates of university enrollments relative to both its total population and its nineteen- to twenty-two-year-olds of any Austrian crown land.[78]

In the expansion of Austrian higher education, unlike secondary education, the founding of wholly new institutions played no major part during the late nineteenth century. The central authorities were hesitant to found new universities and technical colleges, although they created many new professorial chairs and institutes as well as several new faculties to meet scholarly and professional needs and public demand for greater access. In the 1850s the Ministry of Religion and Instruction added professors and institutes to various universities, but, as already noted, the ministry acted to dissolve what remained of the old universities in Salzburg and Olomouc, leaving only free-standing Catholic theological faculties in those cities. Beyond establishing the University of Chernivtsi in 1875, the central authorities were willing to expand the university network only by dividing Prague's Charles-Ferdinand University into separate Czech and German institutions after 1882, adding a theology faculty in Innsbruck in 1857, and establishing medical faculties in Graz in 1863, Innsbruck in 1869, and L'viv in 1894. In 1904 the central government attempted unsuccessfully to open a new law faculty with Italian-language instruction in Innsbruck.[79] At the turn of the century, the central authorities resisted proposals for a new university in Salzburg, a new Czech university in Brno, or an Italian university in Trieste or Trento.

The Ministry of Religion and Instruction and the provincial governments, which operated most of the technical colleges until the early 1870s, followed similar policies for higher technical education. During the second half of the century, the ministerial and provincial authorities radically reformed the technical colleges in several phases, but they opened no new institutions except by the division of the technical institute in Prague into separate Czech and German schools in 1869 and the similar division of the technical college in Brno in 1900.

Compared with Germany's educational authorities, Austrian officials proceeded with great caution during the late nineteenth century in developing specialized *Hochschulen* in the arts or applied sciences. For the arts, only the Akademie der bildenden Künste (Academy of Fine Arts) in Vienna won the status of a *Hochschule* with its own rector in 1872. Up to 1918 the Ministry of Religion and Instruction never accorded that rank to the other arts academies and conservatories in Vienna and other cities.[80] After 1849 advanced schools of mining and metallurgy (*Montan-Lehranstalten,* later called *Bergakademien*) operated in Leoben, Styria, and Příbram, Bohemia, both with German-language instruction. Initially, they offered only two-year programs and had inferior status to the technical colleges. The two mining schools only gained the rank of *Hochschulen* in 1904 and the authority to grant doctoral degrees in 1906.[81] Many of the technical colleges carried on some instruction and research in agronomy. After the central government created a separate Ministry of Agriculture in 1867, however, it established in 1872 the College of Agriculture (Hochschule für Bodenkultur) in Vienna. Anyone with a *Gymnasium* or *Realschule Matura* could be admitted to it as a regular student, but only as late as 1911 did enrollments exceed 1,000.[82] No other independent agricultural college opened in Austria before 1918.

The cautious policies on institutional expansion resulted in Austrian university education being concentrated in a small number of institutions. Germany, with its traditions of *Landesuniversitäten,* had more than twenty universities at the end of the century. After 1882 the Austrian half of the Habsburg Monarchy had eight universities: in Vienna, Prague (Czech and German), Graz, Innsbruck, Krakow, L'viv, and Chernivtsi. By 1900 all had a full complement of four faculties except Chernivtsi, which lacked medicine. The rising enrollments in Galicia after the 1880s resulted in substantial growth for the University of L'viv, from only 1,091 matriculated students in winter 1889–90 to 4,309 in winter 1909–10, and the University of Krakow, from 1,113 in 1889–90 to 2,858 in 1909–10. Otherwise, the two oldest of the Austrian universities, Vienna and Prague, continued to attract the largest numbers of students throughout the late nineteenth century. Two-thirds or more of all the matriculated university students in Austria were enrolled in Vienna and Prague in the 1850s, 1860s, and 1870s. In winter 1909–10, the Vienna University with 7,579 students and the two Prague universities with 4,808 students still accounted for 54 percent of all the matriculated university students in Austria.[83] The universities in Graz and Innsbruck remained small, with only 1,643 matriculated students in the former and 1,006 in the latter in winter 1909–10.

At the beginning of the twentieth century, Austria had a larger number of technical colleges compared with population than did Germany. After 1900 there were seven Austrian technical colleges: in Vienna, Prague (Czech and German), Brno (Czech and German), Graz, and L'viv. Imperial Germany, with two and one-quarter times the population of Austria, had only eleven technical colleges in 1910.[84] As elsewhere in Central Europe, the individual Austrian technical colleges attracted smaller numbers of students than did most universities. Here, too, the institution in the imperial capital drew the largest enrollments. In winter 1909–10, the Vienna Technical College had 3,015 matriculated students. It was followed by the Czech Technical College in Prague with 2,854 students and the Technical College of L'viv with

1,660. In winter 1909–10 each of the other four colleges had fewer than one thousand matriculated students.[85]

The concentration of university and technical college students in a relatively small number of institutions made some of the Austrian schools unusually large by European standards. In 1910 only the Berlin University with its 9,700 matriculated students exceeded the Vienna University as the largest university in Central Europe, the Low Countries, and Italy. The Vienna Technical College and the Czech Technical College in Prague had the largest enrollments of any such institutions in Central Europe and Italy. Among individual faculties, the Vienna law faculty, with 3,418 matriculated students in winter 1909–10, easily surpassed the largest of its German counterparts in Berlin and Munich.[86] Officials in the Austrian Ministry of Religion and Instruction could defend on fiscal grounds their policies of keeping low the number of universities and technical colleges, but students repeatedly faced severe overcrowding in lecture halls, seminars, and laboratories from the late 1860s onward.[87]

The addition of new teaching positions, institutes, and programs in Austrian higher education during the late nineteenth century came roughly in three waves: as part of the Thun-Exner reforms of the 1850s, under the German liberal cabinets between 1867 and 1879, and during the great growth period for all public education after the mid-1890s. Despite limited financial resources, the ministerial authorities in 1848 and the 1850s aggressively recruited new professors and established new seminars and institutes in the universities to meet the new curricular requirements and replace some of the least able older professors.[88] Engelbrecht cites the philosophical faculty of the Vienna University as indicative of the substantial growth after 1848: from only 17 professors and *Privatdozenten* in 1848 to 47 in 1868 and 109 in 1888.[89] The number of professors in Austrian universities altogether nearly tripled between 1847 and the early 1870s.[90] Although university enrollments grew only modestly between 1870 and 1880 and economic growth slowed after the crash of 1873, the German liberal cabinets in the 1870s approved many new institutes, seminars, and clinics in a range of specialties from history and philology to all the natural sciences, law, and medicine. Some of the technical colleges, however, experienced slower growth in the numbers of teaching positions and institutes than did the universities between the 1850s and 1880s.

Nearly all of Austrian higher education shared in the new round of expansion that began in the 1890s. The great rise in enrollments provoked calls by student groups, professors, elected politicians, and popular organizations for more teaching personnel and expanded facilities in all the universities and technical colleges. A proliferation of new academic specialties also created pressure for the creation of new seminars and institutes, and the ministry generally responded as best it could. The smaller universities and technical colleges benefited along with the larger ones from the addition of new professorial chairs and institutes.[91] Educational expenditures, of course, had to compete with other urgent demands on the state budget; and the ministerial officials had to admit that, despite all they accomplished, they were not keeping up with the growing needs of higher education.[92]

Enrollment trends after the mid-nineteenth century in the various university faculties and in the particular schools within the technical colleges reflected shifts in popular demand and changing career opportunities. Already in the mid-1870s, government statisticians were commenting on the clear relationship of employment opportunities, the oversupply of newly educated professionals in some fields, and specific enrollment trends in the medical, philosophical, and theological faculties.[93] Nonetheless, some of the Austrian enrollment patterns also showed a stronger persistence of older attitudes regarding higher education and preparation for professional careers than was the case in Germany.

As in the German universities, the faculties of law and public administration (*Rechts- und Staatswissenschaften*) had the largest enrollments among the Austrian university faculties during the late eighteenth and early nineteenth centuries, and throughout the period from 1860 to World War I the law faculties continued to draw between 38 and 60 percent of all matriculated Austrian university students (see table 2 in the appendix). In the last years before 1914, though, Austrian youth were enrolling in the law faculties at more than twice the German rate. In 1910, the Austrian law faculties had 6.11 matriculated students per thousand inhabitants aged nineteen to twenty-two years, compared with only 2.75 law students per thousand inhabitants aged twenty to twenty-three years in Germany in 1911. In the latter year, the law faculties enrolled 51 percent of all the matriculated university students in Austria, compared with only 25 percent in Germany.[94]

In total numbers, enrollments in the Austrian medical faculties generally ranked second behind the law faculties from the mid-nineteenth century until after 1900, when the philosophical faculties overtook medicine. The medical faculties passed through several waves of expansion and contraction during the second half of the century (see figure 2 above and table 2 in the appendix). Increasing numbers of *Gymnasium* graduates in the late 1850s and 1860s, new medical faculties in Graz and Innsbruck, and the phasing out of the Josephs-Akademie after 1868 all contributed to strong increases in total medical faculty enrollments between 1860 and the early 1870s.[95] By 1870 many of the courses were badly overcrowded, and fears began to spread in the medical profession and the educational bureaucracy of a surplus of newly trained physicians. The cumulative costs and duration of medical training greatly exceeded those for the other learned professions. Overcrowding in the medical faculties and rising competition among new graduates for hospital appointments could easily discourage new enrollments. This and the uncertain economic conditions of the middle and late 1870s led to significant declines in the numbers of Austrian medical students.[96] Germany, which experienced many of the same economic and professional trends, also saw some decline in medical enrollments between 1872 and 1875.[97] The new, more demanding curriculum introduced in Austria in 1872 may have also had a dampening effect.[98]

During the 1880s Austrian medical enrollments recovered strongly along with university enrollments in general. Enrollments in the Vienna University's world-renowned medical faculty reached particularly high levels in the mid-1880s: in winter 1884–85, for instance, there were 2,291 matriculated students along with 164 nonmatriculated students.[99] The closing of the old surgical schools (*Wundärztliche Schulen*) in the 1870s sharply reduced the supply of medical practitioners from outside the universities and contributed, by the 1880s, to a widely perceived shortage of physicians. The largest cities might be well supplied, but small town and rural interests complained of inadequate numbers of practitioners. In 1891 the Society of Physicians in Vienna's First District, for instance, supported dropping the per-hour tuition fees (*Kollegiengeld*) for medical students and substituting lower flat fees to help supply more physicians to the countryside.[100] Germany's medical faculties had much the same experience as Austria's during the 1880s as their enrollments grew in response to rising demand for medical services and the continuing professionalization of medical training and practice.[101]

By the mid-1890s, a reaction set in to the increase in numbers of Austrian medical students and graduates so that medical enrollments declined significantly until around 1905. In Germany the reaction had already begun in 1889–90.[102] Medical enrollments rebounded in both countries after 1905 as the attraction of medical careers grew again in a period of strong economic expansion. In both Austria and Germany the numbers of medical students nearly doubled in the five years between 1905 and 1910.[103]

To some extent, the trends in enrollments in medical faculties throughout Central Europe during the late nineteenth century showed an inverse relationship to changes in the numbers of law students. In Austria, the law faculties grew strongly during the 1870s, while medicine lost significant numbers of students, and philosophy and theology declined modestly. The trends in medical and law enrollments reversed between 1885 and 1890, when the numbers of medical students increased by 25 percent and law students decreased by 4 percent. Between winter 1889–90 and winter 1904–5, the absolute numbers of matriculated law students in Austria increased by 75 percent, while the numbers of medical students fell by 58 percent. Enrollments in law and medicine also showed an inverse relationship in Germany between the 1880s and 1905.[104] This inverse relationship suggests that legal and medical studies competed directly with each other for some segments of the student population. This will be borne out later by the analysis of the socioeconomic origins of students in the various faculties, which shows strong parallels between the law and medical students.[105] Probably few students changed from medicine to law or vice versa once they began university studies; the great differences in curricula made that difficult. Apparently, though, many youth during their studies in the *Gymnasien* envisioned as a general goal a career in a respected, secure profession and were choosing *between* law and medicine as they approached entry into a university.[106]

Enrollments in the philosophical and theological faculties were also governed to a great degree by popular estimations of career opportunities and the relative prestige and financial rewards of the professions those faculties served. Here, too, though, persisting older traditions of Austrian higher education played a part. The Austrian university reformers of the 1850s and 1860s gave great importance to improving and expanding the philosophical faculties, but those faculties drew few students compared with law and medicine until after 1900. Only 17 percent of all matriculated Austrian university students were enrolled in the philosophical faculties in 1861 and 1880 and only

15 percent in 1900. By winter 1909–10, however, that portion had risen to 24 percent. In Germany, by contrast, where philosophical faculties tended to split into separate faculties of humanities and natural sciences, enrollments in these faculties taken together grew from 33 percent of all university students in 1865–66 to fully 52 percent by 1910–11.[107]

Before the mid-nineteenth century, few Austrian students had gone to the universities to study in the humanities and natural sciences, and traditional preferences in this regard apparently persisted to a greater extent in Austria during the late nineteenth century than in Germany during the same period. Even after 1900, when enrollments in the Austrian philosophical faculties began to increase significantly as compared with the other faculties, those numbers grew more slowly than in Germany. This increase occurred in a period when throughout Central Europe employment in secondary school teaching was expanding, the humanities and natural sciences gained greater prestige, and more of the school-aged population was enrolling in higher education than ever before.[108]

Throughout the late nineteenth century, Austria's university-based theological faculties, all of them Catholic except for an Eastern Orthodox faculty in Chernivtsi, attracted fewer students than did the faculties of law, medicine, or philosophy. Germany's universities showed similar trends from the early 1870s onward.[109] In 1866 only 15 percent of all the matriculated Austrian university students were enrolled in theological faculties, compared with 26 percent of all university students in Germany. After the 1860s and 1870s, all of Austria's university-based theological faculties suffered significant declines compared with the other faculties except in Innsbruck. In 1910 the Austrian theological faculties enrolled only 6 percent of all matriculated university students, again lower than in Germany, where the Protestant and Catholic faculties together drew 8 percent of the university students.[110] Young men in Austria who wished to join the clergy could also study Catholic, Orthodox, or Protestant theology in diocesan seminaries, monastic institutions, and several independent theological faculties. Nonetheless, by 1900 the low attraction of theological studies and clerical careers resulted in generally low enrollments in the other institutions as well. In the winter semester 1904–5, for instance, all of Austria's Christian seminaries and independent theological faculties had an enrollment of only 2,076, compared with the 1,197 matriculated students in the university theological faculties, 16,416 in the secular university faculties, and 7,656 in the technical colleges.[111]

The preferences of Austrian technical college students for the various schools within the colleges fluctuated relatively little during the late nineteenth century. Overall, the schools of general engineering had the largest enrollments for nearly the whole period from the late 1870s to World War I. Chemical engineering with its related fields (the *Chemisch-technische Schulen)* gained strongly in the 1870s, but those schools lost students as did all the others during the depression of the 1880s. During the expansion of higher education between the early 1890s and 1914, the general engineering schools and the *Maschinenbauschulen* for mechanical engineering and related fields showed the strongest growth. The schools of civil and structural engineering (*Hochbauschulen*) consistently had the smallest enrollments within the Austrian technical colleges. This contrasted with the *Bauschulen* in many of Germany's technical colleges, which had relatively larger enrollments. The Austrian technical colleges, however, undertook little of architectural training, leaving the primary role to the Academy of Fine Arts in Vienna. Within the individual technical colleges, the distribution of students among the various schools tended to follow the general pattern except for the two Czech technical colleges in Prague and Brno. In those two institutions after 1900, as elsewhere, the general engineering schools led in enrollments; but they were followed in the Czech colleges by the "general departments," which taught diverse subjects such as applied mathematics, actuarial science, and some business specialties, and then by the mechanical engineering schools.[112]

Many forces caused Austria's academic secondary and higher education to expand and the student numbers to increase during the second half of the nineteenth century. The unevenness of growth over time and the variations among the various segments of the educational system suggest that no one factor had primacy. An expanding school-aged population was an obvious prerequisite for general growth in enrollments, but the increasing share of that population that pursued advanced education also represented qualitative changes in values and behavior. The ministerial authorities in Vienna controlled part of the process by deciding where and when to expand the educational institutions that the ministry funded, but one cannot say that the central government intended or even managed to control all the growth that occurred, because much initiative in expanding secondary education came from local governments and voluntary associations. In any case, the institutional expansion often failed to keep pace with the increasing student numbers. Once the central government had established the legal principle that those who earned the *Matura* from the appropriate secondary school, along with acceptable course grades, were entitled to admission to a university or technical college, it could not control the growth in enrollments in higher education except by introducing extraordinary numerical limits and risking public outcry.[113]

With regard to economic forces, the government authorities considered what educational initiatives seemed appropriate to assure growth and prosperity and what expenditures their budgets could sustain. Various officials, elected representatives, and educators differed, though, over what educational measures might best contribute to popular well-being. The neo-absolutist reformers of the 1850s thought that improving the quality of academic secondary and higher education, although not necessarily the quantity, was necessary to the general welfare of state and society. The German liberal ministers of the 1860s and 1870s pursued educational policies that both improved advanced education and broadened access to it, and until 1873 they benefited from an economic boom that recommended such action and made it affordable. The more conservative figures who framed policies in the 1880s and early 1890s faced straitened economic conditions, and they argued for increased vocational training and against expanding academic education. Nonetheless, they could not stop the growth during the 1880s of *Gymnasium* and university enrollments at the expense of the *Realschulen* and technical colleges that was motivated by reduced employment opportunities in industry and commerce and heightened interest in more traditional professions. Renewed economic development after the mid-1890s encouraged government officials to resume the expansion of educational facilities on a broad front, but they failed to keep up with the ballooning enrollments in the secondary schools, universities, and technical colleges.

In considering educational issues, Austrian government officials, like their counterparts elsewhere in Europe, might try to influence popular attitudes in hopes of stemming the growing appetite for advanced education. The ministerial authorities in Vienna attempted to reduce enrollments when they introduced the admissions examinations for secondary schools in 1870 and, as will be seen, they made additional efforts in the 1880s and 1890s.[114] Nonetheless, the state could do little to control the rising popular aspirations for secondary and higher education and for careers in learned professions. Indeed, the ministerial officials, along with the provincial and local governments, often helped encourage those aspirations by modernizing the curricula and expanding the institutions After the late 1850s, though, they were often only responding to growing popular demand as expressed in the overcrowding of facilities and calls by elected politicians and voluntary associations for more schools.

While economic trends and government policies helped fuel popular demand for educational opportunities, those popular aspirations had something of their own dynamic. It was no accident, of course, that the boom years of the 1860s and early 1870s and the new boom era around 1900 saw strong increases in enrollments, particularly in the more modern and technologically oriented segments of secondary and higher education. A developing economy encouraged beliefs that new opportunities were opening in industry, commerce, and finance as well as in the more familiar pursuits of higher state service, law, medicine, and secondary school teaching. The difficult economic conditions of the 1880s and the government's fostering of vocational education stopped for a decade the growth in the portion of all eleven- to eighteen-year-olds attending the academic secondary schools. Nonetheless, popular aspirations for advanced education and hopes for careers in a learned profession continued to increase during the 1880s, as the percentage of the nineteen- to twenty-two-year-olds who went on to universities continued to grow.

Social and political competition among Austria's various ethnic and national groups often focused on educational issues, and ethnic or national competition surely contributed to the growth in popular demand for advanced education. Czechs in the Bohemian lands and Slovenes in the southeastern portions of the Alpine lands raised demands for secondary and higher education in their mother tongues as part of their challenges to the historic dominance of German-speakers, just as did Ukrainians in their struggle with Polish elites in eastern Galicia. After the 1860s nationalist politicians often succeeded in winning increased educational opportunities for their peoples, but they typically used their peoples' educational aspirations only as part of broader efforts to mobilize them for social and political action. Nationalist leaders encouraged and exploited popular educational aspirations, but they seldom created them.

The spread of desires for advanced education and entry into learned professions to larger segments of the population than before the mid-nineteenth century was only another by-product of the larger transformation from the traditional economy and corporate society to a modern industrial market economy and class structure. That transformation also worked to spread modern national identities and provided the social fodder for the nationalist political movements themselves. In the Bohemian lands, for instance, there was an "educational competition" between Czechs and Germans, as Friedrich Prinz puts it, which surely added to the development of the educational network and to increasing enrollments,[115] but these crown lands also experienced some of the most rapid economic and social development of any part of Austria during the nineteenth century. If ethnic competition worked as a critical independent factor in increasing both popular demand and access to advanced education in imperial Austria, then it would be hard to explain why Moravia consistently had relatively higher enrollments for its youth in secondary and higher education than did Bohemia, where the Czech-German conflict was more intense, or why secondary enrollments were particularly strong in ethnically homogeneous, but well-industrialized Vorarlberg (see tables 2/5 and 2/6). The Slovenes in Carniola, southern Styria, and southern Carinthia had as much reason as the Czechs to want to use education to help overcome the social dominance of ethnic Germans. Nonetheless, the poorer economic conditions and slower development of those lands, along with the Slovenes' smaller numbers, resulted in the Slovene national political movement and Slovene advanced education evolving more slowly than the Czech counterparts. Ethnic competition was only part of a complex, evolving social and political matrix that produced increases in school attendance and ultimately the growth of the professions.[116]

Whatever the force of government policies, economic conditions, and ethnic competition, those factors were refracted by popular perceptions in influencing the growing demand for advanced education. The individual calculations of youth and their parents and their beliefs about the value of education and the prospects for careers in educated pursuits determined who enrolled in the secondary schools, universities, and technical colleges. On the eve of World War I, advanced academic education still remained the province of an elite in simple numerical terms: in spring 1910, only 3.06 percent of all eleven- to eighteen-year-old males and females throughout Austria were attending academic secondary schools. In winter 1909–10, only 1.2 percent of the nineteen- to twenty-two-year-old males and females were matriculated students in universities with only 0.42 percent of all eighteen- to twenty-two-year-olds matriculated in technical colleges. Nonetheless, those rates of enrollment represented more than twofold gains for the secondary schools and universities over the rates in 1870 and a quadrupling in the rate for the technical colleges. Aspirations for advanced academic education, the privileges it conferred, and the professional careers to which it led were clearly increasing among the Austrian population, as elsewhere in Western and Central Europe during the late nineteenth century.

Many contemporary observers considered the increasing enrollments in secondary and higher education and the apparent broadening of access to the educated strata as signs of progress, but others were less sanguine. In Austria, already by the 1870s and increasingly in the 1880s and 1890s, conservative officials, politicians, and educators warned against producing larger numbers of people prepared for professions than society actually needed. Pessimists feared the raising of misplaced hopes among the lower classes for upward social mobility through education. In 1889 one anonymous commentator on Austrian education voiced such worries in particularly somber terms:

> This aiming high above one's status, often notwithstanding all conditions, is, in fact, a dark side of our social relations, for it accords with a basic misjudgment of the value and importance of a trained agricultural and craft element, a sad delusion about the good fortune of becoming something "better," a mistake which often must be paid for with the bitterest disappointment, a mongrel life, and the dire circumstances of pressing occupational responsibility and an increasing struggle for survival, and which raises up that multifarious proletariat in office garb that is worse off than the proletariat with the callused hands of labor.[117]

Such critics feared that expanding educational opportunities were bringing into the circles of the educated and semieducated too many from the lower middle classes and working classes, who might not be suited to professional callings, would not have careers up to their expectations, and in frustration might contribute to political radicalism and social unrest. These fears were shared by high officials in the Ministry of Religion and Instruction after 1879, when a conservative cabinet came to power. The central government after the early 1880s made repeated, although largely fruitless, efforts to limit the growth of secondary and higher education. Indeed, the pressures favoring the further growth and development of advanced education became so strong after the mid-1890s that the state authorities saw a gradual erosion of their powers to control change.

CHAPTER 3

Guarding the Gates

The Social Politics of Education after 1880

The expanding enrollments in Austrian secondary and higher education during the late nineteenth century evoked much concern among officials, professional groups, and interested citizens. Some educators worried about the effects of overcrowding on students and on the quality of their education. Some students and their parents also feared the impact on prospects for successful professional careers. Conservative officials and elected representatives worried about the threats to social stability of producing more educated persons than were actually needed. They complained that the popular infatuation with academic education and the professions was only denying to other necessary occupations talented youth who might be better off there.

In 1881, for example, Armand Freiherr von Dumreicher (1845–1908), an official in the Ministry of Religion and Instruction, decried the consequences of developments in the *Realschulen* after 1867. Dumreicher believed that strengthening the academic subjects and downgrading the vocational elements in the *Realschule* curriculum had only added to the difficulties of craft producers:

> On the one hand, an expansion in the purely theoretical schools was induced beyond healthy needs; and this increased the danger posed to the state by a Catiline social element and to the intellectual culture by a demi-monde of the educated. On the other hand, an important segment of the population, the artisanal class, was deprived of an educational institution which it had possessed for sixteen years and which it could not do without.[1]

In contrast to those who feared the rapid growth in secondary and higher education, most Czech nationalist leaders in the late nineteenth century championed increasing access to advanced education as part of the efforts to emancipate their people from domination by ethnic Germans. By the beginning of the twentieth century, however, the great increases in enrollments had convinced some more conservative Czech politicians of the need to limit further growth. In 1914

Dr. Karel Mattuš (1836–1919), who served many years as an Old Czech deputy in the Reichsrat and sat in the Austrian House of Lords after 1899, offered such a view:

> The previous lack of Czech secondary schools has not only been completely overcome, but at the moment we have to endure a painful surplus of secondary schools and, because of this, an overproduction of people with higher education, who cannot find the positions for which they prepared themselves. . . . Under the current circumstances, every expenditure for the establishment of new secondary schools must be considered uneconomical, a pure luxury.[2]

Fears of excessive growth in advanced education engendered repeated attempts to reduce enrollments. Already in 1870, as we have seen, the Ministry of Religion and Instruction acted to tighten admissions to the secondary schools. The government, led by German liberals at the time, wanted to assure that students in the secondary schools would meet academic standards appropriate to the modern educational system it was consolidating. Under more conservative leadership after 1880, the ministry made new efforts to restrict secondary school admissions as part of broader programs to bolster craft manufacture and agriculture and to deter lower-middle-class youth from aspiring to professional and bureaucratic careers that few could ever realize.

As will be seen, social, political, and institutional realities made it difficult to limit growth in enrollments or, indeed, to change substantially the standards and practices for admission to secondary and higher education. Loyalties to established principles and procedures proved strong among the instructors, school administrators, and many permanent officials despite the worries about excessive enrollments and overproduction of graduates. The ministerial officials also faced pressures from a number of popular interests to continue the expansion of educational opportunities. Even though most of the attempts to restrict growth in enrollments failed, examining them and the major curricular and organizational reforms made after 1880 reveals much about the social politics of advanced education during this era and about what could and could not be done to change the educational institutions. The efforts to control the growth of advanced education occurred at irregular intervals between 1880 and 1914 and had varying sources. The enrollment trends, changes in the balance of political forces, and economic cycles all helped precipitate the initiatives; and it is hard to chart a continuous chain of development in the central government's educational policies. It is best then to analyze some of the most important individual initiatives and derive such insights as may be drawn about the larger forces that were at work.

The Conservative Search for Social Balance

In 1879 a new Austrian cabinet came into office led by the emperor's old friend Count Eduard Taaffe. The German liberal leaders in the Reichsrat had angered the emperor in the preceding years by sponsoring more anticlerical legislation and opposing the occupation of Bosnia-Herzegovina, and their own ranks were now split. Count Taaffe initially tried to include some German liberals in his cabinet, but after 1880 his government rested on a coalition of Catholic conservatives, moderate Czech nationalists, and Polish conservatives, united as the so-called Iron Ring around their opposition to the German liberals.[3] Count Taaffe's government reduced the suffrage requirements for the Reichsrat in 1882 to increase the voting strength of the lower middle classes and weaken German liberal entrepreneurial and professional interests. During its tenure up to 1893, the Taaffe government made important concessions to Slavic nationalist demands at the expense of German middle-class interests. Otherwise, Count Taaffe's policies on social and educational issues showed strongly conservative, traditionalist tendencies. The Taaffe cabinet appealed to the corporative social ideals that were reviving throughout Central Europe during the 1880s in its efforts to build an alliance of noble landowners, peasant farmers, craft producers, and shopkeepers from all nationalities. In Germany after 1879, Otto von Bismarck's government tried to unite the interests of agriculture with big industry, but it offered relatively little beyond rhetoric to assist struggling craft producers. Count Taaffe's government showed a stronger commitment to assisting independent artisans. Regarding cultural and educational issues, the conservative Catholics in the coalition thought that the German liberals' anticlerical policies had gone too far, and they wanted to revive the influence of the Catholic Church over primary schools.

During the 1880s Austria's conservative political forces reacted to the former policies of educational expansion by trying to cut back parts of public education and limit further growth. In the interests of social balance, conservatives expected vigorous bodies of peasant farmers, independent craft producers, and skilled workers to continue in society even if this required some government protection. Many peasant farmers opposed from the outset the increase from six to eight years of mandatory primary education that was introduced in 1869. Many community governments also complained about the costs of the expanded primary schools. Conservative political thinkers were sympathetic to such views and thought that increased access to *Gymnasien* and *Realschulen* was diverting some of the ablest youth away from farming and craft production.

The Taaffe government developed its educational policies gradually and tended to give less attention to public education than to other social and economic issues.[4] Still, during the 1880s the central government made a series of initiatives to reduce what it viewed as superfluous primary education, diminish access to academic secondary schools, and promote vocational training. The German liberal, Stremayr, continued as Minister of Religion and Instruction in 1879–80; but in June 1880 it became known that Count Taaffe wanted to appoint someone favored by Catholic conservatives. In the face of German liberal opposition, though, the minister-president backed down and chose the erstwhile governor of Lower Austria, Siegmund Freiherr Conrad von Eybesfeld, who would be more acceptable to those interests.[5] Like many Austrian cabinet members in the constitutional era, Conrad-Eybesfeld came not from the parliamentary benches or academic life but from the state administration. The Taaffe government's educational policies took shape under Conrad-Eybesfeld's sometimes ambivalent leadership.

In late 1879 and early 1880, Catholic conservatives moved quickly to demand changes in primary education, hoping to force a commitment from the new cabinet. The Catholic bishops in Bohemia, for instance, demanded that the government restore the religious character of primary schooling. In February 1880, Prince Alois von Liechtenstein—one of the founders of Catholic social thought in Austria—and another Catholic conservative, Georg Lienbacher, each introduced bills in the Reichsrat to restore the powers of the provincial diets over primary education, reduce the basic educational requirement to six years, and allow the individual crown lands to set any additional requirement for the seventh and eighth years.[6] Conrad-Eybesfeld persuaded Liechtenstein to withdraw his proposal pending the government's full reassessment of the 1869 school law, but Lienbacher won a majority of the lower house for his amended bill. This attack on the 1869 school law put the government in an awkward position. When the Lienbacher bill reached the House of Lords in 1881, Conrad-Eybesfeld offered no more than equivocal support, and German liberals defeated it there.[7]

In January 1882, Conrad-Eybesfeld proposed a new law on primary education that tried to appease Catholic conservatives while preserving the foundations of the 1869 legislation. The government's bill affirmed the purpose of the public primary schools to train children "religiously and morally," reversing the order of the previous formulation. The bill would allow parents or community governments in all crown lands to substitute part-time or half-day instruction for the seventh and eighth years of the *Volksschule*. In addition, each teacher would have to prove his or her competence to give religious instruction in the faith of the majority of the pupils. With this latter measure, the government hoped to answer Catholic conservative objections to the employment of Jewish teachers, particularly in Lower Austria. Still, Catholic conservative deputies added a new requirement that the religious affiliation of any new school director must correspond to that of the majority of the pupils, except in Galicia and Dalmatia. This exception would permit Latin-rite Catholics to direct schools attended by Orthodox Christians and Uniate Catholics, a particular concern of the Polish elites in eastern Galicia. German liberals, some of the more liberal Czech nationalists, and some Ukrainian deputies opposed the revision of the primary school law; but the bill passed both houses of the Reichsrat by April 1883. In practice, some of the poorest and least-developed crown lands had already exempted children from the seventh and eighth years of primary schooling; and the Taaffe government had been permitting a religious test for teaching appointments in some localities despite the violation of civil rights which that involved.[8]

As early as August 1880, the Taaffe government voiced concern about what it viewed as excessive numbers of students enrolling in *Gymnasien* and *Realschulen*. In some ways the government only followed the example of the 1870 measure that stiffened admissions requirements, but the Taaffe cabinet connected its effort to reduce enrollments in secondary schools with steps to promote vocational education. On 20 August 1880, Conrad-Eybesfeld issued a decree to all directors of state-recognized secondary schools calling for detailed annual reports on the admissions examinations. In view of the strong growth in enrollments since the mid-1870s and many students' failure to complete full programs of study, the ministry ordered the school directors to discuss with all applicants for admission and their parents the purposes of secondary education to prepare for university and technical college study. The directors were "to warn against attending a general educational institution those pupils whom one, from the outset, would not expect to want to use the secondary school to prepare for higher education or to be able to, and to warn those whom one, from experience, would not expect to be successful in a secondary school." The school directors were to recommend that such youth enroll instead in intermediate vocational schools for manufacture, commerce, and agriculture.[9]

The August 1880 decree indicated the government's general social goals regarding secondary education. The text recognized the continuing expansion of secondary education as "doubtlessly one of the most gratifying phenomena of recent times in our educational situation," but went on to assert that "there must be questionable consequences for the economic and social interests of the population when the crowding of students into the *Gymnasien* and *Realschulen* begins to exceed the limits of the professional and employment possibilities connected with such studies." The decree cited the numerous youth from agricultural, commercial, and craft backgrounds who sought admission to the schools even though they lacked "the economic and intellectual prerequisites" that were needed to gain real advantage from such long and costly studies. Many talented youth, it predicted, might have successful careers in manufacture and agriculture if they attended vocational schools rather than *Gymnasien* and *Realschulen*. The decree asserted the duty and power of "the state administration and especially the educational authorities to counteract the tendency of the population that would deprive agriculture and the crafts of some of the best talents on the one hand and would create on the other hand an unproductive and dissatisfied proletariat of unemployed educated persons."[10] In the name of general social welfare, the ministry was openly trying to reduce the numbers of youth from the traditional lower middle classes who enrolled in academic secondary schools and aspired to careers in educated and semi-educated professions.

Whatever the Taaffe government's conservative agenda, permanent officials who were products of the German liberal era encouraged and aided the drafting of the decree on secondary school admissions. These included Heinrich Schramm, a provincial school inspector in Lower Austria, and Dumreicher, who had had responsibilities in the Ministry of Religion and Instruction for developing vocational education since the mid-1870s. In July 1880 Schramm submitted to the ministry a long report that proposed some of the new procedures that appeared in the August decree and articulated parts of the basic rationale.[11] Schramm noted that in recent years the ministry had laid the foundations for a good system of vocational education, but the public was slow to take advantage of the opportunities. He complained that "every year the state educates too many people who only write and speak and too few who can work." In addition to popular ignorance of the possibilities for vocational training and the widespread bias in favor of academic education, existing laws and institutional relationships contributed to the problems. The various privileges accorded to graduates of *Gymnasien* and *Realschulen,* particularly the one-year, volunteer military service, also increased those schools' attractiveness over vocational training. Schramm noted as well that *Gymnasium* and *Realschule* directors, particularly in smaller schools, had a vested interest in protecting and increasing their enrollments.

Armand von Dumreicher also played a major role in drafting the August 1880 decree.[12] The son of Johann Baron Dumreicher von Österreicher, a professor in the Vienna medical faculty, he was a moderate German liberal who believed in centralized policy making for educational affairs. In 1881 he published a lecture justifying the efforts to steer lower-middle-class youth into vocational schools and away from academic secondary education.[13] Like Schramm, Dumreicher lamented the abandonment of agriculture and the crafts by youth who aspired to enter educated professions. He rejected the charge that it was a reactionary policy to divert sons of craft producers and peasant farmers away from education for white-collar employment and the professions. Dumreicher argued that it was really in the best interests of modern manufacturing and agriculture to encourage more of the most-gifted youth from handicraft, small manufacturing, and farming backgrounds to pursue vocational training and remain in those economic sectors. In truth, he suggested, popular prejudices in favor of "the pen over the tool" were reactionary, for they harked back to the "time of the absolute monarchy with its all-powerful officialdom, in which the smallest office had a much higher prestige than the most productive workshop."[14] A moderate liberal bureaucrat such as Dumreicher could agree with conservatives that academic education should serve a limited constituency and the state must try to maintain social balances.

The ministry's efforts to stem the rising enrollments in Austria's academic secondary schools paralleled developments in Germany that began in the late 1870s. One can assume that many Austrian educators and ministerial officials were informed of discussions in German educational circles from newspapers, journals, and personal contacts, although Austrian official statements generally did not mention initiatives in Germany. During the difficult years after the financial crash of 1873, Prussian state officials, conservative politicians, and some educators became concerned about the filling of the *Gymnasien* with a large "ballast," as they termed it, of students from lower-class origins, many of whom did not graduate or go on to higher education. Many conservatives and moderate liberals in Prussia supported the social segmentation of secondary education and wanted to reaffirm the elitist traditions of the *Gymnasien* by reducing the lower-class "ballast." The Prussian educational authorities found it difficult, though, to achieve any consensus on practical measures.[15] Prussia and some of the other German states stiffened admissions and transfer requirements for secondary schools during the late 1870s and again in the 1890s, but significant portions of the German public still expected secondary education to offer opportunities for upward social mobility. The Prussian education minister between 1881 to 1891, Gustav von Gossler, attempted to reduce the "ballast" in the *Gymnasien* primarily by working to increase the attractiveness of other intermediate schools and opposing local initiatives to expand the *Gymnasien* and *Realgymnasien*.

The responses of Austrian secondary school directors to the August 1880 ministerial decree demonstrated how hard it was for the central authorities in Vienna to change popular expectations regarding advanced education or to alter how the schools dealt with the public. Despite the fact that the decree came out in late August, it called for immediate implementation and asked for early reports on the results. Some school directors replied bluntly that the new regulations only reached them in mid-September after they had finished admitting all their new students; others reported that giving the prescribed advice to the new applicants and their parents had only limited success.[16] Several directors explained that it was hard to dissuade parents from enrolling their sons in the *Gymnasium* or *Realschule* when the boys at age ten were not sure what career they would pursue and the nearest vocational school was some distance away. Even if a child ultimately might not go on to a university or technical college, the parents thought that he would learn more during a few years at an academic secondary school than in a *Bürgerschule* or the last years of a *Volksschule.* Many parents asked why their child should not have the opportunity to try a *Gymnasium* or *Realschule* like anyone else's and decide after a year or two whether that was the right choice. Some school directors reported to the ministry that they could not change the widespread belief that *Gymnasium* and *Realschule* education was more valuable than that of a *Bürgerschule* or the various vocational schools.[17] Finally, as one Carinthian *Gymnasium* director commented, many parents considered the choice of schools a family matter and they resisted instinctively advice from an official.[18]

In the Taaffe era, the Ministry of Religion and Instruction pursued an apparently simple purpose in trying to reduce enrollment in *Gymnasien* and *Realschulen* by discouraging students whom it thought unlikely to finish and pointing them to vocational schools instead. That goal collided, though, with the realities of existing institutions and popular attitudes that resisted government-initiated change. Baron Karl Korb von Weidenheim, the governor of Moravia, summed up the difficulties when he reported to the ministry in late 1880 on the results of the new admissions procedures in the Moravian secondary schools.[19] He agreed that there was a "disproportionate and unnatural" press of youth into the *Gymnasien* and *Realschulen* but doubted that the new measures would have any effect. Academic secondary education had become so accessible and the immediate economic prospects for craft producers, small manufacturers, and farmers were so grim that it was hard to persuade lower-middle-class youth to opt for vocational schools. To make any difference, Baron Korb-Weidenheim argued, required more publicity for the vocational schools, opening more of them, closing superfluous *Gymnasien* and *Realschulen,* and terminating all special preparatory classes for academic secondary schools. The governor noted that he would happily close all of Moravia's independent public *Untergymnasien* and *Unterrealschulen,* i.e., schools that offered only the first four forms; but local interests would stoutly oppose such action.

Beyond the popular preferences for academic secondary education, institutional realities made it difficult to shift enrollments to the vocational schools. The larger number and closer proximity of *Gymnasien* and *Realschulen* were critical factors in many districts. In addition, some of the vocational schools, particularly the commercial academies, expected prior attendance at an *Untergymnasium* or *Unterrealschule.* Provincial school boards and secondary school directors understood this; but ministerial officials in Vienna, who wanted rapid changes, apparently needed reminders of these simple facts.

The Taaffe government based its policies governing secondary school admissions on the proposition that *Gymnasien* and *Realschulen* had the primary purpose of producing graduates ready for higher education or qualified white-collar employment. The new policies underestimated the broader functions that were served by the lower forms of the secondary schools. Despite the realities, the ministerial decree of August 1880, Dumreicher's 1881 lecture on educational policy, and Baron Korb-Weidenheim's report, for example, all bespoke narrower, more elitist assumptions about the purposes and clientele of secondary education that were widely held among higher officials, regardless of whether Catholic conservatives or German liberals were in control.

Throughout the 1880s, the Ministry of Religion and Instruction continued to collect annual reports on admissions to the secondary schools and looked for ways to limit enrollments. The emperor's speech at the opening of the Reichsrat in September 1885 noted the "exceedingly large numbers of youth flooding into the secondary schools" and repeated the government's desire to divert some of them into vocational education.[20] In June 1887, the ministry issued regulations to tighten the age requirement for entry into *Gymnasien* and *Realschulen.* Without exception, admittees were now expected to complete their tenth year of age during the calendar year in which their first semester of study began.[21]

In November 1885, Paul Freiherr Gautsch von Frankenthurn, a career official, succeeded Conrad-Eybesfeld as minister of religion and instruction. Citing low enrollments and budgetary constraints, Gautsch ordered in July 1887 the closing of the *Realschule* in Steyr, Upper Austria; *Gymnasien* in Bolzano and Roveredo, Tirol; the *Gymnasium* in Kranj (Krainburg), Carniola; a *Realschule* and *Gymnasium* in Kotor (Cattaro), Dalmatia; and the *Untergymnasium* in Sereth, Bukovina. Gautsch also declared the ministry's opposition to putting any additional communal or provincial secondary schools on the state budget, stopped plans to expand several existing state schools, and revoked subventions for the communally operated Czech-language secondary schools in Čáslav and Nový Bydžov, eastern Bohemia.[22]

By the mid-1880s the Austrian public had become accustomed to the central government's support for continuing expansion of secondary education, and Minister Gautsch's initiatives elicited protests from the affected communities. Czech politicians expressed outrage because the Taaffe cabinet was reneging on commitments, and they accused the government of betraying them when it needed their support. The emperor tried to reassure Czech leaders that the government's school policies were not directed against their interests, but he also voiced concerns about excessive numbers of students in *Gymnasien* and *Realschulen*.[23] The government retreated on some of the most draconic orders to close schools but pressed forward with other measures. In the end, most of the schools in the Alpine lands that Gautsch's orders had targeted for closure survived.

In early May 1888, Minister Gautsch explained to deputies in the Reichsrat the rationale for continuing to try to reduce enrollments in the academic secondary schools.[24] He decried the fact that many more students were enrolling in secondary schools, universities, and technical colleges than ever graduated or managed to enter educated professions. By the ministry's reckoning, only 2 percent of the male population were engaged in educated professions at the time, although 4.1 percent of the male youth between ages 11 and 18 attended *Gymnasien* and *Realschulen*. Gautsch asserted that positions in government offices were full and those who wished to teach in secondary schools also faced poor prospects. Technical college enrollments had declined greatly during the preceding decade, but that derived, in the minister's view, from the competition of vocational schools and an oversupply of engineers and other educated technical personnel.

The surplus of graduates compared with employment opportunities was a different problem from the crowding of schools with ill-suited students, but Gautsch focused on the excessive enrollments as the root of the difficulties. He cited the ballooning of secondary school attendance since the 1840s, a 60 percent increase in university enrollments between 1882 and 1886, and appallingly high attrition rates in secondary and higher education. Less than one-third of those who entered the *Gymnasien* actually completed their studies and passed the *Matura*. The university faculties of law and medicine had similarly high rates of attrition.[25] While more than 90 percent of the *Gymnasium*

Maturanten went on to higher education of some kind, only 43 percent of the *Realschule* graduates were going on to technical colleges. Gautsch suggested that lax standards for admitting students to the secondary schools and exempting them from tuition fees were helping cause the excessive enrollments and high attrition rates. All these circumstances, in the minister's view, justified steps to tighten admissions for the *Gymnasien* and *Realschulen* and steer youth to vocational schools instead. The government recognized an obligation to meet popular aspirations for advanced education, but there must be some balances, the minister argued, "between the educational needs of the population and the requirements of the state" and among the various public educational institutions.[26]

Gautsch did not discuss in detail in May 1888 any opposition to the government's policies. Austria's smaller ethnic groups and the lower middle classes in general desired even broader access to advanced education. The Ministry of Religion and Instruction, however, had considerable power to establish regulations for all public education without specific legislation from the Reichsrat or the provincial diets. Moreover, in 1888 mass political parties were only just coming to the fore, and legislative efforts to reverse the ministry's restrictive policies on secondary education might not have passed both houses of the Reichsrat.

In themselves, the government efforts to limit secondary school enrollments and promote vocational education during the 1880s had only limited effects. Total enrollments in the *Gymnasien, Real-Gymnasien,* and *Realschulen* did stop increasing relative to Austria's total population between 1879–80 and 1889–90; and enrollments relative to the eleven- to eighteen-year-old age group declined slightly during that period (see tables 2/1 and 2/2 above). This change, however, probably resulted as much from the depressed conditions in agriculture and the reduced growth of commerce and industry in the 1880s as from anything else. The declining *Real-Gymnasien* lost more than one-eighth of their enrollments during the decade, while the *Realschule* students increased by a little more than 2 percent (see table 1 in the appendix). The fact that *Gymnasien* enrollments still grew by 16 percent in absolute terms worried the ministry and encouraged further efforts to reduce the numbers.

During the 1880s, however, the alternative of vocational education grew only slowly. Since the 1860s the *Bürgerschulen* had done more to provide basic education to children from the lower middle classes and laboring strata than to offer vocational training, and that tendency continued during the 1880s and after. The Ministry of Religion and Instruction worked to expand advanced state craft schools (*Staats-Gewerbeschulen*) from the mid-1870s onward, but with limited results. By 1895 in the Alpine lands, for instance, such schools existed only in Vienna, Graz, Salzburg, and Innsbruck. General craftsman's schools (*Allgemeine Handwerkerschulen*), funded primarily by local and provincial authorities, began in the 1880s; but in the Alpine lands only three such institutions were operating by 1890. Specialized trade schools (*Fachschulen*) developed during the last decades of the century, but they were scattered haphazardly over the Austrian territory. By the mid-1880s, Dumreicher, one of the chief advocates for vocational education in the ministry, found himself increasingly out of sympathy with the Taaffe government's conservative Catholic and federalist tendencies. Having defined much of the organizational structure for vocational education, he left the ministry in 1886.[27]

The central authorities made admission to *Gymnasien* and *Realschulen* the primary focus for their efforts to limit growth for both secondary and higher education. Any attempt to make the secondary school curricula more difficult would have been beside the point: attrition rates were already high, and there was already too great a disproportion between the high enrollments in the lower forms and the smaller numbers in the upper. Perhaps the ministry might have asked the provincial school councils and their school inspectors to make the *Matura* examinations more stringent, but it would have been difficult to force any significant changes in this regard on school directors and professors who knew the examinees and had to face them and their parents. As it was, Austrian educators in the 1880s were already hearing public complaints about the excessive demands of the *Matura* and the burdens of secondary school studies, particularly in the *Gymnasien*.

While the Austrian educational authorities tried repeatedly to tighten admissions to the secondary schools, they did not attempt to change significantly admission requirements for higher education. Establishing additional requirements for entry into the universities and technical colleges beyond satisfactory completion of *Gymnasium* or *Realschule* studies and passing the *Matura* would have contradicted the basic assumption that the academic secondary schools were to prepare students adequately for higher education. Also, by the 1870s, if not already in the 1860s, the *Matura* from an Austrian *Gymnasium* and the parallel examination in a *Realschule* had acquired a hallowed status in Austrian academic culture, parallel to the *Abitur* in Germany, as the critical entrance requirement for higher education. Over the years after the establishment of the *Matura* in 1849, the Austrian public came to consider admission to a university or technical college on the basis of passing the appropriate *Matura* as a legal entitlement.

Apparently, the legalistic mentality of the state officials respected that notion of entitlement. Individual professors in the universities and technical colleges could put numerical limits on enrollments for particular courses and clinics;[28] and in emergencies the ministerial authorities might limit total enrollments for individual institutions to deal with overcrowding. Otherwise, demanding any additional general requirements for admission to higher education would have broken the implied contract with the public regarding the functions of *Gymnasium* and *Realschule* studies and the *Matura*. Such action also might have cast doubt on the basic quality of the academic secondary schools and the soundness of the *Matura*. Under those circumstances, any formal measures to control growth in enrollments for Austrian higher education, other than emergency actions, would be difficult and had to be indirect if they were tried at all.

Deluge at the Turn of the Century

The powerful wave of increasing student numbers after the early 1890s put enormous strains on Austrian secondary and higher education. The *Gymnasien* could hardly keep up with a two-thirds increase in their enrollments between 1895 and 1910, and the number of *Realschule* students nearly doubled in those same years (see table 1 in the appendix). The universities faced a 75 percent increase in the number of matriculated students in this period, while the numbers in technical colleges quadrupled (see table 2 in the appendix). In Austria and throughout Central Europe, the stresses of expanding enrollments after the early 1890s added fuel to a growing public debate about advanced education. Professional groups, educators, political leaders, and parents questioned whether the schools were meeting the needs of youth or the requirements of employers and professional practice. Parents and educators lamented the overcrowding of institutions, the costs and duration of studies, and the high attrition of students. Many claimed that students, particularly in the *Gymnasien,* were overburdened with studies of dubious value and were suffering psychological and physical harm. Critics of secondary education also complained about excessive reliance on memorization, the tyranny of daily graded recitation, inadequate development of reasoning abilities, and the rigors of the *Matura* examinations.[29]

In Austria as well as Germany, as will be seen, the majority of secondary school students were the offspring of medium and small business owners, white-collar employees, craft producers, and agricultural proprietors who had little experience with advanced education themselves. Many of these students and their parents found irrelevant the intellectual values that underlay the classical *Gymnasium.* After 1890 growing numbers of parents and sympathetic educators called for changes in the *Gymnasien* and questioned why other forms of academic secondary education continued to have inferior status.[30] They challenged the requirements for Latin and Greek and asked why modern languages such as English or French could not be substituted for Greek. Some in Austria pushed for a new secondary school modeled after the Prussian *Realgymnasium,* for which they demanded full equality with the classical *Gymnasium* in preparing students for the universities. In both Germany and Austria, there were increasing calls for equal status for graduates of all academic secondary schools. At the same time, advocates of advanced education for women campaigned for their admission to the classical *Gymnasien* and for girls' secondary schools to have equal status with the boys'.

Austria's Ministry of Religion and Instruction and the provincial educational authorities were hard-pressed to respond to the growing public appetite for advanced education and the varied calls for reform of the secondary schools. In December 1895, Gautsch, who returned as minister in the cabinet of Count Kasimir Badeni, tried once again to limit enrollments in the secondary schools by ordering stricter standards for the admissions examinations.[31] While the ministry considered additional measures, it ordered school directors to send forward samples of the examination records and the written essays of all applicants for admission beginning in summer 1896. The ministry explained that it was trying to exclude "immature elements" and raise the quality of education for the students who were accepted. Still, like the earlier efforts, this new action failed to stem the increase in enrollments.[32]

Indeed, as Engelbrecht has pointed out, Austria's central authorities experienced a decline in their ability to set the direction of educational policy after the mid-1890s.[33] The Ministry of Religion and Instruction still had great power over secondary and higher education, but it was constrained in policy making by fiscal stringency and the circumstance that no less than ten cabinets served between the fall of Count Badeni in November 1897 and the outbreak of war in summer 1914, with few of them commanding a parliamentary majority for long. Partisan politics in the Reichsrat and the provincial diets and growing public debate of educational issues put increasing pressure on the ministerial officials. While the Reichsrat and the provincial diets did not achieve legislative control over many areas of public policy and the Reichsrat at times had difficulty in passing any legislation, the ministry faced bruising parliamentary debates about educational affairs, agitation in the partisan press, and intensive campaigning by interest groups.

Even if effective parliamentary government did not take hold in late imperial Austria, the activity of the emerging mass parties and popularly based interest groups increasingly influenced educational policy making. As Boyer has emphasized, the larger municipalities and most of the provincial governments after the 1880s experienced significant growth in their activity and powers regarding welfare programs, public health, economic development, and primary education. The city and provincial governments thereby became stages for a kind of representative democracy where the mass parties and interest groups could shape public policy in a number of important areas.[34] That activity inevitably influenced policy making by the central authorities. The Ministry of Religion and Instruction retained its authority to issue regulations for all sectors of public education, but increasingly it had to take into account popular political forces.

None of the largest Austrian parties at the turn of the century treated education as a primary concern, but partisan forces could affect decisions about funding, personnel matters, and some curricular questions.[35] The Christian Social Party did not work out a full-fledged educational program before World War I, but it and the older Catholic conservative interests pushed to increase the influence of the Catholic Church in primary education.[36] The Social Democrats campaigned for equality of access to free, secular public education; but they focused primarily on elementary education. The Social Democrats otherwise tended to join with the remaining German liberals and German nationalists in combating clerical influences and defending the liberal educational system. For their part, the German liberals and nationalists zealously defended German-language instruction against the inroads of education in Czech, Slovene, Polish, and Austria's other non-Germanic languages.[37]

Catholic conservatives and the Christian Social movement worked through the provincial governments in the Alpine lands to increase the power of elected local officials in the hiring of primary school teachers and to enhance the role of the Church in provincial school boards. Catholic political forces also wanted greater influence in secondary and higher education and pressed for increased deference there to Catholic social and religious values.[38] The case of Ludwig Wahrmund (1860–1932), a professor of canon law in the law faculty of the University of Innsbruck, illustrates how the Ministry of Religion and Instruction found itself buffeted by conflicting mass political forces after the mid-1890s. Wahrmund became increasingly identified with German nationalist politics after 1902, and he criticized Catholic political causes and Church dogma in his teaching and public statements. In a 1908 public lecture in Innsbruck, he particularly angered Catholic circles by attacking several pronouncements of Pope Pius X. Pressured by Catholic conservatives, the papal nuncio, and Christian Social politicians, Gustav Marchet—minister of religion and instruction in the cabinet of Max Freiherr von Beck—removed Wahrmund from the Innsbruck faculty. Marchet, with Wahrmund's consent, reassigned him to the German University of Prague, although it had no vacancy in canon law at the time.

In fact, this was one of the few cases during the whole constitutional era in Austria in which the ministry removed a professor for political reasons; and Wahrmund had actually overstepped the customary limits of academic freedom by giving a popular lecture with partisan implications.[39] Nonetheless, liberal, nationalist, and socialist circles vehemently protested the government's bowing to Catholic pressures and what they believed was an infringement of academic freedom and Wahrmund's personal liberty of conscience. Student protests in support of Wahrmund led to the temporary closing of the University of Innsbruck and a general strike in all universities in the Alpine and Bohemian lands. Czech and German students in Prague even joined together to protest the government's action. Wahrmund remained in Prague after the affair, but the Beck government succeeded in angering nearly all major political parties in the Alpine and Bohemian lands.

At the turn of the century, the popular nationalist parties of the Czechs, Slovenes, Poles, Ukrainians, and the smaller ethnic groups campaigned aggressively for expanded secondary and higher education in their mother tongues. Facing such agitation along with the general growth in demand for advanced education, the ministerial and provincial authorities often found it expedient to expand the educational system where they could, at least at the primary and secondary levels. Whatever the sentiments of the more conservative officials and politicians against the rapid growth of secondary and higher education, they could find little political support after the mid-1890s for stringent measures to limit further increases in enrollments.

The lower costs of expanding primary and secondary schools and the essentially local character of those institutions, of course, made it easier for the provincial and central authorities to satisfy popular aspirations at those levels than in higher education. In 1895, however, the Austrian cabinet set off a political firestorm among Austrian German political groups when it decided to fund Slovene parallel classes in the *Gymnasium* of Celje (Cilli), a German-speaking town in largely Slovene southern Styria.[40] The issue ultimately brought down Prince Alfred Windischgrätz's coalition government and left a dire warning to later cabinets of what could happen if they became caught in a nationalist cross fire over educational issues.

The central government found it much more difficult to appease nationalist demands or meet the rising popular appetite for higher education. The financial costs of any new institutions would be high, and all the nationalist interests attached such great importance to extending or, for the Germans and Poles, protecting university and technical college education in their respective languages that any changes could become incendiary issues. At the University of Innsbruck, for instance, the faculties of law, medicine, and philosophy offered some instruction in Italian after the mid-1860s; but in November 1904, Ernest von Koerber's cabinet evoked German nationalist protests, student riots in Innsbruck, and demonstrations in Graz and Vienna when it opened a separate Italian law faculty in Innsbruck. By the end of December 1904, the protests forced the government to close that faculty; and the Innsbruck academic senate declared German as the language of instruction and administration in the university.[41] German and South Slav nationalist politicians in Austria blocked subsequent proposals to open an Italian law faculty in Trieste or Vienna. In the meantime the central government did nothing to meet Czech nationalist demands for a Czech university in Brno.[42]

In practice, the Austrian educational authorities found that they could do little to restrain the rapid increases in enrollments in secondary and higher education at the turn of the century. The fruitless effort to stiffen the admissions examinations for *Gymnasien* and *Realschulen* in 1895–96 represented the most aggressive step to restrict growth in the numbers of students in these institutions during the last two decades before 1914, and the ministry tried no further direct measures in secondary education after 1895. The rapid increase in enrollments in the universities and especially in the technical colleges caused much concern among professors and state officials about overcrowded facilities, the high attrition of students, and the possible oversupply of graduates in some fields. As in the 1880s, though, few educators or bureaucrats were eager to break traditions and raise admissions requirements for higher education.

Occasionally, some officials and professors suggested capping enrollments in higher education, but more typically they tried to accommodate the rising numbers. The ministry stretched its budget to establish new professorial chairs, institutes, and laboratories in the universities.[43] Between 1893 and 1903, the ministry also took steps to shorten the length of university studies by streamlining examinations and degree requirements in a number of subjects and encouraging students to complete programs in a timely fashion. A reform in the curriculum of the law faculties in 1893 allowed students to take the state examination in legal history after the third semester of study. In 1897, when the expanding secondary schools faced a shortage of new teachers, the ministry approved new requirements for teacher certification that shortened the examinations and encouraged candidates to complete earlier the various required essays. In 1899 the ministry modified the doctoral requirements for the philosophical faculties to facilitate more rapid completion of degrees. Changes in the examination system for the medical faculties enacted between 1899 and 1903 shortened somewhat the course work and realigned and consolidated the examination fields. With such measures, though, neither the ministry nor the various university faculties intended any fundamental lowering of academic standards.[44]

The prolonged debates about Austrian medical education between the late 1870s and 1900 illustrate the interaction of intellectual and scientific developments, professional needs, enrollment pressures, and bureaucratic and institutional factors in shaping the evolution of higher education. State officials, professors, and the medical profession all wanted to find balances between scientific education and clinical training and between the supply of well-prepared new physicians and society's demand for them. As already noted, total enrollments diminished significantly in the Austrian medical faculties during the 1870s in response to the previous overcrowding, the more stringent doctoral requirements adopted in 1872, and the economic slowdown after 1873. The numbers of medical students increased again after 1880, and in the late 1880s enrollments reached a peak for the whole period between 1848 and 1910 (see table 2 in the appendix). In the meantime, the medical faculties struggled to provide sufficient teaching personnel and facilities to keep up with a proliferation of new medical specialties and the growing student numbers. In the 1860s and again in the 1880s and early 1890s, students and professors complained about insufficient course offerings, teaching personnel, and facilities.[45]

When the ministerial authorities considered changing the medical curriculum, they consulted with public health officers and representatives of independent practitioners; but they tended to defer to the professors, particularly those in the eminent Vienna medical faculty. This contrasted somewhat with deliberations over the curriculum in law, where government officials and occasionally even the emperor asserted more forcefully state interests in the training of future bureaucrats and judicial officers.[46] In 1886 Minister Gautsch informed the Vienna medical faculty that the ministry could not afford to continue expanding its departments and clinics to meet the rising enrollments and asked the professors to consider limits on the numbers of students. Many professors were troubled by signs of overcrowding, but the great majority strongly opposed a *numerus clausus*.[47] Many believed that the ability of the faculty to attract students from throughout the monarchy and all over Europe was a great virtue and preferred augmenting the facilities and teaching personnel over imposing a limit on enrollments.[48] Most of the other Austrian medical faculties also experienced overcrowding, and many of their professors opposed limits on enrollments even more strongly than did their Viennese colleagues. In the Bohemian lands and Galicia, nationalist politics as well as popular aspirations for professional careers put heavy pressure on the faculties to accept growing numbers of students.

Throughout the 1880s and early 1890s, the Austrian medical faculties and physicians' groups debated how to modify the curriculum to deal with scientific developments, changes in clinical practice, and enrollment pressures. The Ministry of Religion and Instruction apparently delayed final action until the professors, led by the Vienna faculty, reached some consensus. In 1894 the ministry collected and printed recommendations from each of the Austrian medical faculties,[49] and on 18 December 1895 delegates from all the provincial chambers of physicians met in Vienna to discuss a package of proposed reforms. The next day the ministry convened interested state officials and representatives of all the medical faculties for an *Enquête* to make formal recommendations for changes in the medical curriculum.[50]

Minister Gautsch opened the *Enquête* by reaffirming the hallowed principles of broad scientific and scholarly inquiry in university studies:

> . . . I am obligated to state from the outset that I shall speak out against all efforts which aim to turn our faculties into trade schools (*Fachschulen*) or training institutions for physicians. I attach the greatest value to preserving the scientific spirit in our universities under all circumstances and to insuring that in the future they will have the ability to provide Austrian physicians with additional scientific education even after they have begun practice.[51]

Nonetheless, while the minister and the representatives of the faculties affirmed the importance of scientific inquiry in medical education, concerns about clinical training and professional practice dominated much of the discussion. Gautsch instructed the participants in the *Enquête* to judge the practicality of the medical curriculum for "students of average talent and adequate industry" in all the medical faculties, not merely the largest and best-equipped institutions. The participants in the *Enquête* approved dropping the preliminary examinations in mineralogy, botany, and zoology in favor of one test in general biology; dividing the ten semesters of study into a four-semester classroom-and-laboratory segment and an augmented six-semester clinical segment; giving greater weight in the doctoral examinations to clinical questions and the newer specialties of dermatology, pediatrics, and psychiatry; and requiring a year of hospital service for new medical graduates.[52] Still, even after the 1895 *Enquête,* the Ministry of Religion and Instruction took several more years to finalize the new regulations, which appeared in ordinances in 1899, 1902, and 1903.[53]

The new requirements for medical degrees modernized the curriculum, adding some new requirements while reducing others. Students were now required to follow a more structured program of studies, and the doctoral examinations would give added attention to clinical expertise and various new specialties. The additional subjects covered in the examinations and particularly the year of required hospital service made increased demands on students. Some professors, who had vested interests, after all, in keeping up student numbers, feared that declines in enrollment might result. On the other side, offering a more structured program and streamlining the basic science curriculum would allow students to progress more rapidly through their studies and emphasized the clinical training they needed for professional practice. Few of the professors and ministerial officials who supported the changes made any claim that they intended to reduce medical enrollments per se. Indeed, the participants in the 1895 *Enquête* expressed concern about the financial costs to students of medical education and the additional burden of the required hospital service; and they recommended that the ministry provide stipends for that year and try to cut the overall costs of studies.[54] The ministerial officials who were developing a new medical faculty in L'viv at this time could hardly be accused of pursuing a consistent policy of trying to reduce access to medical education.

It was clear in the extended debate over medical education that as a practical matter, neither professional organizations, professors, nor the ministerial authorities could change a university curriculum quickly or easily. Even when a range of interests agreed on the need for new requirements in the medical program, producing a new curriculum involved a long process. The central government nominally possessed great powers in establishing such regulations, but the Ministry of Religion and Instruction wanted some consensus among educators, professional groups, and interested popular representatives before it made a significant change. Achieving any broad agreement required reconciling the conflicting demands of scientific education and clinical training, harmonizing the traditions of academic freedom with the need for a well-rounded program of study, and balancing popular expectations about access to professional education with budgetary constraints and practitioners' concerns about the numbers and quality of graduates.

To deal with the ballooning enrollments in the technical colleges after the early 1890s, the ministry augmented facilities and teaching personnel where possible and in 1900 adopted a new format for the state examinations, which reduced the period of study in several fields.[55] Still, many institutions were unable to keep up with the huge increases in student numbers. The central government faced a serious budgetary dilemma if it were to maintain academic standards, since the technical colleges had relatively high instructional costs. In 1886–87, for instance, the Austrian state spent on average nearly twice as much per student in the technical colleges as in the universities. The enrollment growth in the technical colleges during the 1890s so far exceeded increases in expenditures, though, that the average outlay per student in 1899–1900 amounted to roughly half the figure of 1886, a lower sum, in fact, than the average spent per university student in 1899.[56] It was one thing to increase lecture space and the number of unsalaried docents or to wink at irregular attendance of lectures in law, the humanities, or the social sciences. Higher technical education was different. The technical colleges around 1900, like the medical faculties earlier, could not long delay either providing adequate facilities for essential laboratory and practical instruction or turning some students away.

Convinced that it could not offer sufficient new space and equipment for the increasing numbers of students, the ministry took the extraordinary step of ordering limits on enrollments for various technical colleges. This began with the Vienna Technical College in 1902, after the total number of matriculated and nonmatriculated students reached 2,525 in 1901–2. The new regulations for admissions in Vienna promised to give preference to students from Lower Austria and those crown lands that had no technical colleges. Students from other crown lands and then foreign students would be admitted thereafter only if space permitted. Total registrations for the Vienna Technical College declined somewhat during the next two years, but enforcement then slackened, so that matriculated and nonmatriculated enrollments reached 3,239 in 1910–11. The ministry imposed similar restrictions on the German Technical College of Prague in 1905 and again in 1913, the Graz Technical College in 1906 and 1908, the German Technical College of Brno in 1912, and again on the Vienna Technical College in July 1913.[57]

Many professors in the technical colleges initially opposed limits on student numbers. Their resistance stemmed from loyalty to established academic principles, institutional self-interest, and recognition of the rising public expectations for access to higher education. Both the German and Czech colleges in Prague, for example, faced dire shortages of space at the turn of the century; and students in both institutions staged protests.[58] Nonetheless, in July 1902 the professors of the Czech Technical College recommended to the Ministry of Religion and Instruction the admission of women as matriculated students despite the additional enrollments that would bring. In March 1903 the professors in the Czech Technical College declined to recommend restrictions when a committee reported on possible limits on student numbers. Gabriel Blažek, a professor of mathematics who also served as a deputy in the Bohemian Diet, spoke out against "any limitation on study at the college, for that would contradict the spirit of higher education, and the proposed illiberal measures would hardly be greeted by the public with approbation."[59] No limit was imposed for Prague's Czech Technical College in 1903, but in 1910 the ministry adopted with the professors' approval a new regulation to deny admission to students from Moravia and Silesia unless the applicants wished to pursue a specialty not offered by the Czech Technical College in Brno.[60]

The steps taken to restrict technical college enrollments between 1902 and 1913 demonstrated vividly the ministry's limited ability to control the growth of higher education at the turn of the century. The ministry had the authority in view of space limitations to restrict how many students might register. In practice, though, it took no such action in the universities during this period and only did so belatedly in the technical colleges. In the end, the ministry was unable to control the rapid increase of enrollments in higher education. While the central authorities resisted establishing new institutions, they expanded many of the existing ones and accelerated programs of study to make room for the growing student numbers. In the technical colleges the ministry invoked emergency measures only when faced with acute instructional problems and while it was still working to increase the institutions' capacity.

Debates over Secondary School Reform

The Ministry of Religion and Instruction retained its basic authority to regulate secondary education, but it faced increasingly powerful forces at the turn of the century that demanded major changes. After the late 1890s the ministry confronted a rising public debate about the relative status of the various types of secondary schools and the content of their curricula. The central authorities' footdragging on secondary education for women was characteristic of their general response: the ministry generally answered calls for change from parents, professional groups, educators, and elected politicians with bureaucratic delays, lengthy deliberations, and limited compromises. The educational bureaucracy had strong loyalties to the system of secondary education established by the neo-absolutist regime in the 1850s and the German liberals in the late 1860s and 1870s, and fiscal constraints only bolstered the officials' defense of the status quo. The circumstance that academicians and civil servants who were sympathetic to German liberal interests served as minister of religion and instruction for most of the period between 1899 and World War I only abetted the resistance to major changes.[61] Wilhelm von Hartel, who served briefly in late 1899 and then between 1900 and 1905, was a former university professor and section chief in the ministry. Marchet, who was minister between 1906 and 1908, had been a professor in the College of Agriculture in Vienna; and the career bureaucrat Count Stürgkh led the ministry from 1909 to late 1911, when he became minister-president.

Around the turn of the century, the Austrian educational authorities, like their counterparts in Germany, faced a growing movement among the public and some educators for the reform of secondary education. Many in the Austrian movement followed the debate in Germany and raised a number of the same issues.[62] Emperor William II initially appeared to favor far-reaching change in secondary education, and in December 1890 he convened in Berlin a conference on school reform for Prussia. That assemblage of secondary school educators, university professors, clergy, and members of the Prussian Diet accepted limited changes in the *Gymnasium* curriculum but in the end reaffirmed the pre-eminence of the *Gymnasien* in preparing students for university study.[63] This meant defeat for the Prussian *Oberrealschulen,* which required neither Greek nor Latin, and for the *Realgymnasien,* which offered Latin and modern languages such as French or English in place of Greek; but another school conference in Berlin in 1900 reversed the decision. Thereafter, the Prussian state government recognized the equal status of all three types of secondary schools in providing general academic education and preparing students for all university faculties.[64]

By the late 1890s many Austrians who were concerned about secondary education were growing impatient with the Ministry of Religion and Instruction for not enacting major curricular reforms or considering equal status for all academic secondary schools. An enterprising social liberal journalist, Dr. Robert Scheu, organized an independent conference on these questions in Vienna in late January 1898. Borrowing the officials' own terminology, Scheu billed the meeting as a *Mittelschul-Enquête.* Along with *Gymnasium* and *Realschule* educators, renowned professors from various institutions of higher learning joined in calling for major reforms of secondary education: Theodor Gomperz from the Vienna philosophical faculty; Edmund Bernatzik, Anton Menger, Adolf Menzel, and Eugen von Philippovich from the Vienna law faculty; the architect Karl Mayreder from the Vienna Technical College; and Artur Oelwein from the College of Agriculture in Vienna.[65] Some of these were prominent left liberals or Fabians who wanted change in popular education as part of a broader agenda of reforms in bourgeois society.

The eminent philosopher Friedrich Jodl (1849–1914) presided over the sessions. A liberal rationalist in his philosophic work, Jodl had strong commitments to civil liberties, women's rights, and adult education. At the 1898 conference he argued that with the increasing specialization of university studies, secondary schools needed more than ever to provide broad general education.[66] Nonetheless, he joined with most of the other participants in criticizing the classical *Gymnasium* curriculum for concentrating on the memorization of Latin and Greek grammar while missing the meaning of classical culture. Several conference members complained that important modern languages such as English and French were taught poorly as elective subjects in the *Gymnasien.* The participants agreed that the *Gymnasium* curriculum was outmoded and that there must be a new division of labor between the *Gymnasien* and *Realschulen*. A number went so far as to urge establishing a unified secondary school to prepare students for all institutions of higher learning with a curriculum including, in one or another format, literature, history, Latin and modern languages, natural sciences, and mathematics.[67]

During the following decade and a half, the debate over secondary education continued in Vienna and various provincial cities in parents' groups, educational and professional societies, and the press. The curriculum of the *Gymnasien* and their graduates' privileges in admission to universities drew much criticism, so much that defenders of the classical program of study felt obliged to establish in early 1906 an "Association of Friends of the Humanistic Gymnasium." Not surprisingly, the founders were primarily conservative university professors; and they named as their first president Count Stürgkh, who was then a deputy in the Reichsrat and the expert on secondary schools for the budget committee in the lower house. Proponents of reform organized the Association for School Reform in 1907.[68]

Oelwein and Scheu, who was now president of the Cultural-Political Society (Kulturpolitische Gesellschaft), staged another *Mittelschul-Enquête* in Vienna between 13 November 1906 and 18 January 1907. Since the 1898 conference, Scheu and the social liberals around him had held conferences on criminal investigative procedures, personal credit and usury, marriage laws, and government arts policy that attracted great interest in intellectual and political circles.[69] The second *Enquête* on secondary education drew an eminent group of participants from academic life, and high officials from the Ministry of Religion and Instruction attended this time. A famed professor of psychiatry from the Vienna University, Julius Wagner Ritter von Jauregg, presided over the opening session. Again some participants advocated a unified secondary school, but a number argued that differentiation of the curriculum was still needed in the upper forms to meet the particular needs of higher studies in the sciences and technology as compared with the humanities or the social sciences and law. Many argued that the current *Gymnasium* curriculum and the *Matura* overburdened students and demanded too much simple memorization. A professor from the Vienna Export Academy complained that teachers in Austrian secondary schools oppressed their students even more with daily recitation than did their Prussian counterparts, despite Prussia's reputation as "the home of drill culture."[70] Scheu bolstered the criticisms of the *Matura* with some six hundred letters from students and secondary school professors who cited frequent cheating on examination essays, prior knowledge of test questions, and special treatment for favored students.[71]

Officials in the Ministry of Religion and Instruction followed closely the public debates about secondary education, but they were slow to enact major reforms. Instead, the central authorities offered a series of minor adjustments. In response to complaints about the overburdening of *Gymnasium* students and the obsolescence of the curriculum, the ministry had already acted in 1887 to reduce the amount of instruction in Latin and Greek grammar. In 1891 the ministry ordered reductions in written home exercises and essays in Latin and Greek. Other changes in the *Gymnasien* during the 1890s cut some of the required coverage in history, geography, mathematics, and the natural sciences; expanded the treatment of modern history; and improved the elective courses in modern languages. In the same period the ministry increased the humanistic part of the *Realschule* curriculum by enhancing the teaching of writing, literature, and the modern foreign languages.

In 1903 Austria's provincial school inspectors showed a readiness for greater changes in the *Realschulen* and called for extending the program of study from seven to eight years, equal to that of the *Gymnasien*. Still, the Ministry of Religion and Instruction hesitated to make any costly changes in the *Realschulen*. In these years the Austrian Finance Ministry wanted to minimize any increases in educational expenditures, whether incurred by adding more secondary schools to the central budget or by expanding existing institutions. Advocates of reform, for their part, expressed no consensus about how many types of secondary schools there should be or what relationship they should have to each other. In response to calls to raise the status of the *Realschulen,* the ministry took only limited steps in 1906, authorizing some *Realschulen* to teach Latin as an elective, reducing the subjects covered in the special examinations that *Realschule* graduates had to pass for admission to the universities, and creating preparatory classes in the universities for *Realschule* graduates.[72]

Advocates of far-reaching reform in secondary education could only be disappointed with the meager results of the formal inquiry that the ministry finally convened in January 1908. The ministry announced that it would solicit a range of views on all issues of school organization, curriculum, and examinations as the basis for a comprehensive reform. In fact, the officials arranged the preparatory surveys, conference agenda, and list of participants to lead toward preordained results.[73] Of the sixty-two persons who attended, thirty-two were representatives of government ministries. Beyond the state officials and several members of the Reichsrat, there were fourteen representatives of higher education and four from commercial and technical occupations, but only ten from the secondary schools themselves. The participants included only three women, and Czechs, Poles, and Slovenes found themselves underrepresented relative to the German-speaking majority.

In his opening statement to the 1908 conference, the minister, Marchet, asked for proposals to reform the *Gymnasium* and *Realschule* curricula. He made it clear, though, that the ministry would welcome steps to transform existing institutions into one or more new types of schools over any radical measures to create a unified secondary school. Several participants in the conference still advocated a unified school or at least a uniform curriculum for the lower forms of all secondary schools, and proponents of equality of status between the *Gymnasien* and the *Realschulen* called for an eighth year for the *Realschule* program and increased instruction in the humanities. In the end, the ministry got from the conference what it had apparently intended: recommendations to moderate and simplify the *Matura* examinations and to authorize, in addition to the *Gymnasium* and the *Realschule,* a new eight-year *Realgymnasium.* Much like the Prussian *Realgymnasium* and unlike the old Austrian *Real-Gymnasium* of the 1860s and 1870s, the new schools would have required courses in Latin, a modern language instead of Greek, drawing, gymnastics, and more science and mathematics than the *Gymnasium.* A *Realschule* graduate would still have to pass supplementary examinations to matriculate in a university, but a *Matura* from a *Realgymnasium* would have the same status as that from a *Gymnasium.*[74]

Between 1908 and 1910 the Ministry of Religion and Instruction moved with uncharacteristic speed to enact the recommendations of the 1908 conference, although the promised comprehensive law on secondary education did not materialize before the outbreak of war in 1914. A ministerial ordinance sanctioned the new *Realgymnasium* in August 1908.[75] Other regulations issued in 1908 called for less reliance on class recitation in the *Gymnasien* and *Realschulen,* simplified the grading systems, and reduced the rigors of the *Matura* examinations. In 1909, after consultation with educators in the *Gymnasien* and the universities, the ministry approved new study plans for the *Gymnasien* that decreased the demands in Latin, mathematics, and physics; enhanced instruction in chemistry, geography, and civics; and added requirements in freehand drawing and gymnastics. The ministry took no action before 1914 to expand the *Realschule* curriculum to eight years, but a new study plan issued in 1909 increased instruction in geography, natural history, and modern languages while reducing the teaching of other subjects.[76]

The *Realgymnasium* quickly proved popular, with new institutions opened in many communities or existing *Gymnasien* and *Realschulen* converted to the new model. The new ordinances also authorized a *Reform-Realgymnasium,* whose lower forms would follow the model of the *Unterrealschule,* with French instruction beginning in the first year and Latin offered only in the upper forms. The curricular options for *Realgymnasien* permitted a revival of the old concept from the 1860s and 1870s of offering common classes for *Gymnasium* and *Realschule* students in the first two forms and then separate tracks within the same school from the third form onward. This enabled smaller communities to provide all the secondary-school options for boys under a single roof.[77] While the reforms in Austrian secondary education after 1908 did not meet the egalitarian ideal of a unified school, the growth of the new-style *Realgymnasien* along with the girls' *Lyzeen* and the privately sponsored girls' *Gymnasien* signified movement toward greater equality among the various school types and a loss in status for the classical *Gymnasien.*

It is tempting to blame the rigidity of the Austrian state bureaucracy for the extended deliberations before any reforms were enacted in secondary and higher education during the last decades before 1914. Ministerial officials generally made the ultimate decisions regarding new regulations, and their conservative attitudes and practices contributed much to the outcomes. Still, educators, elected representatives, professional associations, other interest groups, and the press often played important parts in the discussions that preceded ministerial decisions. If Austrian secondary and higher education proved unable to adapt quickly to the many pressures for change, this was due not simply to the conservatism and unresponsiveness of the bureaucrats but also to an inelasticity in the whole educational system that was rooted deeply in the established principles and procedures and perpetuated by educators and students as well as officials.

Even if their actions were belated or half-hearted, the Austrian authorities accepted changes in secondary education after 1900 that departed significantly from the original designs of Exner, Bonitz, and Leo Thun. These innovations paralleled the steps taken after the early 1890s to reform the doctoral and state examinations in the universities and technical colleges but went farther in some ways. The ministerial officials and educators changed some of the basic principles and traditions of secondary education when, for example, they established the new-style *Realgymnasium,* increased instruction in the humanities and social sciences in the *Realschulen,* and allowed, albeit grudgingly, the emergence of eight-year private women's *Gymnasien.*

The state officials and educators made the organizational and curricular changes while they were struggling to accommodate rapidly growing enrollments in both secondary and higher education. In the process, they accepted some change in the old assumptions about advanced education being aimed primarily at a select, male intellectual elite. Neither Austria nor the German states had recognized any general popular right to academic secondary education during the early nineteenth century, and while Exner and Bonitz had initially foreseen a broad popular constituency for the *Realschulen,* they and the other midcentury Austrian reformers recognized no universal right to study in *Gymnasien* or universities. By the 1890s Austrian secondary school teachers, university professors, and ministerial officials alike had to recognize that a significant change was taking place in popular expectations regarding advanced education. The educational authorities still intended the *Gymnasium* and *Realschule* curricula for a qualified elite, but growing numbers of the public now treated access to at least the initial forms of the secondary schools as more of a general right. This was already clear in the early 1880s in parents' resistance to the official efforts to restrict admissions to secondary schools and divert youth to vocational education. Parents insisted on their children's right to enter the *Gymnasien* and *Realschulen* even if many might not stay beyond the lower forms. In 1880 a *Gymnasium* director in Graz reported to the Styrian provincial school board the statement of a number of parents: "I pay taxes, too, and therefore have the right, like others, to an education for my son in a state *Gymnasium.*"[78]

In simple numbers, Austria and the rest of Central Europe were still a long way from the mass secondary education that developed later in the twentieth century; but the growth in enrollments after the mid-1890s was unprecedentedly strong and unremitting. In 1870 under German liberals, in the 1880s under the Taaffe government, and in 1895 when Gautsch served again as minister, the Austrian Ministry of Religion and Instruction tried to limit the increase in student numbers in academic secondary schools. Thereafter some of the highest officials, such as Count Stürgkh, might still oppose rapid growth in enrollments, the opening of advanced education to new constituencies such as women, or major changes in the curricula; but they could not stop the forces of change. After the mid-1890s the ministerial officials increasingly bowed to the growing popular appetite for advanced education and modified curricular requirements and examinations that were criticized as outmoded or unreasonable. Certainly, some of the substantive changes in secondary school curricula resulted from intellectual developments and pedagogical judgments by educators. Otherwise, though, desires to accommodate larger enrollments and reduce requirements that were popularly viewed as unnecessary barriers for students influenced many changes in programs, whether it was reducing requirements in Latin and Greek in the *Gymnasien,* moderating the *Matura* examinations, or accelerating the completion of diplomas in the universities and technical colleges.

No one should have been surprised that there was so much conflict at the turn of the century between established academic practices and the changing requirements of contemporary society. European education had faced such crises before during periods of rapid economic, social, and cultural development. The dilemma was particularly acute in this instance because the concurrent forces of population increase, far-reaching social and economic transformation, and the expansion of public and private bureaucracy during the second half of the nineteenth century caused a rapid broadening of demand for advanced education and the emergence of many new academic specialties. The expansion of popular demand in Austria resulted in significant changes in the ethnic, religious, and class composition of the students in secondary and higher education, which must now be examined.

CHAPTER 4

The Changing Ethnic and Religious Recruitment of Students

We have contradictory notions about the recruitment and social status of educated elites in Central Europe during the late nineteenth century. Even on the eve of World War I, no more than 3.0 percent of the school-aged population in Germany and Austria attended academic secondary schools, and only around 1.5 percent of the prime age groups were enrolled in universities and technical colleges. In numerical terms secondary and higher education still served only small segments of the German and Austrian populations, and advanced education brought considerable privileges and prestige. Reporting to the Silesian Provincial School Board in 1880, one Austrian school director summed up popular beliefs about the value of *Gymnasium* education: "The public holds the view, and indeed with a certain amount of truth, that all paths for the future stand open to the *Gymnasium* graduate."[1] The *Realschule* might have less status than the classical *Gymnasium,* but after the early 1870s students in Austrian *Realschulen* could take their own *Matura* and were also entitled to advantages such as the one-year, volunteer military service, eligibility for certain jobs, and admission to a technical college. Those who went on to universities or technical colleges and eventually passed state examinations or earned degrees carried their diplomas and titles as badges of accomplishment. They expected special respect, regardless of their own social origins or the circumstances of their actual employment. Still, while graduates of academic secondary schools, universities, and technical colleges enjoyed special status, many of them were known to have come from relatively humble social origins. Memoirs and popular fiction that portray the deference to academic and professional titles also frequently celebrate the modest origins of many of the diploma-holders. The educated were characterized by greater diversity of social origins than one might expect for a small, privileged segment of the population. Studies of secondary and higher education in the German states show that throughout the nineteenth century many students came from the families of schoolteachers, clerks, petty government employees, Protestant pastors, small business owners, master craft producers, or peasant farmers.[2]

To appreciate the actual social experience of the educated elites, one must also recognize that many who studied in universities and technical colleges went on to careers of relatively limited income and moderate status in lesser state offices, finance, industry, secondary schools, or churches. When observers of German and Austrian education in the late nineteenth century warned against the dangers of an "academic proletariat," they feared not merely the threat for the future posed by expanding enrollments but also the present reality of frustrations among those who had expected education to bring them greater social and financial advantages than they actually achieved.[3]

The primary criteria for measuring the changing recruitment of the educated elites in the German states during the nineteenth century have been occupation and class, with regional, religious, ethnic, and urban-rural differences also given consideration. For old Austria, though, like the United Kingdom and North America, the ethnic and religious diversity of the population make those factors as important as occupation or class for analyzing the origins of the educated and measuring the social opportunities offered by advanced education. As will be seen, the ethnic and religious composition of students in Austrian secondary and higher education changed strikingly, as Czechs and Poles, among the larger ethnic groups, and the Jewish and Protestant religious minorities greatly increased their representation while the German-speaking Catholics' fraction of total enrollments gradually declined. This was tangible proof that the expansion of the educational system gave increased access to segments of the population that were more poorly represented before the mid-nineteenth century. In the process, the recruitment of students from the various social classes also changed, but, as will be seen in the following chapter, that transformation was in many respects more subtle and gradual.

The Early Modern Heritage

During the eighteenth and early nineteenth centuries, access to Austrian secondary and higher education was contingent on students' ability, financial means, language, and, to a diminishing degree, religion. Joseph II's educational reforms envisioned a reduced network in which the students would choose between *Lyzeen* or *Gymnasien* leading to the universities and which would produce no more graduates than the state deemed necessary for practical purposes. The old

Jesuit-run secondary schools of the early eighteenth century levied no tuition fees, but after 1784 the institutions of secondary and higher education charged tuition and other fees to help meet costs and to discourage youth of limited talents, doubtful dedication, or modest means.[4]

Secondary and higher education in the Alpine and Bohemian lands during the late eighteenth and early nineteenth centuries meant essentially German-language instruction. Under the reforms of Maria Theresa and Joseph II, primary school instruction began in the students' mother tongue, but teaching switched to German after the first few forms. During the early nineteenth century, instruction in all the public *Gymnasien, Realschulen,* universities, and technical institutes in those provinces was in German with the exception of some courses taught in Latin. By the 1830s and 1840s, several Austrian universities offered courses on various Slavic languages and literatures; but students from the Slavic groups in the Alpine and Bohemian lands had to do nearly all their academic work in German. The Austrian educational authorities did not collect data on students' ethnicity or mother tongues on a systematic basis before the mid-nineteenth century, but clearly youth who did not come from German-speaking homes faced a serious disadvantage of having to study primarily in an acquired language.[5] In the meantime the Austrian authorities Germanized most of secondary education in Galicia during the first half of the nineteenth century, and they made first Latin and later German the principal language of instruction at the university they developed out of the old college in L'viv.[6] Only in northern Italy and some of the Adriatic coastal towns did the Austrian officials make an exception to the Germanizing policies and provide secondary and higher education in Italian.

The eighteenth-century reforms asserted the authority of the state over the Catholic Church in public education and under Joseph II granted religious toleration to non-Catholics, but significant Catholic influences persisted in Austrian education through the early nineteenth century. After the late eighteenth century, Protestants, Eastern Orthodox Christians, and Jews were able to operate their own officially recognized primary schools; and their youth could enroll in the state-run *Gymnasien,* technical institutes, and all university faculties except the Catholic theological faculties. Protestants could receive university degrees after 1778, and the government lifted some of the restrictions on Jews, so that after 1782 they could enroll and earn degrees in the faculties of law and medicine.[7] Nonetheless, Catholic religious influence remained strong. Through the 1830s the great majority of Austria's *Gymnasium* teachers were still members of Catholic religious orders, and many in orders continued to teach in the universities.[8]

The social and economic constraints of the traditional corporate society strongly affected the recruitment of youth to secondary and higher education during the first half of the nineteenth century, but the students did not come from as narrow a segment of the prosperous and privileged as might be expected. Tuition costs were low, exemptions from tuition could be easily obtained, and there were some scholarships. Still, most peasant households and families in craft production and petty commerce could not readily sustain the loss of income from sons who studied or bear their living costs if they had to go away to school. The fragmentary knowledge that we have indicates nonetheless that significant portions of the students in the *Gymnasien,* universities, and technical institutes actually came from the intermediate strata of shopkeepers, independent craft producers, schoolteachers, and some peasant farmers—the *Mittelstand* in the terminology of Central Europe's old corporate society. In the *Gymnasien* of Lower Austria's monasteries and smaller cities, for instance, only around 6 percent of the students in 1833–34 and 1840–41 were children of professionals with higher education—physicians, lawyers, judges—with another 35 percent the offspring of officials and employees. In these years the sons of craft producers constituted fully 45 percent and those of peasants 10 percent of Lower Austria's *Gymnasium* students outside Vienna. In Vienna's *Gymnasien,* the children of officials and employees accounted for 54 percent of the students, those of craft producers 31 percent, and those of educated professionals again only 6 percent.[9]

The social origins of *Gymnasium* students in Lower Austria's lesser cities and monasteries differed little, in fact, from the general pattern for Prussian *Gymnasien* in the period between 1815 and 1848. Studies of the Rhineland and Westphalia show that the recruitment of students went well beyond the offspring of the existing educated elites, estate owners, and the urban patriciate and embraced broadly the middle strata of the cities and towns.[10] The Lower Austrian *Gymnasien* in the 1830s, apparently like their Prussian counterparts, served more than merely the educated and propertied elites, although they drew few students from the urban underclasses or from families of peasant farmers and agricultural servants relative to those groups' numbers in the total population.

The available studies of Austrian education before 1848 suggest that while universities and technical institutes functioned more to reproduce the existing educated elites than did the *Gymnasien,* the major institutions of higher education also tended to recruit the majority of their students broadly from the middle strata. In the philosophical faculty of Prague's Charles-Ferdinand University, for instance, the share of the students whose fathers or guardians were educated or semieducated, including governmental and private officials, lawyers, physicians, surgeons, pharmacists, military officers, and teachers, ranged from nearly 30 percent in 1820 to over 39 percent in 1835. Sons of the nobility and estate owners typically studied privately or in academies like the Theresianum in Vienna, and they accounted for no more than 2 to 4 percent of the students in the Prague philosophical faculty. Only around 5 percent were the sons of urban property and factory owners. In contrast, the share from craft and commercial backgrounds fluctuated between 37 and 46 percent of the enrollments in the Prague philosophical faculty, and sons of peasant farmers, small tenants, and agricultural laborers constituted another 8 to 16 percent of the total.[11] The composition of students enrolled in the philosophical faculty may not be representative of those who actually completed diplomas and degrees in all faculties, but since the Austrian philosophical faculties functioned in this period mainly to prepare students for the other university faculties, the recruitment to the Prague philosophical faculty suggests at least who was entering the other faculties in the Bohemian capital.

Students from the urban and rural *Mittelstand* also accounted for a substantial share of the Vienna University's enrollments during the early nineteenth century. Here, as in many parts of Western and Central Europe, the poorest social strata actually commanded a larger share of the small numbers of university students at the beginning of the nineteenth century than among the larger total enrollments at the beginning of the twentieth.[12] Hans Kudlich, the famed advocate of Austrian peasants' rights in the 1848 parliament, later recalled how the Vienna University in the 1840s drew students from nearly all social strata and ethnic groups, including some from the poorest peasant families like his own in Silesia. The poorer students had to struggle to meet living expenses, but, as Kudlich recalled, with stipends and liberal exemptions from fees, "from entry into the *Gymnasium* to my *Rigorosum,* I never had to pay a single *Kreuzer* of tuition."[13]

A study of the Prague Polytechnic Institute shows parallels with the universities in regard to the social origins of students. In 1845–46, 28 percent of the Prague technical students were offspring of public and private officials and 7 percent of learned professionals and educators. The urban *Mittelstand* was represented by the nearly 25 percent of the students who came from craft families and the 12 percent who were sons of various urban business owners and house owners. Ten percent were sons of peasant farmers.[14] Here, too, exemptions from tuition fees aided the poorer elements from the *Mittelstand:* the majority of students in the Prague Polytechnic during the late 1830s and 1840s paid no tuition.[15]

Access to Austrian higher education before the reforms of the 1850s and 1860s differed somewhat from the patterns in the German states. A smaller portion of Austria's total population studied in universities during the early nineteenth century, and even in the mid-fifties the Austrian universities enrolled students at a rate relative to total population that was less than 60 percent that for the German states.[16] During the first half of the century, however, the Austrian universities appear to have recruited students more broadly in socioeconomic terms than did those in Prussia or the German states overall.[17] If the Prague philosophical faculty is representative, only around one-third of the Austrian university students during the 1820s and 1830s were the offspring of the educated; the sons of noble and bourgeois propertied elements, no more than one-tenth; and children of small business owners, independent craft producers, and peasant farmers, fully half or more of the university students. In contrast, sons of educated middle-class officials and professionals apparently accounted for nearly one-half of all the non-noble university students in the German states between 1800 and 1860. Requiring a classical *Gymnasium* education with the *Abitur* for admission to university studies after 1834 only strengthened the tendencies toward self-recruitment among the educated middle classes in Prussia and other German states.[18] The share of the nobility among German university students ranged from 18 percent around 1800 to under 10 percent in the 1860s, while the as yet limited propertied middle class provided no more than 15 percent of the students before 1870. Youth from families in the crafts, petty commerce, and peasant farming were more strongly represented in the German universities than either the offspring of noblemen or the propertied middle class but still accounted for only around 20 percent of all the students around midcentury. These *Mittelstand* elements constituted the second-largest segment in the German universities, surpassed only by the educated middle class. Nonetheless, segments of society privileged by birth, property, or advanced education accounted for more than three-quarters of all German university students in the early and mid-nineteenth century. The children of servants and laborers were virtually excluded, constituting no more than 1 percent of the students.[19]

The Austrian government's conservative educational policies in the early nineteenth century assured that the universities continued to perform their old functions of training civil servants, physicians, Catholic clergy, and secondary school teachers in what were becoming old-fashioned ways compared with the innovations made in many German universities after the late eighteenth century. Austria's traditional economy and corporate social structures were clearly waning, but social and economic development was more rapid in some of the western and northern German states. Even the Austrian state bureaucracy developed only fitfully during the 1820s and 1830s. Strong growth in the numbers of higher state officials between 1801 and 1821 was followed by stagnation between 1821 and 1831 and then more rapid expansion during the 1830s.[20] Until the 1840s, Austria's central government maintained rigid policies for the universities and displayed no interest in developing modern and broadly educated bureaucrats and professionals comparable to those produced by the reformed German universities after the Napoleonic Wars.

The different recruitment of university students in Austria in the 1830s and 1840s reflected the government's more conservative educational and social policies, a more traditional social structure, and the slower evolution of its educated professional and bureaucratic strata than in some of the German states. Compared with Germany, less is understood about the evolution of governmental structures and relations between state and society in Austria during the early nineteenth century.[21] It appears that limits on public employment in Austria, slower economic development, and tendencies toward stagnation in the state bureaucracy and much of advanced education from around 1820 to the 1840s resulted in more limited opportunities for the growth of the educated middle class than in many of the German states. More precise statistics are needed, but compared with the most advanced parts of Germany, it appears that Austria had relatively fewer children of the educated strata and fewer offspring of a new entrepreneurial middle class positioned to use the opportunities for university education that existed. As a result, a larger share of the Austrian university students during the 1830s and 1840s came from peasant households and particularly from the urban *Mittelstand* of craft producers, shopkeepers, and petty employees than in many of the German universities. As will be seen, the offspring of the old urban and rural *Mittelstand* remained a significant presence among Austria's university and technical college students during the late nineteenth century.

Measuring the Representation of the Major Ethnic and Religious Groups

As secondary and higher education expanded after the mid-nineteenth century, nearly all of Austria's ethnic and religious groups eventually won increased opportunities for study. The advances were uneven, though, and the extent to which the various ethnic and religious groups were represented among the enrolled students became a major political issue. Statistics on the representation of the various groups at all levels of education attracted serious public attention.

Measures of each ethnic or religious group's representation must be based on students' declarations of their mother tongue and religious affiliation in school registries and comparisons with the Austrian census statistics on language use and religion for the total population. Government statistics on public education analyzed enrollments in the 1850s by nationality and religion and after the 1860s by mother tongue, religion, and land of birth or citizenship. Generally there is no reliable way to adjust either the school registration statistics or the census totals to separate out those individuals who changed their ethnic identification or their religion. Even where one has individual names in school registries or manuscript census returns, one cannot use names to determine ethnic or religious origin for populations that experienced centuries of migration, intermarriage, and assimilation, often without any accompanying changes of surname.

To change one's religion, however, or to declare oneself formally "without religion" was no simple matter. Anyone doing so had to go through bureaucratic formalities as well as face the possible opprobrium of family or community. Throughout the late nineteenth century, the Austrian government required that individuals register their religious affiliation in a range of public documents. The state relied on baptismal records or other religious documents for proof of birth, required religious instruction for pupils in primary and secondary schools, and obliged members of minorities to pay special taxes to maintain their religious institutions. Anyone wishing to convert or to declare oneself "without religion" had to file documents with several state agencies to resolve tax obligations and the matter of religious instruction in school if children were involved.

Members of religious minorities, particularly Jews, faced some pressures to convert or to declare themselves "without religion" if they aspired to upward economic and social mobility, but the total numbers of Austrian citizens who converted or declared themselves "without religion" each year remained low to the beginning of the twentieth century. The numbers of Austrian Jews who formally gave up their Jewish religious affiliation each year rose slightly between the 1870s and 1900, particularly in Vienna and some of the other larger cities; but overall, few Jews converted. Even in Vienna, where 146,926 Jews resided in 1900, only a total of 9,085 changed their religious affiliation between 1868 and 1903, over half of these becoming Catholic, nearly one-quarter Protestant, and only one-fifth "without religion."[22] In 1910, less than 1.7 percent of the total Austrian population was registered as "without religion." Of the 27,531 matriculated and nonmatriculated university students in Austria in winter 1909–10, less than half of one percent were "without religion," compared with 17.5 percent registered *Israeliten*. Of the 91,546 students in the Austrian men's *Gymnasien* at the end of the 1909–10 school year, 14,518 (16 percent) were Jews, and only 94 fell in the "other" category, which included Moslems, the smallest Christian sects such as the Old Catholics, and those "without religion."[23]

Given the disproportion between the large numbers of registered Jewish students in Austrian secondary and higher education and the very small numbers of Jews who converted or declared themselves "without religion," one can accept the official statistics on Jewish students as a fair overall measure of Jewish representation. The rise of political anti-Semitism in Austria actually worked against conversion in some cases as Jews grew defiant of anti-Semitic agitation or concluded that conversion would bring no real social benefits. The historian Marsha Rozenblit has found that the percentage of all Viennese Jews who renounced Judaism each year who were students actually declined from 19 percent of all such converts in 1890 to only 8 percent in 1910.[24] Analyzing the recruitment of particular professional groups would be a different matter. In some specialized professions Austrian Jews did face strong pressures to convert if they were to enter or advance, and ideally one would like some measure of the Jews or members of other minorities who converted or declared themselves "without religion" for such purposes.

Since language functioned as a crucial indicator of ethnic and national allegiances in Central and East-Central Europe during the late nineteenth century, individual declarations of mother tongue in the Austrian school registries or of "language of everyday use" (*Umgangssprache* in German or *obcovací řeč* in Czech) in the Austrian censuses after 1880 were widely viewed as signs of ethnic identity. With some reservations, one can accept the official statistics on the mother tongue of students and the census data on language of everyday use as reasonably accurate measures for the strength of each ethnic or national group.[25] In using the census statistics on language, one must allow for some underreporting of Czechs and Slovenes in certain ethnically mixed districts where they were subject to economic pressures and bureaucratic chicanery from ethnic Germans. Some Slovenes, Croats, and Serbs in the Adriatic coastal towns faced similar treatment from ethnic Italian employers and officials. In Galicia, Polish officials and landowners were able to sway some Jews and Ukrainians there to report Polish as their everyday language or occasionally managed to adjust the official statistics in favor of Polish.[26]

There was an additional problem regarding the languages reported in school records and censuses, particularly in Galicia and Bukovina, because Austrian law after the 1860s recognized only certain principal ethnic groups or peoples (*Volksstämme*) and distinguished between the principal languages spoken in each crown land (*landesübliche Sprachen*) and strictly local (*ortsübliche*) languages or dialects, which could not be reported in school registries or the census.[27] The Austrian authorities accepted as *landesüblich* the language or particular dialects spoken by the ethnic Ukrainian population in Galicia and Bukovina under the rubric "Ruthenian" (*Ruthenisch*), but they treated strictly as local languages the Yiddish dialects spoken by 90 percent or more of the Jews in those lands. Jews had to report Polish, German, Ruthenian, or, in Bukovina, Romanian in the censuses and school registries.[28]

The ambiguities of ethnic and national loyalties for many Austrian Jews present one of the greatest problems in using official data on students' mother tongue to measure the various ethnic groups' representation in the educational system during the late nineteenth century. Austrian law during the constitutional era recognized Jews as a religious group, not as an ethnic or national group. By the mid-nineteenth century, the great majority of the Jewish population in the Alpine and Bohemian lands gave up speaking Yiddish dialects in favor of their Christian neighbors' languages. Between the 1840s and the 1890s, most Jews in these areas aligned themselves in civic life with the ethnic Germans, Italians, or, in Bohemia after the 1880s increasingly, Czechs. For most Jews in the western provinces, their declarations of everyday language in the census could be taken as a statement of national allegiance in public affairs. Where Jews or others were bilingual or multilingual, though, individuals could easily declare one language as their everyday language in the census while registering their children in school with another mother tongue if it was expedient. Many Bohemian Jews who identified politically with the Czechs around 1900 chose to send their children to German schools, where they registered as German-speaking.[29] Only with the rise of political anti-Semitism after the mid-1880s did Jews in the Alpine and Bohemian lands begin to have serious doubts about national identification with the other peoples, and after 1890 various forms of Jewish nationalism slowly began to win adherents. For the Alpine and Bohemian lands through most of the late nineteenth century then, one can reasonably argue for treating the Jewish population essentially as a religious group, not as a nationality, just as did Austrian law, most of the Jews themselves, and many liberals in the various nationalist political movements.

In general, the census statistics on language use and the data on students' mother tongues from school registries are more doubtful measures for the strength of the various ethnic groups in the Carpathian lands than in the western provinces. Polish provincial officials sometimes manipulated official statistics at the expense of the Ukrainians in eastern Galicia until after 1900, when Ukrainian political groups grew strong enough to protest and resist.[30] Fewer Jews in Galicia and

Bukovina actually identified with the Polish, German, Ukrainian, and Romanian nationalities than reported those languages in the censuses and school registries. Some Jews in the larger cities and towns of Galicia who wanted social mobility did pursue assimilation, first with the ethnic Germans and then increasingly with the Poles after the 1880s. In Chernivtsi, Bukovina, during the last decades of the century, a number of Jewish residents identified with the Austrian Germans, although others did not. The great majority of Jews in Galicia and Bukovina lived in poverty in heavily Jewish communities and did not assimilate with the Christian population or identify with their national groups. Regardless of the Austrian government's definitions of *Volksstämme,* the Jews of the Carpathian lands who lived in mostly Jewish small towns had the culture and social existence of a separate people; and many more of them rallied to Jewish nationalism and Zionism at the turn of the century than among the Jews of the Bohemian lands or Lower Austria.[31]

For Galicia and Bukovina then, using the census statistics on everyday language and data from school registries on students' mother tongue may well present an inflated measure of the strength of the Poles or Germans by including Jews, Ukrainians, or others. In some cases Jewish and Ukrainian students who were registered with a Polish or German mother tongue can be separated out on the basis of their religion. One cannot easily adjust, though, the aggregate census statistics on everyday language to distinguish Jews or other religious minorities, since the published returns rarely included any cross-tabulation of language with religion. Under the circumstances, one has no choice but to use the official statistics on language and religion for the Carpathian lands and all of Austria as best one can, noting where necessary the indeterminacy of the numbers. In such cases, lacking other evidence, one can do no more than report the numbers of people who were *recorded* as speaking one or another language. It may be clumsy to use the formulations "Polish speakers" or "German speakers" rather than discussing simply ethnic Poles and Germans, but social realities and the ambiguities of the sources make it impossible to derive more precise aggregate measures for the various ethnic groups.

The inclusion of foreign students in statistics on Austrian education creates additional problems in measuring the representation of the indigenous ethnic and religious groups. The published official statistics included no cross-tabulations of students' mother tongue and religion with their country of birth or citizenship. Where the enrollment of a particular ethnic or religious group was small, the presence of foreign students could make the representation of the indigenous group appear to be much larger than it actually was. In general, however, the inclusion of foreign students does not present great problems for analyzing the aggregate secondary school enrollments after the early 1880s, since thereafter usually close to 98 percent of all students were Austrian citizens. Typically, though, a larger share of the university and technical college students were citizens of Hungary and foreign countries. In winter 1879–80, for instance, more than one-sixth of all matriculated and nonmatriculated students in the Austrian universities and close to that share in the technical colleges were citizens of Hungary or foreign countries. The percentage of foreigners among students in Austrian higher education dropped considerably after the 1890s, particularly as the Hungarian government invoked policies against accepting foreign diplomas and the numbers of Hungarian students declined in the Austrian institutions. Nonetheless, in winter 1909–10, individuals who were not citizens of Austria still accounted for 10.0 percent of all university enrollments and 11.2 percent of all technical college students.[32] The numbers of Romanians, Serbs, Protestants, or Eastern Orthodox Christians in general who were enrolled in Austrian higher education included significant numbers of foreigners. In some circumstances one can estimate the share of foreign students in the aggregate totals for the smaller ethnic and religious groups, but in many cases one cannot.

In measuring the representation of the various ethnic, religious, or socioeconomic groupings in the educational system, it is preferable to compare their enrollments with their respective shares of the school-aged population.[33] Such an analysis, however, cannot be readily presented for Austria during the late nineteenth century, since the government produced statistics on the age stratification of the male and female populations in each crown land but *not* for the various linguistic, national, religious, or occupational groupings. On the few occasions when statisticians analyzed the age stratification for such groups, they published figures only for particular cities or provinces, typically in five- or ten-year age cohorts. Rather than try to approximate age stratifications for the ethnic, religious, and occupational or class groupings, this discussion will simply analyze the enrollments in secondary and higher education compared with each group's share of the total population.

If the differences in the representation of various groups in the educational system relative to total populations prove to be large enough, they will outweigh most conceivable differences in the groups' birthrates and age stratification.

The Major Ethnic and Religious Groups in Secondary Education

Overall, the enrollments in Austrian secondary education between the late 1850s and 1914 showed a pattern of continuing but steadily declining overrepresentation of the German-speaking population. The German-speaking population obviously benefited in advanced education from the long predominance of German-language instruction and German speakers' historic leadership role in Austrian government and society. Beginning with the Czechs and Poles in the 1850s and 1860s, however, some of the non-German groups made rapid gains, either by attending German-language institutions or, after 1860, by enrolling in the growing numbers of schools that taught in Czech or Polish. With regard to religion, the representation of Catholics in the secondary schools was noticeably less than their 90 percent share of the total population from the late 1850s onward. The Jewish and Protestant minorities achieved significant overrepresentation relative to their populations.

Austria's German-speaking population had higher secondary school enrollments per capita than any other major ethnic or national group until after 1900 (see table 4/1).[34] During the 1850s Austria's Christian German inhabitants accounted for only 36 percent of the total population, but 47 percent of all students in academic secondary schools in 1856–57 were German by nationality, not counting the German-speaking Jews. The enrollment statistics from 1869–70, which reported the students' mother tongue rather than nationality, make the representation of the German population appear even stronger, although then and thereafter the German totals in the Alpine and Bohemian lands included significant numbers of Jewish students. Between the late 1850s and the late 1870s, Czech enrollments made noticeable gains. The enrollments of Polish speakers also increased significantly in the 1860s and 1870s.[35] Not surprisingly, the German speakers' share of the secondary school enrollments declined most rapidly during the great growth period of Austrian secondary education after the 1890s, when nearly all of the Slavic groups made relative and absolute gains.

TABLE 4/1
Mother Tongue of All Students in Austrian Academic Secondary Schools, 1880–1910*

Secondary Enrollments Analyzed per Thousand Inhabitants for Each Language, 1880–1910*

End of Acad. Yr.	Total	German	Czech	Polish	Ukra.	Slove.	Serb./Cro.	Ital.	Rom.	Magy.
1879–80	3.03	3.88	3.65	2.74	0.68	1.25	1.16	3.29	1.81	38.9
1889–90	3.04	4.04	3.37	2.78	0.71	1.65	1.20	3.88	1.78	30.2
1899–1900	3.74	4.61	4.24	3.77	1.06	2.45	2.01	4.48	2.93	23.0
1909–10	5.03	5.88	5.01	6.05	2.29	3.05	2.26	6.01	4.03	22.8

Sources: *Statistisches Jahrbuch für das Jahr 1879; Öster. Statistik* 28, no. 4 (1892); 68, no. 3 (1903); n.s., 7, no. 3 (1913); and Urbanitsch 1980, 3, pt. 1: 38, table 1.

* *The enrollment totals include all students, matriculated and "private."*

In 1909–10, the number of German-speaking students in Austrian secondary schools relative to their total population still significantly exceeded the rate of enrollment for Czechs and was nearly double the rate for Slovenes and more than double that for Ukrainians. The huge growth in Polish-language secondary education in Galicia after the 1890s resulted, though, in Polish speakers having an even higher overall rate of enrollment in *Gymnasien, Realgymnasien,* and *Realschulen* in 1909–10 than did Austria's German speakers (see table 4/1). The German speakers' share of all *Gymnasium* students in 1909–10 was barely larger than the 35.6 percent of the Austrian population that reported German as its language of everyday use in the 1910 census.

Throughout the period from the 1860s to World War I, the German-speaking population was represented even more strongly in the *Realschulen* compared with the Slavic groups than in all types of *Gymnasien.* Like all major ethnic groups, the German-speaking inhabitants generally still ascribed higher prestige to a *Gymnasium* than to a *Realschule* education. Compared with most of the Slavic groups, though, the German-speaking population generated greater demand for *Realschule* schooling during this period. The appetite for *Realschule* education seems to have depended largely on the level of industrial and commercial development experienced by a particular population. *Realschulen* developed most rapidly and remained most highly concentrated in the larger cities; among the various crown lands they were most numerous in the Alpine and Bohemian provinces, where economic development and urbanization were most rapid and the German-speaking population lived in greatest numbers. The Czechs also experienced much more rapid industrial and commercial development than did the Poles, Ukrainians, or South Slavic groups; and like the German-speaking population, the Czechs generated a strong demand for *Realschule* study. Indeed, the Czech appetite for *Realschule* education became so great after 1900 that Czech-speaking students enrolled in roughly equal numbers in *Gymnasien* and *Realschulen*.[36]

Austria's small Italian minority was the only other significant ethnic group besides the German speakers whose representation in secondary education noticeably exceeded its share of the total population during much of the late nineteenth century.[37] The Italian speakers who remained under Habsburg rule after the unification of Italy accounted for only between 2.6 and 2.8 percent of the Austrian population, but they included significant numbers of entrepreneurs, professionals, small business owners, and white-collar employees, particularly in the Adriatic coastal towns. Except for a few courses in Innsbruck, however, Austria provided no Italian-language university education after the 1860s. Nonetheless, the Italian minority had public secondary schools with Italian instruction in southern Tirol, the maritime lands, and Dalmatia; and Italian speakers typically accounted for between 3.7 and 3.3 percent of all secondary school students in Austria (see table 3 in the appendix).[38] Ethnic Italians had strong representation in secondary education, even allowing for the presence of Slovenes, Serbs, and Croats among the students reported with Italian mother tongue on the Adriatic coast. In 1910 the Italian speakers' enrollment relative to their population, like that of Polish speakers, slightly exceeded even the rate for German speakers in Austria (see table 4/1).

The various Slavic groups increased their enrollments in secondary education during the late nineteenth century at markedly differing speeds. Czechs benefited from the relatively dense network of schools in the Bohemian lands, and Czech demand for advanced education was already strong in the 1840s and 1850s, when there was still little Czech-language instruction. In 1857 the Czech speakers' share of all secondary enrollments in Austria already approached their 23 percent of the total population. Except for the depression years of the 1880s, Czech-speaking enrollments in secondary schools increased steadily during the late nineteenth century as Czech-language instruction grew. In 1909–10, the Czechs' representation among all Austrian secondary students, measured by mother tongue, almost exactly equaled their share of the population; and they ranked just behind the Polish, Italian, and German speakers in enrollments relative to total population (see table 4/1 above and table 3 in the appendix).

Next to the Czechs, the secondary school enrollments of Polish speakers grew most rapidly during the 1850s and 1860s, reaching 15 percent of the Austrian total in 1869–70. It is difficult to determine exactly how many youth of Ukrainian origin may have been among the students registered with Polish mother tongue, but the Polish enrollments were apparently not greatly inflated by the inclusion of Ukrainians. Youth of Ukrainian origin who were Latin-rite Catholics might easily be included among the totals for Polish speakers, but more than 98 percent of the Ukrainian population in Galicia were Uniate Catholics, or "Greek Catholics" in Austrian official parlance. Only 6 percent of the Polish speakers in Galicia in 1910, for instance, were Uniates.[39] Since Uniate Catholics were entitled to their own religious instruction, the school authorities were under some constraint to report Ukrainian enrollments fairly honestly so that there would be no great discrepancy between the statistics for religion and those for mother tongue. In 1870, for instance, 1,687 secondary school students in Galicia were recorded with Ukrainian mother tongue, compared with 1,708 Uniate Catholics. The 1870 total of 6,149 Polish-speaking secondary school students in Galicia already included, however, at least several hundred Jews. At the end of that school year, 734 Jewish students were registered in the Galician secondary schools. Only a total of 478 secondary school students in Galicia in 1870, however, were recorded with German mother tongue, and this figure included Catholics and Protestants as well as Jews.[40]

With the great enrollment boom after the mid-1890s, the representation of Polish speakers in Austrian secondary education quickly grew to exceed their share of the total population (see table 4/1 and table 3 in the appendix). In 1910, though, Jews accounted for more than one-quarter of the 28,804 Polish-speaking students in Galician secondary schools.[41] If one subtracted *all* the Jewish students in Galicia from the total registered with Polish mother tongue, the Polish share of all Austrian secondary school students in 1910 would still slightly exceed the 14.9 percent of the Austrian population that was recorded in the 1910 census as using Polish for its everyday language and as not Jewish.[42] As late as 1910, only 12 percent of all the Polish-speaking secondary school students in Austria were enrolled in *Realschulen,* compared with 40 percent of all German-speaking secondary students. This reflected the slow development of modern economic and social structures in Galicia and the persisting preferences of Polish-speaking youth for *Gymnasium* studies.

Austria's smaller, poorer, and more traditional ethnic groups were much slower than the Czechs and Poles to increase their representation in secondary education. Between 1880 and 1910, Ukrainian speakers' rate of enrollment in academic secondary schools more than tripled relative to their total population; but even in 1910, students who reported their mother tongue as Ukrainian still accounted for less than 6 percent of all Austrian *Gymnasium* and *Realschule* students, less than half their share of the total population (see table 3 in the appendix). This does not include, of course, youth of Ukrainian origin who were Latin-rite Catholics and reported Polish as their mother tongue in school registries. Poles kept a strong grip on government offices and estate ownership throughout Galicia, where more than nine-tenths of Austria's Ukrainian population resided; and Polish Catholics and Jews dominated the professions there during the late nineteenth century. In general, Ukrainians who aspired to professional careers in Galicia outside the clergy and primary school teaching felt pressure to assimilate with the Poles.[43]

The Ukrainian population in Bukovina also made advances in secondary education at the turn of the century, but Romanians there did even better. In 1910 Austria's Romanian minority numbered only 275,115 altogether. Nonetheless, between 1880 and 1910 Romanian enrollments in academic secondary schools, including foreign students, relative to Austria's total Romanian population were generally twice as high as the Ukrainians' rate of enrollment (see table 4/1).[44]

Slovene enrollments in Austrian secondary schools grew fairly steadily from the 1860s to World War I, but the portion of all students who registered with Slovene as their mother tongue never exceeded a little more than half the Slovene share of the total population. One can only guess at how many students of Slovene origin reported German or Italian as their mother tongue. By the turn of the century, the social and economic position of Slovenes had advanced significantly in Carniola and its capital city, Ljubljana (Laibach); but elsewhere in

Styria, Carinthia, and the maritime lands, Slovenes remained disadvantaged and under pressure to assimilate with Germans or Italians if they desired social advancement.[45] Of the other South Slavic groups in Austria, the small Serbian and Croatian minorities, who had less than 3 percent of the total population together, also had weak representation in the secondary schools with no more than 1 to 1.5 percent of the total enrollments at any time during the late nineteenth century.

Austria repealed its last discriminatory laws against religious minorities during the 1848 revolution and as part of the economic and constitutional reforms enacted between 1859 and 1867. Legal emancipation and the general growth of educational opportunities after the 1850s allowed Jews and Protestants to increase substantially their representation among secondary school students. By the end of the 1860s, the Jews' 10 percent share of total enrollments in Austria's *Gymnasien* and *Realschulen* was twice as large as their portion of the total population.[46] After around 1880 the Jewish presence in secondary schools was roughly three times the Jewish share of the total population (see table 4/2 and table 4 in the appendix). At the end of the nineteenth century only a little more than 2 percent of all Austrian inhabitants were Protestants, but from around 1890 Protestants accounted for 3 percent or more of all secondary school students. In 1909–10 then, Austrian Jews were enrolling in academic secondary schools at more than three times the rate of the Catholic majority, relative to total population, while Protestants attended at nearly twice the rate of Catholics (see table 4/2). No statistics are available on the age stratification of the various religious groups, but if one assumes a lower birthrate and slightly older population for the, on average, more urbanized Austrian Jews and Protestants than for Catholics, then the overrepresentation of these religious minorities was even greater than what is suggested by their enrollments relative to their total populations.

In contrast, the Eastern Orthodox and Uniate Catholic minorities were significantly underrepresented in the *Gymnasien* and *Realschulen* throughout the late nineteenth century. This was true even with the counting of students who were citizens of Romania, Hungary, and Bosnia-Herzegovina, which was governed separately from both the Austrian and Hungarian halves of the monarchy. Most of Austria's Eastern Orthodox and Uniate Catholic citizens were concentrated in regions that remained the poorest and relatively least developed of the Austrian lands: eastern Galicia, Bukovina, and Dalmatia. Over 80

TABLE 4/2
Religion of All Students in Austrian Academic Secondary Schools, 1870–1910*

End of Acad. Year	Total Enroll.	Per thous.	All Cath.	E. Orth.	All Prot.	Jewish
			Total Secondary Enrollments per 1,000 Inhabitants of Each Religion, 1869/70–1909/10			
1869–70	43,734	2.14	3.0	1.09	2.81	5.32
1879–80	65,935	3.03	2.66	1.28	4.39	9.59
1889–90	71,295	3.04	2.68	1.14	5.11	8.89
1899–1900	95,914	3.67	3.33	1.81	5.57	10.41
1909–10	140,545	4.92	4.34	3.08	8.26	15.72

Sources: *Statistisches Jahrbuch für das Jahr 1869; Statistisches Jahrbuch für das Jahr 1879; Öster. Statistik* 28, no. 4 (1892); 32, no. 1 (1892); 63, no. 1 (1902); 68, no. 3 (1903); n.s., 7, no. 3 (1913); and Urbanitsch 1980, 3, pt. 1: 54, table 5.

* *The enrollment totals include all students, matriculated and "private."*

percent of the Eastern Orthodox Christians were Ukrainians and Romanians in Bukovina and eastern Galicia with the remainder mostly Serbs in Dalmatia, Istria, and Trieste. The Eastern Orthodox share of the total secondary enrollments rose to 1.5 percent in 1909–10, still less than their 2.3 percent of the total population. Attendance in the Austrian secondary schools by Uniate Catholics, who were overwhelmingly Ukrainian, increased only slightly, reaching 5.5 percent in 1909–10, less than half the Uniate Catholics' 12 percent share of the total population.[47] If the Uniate Catholics and Eastern Orthodox Christians in the less developed regions tended to have higher birthrates and younger populations than the average for Latin-rite Catholics throughout Austria, then their rate of enrollment in secondary education relative to school-aged population was even lower compared with all Catholics or compared with the Jews and Protestants than the rates relative to total population would suggest.[48]

The growth of Jewish enrollments in both secondary and higher education after the 1850s and 1860s was so strong that it attracted much contemporary notice and antagonism.[49] Wherever Jews resided in significant numbers, their attendance in Austrian *Gymnasien, Realschulen,* universities, and technical colleges expanded rapidly between the 1860s and 1880s and continued to increase thereafter. In the Bohemian lands, for instance, Jews accounted for only 1.8 percent of the population in 1880 but 13 percent of the academic secondary students at the end of the 1881–82 school year. By 1910 the Jewish population in Bohemia, Moravia, and Silesia had declined to 1.4 percent of the total, but Jews still provided 9.4 percent of the secondary school students.[50] The growth in Jewish attendance of the Galician secondary schools around the turn of the century outpaced the strong increases in Polish Catholic enrollments, so that the Jewish share of the total reached 24 percent in 1909–10, more than twice the Jewish share of the Galician population.[51] In the city of Vienna (districts I–X) in 1875, Jews accounted for nearly 10 percent of the population but fully 30 percent of all *Gymnasium* and *Real-Gymnasium* enrollments. Jewish students retained approximately the same share of the secondary school enrollments in the expanded city limits up to World War I.[52]

Preferences for the different types of secondary schools varied among the major religious groups. In 1879–80 a little more than one-quarter of all Jewish secondary students in Austria attended *Realschulen,* a fraction equal to that among all Austrian Catholic students. By 1909–10, the share of all Catholic secondary school students who were enrolled in *Realschulen* had risen to more than one-third, while still only one-quarter of all Jewish secondary students attended *Realschulen.* The low share of Jewish secondary students enrolled in *Realschulen* derived primarily from the slow development of *Realschulen* and advanced technical education in the Carpathian lands, where nearly three-quarters of Austria's Jewish population still resided in 1910. Eastern Orthodox enrollments in Austrian *Realschulen* were minimal throughout the late nineteenth century, but the Protestant minority displayed a strong interest in scientific and technical education. Thirty-five percent of all Protestant secondary school students in Austria in 1879 were enrolled in *Realschulen,* and 43 percent in 1909–10.[53] As will be seen later, this accorded with strong enrollments of Austrian Protestants in the technical colleges.

The Recruitment of University and Technical College Students

As might be expected, many of the trends in the representation of Austria's various ethnic and religious groups in secondary education were repeated in the universities and technical colleges despite the attrition of students along the way (see tables 4/3 and 4/4 and tables 5 and 6 in the appendix). The economic and social impediments to access were greater for higher education, of course, than for secondary schooling. Average total costs for a year of study in a university or technical college greatly exceeded those for a year in a secondary school. With universities and technical colleges located in only eight Austrian cities after 1874, a much larger share of the students at this level than in secondary education had to leave home and go to live in a strange, perhaps distant city. Besides economic and geographic con-

TABLE 4/3
Religion and Mother Tongue of Austrian University Students, 1870–1910

Religion and Mother Tongue of Matriculated and Nonmatriculated University Students per 1,000 Inhabitants of the Same Religion or Language

RELIGION

Winter Sem.	Tot. stud./ 1000 pop.	Cath.	Jew.	Prot.	E. Orth.
1869–70*	0.44	0.38	1.38	0.92	0.36
1879–80	0.43	0.37	1.44	0.81	0.53
1889–90	0.64	0.50	2.66	1.37	0.91
1899–1900	0.67	0.56	2.34	1.15	0.81
1909–10	0.98	0.80	3.67	1.58	1.27

MOTHER TONGUE

Winter Sem.	Tot. stud./ 1000 pop.	Ger.	Cze.	Pol.	Ukra.	Slove.	Serb./Cro.	Magy.	Ital.
1869–70*	0.44								
1879–80	0.43	0.57	0.30	0.49	0.17	0.17	0.47	41.1	0.48
1889–90	0.64	0.81	0.59	0.62	0.18	0.13	0.71	58.1	0.67
1899–1900	0.67	0.87	0.59	0.70	0.20	0.32	0.86	14.2	0.72
1909–10	0.98	1.12	0.70	1.35	0.42	0.43	1.07	15.2	0.85

Sources: *Statistisches Jahrbuch für das Jahr 1869; Statistisches Jahrbuch für das Jahr 1879; Öster. Statistik* 28, no. 4 (1892); 32, no. 1 (1892); 63, no. 1 (1902); 68, no. 3 (1903); n.s., 7, no. 3 (1913); and Urbanitsch 1980, 3, pt. 1: 38, (table 1), 54 (table 5).

* *The 1869 Austrian census did not include any question on language. Statistics on everyday language were included in the 1880 census returns and in censuses thereafter.*

siderations, the language of instruction remained a barrier in higher education for many youth long after secondary education became available in nearly all the major languages. On the eve of World War I, nine of the fifteen Austrian universities and technical colleges still taught principally in German. The German-speaking population of the Alpine and Bohemian lands was as strongly overrepresented among university and technical college students relative to its total numbers as it was among the secondary school students. Here too, though, the German speakers' overrepresentation gradually declined from the 1860s to World War I.

TABLE 4/4
Religion and Mother Tongue of Austrian Technical College Students, 1870–1910

Religion and Mother Tongue of Matriculated and Nonmatriculated Technical College Students per 1,000 Inhabitants of the Same Religion or Language

RELIGION

Winter Sem.	Tot. stud./ 1000 pop.	Cath.	Jew.	Prot.	E. Orth.
1869–70*	0.11	0.10	0.27	0.25	0.06
1879–80	0.15	0.12	0.54	0.37	0.11
1889–90	0.08	0.06	0.25	0.24	0.09
1899–1900	0.21	0.17	0.78	0.65	0.09
1909–10	0.39	0.32	1.17	0.93	0.28

MOTHER TONGUE

Winter Sem.	Tot. stud./ 1000 pop.	Ger.	Cze.	Pol.	Ukra.	Slove.	Serb./Cro.	Magy.	Ital.
1869–70*	0.11								
1879–80	0.15	0.20	0.18	0.11	0.004	0.03	0.12	16.4	0.09
1889–90	0.08	0.11	0.08	0.06	0.004	0.02	0.06	5.9	0.06
1899–1900	0.21	0.29	0.24	0.19	0.013	0.02	0.15	5.0	0.14
1909–10	0.39	0.47	0.52	0.36	0.023	0.08	0.30	1.6	0.26

Sources: *Statistisches Jahrbuch für das Jahr 1869; Statistisches Jahrbuch für das Jahr 1879; Öster. Statistik* 28, no. 4 (1892), 32, no. 1 (1892); 63, no. 1 (1902); 68, no. 3 (1903); n.s., 7, no. 3 (1913); and Urbanitsch 1980, 3, pt. 1: 38 (table 1), 54 (table 5).

* *The 1869 Austrian census did not include any question on language. Statistics on everyday language were included in the 1880 census returns and in censuses thereafter.*

Between the late 1860s and 1900, matriculated and nonmatriculated students registered with German mother tongue made up approximately 45 to 50 percent of the total in the Austrian universities and between 42 and 53 percent of all technical college students. Those percentages easily exceeded the German speakers' 35 to 37 percent of the Austrian population (see tables 5 and 6 in the appendix).[54] In higher education, though, the presence of foreign students must be kept in mind. As late as the early 1880s, around one-tenth of the students in the Austrian universities and technical colleges came from Hungary and Croatia, and these included a significant number who registered as German speaking. After the 1890s, however, the numbers of students from Hungary and Croatia declined substantially. With no more than 1 or 2 percent of the students in Austrian higher education at any time coming from Germany and Switzerland, those particular foreign students did not inflate the totals of German-speaking students in the Austrian universities and technical colleges.[55] The presence of foreign-born students did more to inflate the apparent representation in higher education of some of Austria's smaller ethnic and religious groups.

While it is necessary to distinguish foreign students from the indigenous in order to measure accurately the representation of Austria's various ethnic and religious groups, one should not simply dismiss the foreign students as having no importance to the formation of Austria's educated elites.[56] Many of the foreign students, of course, expected only to study in Austria and then to return to their native lands or perhaps move on elsewhere. Still, even the foreign students who subsequently left Austria contributed to the intellectual and social environment in the universities and technical colleges to which Austrian students were exposed. Others among the foreign-born students, including many of the Jews and some of the Catholics and Orthodox Christians who came from Hungary, the Russian Empire, and the Balkan countries, remained after their studies to become part of Austrian society. Some had immigrated earlier to Austria, while others first came as students and then settled there permanently.

Among Austria's various Slavic groups, the Czechs' university enrollments approached parity with their share of the total population by the late 1880s. Czech speakers' enrollments in technical colleges already exceeded their share of the population by a considerable margin in the late 1870s. Still, as late as the winter semester 1909–10, the representation of German speakers in the universities relative to their total population was 60 percent higher than the Czech speakers' rate (see table 4/3). In the technical colleges during that same semester, the Czech rate of enrollment relative to their total population exceeded the German speakers' rate by around 10 percent (see table 4/4).[57] The numbers of students who were registered in Austrian universities and technical colleges with Czech mother tongue always included some Slovaks from the Kingdom of Hungary, but the Slovak numbers were generally so small that one can accept the official statistics as fair measures of the Czechs' growing representation. In winter 1889–90, for instance, the Czech University in Prague had a total of 2,528 matriculated and nonmatriculated students, of whom 2,514 were recorded with Czech mother tongue. Only 18 out of the total student body were citizens of Hungary. A sample of the registration records for 652 matriculated students in the Vienna University in winter 1879–80 included 43 non-Jewish students who reported Czech as their mother tongue. All 43 were born in Bohemia, Moravia, or Silesia.[58]

As in secondary education, after 1900 the enrollment of Polish-speaking students in the Austrian universities grew to exceed the Polish speakers' share of the total population, although the many Jews in the universities of Krakow and L'viv and the smaller numbers of students from the Russian Empire and Germany worked to inflate the totals of Polish-speaking students.[59] The Polish speakers' rate of enrollment in Austrian universities (including Jews and foreign students) relative to the Polish-speaking population approached that for German speakers in 1900 and actually exceeded the German speakers' rate in winter 1909–10 (see table 4/3). The 6,716 students with Polish mother tongue who were registered in Austrian universities that semester, however, included in Krakow and L'viv more than 1,100 Jews, around 800 students who were citizens of Russia (all religions), and around 50 from Germany.[60] Moreover, some of the Polish-speaking university students were surely of Ukrainian origin. If one subtracts from the total of Polish-speaking university students all the Polish-speaking Jewish students and all students from Russia and Germany who were registered in Krakow and L'viv and adjusts the total of Polish speakers in the Austrian population to exclude Jews, then Poles attended Austrian universities in winter 1909–10 at a rate of 1.15 students per thousand in the indigenous Polish population, allowing still for the inclusion of some Ukrainians in the Polish totals. This adjusted rate still marginally exceeds that for Austria's German-speaking population in 1909–10.

Throughout the late nineteenth century the Polish-speaking population generated much less demand for higher technical education than did the German and Czech speakers. As late as winter 1909–10, the enrollment in the Austrian technical colleges of Polish speakers, including Jews and foreign students, relative to the total Polish-speaking population was 23 percent less than the German speakers' rate and 30 percent less than the Czechs' (see table 4/4). The slow economic development and limited industrialization of Galicia surely influenced the low interest of Polish-speaking students in technical education. In winter 1909–10, Ukrainians, Slovenes, Romanians, Serbs, and Croats had even lower rates of enrollment in Austrian technical colleges than did the Polish speakers.

Relative to population, the overall enrollments of Ukrainians, Slovenes, Romanians, Serbs, and Croats in Austrian higher education tended to improve at the end of the nineteenth century but still lagged far behind the rates for the German-, Czech-, and Polish-speaking populations (see tables 4/3 and 4/4). Austria's small Romanian minority was, in fact, overrepresented in the universities after the 1880s compared with its share of the Austrian population. This was due primarily to strong Romanian enrollments in the University of Chernivtsi. On paper, the rate of enrollment in Austrian higher education by Serbs and Croats relative to their population approached more closely the levels of the Czechs and Poles than did the rates for the Ukrainians and Slovenes. Austria's indigenous Serbian and Croatian populations were so small, though, that the presence of even small numbers of students from Croatia, Serbia, and Bosnia-Herzegovina could significantly affect the apparent representation of those groups. Probably a majority of the students in Austrian higher education at the turn of the century who reported Serbian or Croatian as their mother tongue were citizens of other countries.[61]

Trends in the religious composition of the Austrian university and technical college students generally paralleled patterns in the secondary schools, allowing for the presence of relatively larger numbers of foreigners in higher education. At all times, Latin-rite and Uniate Catholics accounted for at least 70 percent of the university and technical college students, but this was much less than their 91 percent of the total population. After the middle decades of the century, Jewish enrollments grew even more rapidly in higher education, particularly in the universities, than in the secondary schools (see tables 4/3 and 4/4 above and tables 5 and 6 in the appendix). In winter 1869–70, for instance, the Jewish share of all matriculated and nonmatriculated university students was three times the Jewish fraction of the total population, and the share of the technical college students was more than twice the Jewish fraction of the total population.[62] This meant that relative to their total population, Jews were enrolling in the Austrian universities at more than three and one-half times the rate of Catholics and one and one-half times the rate of Protestants. During the succeeding four decades, the numbers of Jewish university and technical college students relative to the Jewish population tended to grow faster than the rates for the Catholic and Protestant populations. In winter 1909–10, for instance, the Jewish representation relative to population among Austrian university students, including foreign students, was more than four and one-half times as great as that for all Catholics in Austria and two and one-third times that for all Protestants. In the technical colleges in winter 1909–10, the Jewish enrollment per capita stood at more than three and one-half times the rate for Austrian Catholics and one and one-quarter times the rate for the Protestant minority (see tables 4/3 and 4/4). Overall between the late 1870s and 1910, Jewish students accounted for between 15 and 20 percent of all Austrian university enrollments and between 14 and 20 percent of all technical college students. This generally exceeded the Jews' 13 to 15 percent share of all academic secondary enrollments during the same period (see table 4 in the appendix).

Foreign students contributed significantly to the Jewish enrollments in Austrian higher education until the 1890s, but the foreign segment declined thereafter. This can be seen clearly in the Vienna University. Through most of the late nineteenth century, the Vienna University had more than half of all the Jewish students enrolled in Austrian universities at any one time, and the concentration in Vienna continued despite the growth of the institutions in Krakow, L'viv, and Chernivtsi. The Vienna Technical College drew a similarly large share of all Jewish technical college students. In both the institutions in Vienna, the percentage of the Jewish students who were born outside Austria declined at the end of the century even while Jewish enrollments were increasing relative to Austria's total Jewish population. In winter 1879–80, a little more than one-third of the matriculated Jewish students in the Vienna University and Vienna Technical College were born in Hungary or foreign lands; but owing mainly to the decline in students from the Hungarian crown lands, only 14 percent of the matriculated Jews in each institution in winter 1899–1900 were born outside of Austria.[63] In universities and technical colleges outside the imperial capital, by far the largest concentrations of Jewish students were in Prague, L'viv, Krakow, and Chernivtsi. Taken together, the institutions in these other cities, however, drew much smaller fractions of their student bodies from outside Austria than did the institutions in Vienna.

Even if one excludes foreign-born students, the enrollment of Austrian Jews in higher education relative to the population at the turn of the century still exceeded that for any other major religious denomination. One can make a conservative estimate for the overall representation of the indigenous Jewish population by reducing the totals for Jewish students in all higher education by the percentage of foreign-born among the Jewish students in Vienna.[64] That would yield an adjusted rate of Jewish enrollment in the Austrian universities in 1900 of 2.01 per thousand in the total Jewish population and in the technical colleges of 0.62 per thousand, nearly four times the rates for all Catholics in the Austrian universities and technical colleges in 1900.[65]

While Jews were significantly overrepresented among Austrian university students relative to their share of the total population during the late nineteenth century, Jews, in fact, were even more strongly overrepresented among Prussian university students. Jews accounted for 10 percent of all Prussian university students in 1886–87, compared with only 1.3 percent of the Prussian population. In 1911–12, 5.6 percent of Prussia's university students were Jewish. Relative to total Jewish population, Jews were enrolled in the Prussian universities in 1886–87 at a rate of 6.12 students per thousand, and 6.62 students per thousand in 1911–12.[66] In comparison, Austria had only 2.66 Jewish university students per thousand in the population in 1889–90 and 3.67 students per thousand in 1909–10 (see table 4/3). Still, with Jews accounting for a larger percentage of the Austrian population than in Prussia, they were a larger presence in the Austrian universities. In winter 1909–10, Jews accounted for one-seventh of all matriculated and nonmatriculated university students in Austria. Whatever the precise degree of Jewish overrepresentation in German and Austrian higher education, the high visibility of Jewish students in the universities and technical colleges of both countries drew loud complaints after the 1880s from anti-Semitic politicians.

The sizable foreign contingents among the Protestant and Eastern Orthodox students in Austrian higher education make it difficult to measure the representation of the indigenous Protestant and Eastern Orthodox populations. It appears, though, that Austrian Protestants enrolled in higher education around 1900 at significantly higher rates relative to their population than did the Catholic majority. For most of the period between the 1860s and World War I, 60 to 80 percent of all Protestant university students in Austria studied in Vienna, and until after 1900 the Vienna Technical College tended to draw the majority of all Protestants enrolled in Austrian technical colleges. Samples of the registration records for winter 1879–80 indicate, however, that only one-third of the matriculated Protestant students in the Vienna University and a little more than two-fifths of those in the Vienna Technical College were native to Austria, with the great majority of the non-native Protestants coming from Hungary and Transylvania. Thereafter, the share of Austrian natives increased among the Protestants enrolled in Austrian higher education as the numbers from the Hungarian crown lands diminished. In winter 1899–1900, for instance, students who were native to Austria accounted for just over four-fifths of the matriculated Protestants in the Vienna University and an equal share of those in the Vienna Technical College. One can make a conservative estimate for the representation of Austria's indigenous Protestants in higher education by reducing the total numbers of Protestant students by the percentage of foreign-born found in the Vienna institutions. That yields adjusted rates of 0.92 native Protestant university students per thousand in the Protestant population and 0.53 Protestant technical college students per thousand in the population for winter 1899–1900, which still exceed significantly the unadjusted rates for Catholics (see tables 4/3 and 4/4).

Despite Eastern Orthodox Christians' increasing attendance of Austrian secondary schools during the late nineteenth century, the representation of the native Eastern Orthodox population in universities and technical colleges advanced only slowly, if at all. Including foreign students, the total numbers of Eastern Orthodox students in Austrian higher education relative to the Orthodox population appear to have increased nearly two and one-half times between 1880 and 1910 (see tables 4/3 and 4/4). In fact, though, for most of the period the majority of the Eastern Orthodox students appear to have come from the Hungarian crown lands and other parts of East-Central Europe beyond the Austrian borders.

Around 1900 the universities of Vienna and Chernivtsi, which had an Eastern Orthodox theological faculty, accounted for three-quarters or more of all the Eastern Orthodox students enrolled in Austrian universities. As late as winter 1909–10, though, apparently less than 5 percent of the matriculated Eastern Orthodox students in the Vienna University were native to Austria, with the largest foreign-born contingents coming from Serbia, Bosnia, Russia, and the Hungarian crown lands.[67] The number of Chernivtsi's Eastern Orthodox students lagged far behind the total for Vienna until after 1900 despite the proximity of Ukrainian and Romanian Orthodox populations in Bukovina and eastern Galicia. By winter 1909–10, however, the University of Chernivtsi had 348 matriculated and nonmatriculated Eastern Orthodox students, only two less than in the Vienna University that semester. More than 80 percent of Chernivtsi's Eastern Orthodox students in winter 1909–10 were native to Austrian territories.[68] Nonetheless, this enrollment was still small compared with the tens of thousands of Eastern Orthodox young people in the surrounding territory.

Among the Austrian technical colleges, the Vienna Technical College and the Czech Technical College in Prague typically had the largest contingents of Eastern Orthodox students. In winter 1909–10 those two institutions accounted for more than three-quarters of all the matriculated and nonmatriculated Eastern Orthodox Christians in Austrian technical colleges. The great majority of these students apparently came from outside Austria. Indeed, during the last years before World War I, the Czech Technical College in Prague became something of a mecca among the Austrian technical colleges for students from Croatia-Slavonia, Bosnia, Serbia, and the Russian Empire.

The enrollment trends indicate that during the second half of the nineteenth century, representation in Austrian higher education increased significantly for nearly all the non-German ethnic and national groups and for the Jewish and Protestant religious minorities. While the overall demand for higher education increased among all these groups, the interest in particular sectors of higher education varied considerably among them. Throughout the period from the

1860s to the eve of World War I, German-speaking students showed a strong preference for university studies over the technical colleges, although their enrollments in technical colleges rose relatively and absolutely after 1890. In winter 1869–70 the German speakers had a ratio of 4.2 university students, matriculated and nonmatriculated, to each technical college student. Because of the depressed economic conditions of the 1880s, that ratio stood at 7.3 to 1 in winter 1889–90; but German-speaking demand for advanced technical education was much stronger by winter 1909–10. In the latter semester, there were only 2.4 university students with German mother tongue for each one attending a technical college (see tables 4/3 and 4/4). Consistent with the greater preference for *Realschule* education among Austria's small Protestant minority than among Catholics, Jews, or Eastern Orthodox Christians, the percentage of students in higher education that enrolled in technical colleges was much larger for Protestants than for the other major religious groups. In winter 1909–10 Protestants had a ratio of only 1.9 university students to each technical college student compared with the Catholics' 2.5 to 1.[69]

At the end of the period, Czech speakers of all religious denominations displayed an even higher commitment to advanced scientific and technical education than did the Protestant population. The ratio of university students to technical college students for Czech speakers declined from 5.4 to 1 in winter 1869–70 to only 1.4 to 1 in winter 1909–10. Czech-speaking enrollments in technical colleges were so high by 1910 that, uniquely among the major ethnic groups, the number of Czech-speaking students in technical colleges considerably surpassed the number of Czech speakers in law faculties, easily the most popular branch of higher education for most of the other major ethnic groups at the time. The Czechs' great appetite for advanced technical education corresponded to the high level of industrial development in the Bohemian lands. By comparison, the lesser degree of industrialization in the Alpine lands beyond Vienna, a few other large cities, and the small province of Vorarlberg limited somewhat the German-speaking population's demand for advanced technical education.

Youth from the other major ethnic groups showed stronger preferences for university studies over technical education than did the German-speaking students. In winter 1909–10, for instance, there were 3.8 university students with Polish mother tongue for each one in a technical college. Among Ukrainian students that semester, the ratio stood at 18 to 1 in favor of university education; among Slovenes, 5.3 to 1; Serbs and Croatians, 3.5 to 1; Italians, 3.2 to 1; and Romanians, 15.4 to 1.[70]

Austria's major ethnic and religious groups also showed differing preferences among the various university faculties (see tables 4/5 and 4/6).[71] The German- and Czech-speaking university students shared much the same educational culture and apparently made similar calculations about career opportunities when they chose faculties. Over the period from the late 1860s to 1910, Czech-speaking students tended to be distributed among the various university faculties along lines similar to the German speakers: Czech- and German-speaking enrollments in the theological faculties declined from 11 or 12 percent of all university students in the 1860s to around 4 percent on the eve of World War I. Law generally had the largest contingents of Czech- and German-speaking students among the secular faculties except during the late 1880s, when medical enrollments boomed. During much of the late nineteenth century, relatively more German- than Czech-speaking students enrolled in medicine, but the German-speaking totals in the medical faculties were inflated somewhat by the inclusion of many Jewish students who declared German as their mother tongue.

Preferences among the various university faculties followed different patterns among the major ethnic groups in the Carpathian and Adriatic lands. Each group's level of economic and social development affected its students' choices among programs in higher education. Ignoring any possible distorting effects due to the inclusion of foreign students, the fractions of the Polish-, Slovene-, Serbian/Croatian-, and Italian-speaking university students that enrolled in theology all tended to decline even more sharply than among German- and Czech-speaking students as these ethnic groups experienced modernization. Otherwise, the Slovene- and Polish-speaking students seem to have held more strongly than did the German and Czech speakers to beliefs, old or new, about the economic and social value of legal education and of careers in law or government service. Slovene- and Polish-speaking university students enrolled in relatively greater numbers in the law faculties and in smaller numbers in medicine than did the German- or Czech-speaking students.

The traditional values and social hierarchies of East-Central European peasant society apparently had a stronger continuing influence on Austria's Ukrainian population during the late nineteenth century than on many of the other peoples. The numbers of Ukrainian-speaking university students hardly grew at all relative to the total Ukrainian population between the late 1870s and 1900. Ukrainians who did enroll in universities generally aspired to careers in the clergy, public or private bureaucracy, or legal practice. Much smaller numbers of Ukrainian-speaking students were interested in medicine, the sciences, or secondary school teaching. In winter 1869–70 and winter 1889–90, more than half the Ukrainian-speaking students in all the Austrian universities studied in theological faculties, with the law faculties accounting for the next-largest contingent (see table 4/5). When the rate of Ukrainian enrollment in universities began to grow after 1900, the law faculties saw the greatest increases of Ukrainian-speaking students, followed by the philosophical faculties. In winter 1909–10, nearly three-fifths of all the Ukrainian-speaking students in Austrian universities were enrolled in law faculties, but more than one-fifth were still in theology.

When Magyar-speaking students from the Hungarian crown lands attended Austrian universities in significant numbers between the 1860s and 1880s, they enrolled disproportionately in the medical faculties (see table 4/5). In the mid- and late nineteenth century, the international distinction of the Austrian medical schools, particularly in Vienna and Prague, helped them to attract by far the largest proportions of students from outside Austria of any of the university faculties. Having to study in what might be a student's second or third language apparently created fewer worries about ultimate success in medical practice than in the law, government service, the clergy, or secondary school teaching, where language mattered much more.

Protestant and Jewish students were distributed among the secular university faculties differently from the Catholic majority. Throughout the period from the 1850s to World War I, the law faculties typically attracted 40 to 50 percent of all Catholics enrolled in the secular faculties; and the Catholic preference for law continued even after the philosophical faculties began to grow at the turn of the century. Through the 1890s, significantly larger segments of the Protestant and Jewish university students, both native and foreign, than of the Catholic students pursued medical education, while smaller percentages of the Protestants and Jews enrolled in the law faculties. Probably the principal reasons for Protestants and Jews preferring medicine over law were continuing impediments to advancement in parts of the state

TABLE 4/5
Distribution of Ethnic Groups by Faculties in All Austrian Universities, 1870–1910

Winter 1869–70

	All matr. & non-matr. students	Mother Tongue: GERMAN	CZECH	POLISH	UKRA.	SLOVE./SERB./CRO.	ITAL.	MAGY.
Theol.	13.7%	11.0%	12.3%	10.7%	58.8%	8.6%	2.7%	8.8%
Law	35.4	36.2	37.3	42.5	25.9	27.0	46.4	16.2
Med.	28.4	31.7	23.5	23.9	3.5	33.8	27.7	54.3
Phil.	22.5	21.1	26.8	22.9	11.8	30.5	23.2	20.6
	100%=	100%=	100%=	100%=	100%=	100%=	100%=	100%=
	8,992	4,102	1,818	1,310	517	488	220	431

	All matr. & non-matr. students	GERMAN	CZECH	POLISH	UKRA.	SLOVE.	SERB./CRO.	ITAL.	MAGY.
Winter 1889–90									
Theol.	9.3%	6.5%	9.0%	7.6%	55.5%	1.9%	3.7%	1.8%	11.6%
Law	36.7	35.8	39.9	49.5	22.9	60.9	25.1	45.5	7.4
Med.	42.4	44.0	41.7	31.0	14.0	28.2	56.9	39.5	77.8
Phil.	11.6	13.6	9.4	11.9	7.5	9.0	14.4	13.3	3.2
	100%=	100%=	100%=	100%=	100%=	100%=	100%=	100%=	100%=
	15,121	6,860	3,233	2,326	571	156	459	451	209
Winter 1909–10									
Theol.	5.5%	4.4%	3.7%	3.6%	21.5%	2.0%	1.8%	0.9%	44.9%
Law	45.5	42.0	43.9	49.1	58.0	71.3	31.1	51.6	22.8
Med.	16.5	17.3	16.5	13.5	4.1	13.6	42.3	17.1	19.2
Phil.	32.5	36.3	35.8	33.7	16.4	13.1	24.9	30.4	13.2
	100%=	100%=	100%=	100%=	100%=	100%=	100%=	100%=	100%=
	27,531	11,146	4,520	6,716	1,477	544	837	655	167

Sources: *Statistisches Jahrbuch für das Jahr 1869; Öster. Statistik* 28, no. 4 (1892); n.s., 7, no. 3 (1913).

bureaucracy, especially for Jews, and the strong occupational traditions of Protestants and Jews in small or intermediate private businesses and manufacture, some of whose mores might be carried over into private medical practice.[72]

The persistence of traditional peasant life for much of Austria's Eastern Orthodox population resulted in disproportionately strong enrollments of Eastern Orthodox university students in theology once an Orthodox theological faculty began to operate as part of the University of Chernivtsi. Otherwise, the Eastern Orthodox university students also had higher percentages in the medical faculties and fewer in law than did the Catholic majority. As already noted, though, foreigners accounted for a particularly large share of the Eastern Orthodox university students in Austria; and foreign-born students were attracted to the Austrian medical faculties by their strong reputation.

Typically, larger shares of Austria's Protestant university students than of the Catholic or Jewish students enrolled in the philosophical faculties throughout the late nineteenth century. This tendency cannot be attributed to the tastes of foreign students, since it persisted even after the fall in the numbers of Protestant students from Hungary; and the numbers of Protestants from Germany and Switzerland were generally small in any case. Protestants' enrollment patterns within the Austrian universities and their stronger preferences for *Realschulen* and technical colleges all suggest a stronger scientific and technical orientation among Austrian Protestants than among the Catholics, Jews, or Eastern Orthodox. Careers in teaching, in scientific and technical research, in engineering and architecture, and in medical practice seem to have had a special attraction for the Protestant minority. It is hard to say how much of this may have resulted from any residual discrimination against Protestants in the state bureaucracy and how much from the Protestants' relatively strong concentrations in craft manufacture and modern industry. During the late nineteenth century a few Protestants did achieve prominence in Austrian government service and politics, but by and large Protestants were much less interested than were Catholics or even Jews in pursuing legal education that might lead to government employment or private legal practice.[73]

Career opportunities and broader social circumstances apparently influenced the Jewish students' choices among the various university faculties. Legal equality, the general freeing of social and economic relationships, and economic development after the 1850s and 1860s all offered new opportunities to Austrian Jews.[74] At the same time, though, structural economic changes and growing competition put increasing pressure on Jews' traditional petty commercial functions in the smaller cities and towns.[75] One way for Jews to find new economic opportunities was migration from their traditional smaller settlements in the Bohemian and Carpathian lands to the larger Austrian and Hungarian cities or abroad. Another was for Jewish youth to enroll in secondary and higher education and to try to enter educated and semieducated professions, and this they did in sharply increasing numbers

Fears of continuing discrimination in some professions affected Jewish students' choice of curricula within the Austrian universities during the late nineteenth century. Even after the final legal emancipation, Austrian Jews found only limited opportunities in government employment. Without converting, Jews could obtain positions in the civil service but generally in lower echelons and less prestigious government agencies.[76] One study has shown that 3.2 percent of the Jewish men in Vienna who married in 1900 worked for the state, provincial, and municipal governments. That percentage, in fact, equaled the share of all the city's working males in civilian public employment that year; but Vienna was unique among Austrian cities with its huge total population, large governmental apparatus, and large Jewish minority, which amounted to nearly 9 percent of all residents in 1900.[77] Elsewhere there were fewer possibilities for government work for Jews, and popular pressures against the employment of Jews in public agencies only increased with the rise of political anti-Semitism during the late 1880s and 1890s. Jewish youth clearly had less incentive than Catholics to enroll in the law faculties. Those Austrian Jews who nonetheless studied law apparently directed their career aspirations more toward private management or independent legal practice.[78]

Austrian Jews also found only limited career opportunities in teaching. During the era of the Concordat between 1855 and the end of the 1860s, only Catholics received regular teaching appointments in the *Gymnasien* and *Realschulen*. In that period Jewish and Protestant teachers were employed only for religious instruction in their respective faiths. Prejudices persisted thereafter among Catholic churchmen, some school administrators, and parts of the public against having non-Catholics teach Catholic children in public schools; and the

Taaffe government's 1883 legislation on the appointment of primary school directors reflected such feelings.[79] In 1890 and 1900, less than 1 percent of all teachers in Austria's public primary schools were Jewish. Jews could be appointed as regular teachers in secondary schools after the reforms of the late 1860s, but apparently there, too, their numbers remained low.[80] Regarding higher education, Count Leo Thun approved the appointment of Jewish scholars to teach in the universities in the 1850s; and during the late nineteenth century an appreciable number became docents and professors in the Austrian universities and technical colleges. Of course, teaching in higher education could offer professional opportunities to only a small fraction of all university and technical college graduates, whatever their religion. Judging from the Jewish enrollments in the philosophical faculties, careers in teaching or scientific research seem to have evoked only limited interest among Jewish university students in Austria until around 1900.[81]

Given the conditions in other professions, medicine had a particular attraction for Jewish students in Austria and indeed throughout Central and East-Central Europe during the late nineteenth century. If there was no great oversupply of medical graduates, Jewish medical students could move quickly into private practice after completing their training and have reasonable prospects for earning comfortable, steady incomes before long. That contrasted sharply with the genteel poverty that most civil servants experienced in beginning positions in Austria and many of the German states, assuming one could even get a post. Austrian government authorities were willing to appoint Jewish physicians to a range of public health positions even if they might offer Jews only limited opportunities elsewhere in the bureaucracy. The military also employed Jewish physicians. According to one reckoning, nearly five hundred Jews served as career medical officers in the joint Austro-Hungarian army between 1848 and 1910.[82]

The prospects of early economic returns for an investment in advanced education were a vital consideration for any students who came from petty commercial, white-collar, or craft backgrounds. Compared with lower-middle-class Jews, however, students from some of the other ethnic and religious groups had a wider range of professional options. Enrollments in higher education of Czech Catholic students from lower-middle-class origins also grew strongly during the period, but they could choose among secondary school teaching, various types of government employment, legal practice, or medicine to achieve higher status and greater security than that enjoyed by their fathers. In this light, the Jewish students' motivations were not altogether distinct. If the Jewish students differed significantly in this connection from Christian students of lower-middle-class origins, it was in the even greater impetus that the long period of life under discriminatory laws gave them to improve their situation and the somewhat narrower range of career options that were immediately available.[83]

Many observers have made much of older Jewish traditions of literacy and religious learning in explaining their overrepresentation in higher education and learned professions in modern Europe and North America. Such Jewish traditions were indeed strong, but it should be remembered that for most Jews, traditional religious studies relied much on memorization and were neither individualistic nor creative. Those studies by their nature also lacked the worldliness and applied orientation of much of university and technical college education.[84] Apparently few individuals of any religious denomination who enrolled in Central and East-Central European higher education during the late nineteenth century pursued learning for its own sake; the great majority did so to prepare for professional careers.[85] Even in the Austrian philosophical faculties and Germany's faculties of humanities and natural sciences, the majority of students were preparing for teaching careers. In any case, the Austrian philosophical faculties remained small compared with law and medicine until around 1900. For the Jews of Central and East-Central Europe, whose final emancipation was as recent as the 1860s and who remained concentrated in commerce and crafts for decades thereafter, advanced education offered chances to achieve some social dignity and higher and more secure incomes. Central and East-Central European Jews became strongly committed to pursuing advanced education as a means of achieving social and economic improvement, but that was only part of the modern liberal emancipationist value system that most of them held during the late nineteenth century.

In this regard, though, Jews resembled to a considerable degree Austria's Protestant minority and the Czech population. Protestants also pursued advanced education in disproportionate numbers to overcome historic discrimination against them and their continuing disadvantages as a small minority in a strongly Catholic environment. Czech nationalists made increased educational opportunities for their people and the development of a fully articulated Czech-language educational system integral parts of their own emancipationist ideology and political demands.[86] Respect for individual learning and advanced education were significant factors in the popular cultures of Austria's Jewish, Protestant, and Czech populations alike during the late nineteenth century, but those values were inseparable from the historical experiences of each of these groups as disadvantaged peoples that motivated them to use education as a vehicle for social improvement. With the consciousness of their historical disadvantages, individuals in all three groups proved less bound by traditional social norms and limits on individual aspirations than were many German-speaking Catholics in the rural parts of the Alpine lands during the nineteenth century. It was to be expected then that, alongside the offspring of Jewish small business owners and white-collar employees, the children of Czech peasant farmers, independent craft producers, and shopkeepers and those of Protestant small manufacturers, business owners, and clerks also enrolled in secondary and higher education in higher numbers relative to their populations than did their more tradition-bound German Catholic counterparts in the Alpine lands.[87] The *degree* of the Austrian Jews' overrepresentation in advanced education relative to their population was indeed much greater than that for Protestants or Czechs, but Jews had suffered greater discrimination and exclusion from the old corporate social and economic structures. Jews had even less to lose and more to gain than did Protestants and Czechs by giving up their old occupations, pursuing education, and trying to enter growing segments of the emerging modern social structure.

Combined with the growth in overall representation of Jews in Austrian higher education, the Jewish university students' strong preference for medical studies through the 1890s had a striking impact on the medical faculties. In winter 1869–70, for instance, Jewish students accounted for 13 percent of all matriculated and nonmatriculated university students in Austria but 23 percent of all medical students. The percentage of medical students who were Jewish peaked in the middle and late 1880s, just before total medical enrollments in Austria reached the high point for the whole second half of the century. In winter 1889–90, for instance, 31 percent of all students in the medical faculties were Jewish, half again as large a percentage as the Jewish share of all university students.

The combination of Jewish preferences for medical studies and the high concentration of Austria's Jewish university students in Vienna resulted in Jews accounting for a majority of the medical students in that city during most of the 1880s. The Jewish share of the total rose from 30 percent in winter 1869–70 to fully 61 percent in winter 1884–85. In that same semester Jews accounted for 36 percent of all matriculated and nonmatriculated students in the Vienna University. Jewish enrollments in the other Austrian medical faculties during the 1880s were generally much lower, although Jewish students accounted for 43 percent of the total in Prague's German medical faculty in winter 1884–85.

The numbers of Jewish students in the Vienna medical faculty crested in the mid-1880s, although Catholic and Protestant enrollments there continued to grow through the rest of the 1880s. By winter 1889–90 the Jewish portion of the Vienna medical students had fallen to 48 percent, although the total number of matriculated and nonmatriculated medical students had increased by more than one quarter since 1885, reaching a colossal 3,105 in winter 1889–90. As Austrian medical enrollments declined during the 1890s, Jewish enrollments in the Vienna medical faculty fell more sharply than did the numbers of Christian students. In winter 1899–1900 the Vienna medical faculty had less than half the total number of students as ten years previously, and now only 39 percent of them were Jewish.[88] By winter 1909–10 the distribution of Austria's Jewish university students among the faculties of law, medicine, and philosophy resembled that for the Catholic students more closely than in previous decades. In winter 1909–10 just over half of all matriculated and nonmatriculated Jewish university students were enrolled in law faculties and one-quarter in philosophical faculties, compared with only 22 percent in medicine (see table 4/6). Jewish students now accounted for only 35 percent of the total in the Vienna medical faculty.

In the meantime, though, the large Jewish contingents among the medical students in Vienna and among the practicing physicians there and in other larger Austrian cities had evoked complaints from anti-Semitic politicians and concern among some professors of medicine. Already in 1876, the eminent professor of surgery in Vienna, Theodor Billroth, published a treatise on medical education in which, in passing, he criticized the inadequate preparation, limited intellect, and lack of scientific interest among the less prosperous students who

TABLE 4/6
Distribution of Religious Groups by Faculties in All Austrian Universities, 1870–1910

	All matr. & non-matr. students	Cath.	Jewish	Prot.	E. Orth.
		Winter 1869–70			
Theol.	13.7%	17.2%	0.0%	0.0%	0.0%
Law	35.4	36.4	35.5	15.2	26.1
Med.	28.4	23.3	51.7	54.3	50.3
Phil.	22.5	23.1	12.7	30.4	23.6
	100%=	100%=	100%=	100%=	100%=
	8,992	7,161	1,131	335	165
		Winter 1889–90			
Theol.	9.3%	12.1%	0.0%	0.0%	17.6%
Law	36.7	40.6	28.5	22.1	23.6
Med.	42.4	34.3	65.8	61.4	46.7
Phil.	11.6	13.0	5.7	16.6	12.1
	100%=	100%=	100%=	100%=	100%=
	15,121	10,856	3,046	598	495
		Winter 1909–10			
Theol.	5.5%	6.5%	0.0%	0.0%	19.9%
Law	45.5	45.3	52.7	32.0	21.7
Med.	16.5	14.4	22.2	21.5	29.8
Phil.	32.5	33.8	25.1	46.5	28.5
	100%=	100%=	100%=	100%=	100%=
	27,531	20,636	4,817	934	848

Sources: *Statistisches Jahrbuch für das Jahr 1869; Öster. Statistik* 28, no. 4 (1892); n.s., 7, no. 3 (1913).

came to the faculty from Galicia and Hungary, many of them Jews. Billroth had no sympathy for popular Jew-baiting, but these published observations and his later call for excluding from the Vienna faculty anyone lacking an Austrian *Matura* outraged Jews and embarrassed many of his colleagues.[89] As we have seen, though, most of the other medical professors proved unwilling to tamper with what had become by then well-established practice for admissions.

Expanding Access to Education and the Question of Social Privilege

Radical German nationalists and some German-speaking Christian Social politicians might lament the increasing representation of Jews and the various Slavic groups in Austrian secondary and higher education, but they could not reverse what was an accomplished fact by 1900. The expansion of opportunities in advanced education after the 1850s benefited virtually all ethnic and religious groups to some degree. During the late nineteenth century, German Catholics increased their enrollments but saw a diminution in their traditional privileged position in education relative to the non-German ethnic groups and relative to the Protestant and Jewish religious minorities. In academic secondary schools, nearly all the non-German ethnic groups experienced significant increases in their enrollments relative to population and in their percentage shares of the students. In higher education the Czechs, Poles, and the small Italian population achieved strong per capita representation, although the Ukrainian, Slovene, Serbian, Croatian, and Romanian populations made only limited advances until 1890 or after 1900. Among Austria's religious minorities, the indigenous Eastern Orthodox improved only slightly their low representation in secondary and higher education during the late nineteenth century, but from the 1850s onward enrollments of Protestants and Jews in secondary schools, universities, and technical colleges relative to their populations greatly exceeded those of the Catholic majority.

The recruitment of students in Austrian secondary and higher education thus broadened significantly during the second half of the nineteenth century in ethnic and religious terms. German-speaking Catholics did continue to enjoy important advantages in education and more broadly in society in the Alpine and Bohemian lands, but even in these regions access widened to the ranks of the educated and semi-educated and, by extension, to the pool of young professionals and semiprofessionals. In itself the weakening of the old linguistic and religious barriers to gaining advanced education represented an important change in Austrian social structure, but the question of whether advanced education helped to perpetuate or transform professional elites in the society must be addressed in terms of occupational and class origins as well as ethnic and religious background. Alongside the changes in students' ethnic and religious origins, it is also necessary to assess the extent to which their occupational and class backgrounds changed during the late nineteenth century.

CHAPTER 5

The Limits of Opportunity

Students' Occupational and Class Origins

The geographical, ethnic, and religious recruitment of students clearly broadened as the networks of Austrian secondary and higher education expanded during the late nineteenth century. Analysis of the students' occupational and class origins confirms the impression of broad recruitment. Secondary and higher education in Austria did more than help perpetuate the status and privileges of propertied and educated elites from one generation to the next. During much of the late nineteenth century, as we shall see, majorities of the students in the universities and technical colleges of Vienna and Prague, for example, were the children of lower-middle-class fathers who lacked large property holdings or higher education.

Austrian educational records do not make it easy to determine students' occupational and class origins. When students registered, they were asked to report their father's or guardian's occupation; but the government authorities never published this data on a broad basis. Here then, one must rely on descriptions by contemporary observers, fragmentary statistics published for a few secondary schools, and samples of the registration records for several of the universities and technical colleges. To be fair, one must take the fathers' or guardians' occupations as reported by students with a grain of salt. The students often used broad designations such as "official," "merchant," "agent," or "farmer"; and some of these might be more elevated than reality warranted. Many of the "merchants" (*Kaufleute,* or *obchodníci* in Czech) and "farmers" (*Bauern* in German or, in Czech, *rolníci* or *sedláci*) were only small proprietors. Moreover, students who were legally adults and desired financial assistance commonly reported no occupation for their fathers or guardians. Still, the registration records for secondary and higher education offer no other reliable indicators of the students' occupational or class origins.[1]

Secondary School Students

The increasing enrollments of formerly disadvantaged ethnic groups such as Czechs and Slovenes and of religious minorities like the Jews and Protestants suggest a widening of social access to Austrian secondary education. It is hard to gauge precisely trends in the students' occupational and class origins, but it appears that the great majority of *Gymnasium* and *Realschule* students in the Alpine and Bohemian lands during the late nineteenth century came from the lower middle classes, although few were children of wageworkers or poorer peasants from remote localities. As will be seen, offspring of the propertied and educated upper-middle and upper strata made up larger shares of the university students in Vienna and Prague; but even among them, between one-third and one-half came from the lower middle classes. Even larger shares of the technical college students in Vienna and Prague came from lower-middle-class families.

Academic secondary schools in Austria's Alpine and Bohemian lands resembled those in much of Germany in drawing the majority of their students from lower-middle-class origins. One study shows that around a quarter of those who passed the *Gymnasium Abitur* in Prussia between 1875 and 1899 were the offspring of educated professionals, officials, and military officers, and less than one-tenth, the children of landowners and industrialists. Almost three-fifths came from the lower middle class: nearly two-fifths were the children of the old lower middle class of farmers, intermediate and small business owners, and independent craft producers with more than one-fifth from the new lower middle class of employees, clerks, and lesser teachers. At most, only a few percent of the graduates from Prussian *Gymnasien* were the children of wageworkers. Around 70 percent of the graduates from Prussian *Oberrealschulen* in the same period had lower-middle-class origins, with less than 10 percent of the total from the educated middle class and 14 percent, the children of landowners and industrialists.[2] Compared with the Prussian secondary schools, the Austrian apparently included an equal or larger share of students from the lower middle classes. Probably two-thirds or more of the students in the Alpine and Bohemian lands came from lower-middle-class families. In August 1880, the Provincial School Board (*Landesschulrat*) in Austrian Silesia, for instance, estimated that nearly 50 percent of the students in the *Gymnasien* and *Realschulen* there came from craft families alone.[3] It must be remembered, though, that there were considerable differences between those who were enrolled at any one time and the much smaller number who managed to graduate.

To some extent the recruitment of secondary school students continued patterns already defined in the early nineteenth century, but the evidence of some individual schools shows significant shifts in the lower-middle-class contingent as proportions increased from the families of petty officials and white-collar employees and those from peasant families declined. In 1862, for example, in the classical *Gymnasium* of Krems an der Donau in Lower Austria's Weinviertel, the sons of peasant farmers and grape growers accounted for 23 percent of the students; of craft producers, 25 percent; and of petty officials and employees, 21 percent, with the sons of educated professionals and rentiers making up only 20 percent. In 1891 youth from farming backgrounds made up only 12 percent of the students in Krems and those from craft families only 15 percent, while the offspring of petty officials and employees had risen to 37 percent and those of professionals and rentiers accounted for 24 percent.[4] Similarly, in 1900–1901 in the *Gymnasium* of the great Benedictine monastery of Kremsmünster in Upper Austria, sons of educated professionals made up only 22 percent of the students, while the offspring of craft producers and small business owners accounted for 31 percent; petty officials, white-collar employees, teachers and officers, 23 percent; and peasants, only 8 percent.[5] Since as late as 1910, 18 percent of the Lower Austrian population (including Vienna) and 47 percent of Upper Austrians were still directly dependent on agriculture, the German-speaking agricultural elements of the Alpine provinces appear to have been markedly underrepresented even in the *Gymnasien* of the provincial towns and monasteries.[6]

The *Gymnasien* of the larger cities had larger proportions of students who were children of public and private officials, white-collar employees, professionals, and commercial or industrial entrepreneurs. In a study of three boys' *Gymnasien* with large Jewish enrollments in Vienna's first, second, and ninth districts in 1890–91, Rozenblit has found that nearly 50 percent of the non-Jewish students' fathers or guardians were military officers and civil servants, around 25 percent educated professionals, 2 to 5 percent industrialists, and 14 to 25 percent merchants and small business owners, while 10 percent or less were wageworkers, 3 to 4 percent craft producers, and 6 to 14 percent business employees. Among the Jewish students in the three schools, only 16 percent were the sons or wards of educated professionals and 7 percent of industrialists while fully 58 percent were the sons or wards of merchants and small business owners, 13 percent of business employees, only 3 percent each of civil servants and craft producers, and less than 1 percent of wageworkers.[7] As yet, there are no precise analyses of the socioeconomic origins of students in the first privately operated girls' *Gymnasien* that appeared at the turn of the century.

Students in the Czech *gymnasia* and *reálná gymnasia* of Prague and other cities in the Bohemian lands also tended to come more predominantly from the lower middle classes than did German-speaking Catholic secondary students in Vienna. The Czech Jewish writer Pavel Eisner, who graduated in 1906 from the Czech *reálné gymnasium* in Prague's New Town (Ječná Street), later recalled the modest circumstances of the great majority of his schoolmates. Even the most prosperous of them tended to be sons of successful independent craft producers. Eisner's father was a commercial agent, and the parents of his friends included a tailor, a street-corner knife and scissors grinder, and a widow who worked as a domestic servant.[8]

Less is known about the social composition of *Realschule* students than of *Gymnasium* students. Several urban *Realschulen* in Austria's Alpine and Bohemian lands that have been studied, like *Oberrealschulen* in Germany, had smaller percentages of students from the propertied and educated elites than did *Gymnasien* in the same cities; and lower-middle-class students predominated even more in the *Realschulen* than in the *Gymnasien*. In fall 1880, for instance, in the first-year class of the provincial *Oberrealschule* in Graz, 3 percent each were the sons of physicians and industrialists, 20 percent the offspring of officials and government employees of all ranks, 18 percent of military officers, 22 percent of merchants and small business owners, and 17 percent of craft producers.[9] In the *Oberrealschule* of Vienna's fourth district, Wieden, between the late 1850s and 1905, the large majority came from families of officials and white-collar employees of the state, the railroads, or private enterprises. Few came from propertied upper-middle-class families or from working-class families despite the proximity of proletarian districts like Favoriten.[10] In the 1880s the social differences between *Gymnasium* and *Realschule* students were reflected in discrepancies in their ages at entry. Between 1881 and 1883, for instance, entering students in the *Gymnasien* were primarily nine to twelve years old, while students who were twelve years or older at entry predominated in the *Realschulen*.[11] The offspring of some petty white-collar employees, craft producers, and small retailers might only be able to begin secondary education, if at all, at a later age than the more affluent.

Indeed, throughout the late nineteenth century the loss of labor from a teenaged child who remained in school and the costs of tuition, books, and lodging and meals if the secondary school was far from home raised barriers to attaining advanced education for youth from the poorest families.[12] By itself, though, the moderate tuition for state secondary schools did not create an insurmountable impediment, and institutions in smaller cities and towns charged lower amounts than those in the largest cities. Moreover, school authorities liberally granted exemptions. An 1870 ministerial ordinance set tuition rates for all types of academic secondary schools ranging from 15 fl. per semester for the upper forms in the Viennese institutions down to 8 fl. per semester for all forms in schools in some smaller cities and towns.[13] In comparison, in 1871 households paid an average annual rent for a flat of 238 fl. in Prague or 160 fl. in Graz and its suburbs.[14] A subsequent ordinance of June 1886 raised tuition to 25 fl. per semester for all state secondary schools in Vienna, 20 fl. for institutions in other cities and towns with more than 25,000 inhabitants, and 15 fl. for all other state secondary schools.[15] Some private secondary schools charged higher tuition and fees.

For most of the late nineteenth century, public secondary school directors could grant exemptions from tuition on the basis of students' good grades, good behavior, and financial need.[16] The essential requirement was that the student submit to the director a "certificate of means" (*Vermögensausweis*) from the head of the home community government and the local priest or pastor that verified the student's need.[17] Most school directors could offer poorer students little assistance, though, beyond waiving tuition, since stipends were limited. In the decade after 1900, for example, typically only 3 or 4 percent of all students in the accredited Austrian *Gymnasien* and around 2 percent of those in the *Realschulen* received stipends.[18] Many school directors granted so many exemptions from tuition, though, that after 1880 ministerial officials complained that too many poor students with meager prospects for success in academic work or professions were enabled to attend secondary schools.[19] Throughout Austria in 1865–66, for instance, 41 percent of the registered *Gymnasium* and *Real-Gymnasium* students and 27 percent of the *Realschule* students were exempted; in the mid-1870s, 48 percent of the *Gymnasium* students, 34 percent of the *Real-Gymnasium* students, and 25 percent of the *Realschule* students did not pay tuition.[20] Fewer students in the

Realschulen received exemptions than in the *Gymnasien,* probably because many of the poorest youth preferred a *Gymnasium* education that might lead eventually to a career in teaching, the clergy, or government employment and there were more *Gymnasien,* more widely dispersed. With the great expansion in enrollments after the mid-1890s, the majority of all secondary students in 1905–6 were receiving exemptions. By then the difference had narrowed between the percentages of students exempted from tuition in *Gymnasien* and *Realschulen:* 53 percent of all *Realschule* students in Austria in 1905–6 were exempted, compared with 59.3 percent of all *Gymnasium* students.[21]

As might be expected, more students were exempted from tuition in the poorer provinces than in more prosperous ones; but ethnic differences also played a role. Nominally following the same procedures and criteria, the *Gymnasien* and *Realgymnasien* that taught in Czech generally exempted more of their students than did the German-language institutions. In 1905–6, for example, Czech-language institutions waived tuition for fully 64 percent of their students, while the German schools exempted only 48 percent of theirs.[22] There is little data available to compare the economic situations of the ethnic German and Czech students, but probably more of the Czech students came from poorer families. The lagging rates of enrollment in Upper Austria, Tirol, and Carinthia compared with the Czech regions suggest that the Czech popular appetite for secondary education significantly exceeded that of the German Catholic population in the more rural parts of the Alpine lands. In addition, ethnic German politicians in Austria became convinced that Czech educators were generally too generous in exempting students from tuition and too eager to advance as many Czech youth as possible through the schools.[23]

Students in Higher Education

As one might expect, the occupational and class origins of students in Austrian higher education diverged noticeably from those of secondary school students. Large numbers of *Gymnasium* and *Realschule* students did not complete their studies or go on to higher education. Around 1900 on average only one-half of any entering first-year cohort in the Austrian *Gymnasien* and *Realschulen* completed the first four years of study, and only one-quarter eventually graduated and passed the *Matura*.[24] Those students who proceeded on to the universities and technical colleges necessarily represented a more exclusive body, numerically and socially, than the secondary school students. Still, in higher education as well, youth from modest lower-middle-class origins accounted for a large share of the students. The significant numbers of lower-middle-class students in both Austrian and German higher education conflicted, in fact, with the widely held image of students as mostly privileged youth who enjoyed a genteel life during their studies before entering the elite ranks of educated professionals and officials. It was true that in Austria, as in Germany, few offspring of wageworkers attended universities or technical colleges; but their relative numbers among Austrian students exceeded noticeably the laboring-class component in German higher education.

The tuition and fees charged by the Austrian universities and technical colleges exceeded the amounts levied by the *Gymnasien* and *Realschulen,* but in Austria, as in Germany, they were still moderate.[25] Also, the Austrian institutions of higher education, like the secondary schools, liberally granted exemptions. The regulations of 1850 stipulated a matriculation charge of 2 fl. and established tuition (*Kollegiengeld*) of 1 fl. per weekly hour of instruction for a semester. A new ordinance in 1886 raised the matriculation charge to 4 fl., but the hourly tuition remained essentially unchanged.[26] The universities assessed additional fees for doctoral and state examinations, acceptance of dissertations, and graduation, ranging from 20 fl. to 65 fl. each. The tuition and fees for the technical colleges varied more among individual institutions and were raised more frequently. In the early 1880s the technical colleges in Prague, for instance, charged a flat tuition of 25 fl. per semester for each matriculated student. In 1892, when Austria went on the gold standard, a new monetary unit, the Krone, replaced the florin (Gulden) at the rate of two Kronen to the florin. Just before World War I, tuition stood at 50 kr. per semester for the Vienna Technical College and the two technical colleges in Prague and at 30 kr. for Graz, L'viv, and the two colleges in Brno.[27]

According to the 1850 ordinance on tuition, university students could apply for half or full exemptions from the tuition fees, which each institution might grant based on the criteria of good behavior, "true neediness," and "excellent scholarly application."[28] The technical colleges used similar criteria, and, as in secondary education, students had to provide a certificate from their communal authorities to verify their lack of means.[29] Special provisions for theological students freed the majority of them from tuition payments. Over the second half of the nineteenth century, ministerial officials tried to make the criteria for exemptions more precise, but the institutions continued to have considerable latitude.

In contrast with German universities, which preferred postponing payments for needy students over waiving tuition, the Austrian institutions typically granted half or full exemptions to from one-quarter to one-third of all students (see table 5/1).[30] There was some variation in practice among individual universities. Prague's Czech and German universities, for instance, generally granted relatively more exemptions than did the Vienna University, whether because they had larger numbers of students from poorer backgrounds or they applied more liberally the criteria for exemptions, or both.[31] The technical colleges tended to grant exemptions to even larger shares of their students than did the universities. Typically, one-third or more of the technical college students had half or full exemptions from the late 1860s to World War I (see table 5/1). Again, the technical colleges in Prague were more liberal than the Vienna Technical College. This was particularly true of the Czech college, which exempted 40 to 50 percent of its students between the mid-1870s and the 1890s and more than half after 1900.[32]

Generous as they were in waiving tuition, the Austrian universities and technical colleges awarded relatively fewer stipends than did many of the institutions in Germany during the late nineteenth century. In the 1880s and 1890s, around 30 to 40 percent of the Prussian university students received stipends, although with increased enrollments thereafter, the rate fell to only 20 percent in 1911–12.[33] Between 1870 and 1900, typically only 10 or 11 percent of all matriculated and nonmatriculated Austrian university students received stipends. Only 7.5 percent had stipends in winter 1909–10. The percentages of Austrian technical college students who received stipends varied greatly over the period but tended to be close to the concurrent level in the universities.[34] Stipends were typically modest, and average awards grew little during the late nineteenth century. The average university stipend stood at 115 fl. in 1869–70, 148 fl. in 1879–80, and 313 kr. in 1909–10. In the technical colleges the average stipend was 181 fl. in 1869–70, 126 fl. in 1879–80, and 327 kr. in 1909–10.[35] With such limited financial aid available, the poorest students had to take up tutoring and other part-time work.[36]

TABLE 5/1
Frequency of Tuition Exemptions in Austrian Universities and Technical Colleges, 1870–1910

Semester	No. matr. & non-matr. students - half exempt	No. matr. & non-matr. students - fully exempt	Half exempt as % of total	Fully exempt as % of total
		ALL AUSTRIAN UNIVERSITIES		
W. 1869–70	654	1,963	7.3%	21.8%
W. 1879–80	1,070	1,563	11.2%	16.3%
W. 1889–90	1,165	2,004	7.7%	13.3%
W. 1899–1900	1,591	2,571	9.2%	14.9%
W. 1909–10	3,076	6,104	11.2%	22.2%
		ALL AUSTRIAN TECHNICAL COLLEGES		
W. 1869–70	--	1,328	--	58.3%
W. 1879–80	271	802	8.4%	24.8%
W. 1889–90	128	455	7.1%	25.3%
W. 1899–1900	494	1,374	9.3%	25.8%
W. 1909–10	811	2,996	7.5%	27.7%

Sources: *Statistisches Jahrbuch für das Jahr 1869; Statistisches Jahrbuch für das Jahr 1879; Öster. Statistik* 28, no. 4 (1892); 68, no. 3 (1903); n.s., 7, no. 3 (1913).

Any precise analysis of socioeconomic origins for Austrian university and technical college students must be based on samples of the original registration records for various institutions.[37] For this study, the two oldest and, during the late nineteenth century, the largest universities in the Alpine and Bohemian lands have been selected, those of Vienna and Prague. These institutions offered the broadest array of academic specialties and were the most respected of the Austrian institutions. Despite the growth of other universities, Vienna and Prague together continued to enroll the majority of all university students in the Austrian half of the monarchy between 1848 and World War I: two-thirds or more of all matriculated students in the 1850s, 1860s, and 1870s, and still 54 percent of the total as late as winter 1909–10.[38] Total enrollment for the University of Graz first reached 2,000 in 1913–14; and in winter 1909–10, Innsbruck had only 1,006 matriculated students. In the same semester the University of Vienna had nearly 7,600, and the two Prague universities, over 4,800 together.[39]

Likewise, the technical colleges in Vienna and Prague have been selected to represent higher technical education. Like their university counterparts, the technical colleges in these cities tended to have the greatest array of academic programs, and they dominated the training of engineers and other educated technical personnel in Austria during the late nineteenth century. In winter 1879–80, their students accounted for 81 percent of all the matriculated technical college students in Austria. In winter 1909–10, the matriculated students in the Vienna Technical College, the Czech Technical College, and the smaller German college in Prague still made up two-thirds of the Austrian total.[40] By 1910, the number of matriculated students in the L'viv Technical College had grown to 1,565, surpassing the nearly 900 in Prague's German Technical College; but the enrollments were still smaller for each of the other colleges in Brno and Graz than for the German institution in Prague.

To analyze trends in the social recruitment of the students, samples of 200 to 1,000 students each were drawn from the registration records of each institution for selected winter semesters: 1859–60, 1879–80, 1899–1900, and 1909–10.[41] Only matriculated students were included, since only they were subject to all the admissions requirements and eligible to take diplomas and degrees. The socioeconomic analysis is based on the reported occupations for the students' fathers or guardians, grouped together into the broader social categories of propertied, educated, new and old lower middle class (*Kleinbürgertum* or *Mittelstand*), and laborers that have been commonly used to describe Central European society in this era (see table 5/2 for the scheme of occupational and class stratification).[42] Some caution must be exercised here in assessing trends in the recruitment of university and technical college students because of the often vague occupational designations in the registration records, the failure of some students to report their father's or guardian's occupations, and the limitations of sampled data. Also, the residual demographic effects of the "Hungry Forties" and the short-term impact of the Austro-Piedmontese War and of the economic downturn of the late 1850s may have skewed somewhat the social composition of students suggested by the samples for 1859–60.

The limitations of Austrian official statistics make it difficult to measure the representation of the various major occupational and class groups in higher education relative to their shares of the total population and impossible to measure that representation relative to

TABLE 5/2
Scheme of Occupational Stratification

Propertied	
estate owner	higher indust./commercial manager
factory owner/director	land/real estate owner
large merchant/banker	independent
Educated Professions	
higher military officer	lawyer
government official	notary
physician	univ. or tech. college professor
dentist	Gymnasium or Realschule professor
clergyman	engineer or architect
Old Lower Middle Class	
peasant farmer	self-employed craft producer
estate manager	small or intermediate businessman/ shopkeeper
New Lower Middle Class	
primary school teacher	govt./private clerk, bookkeeper
lower indust./commercial manager	unskilled salaried personnel
lower military officer	self-employed subprofessional
Laborers	
factory worker	unskilled worker
craft worker	day-laborer
commercial laborer	

their segments of the school-aged population. From 1880 onward, the published occupational statistics from the Austrian censuses included totals for all the self-employed persons or "independents" in each occupational sector regardless of the size of enterprise or property and made no distinction between industrial and craft production in each manufacturing sector. For salaried employees the census statistics included totals for each economic sector without differentiating between educated and uneducated employees.[43]

The samples of the registration records indicate that in broad class terms the recruitment of university students in Vienna and Prague changed only gradually during the half century after 1860 despite population growth, economic development, and the expansion of education during the era (see figs. 3, 4, and 5 and table 7 in the appendix). Generally, the matriculated students of the Vienna University included a somewhat larger share from the propertied and educated elites than was found among the university students with German mother tongue in Prague and a much larger share than among the Czech-speaking university students there. The most salient trends in the representation of the various social classes over the period were a near doubling of the percentage of students from the new lower middle class of white-collar employees, clerks, and elementary school teachers and a smaller decline in the share of students from the old lower middle class of independent craft producers, small and intermediate business owners, and peasant farmers. In contrast with the Prussian universities, the university enrollments in Vienna and Prague indicate no significant sustained growth during the late nineteenth century in the percentage from propertied families.

University education in Austria functioned to some extent to perpetuate social advantages from one generation of educated professionals

FIGURE 3
Social Origins of Matriculated Vienna University Students, 1860–1910

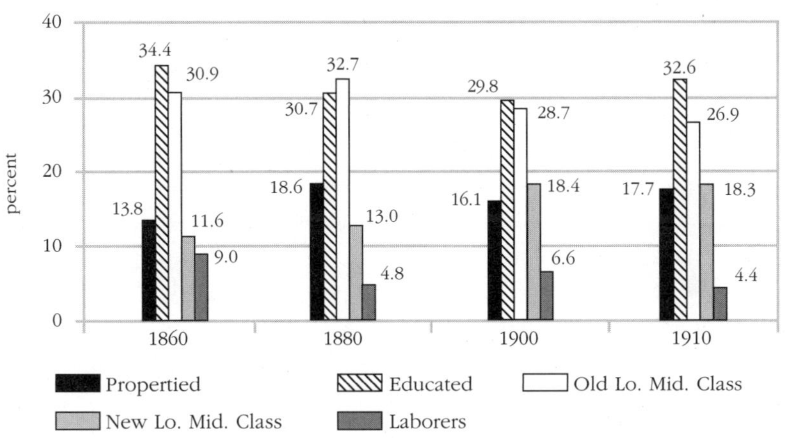

FIGURE 4
Social Origins of Matriculated University Students, Prague, 1860–1910

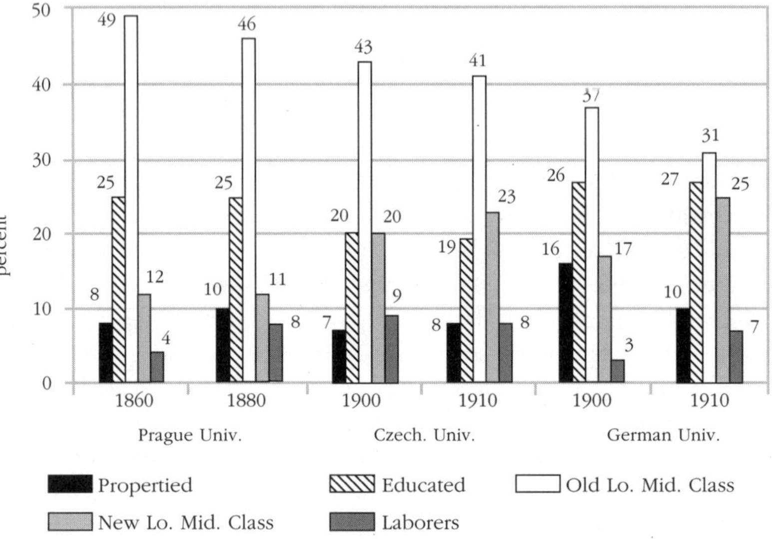

FIGURE 5
Social Origins of Matriculated University Students, Vienna and Prague, 1880–1910

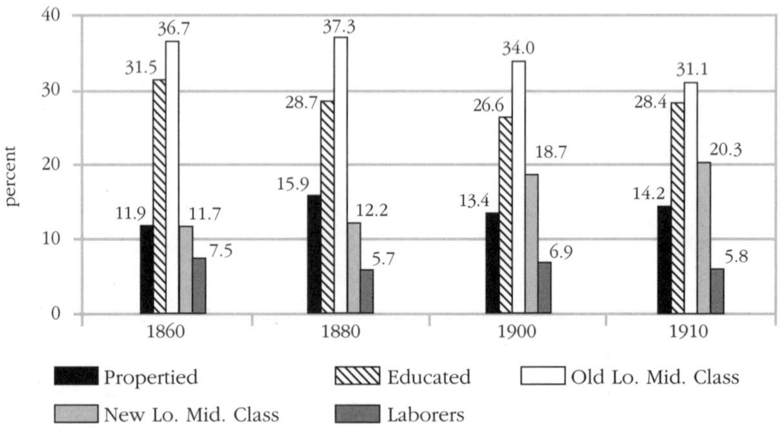

Sources: Samples of the registration records in the *Katalogen der Hörer, Katalogy posluchačů, Nationalen* and *Nationaly* for the respective winter semesters, Archiv der Universität Wien, Vienna, and Archiv Univerzity Karlovy, Prague.

Confidence Intervals: largest—all lower-middle-class students in the Vienna Univ., w. 1859–60: 42.5% ± 4.5%; smallest—laboring-class students in the German Univ. of Prague, w. 1899–1900: 3.3% ± 1.1%

to the next, despite the increase in enrollments relative to the school-aged population and the growing representation of formerly disadvantaged ethnic and religious groups. From 1860 to 1910, a fairly steady figure of between 25 and 30 percent of the matriculated university students in Vienna and Prague were offspring of educated higher government officials, higher military officers, professors, and educated professionals.[44] In Prussia, by contrast, children of the educated elites made up between 40 and 50 percent of the university enrollments during the early and mid-nineteenth century and fell to only around 20 percent just before World War I.[45] The children of Austria's civilian government officials—not counting the professors in the public secondary schools and higher education—were particularly prominent among offspring of the educated in the Vienna and Prague universities during the late nineteenth century, making up about one-half the representation of the educated elites there. Educated officials and professionals, of course, represented a newer and smaller segment of the Czech population than of the German-speaking citizens. Children of the educated accounted for around one-fifth of the Czech-speaking university students in Prague after 1880, but that share also remained fairly constant through 1910 (see tables 7 and 9 in the appendix). After the offspring of government officials, those of physicians, lawyers, military officers, and professors in secondary or higher education, in that order, were most strongly represented among the children of the educated in the Vienna and Prague universities. Czech-speaking students in Prague included relatively few children of higher military officers, since the higher Habsburg officers were heavily German-speaking.[46]

As Austria's propertied upper middle class grew during the late nineteenth century, the numbers of students from those strata in the Vienna and Prague universities kept pace with the growth of total enrollments; but they did not increase their percentage of the total after 1880 (see fig. 5 above and table 7 in the appendix). In the Prussian universities, by contrast, the representation of the propertied elites grew strongly, so that their share eclipsed that for the educated in the late 1890s, reaching approximately 40 percent of the students in 1900. The propertied elites' share of the Prussian students fell back somewhat with the rapid growth of the universities in the next decade, so that their offspring accounted for less than 20 percent of the total in 1911–12 (see fig. 6). That figure still clearly exceeded the percentage for the propertied elites among the university students in Vienna and Prague, although not the share in the Vienna University taken by itself.[47] Modern commerce, finance, and industry, of course, developed on a larger scale in northern Germany than in Austria during the late nineteenth century. The stronger representation of the propertied elites among the Prussian university students may have stemmed largely from their greater numbers in the Prussian population.

In Austria, as in Germany, few sons of the nobility studied in universities during the late nineteenth century. Austrian aristocrats still tended to stand aloof from bourgeois society, and university education was not a practical necessity for the many Austrian noblemen who were engaged in managing their properties. Those aristocrats who wanted careers in the military, diplomatic service, or the Catholic Church might attend the military or consular academies, the Theresianum, or various seminaries without studying in the universities or technical colleges.[48] Even in the Vienna University, aristocrats typically accounted for less than 1 percent of the matriculated students. Slightly more numerous were students with petty titles, most of them children of the "second society" (*zweite Gesellschaft*), bearing the titles of *Edler, Ritter,* or simply *von.* Students with such lesser titles accounted for close to 8 percent of all matriculated students in the Vienna University in winter 1859–60, and around 4 percent of all matriculated university students in Vienna and 2 percent or less of all those in Prague in winter 1899–1900.[49]

The Vienna University consistently had a larger percentage of students drawn from the propertied and educated elites than did the two universities in Prague, amounting to nearly half of all the matriculated students in Vienna throughout the era after 1860. Among the 868 respondents to a survey of the matriculated and nonmatriculated students in the three secular faculties in 1909–10, 56 percent reported that their parents owned some property, whether land, a house, or a business, small or large.[50] But the glass was half empty as well. Even in the Vienna University, throughout the late nineteenth century half of the matriculated students came from modest lower-middle-class and some laborers' families. Even larger segments of the university students in Prague came from such circumstances.

The general expansion of the new lower middle class of lesser public and private managerial employees, clerks, and elementary school teachers during the late nineteenth century fueled the strong growth in its representation among university students in Vienna and Prague between 1860 and 1910. Nonetheless, the old lower middle class of peasant farmers, estate managers, independent craft producers, and owners of small and medium-sized businesses still made up a much larger segment of the population in the Alpine and Bohemian lands. In 1910, for instance, white-collar and supervisory employees of all types, including the educated, accounted for 6 percent of the 5.62 million self-supporting (*berufstätig*) individuals in Austria's German-speaking population. The employees were greatly outnumbered, though, by the independent or self-employed in agriculture, manufacture, commerce, and transportation, who amounted to 20.2 percent of all self-supporting German speakers; and the great majority of these had no more than small or intermediate enterprises (see table 10 in the appendix).[51] Self-employed farmers, manufacturers, craft producers, and business owners accounted for even larger shares of the self-supporting population among the Slavic ethnic groups than among the German speakers.

The percentage of matriculated university students in Vienna and Prague from old-lower-middle-class origins declined somewhat between 1860 and 1910, but through the last prewar years they continued to exceed the offspring of the new lower middle class in all three institutions (see figs. 3–5 above and table 7 in the appendix). In Germany as well, the old lower middle class still constituted a significant part of the population; and some of its children attended universities. By 1911–12, however, the percentage of the students in Prussian universities who came from the new lower middle class had overtaken that from the old lower middle class, 32.6 percent to 29.1 percent (see fig. 6).[52] In the Vienna University in winter 1909–10, 27 percent of the matriculated students came from the old lower middle class compared with only 18 percent from the new lower middle class. At the same time, fully 41 percent of the matriculated students in Prague's Czech University were of old-lower-middle-class origins, including a remarkable 20 percent of the total from farmers' families. The German University in Prague also had a larger share from the lower middle classes than did the Vienna University, although the percentage of farmers' children was smaller than in the Czech University.[53] Overall, though, the old- and new-lower-middle-class contingents in Prague's Czech and German universities in winter 1909–10 approximated the 62 percent of Prussian university students in 1911–12 who came from lower-middle-class origins.

Few children of wageworkers enrolled in the Vienna and Prague universities during the second half of the nineteenth century, and their share of enrollments showed no clear growth trend after 1900. In 1910, wageworkers (and apprentices) in all sectors of the economy accounted for 47 percent of Austria's self-supporting German speakers and 48 percent of the self-supporting Czech speakers (see table 10 in the appendix). After 1880, the offspring of wageworkers made up between 4 and 7 percent of the matriculated students in the Vienna University, a roughly comparable percent of the German University in Prague, and slightly more, 8 or 9 percent, of the matriculated students in the Czech University (see table 7 in the appendix). One must be cautious in generalizing from such small numbers in sampled data, but few of these were the children of industrial workers. More were offspring of wageworkers in the crafts, commerce, and agriculture.

Although small, the presence of workers' children in Austrian universities contrasted with their virtual exclusion from German institutions. In 1911–12 only 0.2 percent of the German citizens enrolled as matriculated students in Prussian universities were the offspring of workers and lesser servants.[54] The social division between the lower middle class and the working class in Austria with regard to higher education was still considerable, but apparently not as wide as in Germany.

Socioeconomic origins, as well as ethnic and religious differences, affected student preferences among the university faculties. The law faculties led to higher government service and legal practice, the longest-established and, in some respects, most prestigious of the secular learned professions. In addition, legal studies, unlike medicine, did not require preparation in the modern sciences or years of clinical training. Through 1900 among German- and Czech-speaking Christian students in Vienna and Prague, strong majorities from all class groupings except wageworkers preferred the law faculties. In 1880 Christian university students in Vienna and Prague from the propertied and educated elites showed the strongest preferences for legal studies, although the medical and philosophical faculties began to draw larger shares of them around 1900 (see table 8 in the appendix).[55] As already noted, poorer employment prospects for Jews than Catholics in government service and secondary teaching limited the shares of Jewish enrollments that went to the law and philosophical faculties.

Compared with the students from the propertied and educated elites, lower percentages of those from lower-middle-class and laboring origins tended to enroll in the law faculties, and larger shares of the students from these strata prepared for secondary school teaching and the Catholic priesthood. One would expect such a pattern for students from lower-middle-class and laboring origins if university education were serving to a great extent to maintain a rigid social hierarchy, but it should be noted that in 1880 and after, in fact, less than half of all lower-middle-class university students were enrolled in the philosophical and theological faculties. Larger percentages of the much smaller number of laboring-class students, however, enrolled in philosophy and theology.

The Catholic theological faculties typically attracted the smallest percentages of students from the propertied and educated strata. At the end of the nineteenth century, total enrollments in the Vienna and Prague theological faculties were small compared with the secular faculties, and typically 4 percent or less of all German-speaking Christian students from the propertied and educated elites were enrolled in theology. Czech-speaking university students who were sons of educated persons were no more prone to enroll in theology than were the sons of educated German-speaking Catholics, although in Prague Catholic theology attracted a somewhat larger share of the Czech-speaking students from propertied families than of the sons of propertied ethnic Germans who studied in Prague or Vienna (see table 8 in the appendix). It should be noted, though, that one-third or more of all offspring of the propertied who were registered as matriculated students in the Czech University at the turn of the century were the children of rural or urban landowners rather than industrial or commercial proprietors. Not surprisingly, smaller shares of the Czech- and German-speaking students in Vienna and Prague from the new lower middle class studied Catholic theology than among the students who were children of peasant farmers, independent craft producers, and small business owners. In most of the samples for the theological faculties in the four selected semesters, well over half of all matriculated students came from the old lower middle and laboring classes, but even so the great majority of the German- or Czech-speaking Christian university students from those social classes studied in the secular faculties.

The long duration and higher costs of medical studies compared with other university programs surely affected the recruitment of medical students. Generally, smaller percentages of the German- and Czech-speaking Christian students from the lower middle and laboring classes enrolled in the medical faculties than in law or philosophy. With reasonable talent and application, a young physician might quickly achieve a comfortable or even high income compared with beginning civil servants or secondary school teachers, not to mention parish clergy. Still, German- and Czech-speaking Christian students from lower-middle- and laboring-class families were apparently deterred somewhat by the higher costs of medical training.

As a result of the varying preferences of students from the different social classes, the university faculties differed markedly in the social composition of their student bodies. In the Vienna University, 50 to 60 percent of the matriculated law students between 1860 and 1910 came from the propertied or educated elites, while students from those strata tended to make up only 40 to 50 percent of the medical enrollments. In contrast, large majorities of the matriculated students in the Vienna philosophical and theological faculties came from the lower middle and laboring classes: in 1860 nearly four-fifths of the total in philosophy and the same amount in theology, and in 1910 just over half in philosophy and nearly three-quarters in theology.[56] The strength of the propertied and educated elites in the Vienna law faculty approximated the situation in the law faculties of the University of Bonn between 1865 and 1914 and the University of Marburg between 1873 and 1913, but the offspring of the propertied and educated also accounted for more than half the matriculated medical students and nearly half the matriculated students in the philosophical faculties of those two German universities.[57]

During the 1860s and 1870s the student body of the still united Prague University had a generally more plebeian character than did that of the Vienna University, and after 1882 the Czech University drew larger portions of its students from the lower middle and laboring classes than did either the German University in Prague or the Vienna University. In contrast with the Vienna law faculty, only one-third of the matriculated students in the Czech law faculty and two-fifths of those in the German law faculty in 1900 were offspring of the propertied and educated elites. Less than 30 percent of the Czech medical faculty's matriculated students in 1900 and 1910 came from propertied or educated backgrounds, compared with around 40 percent or more in the German medical faculty. At the turn of the century, the Czech philosophical faculty drew 80 percent or more of its matriculated students from the lower middle and laboring classes, compared with between 55 and 65 percent in the German philosophical faculty. At the same time, 75 to 85 percent of the matriculated Czech and German theological students in Prague came from lower-middle- and laboring-class origins.[58]

Judging from studies of the Vienna University, it appears that the first matriculated women in the Austrian universities around 1900 came from a narrower segment of society than did the male students. A significantly larger fraction of the fathers or guardians of the first female students in Vienna were educated professionals and public and private officials, while fewer came from the lower middle classes and almost none from the laboring strata. For the period between 1899 and 1914, typically between 44 and 50 percent of the matriculated women in the philosophical faculty had educated fathers or guardians. Less than one-fifth of the total were from the propertied strata, only one-third or slightly more from the lower middle class, and almost none from the laboring class (see table 9 in the appendix).[59] During the first years that women were able to matriculate in the Vienna medical faculty, they, too, were strongly recruited from the families of educated professionals and officials although the larger contingent of daughters of small and intermediate business owners meant a greater lower-middle-class share.[60]

The first matriculated women students in the Vienna University also had a distinct religious composition. In winter 1899–1900, 68 percent of all matriculated and nonmatriculated students in the Vienna philosophical faculty were Catholic, 19 percent Jewish, and 7.2 Protestant; but only 44 percent of the matriculated women there were Catholic, with 44 percent Jewish. In the first decade of the new century, Jewish women made up around one-third of all matriculated women in the Vienna philosophical faculty; and they accounted for an even larger share of the early women medical students, ranging between one-half and two-thirds of the total.[61]

For a woman to matriculate in a university was still an extraordinary phenomenon in Austria or Germany before World War I, an act that required special dedication from any woman student and unusual support from her family. In Austria, as in Germany, the early women students were more likely than male students to come from the families of educated professionals, higher officials, or comfortable entrepreneurs in the cities than from the urban lower classes or rural elements altogether.[62] Since there was little public funding for the limited *Gymnasium* education available to Austrian women before 1914, they had to sustain substantially higher costs than did men simply to reach the universities.[63] The families of the early women students had to believe in the value of university education for their daughters and bear the financial burdens at a time when few learned professions would admit women.

Although the technical colleges in Vienna and Prague had consistently fewer students than did the universities, their enrollments after 1880 included significantly larger percentages of lower-middle-class youth than those in the universities, ranging from six to twelve percentage points higher in the sampled years. In 1900 close to three-quarters of the matriculated students in the three technical colleges came from lower-middle- and laboring-class origins (see figs. 7, 8, and 9 and appendix table 11).[64] Children of educated professionals and higher public and private officials consistently showed stronger preferences for university education over technical college studies than did youth from the propertied elites or the lower middle class. As a result, the representation of educated professionals and higher officials among matriculated university students in Vienna and Prague typically surpassed the level in the corresponding technical college by 8 to 15 percentage points. The proportions of technical college students who came from propertied origins tended to be roughly comparable between each technical college and the corresponding university in Vienna or Prague.

The increases in representation of the new lower middle class among technical college students in 1900 and 1910 reflected the growth in Austria in the numbers of white-collar employees, managerial personnel, petty officials, and teachers and the attraction for their children of expanding employment opportunities for engineers and other educated technical personnel. The percentages from the new lower middle class were up in all three universities and the three technical colleges in 1900 and 1910, but the percentage for the new lower middle class among the matriculated students in each technical college surpassed by a significant margin the percentage in the corresponding university.

Despite the many impediments that poorer youth faced in the educational system, a remarkably large share of Austria's university and technical college students during the late nineteenth century came from lower-middle- and laboring-class backgrounds. Already in 1860

FIGURE 6
Social Origins of University Students in Prussia and Vienna-Prague, 1910–12

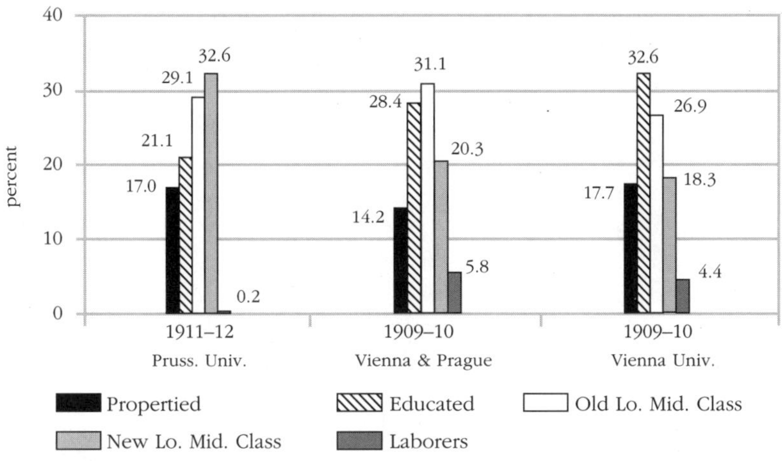

Sources: Samples of the registration records in the *Katalogen der Hörer, Katalogyy posluchačů, Nationalen,* and *Nationaly* for the respective winter semesters, Archiv der Universität Wien, Vienna, and Archiv Univerzity Karlovy, Prague. Statistics on the Prussian universities derive from Petersilie 1923, 236: 147.

Confidence Intervals: largest—all lower-middle-class students in the Vienna Univ., w. 1859–60: 42.5% ± 4.5%; smallest—laboring-class students in the German Univ. of Prague, w. 1899–1900: 3.3% ± 1.1%

FIGURE 7
Social Origins of Matriculated Students in the Vienna Technical College, 1860–1900

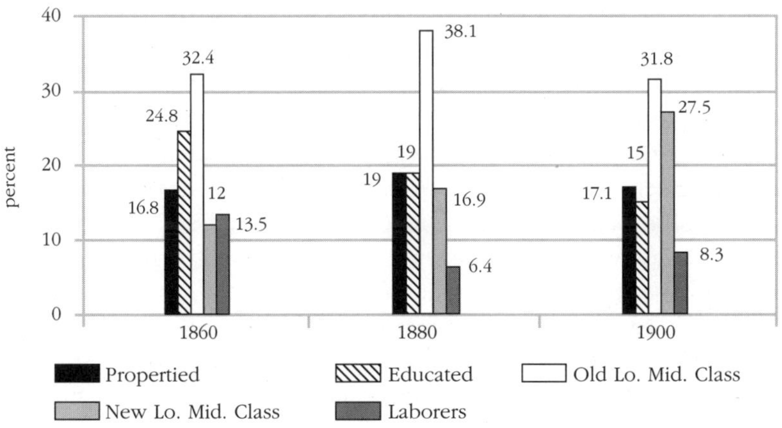

See figure 9 for sources and confidence intervals.

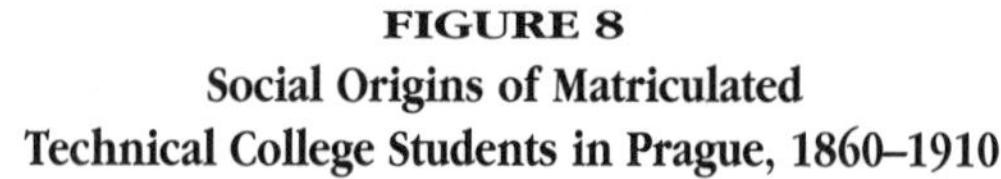

FIGURE 8
Social Origins of Matriculated Technical College Students in Prague, 1860–1910

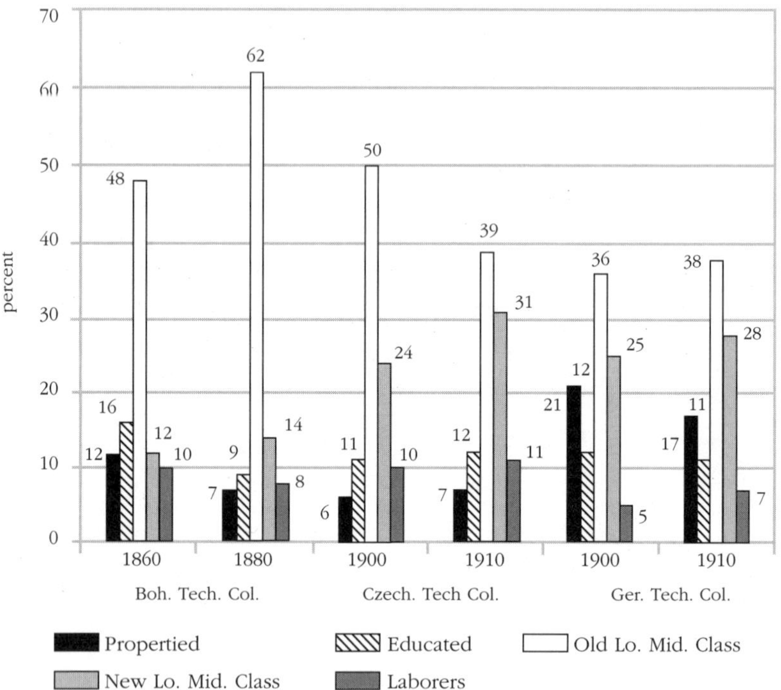

See figure 9 for sources and confidence intervals.

a majority of the matriculated university students in Vienna and Prague came from those strata, and that majority held steady during the succeeding five decades, while the percentage of Austria's nineteen- to twenty-two-year-old population that was matriculated in universities more than doubled. Between 1860 and 1910, around half the matriculated students in the Vienna University tended to come from the propertied and educated elites. In Prague, however, around 70 percent of the Czech university students and between 55 and 60 percent of the German-speaking university students came from the lower middle and laboring classes. The share of matriculated technical college students in Vienna and Prague from those lower strata rose from around 60 percent in 1860 to over 70 percent at the end of the period, while the number of matriculated students in all Austrian technical colleges quadrupled relative to the eighteen- to twenty-two-year-old population between 1870 and 1910.

The growing numbers of students from the Slavic ethnic groups and religious minorities contributed much to the strength of the lower middle and laboring classes in Austrian higher education during the late nineteenth century. As we have seen, the largest of those ethnic and religious groups who increased their representation in higher education in the Alpine and Bohemian lands were the Czechs, primarily Catholic with a Protestant minority, and the Jews, recorded primarily as German-speaking but with a Czech-speaking minority at the end of the period. The rising numbers of Czech Christian and Jewish students from lower-middle-class and some laboring-class families may be the most revealing indication of the broadening access to advanced education in Austria's western provinces, but the strong representation of Czechs and Jews from those strata suggests how their distinct values and experiences as Czechs and Jews affected their demand for education as

FIGURE 9
Social Origins of Matriculated Technical College Students in Vienna and Prague, 1860 and 1900

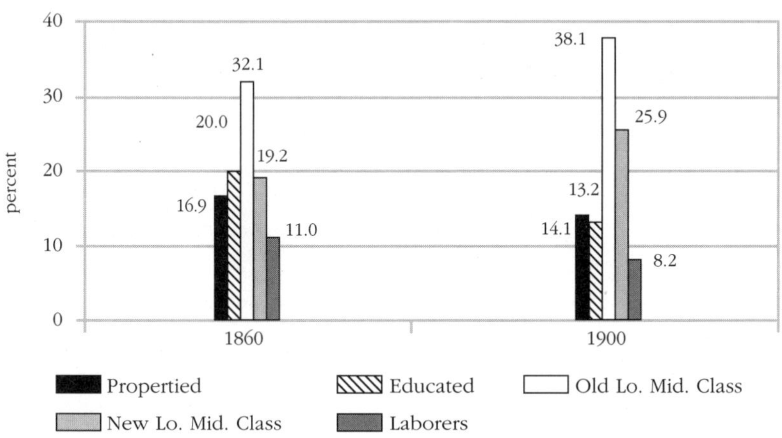

Sources: Samples of *Katalogen der Hörer, Katalogy posluchačů* for the respective winter semesters in the Archiv der Technischen Universität Wien, Vienna, and the Archiv Českého vysokého učení techického, Prague.

Confidence intervals: Largest—all students from the lower middle classes in the German Technical College, w. 1899–1900: 61.2% ± 6.8%; narrowest—students from the laboring strata in the Vienna Technical College, w. 1879–80: 6.4% ± 1.9%.

compared with German Catholics from similar occupational and class origins.

Social Class, Group Culture, and the Demand for Advanced Education

Compared with the German-speaking Christian students in Vienna and Prague, much larger percentages of the Czech-speaking Christian students in higher education came from lower-middle- and laboring-class families, while greater percentages of the Jewish students came from lower-middle-class origins (see tables 9 and 12 in the appendix).[65] In part, the social recruitment of the Christian Czech and the Jewish students only reflected the distinct compositions of their populations. Austria's Czech and Jewish populations, after all, included smaller segments of propertied and educated elites through the late nineteenth century than did the German-speaking Christian population. Nonetheless, if the children of peasant farmers, craft producers, shopkeepers, clerks, and workers were more strongly represented among the Christian Czech-speaking students than among the Christian German-speaking students; and the offspring of shopkeepers, traders, and white-collar employees were more strongly represented among the Jewish students, this also signified greater aspirations for higher education and entry into educated professions among those strata of the Czech and Jewish populations than among the corresponding segments of the German-speaking Christians. The lower middle class and laborers still made up the great majority of the self-supporting German-speaking Christians in the Alpine and Bohemian lands, and conceivably more of their children could have enrolled.

For purposes of this analysis, students of all Christian denominations and those without religion have been grouped together and that total cross-tabulated with their reported mother tongue. The samples from the registration records of the universities and technical colleges include numbers of Protestants and students without religious affiliation that are too small to be statistically significant. All Jewish students, identified positively by their reported religion, have been grouped together regardless of what they indicated as mother tongue. Throughout the late nineteenth century, Catholics, of course, made up the overwhelming majority of all Christian students in Vienna and Prague. In winter 1909–10, for instance, Catholics accounted for more than 80 percent of all the non-Jewish matriculated and nonmatriculated students in the university and technical college in Vienna and over 90 percent in the universities and technical colleges of Prague.[66]

The Czech-speaking Christian students in the Vienna and Prague universities included much larger fractions from modest social origins than did the German-speaking Christians (see table 9 in the appendix). In the winter semesters of 1859–60 and 1879–80, over half of the matriculated Czech-speaking Christian university students in Prague and in winter 1879–80 nearly half of those in the Vienna University were the children of peasant farmers, independent craft producers, and small or intermediate business owners. The modern middle-class and lower-middle-class elements grew significantly in the Czech population during the last decades of the century, however, and by winter 1909–10 the emerging Czech middle class of property and education accounted for nearly 28 percent of the Czech-speaking Christian students in the Czech University. In that same semester the new lower middle class of white-collar employees and schoolteachers provided nearly one-quarter of the matriculated Czech-speaking Christian university students in Prague.[67] Still, as we have seen, even as late as 1910, fully 20 percent were the offspring of Czech peasant farmers. Another 8 percent were the children of independent craft producers, and nearly 9 percent, of small and medium-sized business owners. The Czech-speaking Christian university students in Prague also included larger contingents of wageworkers' children than did the German-speaking Christian or Jewish university students in Vienna or Prague, accounting for nearly 10 percent of the matriculated Czech-speaking Christian university students in Prague in 1880, 1900, and 1910.

Throughout the half century after 1860, at least as large a share among the Jewish as among the Czech-speaking Christian university students in Vienna and Prague came from lower-middle-class origins. In each of the four selected semesters between 1860 and 1910, over 60 percent of the Jewish matriculated university students in Vienna and Prague came from the lower middle class, but these were predominantly the children of small and intermediate business owners. In winter 1859–60 nearly three-quarters of the matriculated Jewish university students in Prague were the offspring of such business owners and some self-employed craft producers. As with the Czech-speaking Christian students, the growth of the modern middle class among Austrian Jews during the succeeding decades affected the recruitment of Jewish university students. In winter 1909–10, 39 percent of the matriculated Jewish students in the German University came from families of the propertied or educated middle class with another 17 percent from the new lower middle class; but still 40 percent were the offspring of small or intermediate business owners.[68] Jewish enrollments in Prague's Czech University and Czech Technical College were minimal compared with those in the German institutions before World War I.

Allowing for the generally larger proportions of students from the lower middle and laboring classes in the technical colleges, the differences in the social recruitment of the German-speaking Christian, Czech-speaking Christian, and Jewish technical college students paralleled the divergences among the groups in the universities (see table 12 in the appendix). The Czech Christian and Jewish technical students in Vienna and Prague tended to include lower percentages from the propertied and educated strata than did the German Christian students, and the Czech Christian and Jewish technical college students tended to have even higher percentages from lower-middle-class origins than did their counterparts in the universities, particularly from the old lower middle class. The representation of wageworkers' offspring among the Czech Christian technical college students was roughly comparable to that among the Czech Christian university students in both cities.[69]

To what extent should the differences in the social composition of the German Christian, Czech Christian, and Jewish students in Austrian higher education be attributed to the differences in their respective populations? Here, it would be desirable to measure the representation of the various occupational and class groupings among the students relative to the numbers for those occupations and classes in the German Christian, Czech Christian, and Jewish populations or, even better, relative to the school-aged populations for the respective occupational and class categories among the three groups. Unfortunately, the published Austrian population statistics do not include any cross-tabulations of occupation, religion, language, and age. Moreover, to be meaningful, any such calculations should gauge the representation of various occupational, ethnic, and religious groups in the *whole* Austrian system of higher education against the total number of school-aged inhabitants for each of those groups. Trying to calculate measures merely for selected universities and technical colleges would raise difficult questions about just which territories and which ethnic and religious groups in all of Austria provided the potential recruitment base for each institution.

Within the limits of the available evidence, it appears that the larger percentages from the lower middle classes among the Czech-speaking Christian and Jewish students than among the German-speaking Christian students in higher education in Vienna and Prague derived only partly from the distinct compositions of the Czech Christian and Jewish populations. The 1910 Austrian census, for instance, reported that 43.2 percent of the self-supporting Czech-speaking population of all religious denominations was engaged in agriculture, a figure that still significantly exceeded the 34.4 percent for the German-speaking population of all denominations.[70] This contributed inevitably to a stronger presence of independent farmers' offspring among Czech-speaking Christian students than among the German-speaking Christians, but the independent farmers' and leaseholders' 20 percent of the matriculated Czech-speaking Christian students in the Czech University in winter 1909–10 was substantially greater than the agricultural proprietors' and leaseholders' 13 percent share of the self-supporting Czech-speaking population in Austria in 1910. During the same semester 18 percent of the matriculated Czech-speaking Christians in Prague's Czech Technical College were the children of farmers and leaseholders.[71] Compared with the early nineteenth century, the absolute and relative numbers of Czech farmers' sons who studied in the Prague University increased significantly in the 1850s and 1860s; and their representation remained strong thereafter among the Czech university students in the Bohemian capital.[72]

In contrast with their high numbers among the Czech-speaking Christian students, independent farmers' children seem to have been markedly underrepresented among German-speaking Christian university and technical college students in Vienna and Prague at the turn of the century relative to the farmers' share of the self-supporting German-speaking population. In 1910 agricultural proprietors and leaseholders made up 10.1 percent of Austria's self-supporting German-speaking population, and one can safely assume that the great majority of these were small farmers and leaseholders. In the winter semester 1909–10, however, independent farmers' children accounted for only 5.8 percent of the matriculated German-speaking Christian students in the Vienna University and 7.2 percent of the German-speaking Christian students in Prague's German University and German Technical College.[73]

The offspring of independent craft producers were apparently also overrepresented among the Czech-speaking Christian university students at the turn of the century compared with the craft producers' share of the self-supporting Czech-speaking population. In 1910 self-employed persons in industry and the crafts, whether small or large entrepreneurs, accounted for 4.6 percent of all self-supporting Czech speakers in Austria, but in winter 1909–10, the children of independent craft producers made up 7.7 percent of the matriculated Czech-speaking Christian students in the Czech University and fully 13 percent of those in Prague's Czech Technical College.[74]

Unlike the situation among the Czech-speaking Christian students, the children of independent craft producers enjoyed no significant overrepresentation among German-speaking Christian students in Vienna compared with the craft producers' share of all self-supporting German speakers in Austria. Among matriculated German-speaking Christian students in the Vienna University in winter 1909–10, only 4.2 percent were the children of self-employed craft producers, while 5.4 percent of Austria's self-supporting German speakers were self-employed in all areas of manufacture and craft production. Equivalent data are lacking for the Vienna Technical College in 1909–10, but in winter 1899–1900 the offspring of independent craft producers made up 5.6 percent of the matriculated German-speaking Christian students in that institution.[75] Bohemia had strong craft traditions and a large industrial sector, and craft producers enjoyed somewhat stronger representation among German-speaking Christian university and technical college students in Prague than in Vienna. In winter 1909–10, 9.8 percent of the matriculated German-speaking Christian students in the German University and 7.7 percent of those in the German Technical College were the children of independent craft producers.[76]

The differing representation of Czech- and German-speaking Christian independent farmers and craft producers among the students in Vienna and Prague suggests divergent social and educational values among those segments of the Austrian population. It should be noted that the matriculated and nonmatriculated students with German mother tongue in the Vienna University and Prague's German University in winter 1909–10 accounted for nearly three-quarters of the German-speaking total in Austrian universities that semester, and together the

Vienna Technical College and Prague's German Technical College accounted for the same share of all technical college students with German mother tongue. In that same semester, the Czech University had fully 90 percent of all matriculated and nonmatriculated Austrian university students registered with Czech mother tongue, while the Czech Technical College in Prague enrolled 84 percent of all technical college students with Czech mother tongue.[77] Assuming no great differences in the age stratifications of the Czech and German Christian lower middle classes, one can only conclude from the enrollments in Vienna and Prague that the offspring of Czech Christian farmers and independent craft producers generated significantly greater demand for higher education than did their counterparts in the German-speaking Christian population of the Alpine and Bohemian lands. It was not easy for most youth coming from independent farming or craft production to reach a university or technical college, whatever their ethnic or religious background, but the children of Czech Christian farmers and craft producers developed greater aspirations for higher education and entry into the professions than did their German Christian counterparts.

Similarly, the stronger representation of small and intermediate business owners' children among matriculated Jewish students in the universities and technical colleges than among Christian students derived only partly from compositional differences in the Jewish population. In 1900, for instance, individuals engaged in commerce and transportation accounted for 40 percent of the self-supporting Jewish population throughout Austria, compared with only 6.4 percent of all self-supporting Catholics, or 10.5 percent of all self-supporting German speakers (all religions) and 7.3 percent of all self-supporting Czech speakers (all religions).[78] While many Jews entered white-collar employment and the professions during the late nineteenth century, the independent or self-employed in commerce and transportation still accounted for fully one-fifth, 20.9 percent, of Austria's self-supporting Jewish inhabitants in 1900. At the same time offspring of small and intermediate independent business owners made up more than twice as large a share of the matriculated Jewish students in the universities and technical colleges of Vienna and Prague: 43 percent of the Jewish students in the Vienna University, 45 percent of those in the Vienna Technical College, and a little over 50 percent of the Jewish students in Prague's German University and German Technical College.[79]

The strong representation of Jewish business owners' children among the Austrian university and technical college students was only a facet of the more general overrepresentation of Jewish youth in Austrian higher education. That broader phenomenon had its roots in the distinct social and economic experience of Austrian Jews and their specific cultural heritage, which affected all Jewish youth to some degree regardless of their parents' particular occupations.[80] Nonetheless, the overrepresentation in higher education of Jewish business owners' children must also have had some connection with the experience and values of small and intermediate commercial proprietors as an occupational group.

In fact, the children of small and intermediate business owners were significantly overrepresented among all Austrian university and technical college students compared with the business owners' share of the total self-supporting population. In 1900, self-employed entrepreneurs or proprietors in commerce and transportation accounted for only 3.7 percent of all self-supporting German speakers and 2.5 percent of all self-supporting Czech speakers in Austria, the great majority of these small or intermediate proprietors.[81] The population recorded with German "everyday language," of course, included many Jewish business owners in the Alpine and Bohemian lands, so that the actual percentage of small and intermediate business owners among the self-supporting German Christian population was smaller. Throughout Austria in 1900, only 2.0 percent of the whole self-supporting Catholic population, regardless of language, and only 1.4 percent of the other self-supporting Christian inhabitants were self-employed in commerce and transportation.[82] Still, during the winter semester 1899–1900, the children of small and intermediate business owners made up between 7 and nearly 10 percent of all matriculated German- and Czech-speaking Christian students in the universities and technical colleges of Vienna and Prague.

It may be that children of shopkeepers and other independent business owners, whatever their religion, were all exposed to certain modes of behavior and encouraged to cultivate traits that proved advantageous in advanced education. Commercial entrepreneurship in larger communities encouraged individualism, competitiveness, and the development of self-discipline and analytic and verbal skills. Children of small business owners might grow up with considerable economic insecurity, but most probably did not know the life of arduous physical work experienced by small peasants, craft producers, and laborers. For the offspring of modest commercial entrepreneurs, salaried white-collar employment and the learned professions offered greater security, higher status, and, many hoped, better incomes than their fathers'. In larger towns and cities, the increasingly accessible *Gymnasien* and *Realschulen* offered the possibility of entry into at least lower-ranking private or public white-collar jobs. With success in university or technical college studies, one might attain a respected bureaucratic position or enter a learned profession.

In the long run, the modern market economy put pressure on peasant farmers and craft producers to develop many of the same traits as commercial entrepreneurs, but one could see those tendencies somewhat earlier and more strongly during the middle and late nineteenth century in the emerging Czech agricultural middle class in Bohemia and Moravia than among Austria's German-speaking rural population.[83] Until the 1880s, particularly in the Alpine lands, many of the German-speaking peasant farmers and small craft producers in villages and smaller towns remained more strongly bound by traditional community values and corporate solidarities than were their Czech-speaking counterparts in Bohemia and Moravia.[84] The German-speaking Catholic peasant farmers in the Alpine and Bohemian lands sent a significantly smaller share of their children to the universities and technical colleges during the second half of the nineteenth century than did their Czech-speaking counterparts. Somewhat higher numbers of students came from the families of German-speaking Catholic independent craft producers, particularly in the more industrialized Bohemian lands, but these were not overrepresented in higher education relative to their share of the self-supporting population, as Czech-speaking craft producers decidedly were.

Through the early and mid-nineteenth century in the rural areas and small towns of the Alpine lands, those children of German-speaking Catholic peasants and craft producers who did pursue advanced education aspired mainly to enter the priesthood, teaching, or the lower levels of government service. Most of these youth apparently perceived higher bureaucratic positions, law, and medicine as beyond their reach. In districts remote from Vienna, Graz, Linz, and Innsbruck, more of them apparently continued to think this way through the late nineteenth century than did the children of Czech Catholic and Protestant peasants and craft producers in the Bohemian lands or the offspring of Jewish business owners almost anywhere in Austria. As Rozenblit has argued, notions of social advancement through education conflicted with traditional corporate social values and respect for established hierarchy that persisted more strongly among the German

Catholic lower-middle- and laboring-class elements in the Alpine lands than among a traditional outsider group like the Jews or, one can add, among Czech peasants and craft producers in the more economically dynamic Bohemian lands.[85]

The children of the educated, of course, had to make no great social or cultural leap in order to pursue advanced education and entry into professions. Throughout the nineteenth century, such youth were strongly overrepresented in Austrian secondary and higher education relative to their fathers' share of the self-supporting population. Aspirations for advanced education also came relatively easily to the children of the new lower middle class of salaried employees, clerks, and schoolteachers. At the beginning of the twentieth century, the new lower middle class was apparently significantly overrepresented in the universities and technical colleges relative to its share of the self-supporting population for Christians and Jews, German speakers and Czech speakers alike (see tables 7, 9, 10, 11, and 12 in the appendix).[86]

Access to Advanced Education and the Limits of Social Change

To what extent did the expansion of Austrian secondary and higher education during the six decades after the mid-nineteenth-century reforms actually broaden educational opportunities for the population and give greater access to formerly disadvantaged social strata? The growth in enrollments relative to the school-aged population indicates that the academic secondary schools, universities, and technical colleges became significantly more *inclusive* in simple numerical terms; but such growth might not necessarily mean that opportunities for the children of economically or socially disadvantaged elements increased at the same speed as they did for those higher in the social hierarchy. One must also ask whether, with increasing inclusiveness, access to advanced education became socially more *progressive,* to use Ringer's useful distinction, by drawing a larger portion of the students from the lower social strata.[87]

Comparisons between Austria and Germany are informative in this connection. Historians of nineteenth-century Germany have debated whether there was any basic tendency there to greater progressiveness in secondary and higher education, demonstrating in the process the difficulties of measuring such changes with the historical data that are typically available. There is agreement that during most of the late nineteenth century the Prussian *Gymnasien* and *Oberrealschulen* recruited students broadly from the middle and lower middle classes, although few enrolled from the laboring strata. From 1875 to the late 1890s, at least 60 percent of the students in the Prussian *Gymnasien* came from the old and new lower middle classes, and the same was true for 70 percent or more of the students in the Prussian *Oberrealschulen.* Scholars differ, though, about whether secondary education in Germany became significantly more progressive as the numbers of students increased. Some, like Detlef K. Müller, have argued that concurrent with the great expansion after the 1890s, the various segments of Prussian secondary education became socially more sharply differentiated with substantially larger percentages of the *Gymnasium* students drawn from the propertied and educated elites than was the case among the *Realgymnasium* and *Oberrealschule* students. Others, though, have disputed Müller's findings and see a significant general advance for the lower middle classes in German secondary education between 1890 and 1914.[88]

The evidence on Austrian secondary school students is fragmentary, but the Austrian schools in general during the late nineteenth century apparently drew as large a percentage of their students from the lower middle classes as did the Prussian institutions, if not more, and a slightly larger percentage from the laboring classes than the minuscule share drawn by the Prussian schools. As in Prussia, notably fewer children of Austria's propertied and educated enrolled in *Realschulen* than in *Gymnasien.* With only limited movement toward greater equality of academic status among the different types of secondary schools in Austria before 1914, their social differentiation was apparently strong and persistent. Still, in view of the increasing percentage of the school-aged population that enrolled in secondary schools and the growing representation of formerly disadvantaged ethnic and religious groups, it seems that, overall, Austrian secondary education became more progressive. To define this more precisely will require quantitative studies for a broader range of institutions and measures relative to the changing occupational and class composition of the school-aged population.

Social trends for German university education during the late nineteenth century have received more extensive and more comprehensive analysis than those for secondary education, but here, too, historians have differed sharply in their findings. Ringer has argued in broad terms that the universities showed progressive trends in the declining tendency for self-recruitment from the educated professionals and higher officials and the growing proportions of students from the new lower middle class. These developments were countered to a considerable degree, however, by the rising percentage of students who were children of more prosperous commercial and industrial entrepreneurs and managers, a decline in representation of small shopkeepers and independent craft producers, and the virtual exclusion of the working class. For Ringer, the recruitment of German university students before World War I reflected the transformation of the middle and upper reaches of German society in the era of mature industrialization but not any significant democratization of higher education.[89] Konrad H. Jarausch has also noted the declining share of offspring of the educated and the growing representation of the propertied elites between the mid-nineteenth century and 1900, but he has argued that German university education became noticeably more progressive with the growing representation of the lower middle class, particularly with the increasing numbers of students from the new lower middle class between the 1890s and World War I.[90]

In contrast with Ringer and Jarausch, John E. Craig has insisted that any changes in the social recruitment of students must be measured relative to the school-aged population for each social group to determine how the educational opportunities for any particular group have changed.[91] Using this stiffer test, Craig found that the representation of shopkeepers and craft producers in German higher education increased during the Second Empire but that of small farmers and the laboring class did not, and few from the lowest social strata enrolled relative to their school-aged population. The new lower middle class was the one broad category most responsible for growth in the total enrollments during the whole period between 1873 and 1933, but that increase failed to keep pace with the rapid expansion in the numbers of school-aged children from the new lower middle class.

The limitations of Austrian population statistics and the available data on higher education make it difficult to measure precisely how progressive were the changes in enrollments during the late nineteenth century. Ultimately, any thorough evaluation of Austrian higher education will require careful analysis of matriculations and enrollments for all the universities and technical colleges and calculation of indices of selectivity for the school-aged population of each occupational and class grouping. Lacking such measures, one can only offer rough assessments of the changing composition of university and technical college students for the Alpine and Bohemian lands based on data from Vienna and Prague without comparisons to the numbers of the school-aged for the various social groupings.

During the early nineteenth century, university education was apparently more progressive in Austria than in much of Germany owing to a stronger representation of shopkeepers', independent craft producers', and petty officials' sons. At the end of the century, higher education in Austria's Alpine and Bohemian lands was more progressive than that in Germany in some ways and less progressive in others, although many of these variances probably derived from differences between the German and Austrian occupational structures. The propertied elites had a smaller representation among university students in Vienna and Prague than in the Prussian universities, but the smaller scale of Austria's modern industry and modern entrepreneurial class surely affected this. In contrast, the educated elites provided a larger share of the university students in Vienna and Prague than in the Prussian institutions. The lower middle classes, old and new, enjoyed strong representation among the university and technical college students in Vienna and Prague throughout the late nineteenth century; and the percentage of students from the new lower middle class roughly doubled during the late nineteenth century. Still, the old lower middle class retained strong representation in the universities and technical colleges of the Alpine and Bohemian lands. In 1910 the percentage of university students in Vienna and Prague from the old lower middle class slightly exceeded the level for all Prussian universities, but the share of the Prussian students from the new lower middle class, fed by the stronger modern commercial and industrial sectors in the northern German economy, greatly exceeded that in Vienna and Prague (see fig. 6). Overall, at the end of the period the Prussian universities may have been more progressive with regard to the representation of the lower middle class as a whole; but the Vienna and Prague universities were more progressive in the inclusion of farmers' and leaseholders' children, at least among the Czech-speaking students, and of wageworkers' offspring more generally.

The technical colleges in the Alpine and Bohemian lands seem to have been socially more progressive than the universities during the late nineteenth century. After 1880 the three technical colleges in Vienna and Prague drew significantly larger percentages of their students from the lower middle classes and usually somewhat larger proportions from the laboring class than did the universities in the two cities (see figs. 5 and 9 above and tables 7 and 11 in the appendix). Historians have given less attention to the social origins of Germany's technical college students than to those of its university students, but studies of the Technical College in Karlsruhe between 1869 and 1893 and the Rhenish-Westphalian Technical College of Aachen between 1870 and 1899 indicate that their students included smaller percentages from the old lower middle class than did German universities, the opposite of the general tendency in Austria between 1880 and 1910. The Karlsruhe Technical College tended to draw more of its students from the propertied and educated elites and relatively fewer from the ranks of independent craft producers, shopkeepers, peasant farmers, and laborers than did Germany's universities on average.[92] At the Technical College of Aachen, the offspring of educated professionals, officials, and the new lower middle class accounted for roughly comparable shares of the enrollments as at the not distant University of Bonn, but the Aachen students included relatively fewer children of independent craft producers and peasant farmers and a larger percentage from laboring backgrounds.[93]

Overall, the class composition of university and technical college students in Vienna and Prague changed slowly and gradually between 1860 and 1910. Only a few of the shifts were large. As in Germany, the new lower middle class strongly increased its representation among Austrian students, roughly doubling its share in the Vienna and Prague universities and nearly tripling in Prague's technical colleges. The percentages of students in Vienna and Prague from the old lower middle class decreased slightly after 1880, but together the offspring of peasant farmers, estate managers, independent craft producers, and small and intermediate business owners still considerably outnumbered the children of petty officials, white-collar employees, and schoolteachers among the students in 1910. In the last years before World War I, the old lower middle class remained somewhat more strongly represented among university students in Vienna and Prague than in Prussia (see fig. 6). The share of the university students in Vienna and Prague who were children of the educated elites held fairly steady throughout the late nineteenth century and in 1910 exceeded by a significant margin the proportion of the Prussian university students who came from similar origins. Children of the propertied elites also had a roughly steady share of the university enrollments in Vienna and Prague between 1860 and 1910, although the percentage of Prussian university students from propertied families increased substantially between 1870 and 1900. In 1910 the share of the matriculated students in the Vienna and Prague universities who came from the propertied elites was slightly smaller than that in the Prussian universities at the same time.

The overall growth in Austrian secondary and higher education during the second half of the nineteenth century surely resulted from the general modernization of the economy, society, and the state. Still, the occupational composition of the Austrian enrollments betokened economic and social structures whose general development lagged behind the pace of change in northern and western Germany. In Prussia, economic and social development caused strong increases in the representation among university students of the propertied elites and private and public white-collar employees; taken together, these strata had significantly weaker representation in higher education in Austria's Alpine and Bohemian lands at the end of the period. Throughout the half century of growth in enrollments, the children of Austria's old lower middle class retained strong representation in higher education; and the offspring of the educated maintained a steady share of the students. As we have seen, relative to either total or school-aged population, enrollments in Austrian higher education slightly exceeded those in Germany in 1870 but lagged behind the growth in Germany's universities between 1870 and the 1890s (see table 2/3 above). The total growth in Austrian higher education after the early 1890s was sufficiently strong to catch up with Germany's by around 1910, but even then the "modern" social strata of propertied entrepreneurs and white-collar employees still had weaker representation among Austrian university students than among the Prussian. These circumstances suggest that, compared with the patterns of growth and transformation in Germany, Austrian higher education was expanding at a tempo that was somewhat faster than the evolution of its economic and social structures, even in the Alpine and Bohemian lands.

Just how progressive Austrian secondary and higher education may have become during the late nineteenth century is a different question, of course, from that of the social recruitment of the various educated professions in Austria. Those who studied in the *Gymnasien* and *Realschulen* became the pool from which probably most petty government officials and private white-collar employees ultimately came. Those who were able to go on to study in the universities and technical colleges provided the potential recruits for the higher public and private officialdom and the medical, legal, and engineering professions. Only a fraction, though, of all those who enrolled actually managed to enter the various professions.

There were numerous examples in nineteenth-century Austria of individuals who came from extremely modest backgrounds and went on to distinguished careers in the professions, politics, or the arts. Carl Friedrich Kübeck (1780–1855), who studied at the Vienna University between 1795 and 1801 and became a high imperial official in the 1840s, demonstrated what the talented and diligent son of a tailor from the Moravian town of Jihlava (Iglau) could accomplish during the early nineteenth century. Ignaz Seipel (1876–1932), Catholic churchman and chancellor of the Austrian Republic during the 1920s, was the son of a sometime cabby (*Fiakerkutscher*) and theater porter.[94] In the early twentieth century, the Czech educated elites included a host of figures from humble backgrounds, epitomized by Tomáš G. Masaryk (1850–1937), the first president of the Czechoslovak Republic. The son of a driver/coachman on a Habsburg estate in southeastern Moravia, Tomáš Masaryk managed to attend the prestigious Benedictine Schottengymnasium in Vienna, earned a doctorate in the Vienna philosophical faculty, and then taught in the Prague University. The composer and conductor Gustav Mahler (1860–1911) shared humble origins in common with many eminent Jewish artists and intellectuals in turn-of-the-century Austria. His grandmother had peddled wares in the villages of southeastern Bohemia, and his father, Bernhard, married the daughter of soap makers and managed to set up a small brandy distillery. Bernhard Mahler had little formal education, but Gustav was able to study in a *Gymnasium* in Prague, graduated and passed the *Matura* in Jihlava, and then went on to the conservatory and some university study in Vienna.

By the 1880s and 1890s, such individual success stories had already become part of a widespread mythology of upward social mobility through education. Such biographical anecdotes encouraged popular belief in advanced education as a means to achieve advancement and fed political debate about both the benefits and potential dangers of an expanding educational system. In this, Austria differed little from the other European and North American countries that carried out liberal educational reforms concurrently with the development of an industrial market economy and the consolidation of a modern class society. The litany of educational success stories was repeated in every country.

In fact, the biographical lore demonstrated only the possibility of upward mobility through education in individual cases. It offered no proof that those fortunate individuals were representative of educated professionals at large or that any large portion of the students in secondary and higher education who came from modest origins actually had successful academic and professional careers. The success stories did not mention the 50 percent or more of the entering secondary school students in Austria who did not proceed beyond the fourth year, the many others who dropped out later to pursue nonprofessional vocations, or the graduates who did not prosper in the professions for which they had prepared. In a parliamentary debate on educational policy in 1891, Tomáš Masaryk himself lamented the seeming waste of talent and effort by many students who were sons of prosperous peasant farmers in Bohemia. Such a young man might toil over studies for years in order to become an educated "gentleman" but then at age twenty-five or thirty might well find himself only an "obscure, lowly clerk and unfree man" (*ein Winkelschreiber und unfreier Mensch*).[95]

Students' social origins probably had a significant influence on whether they successfully completed their academic work and entered various professions. In the western Prussian provinces under the Second Empire between 1870 and World War I, for instance, between one-third and one-half of all the higher government officials came from educated backgrounds with another one-fifth to one-third from the propertied bourgeoisie, while two-thirds of the free professionals there came from the educated or propertied middle class.[96] There has been little comparable research on the social recruitment of the professions in Austria's Alpine and Bohemian lands, but there was clearly some self-perpetuation from one generation to the next among state officials. Hermann Bahr wrote in 1909 of the higher Austrian officials performing the role of a "second nobility" and sarcastically described the phenomenon of bureaucratic families that bequeathed "from father to son the holy mystery of the routine."[97] One partial study of the sons of higher Austrian state officials who received noble titles between 1868 and 1884 found that 58 percent of them went on to careers in the state bureaucracy with another 18 percent becoming military officers.[98]

Historians have a natural tendency to emphasize signs of change and development, but in analyzing enrollments in Austrian secondary and higher education, one should not overlook evidence of stability and continuity. As we have seen, most of the changes in the social recruitment of students in the Alpine and Bohemian lands between the 1860s and World War I were gradual. Population growth, the need for greater numbers of educated personnel to serve a developing economy and a growing public and private bureaucracy, and the increasing appetite for education among wider segments of the citizenry had powerful effects on advanced education in all Western societies during the period. Nonetheless, those forces of transformation were moderated by institutional and legal structures and older popular values about education, many of which changed only slowly.

Once Austria established its modern systems of advanced education, anyone coming to study, whatever the social background, had to meet a range of institutional expectations. The particular ages at which youth completed various requirements and moved from one level to the next provide a telling illustration. School regulations incorporated definite expectations about when a child would begin primary school and at what age he or she might go on to a *Bürgerschule, Gymnasium, Realschule,* or girls' *Lyzeum.* Stipulations were less firm about the age at which the *Matura* or *Reifeprüfung* must be passed in order to proceed on to higher education, but delays or failure carried a stigma, and there were expectations of conformity here, as well. In higher education, of course, the traditions of freedom of study allowed students latitude in when they completed their studies; but the requirements of state and doctoral examinations, admission to certain courses, diploma essays, and dissertations put at least some pressure on students to conform here, too.

One might expect that students from poorer, socially disadvantaged backgrounds would be older when they reached higher education and take longer to complete their studies, but, in fact, the requirements and expectations of the educational system enforced a high degree of conformity with regard to age. The average ages of matriculated students who were offspring of the educated elites or of white-collar employees and schoolteachers tended to be slightly lower than the average for students from the laboring strata or the old lower middle class, but the differences were remarkably small. In the sampled registration records for the Vienna University in winter 1879–80, for instance, the mean age for matriculated students from the educated strata was 20.7 years, and those from the propertied elites had virtually the same mean age, while the mean for the old lower middle class was 21.4, and for those from laboring backgrounds, 22.2.[99] One can use median ages to screen out the effect on mean ages of older individuals who returned to studies, but the median ages generally varied by no more than one year among university students from the various social classes or among the German-speaking Christian, Czech-speaking Christian, and Jewish students. Even the pioneering women in the Vienna philosophical faculty in winter 1899–1900 had a median age no higher than that for the university as a whole.[100] Among technical college students in Vienna and Prague from the four sampled semesters, the median ages for the various class, ethnic, and religious groups differed by no more than one or two years.[101]

To be prepared for entry into the educated and semieducated professions presumably required satisfying a whole range of intellectual, behavioral, and social norms beyond surmounting the various academic hurdles at the appropriate ages. The formal academic requirements and the selection processes for advanced education, of course, did much to assure that students would meet those norms by the end of their studies. Along with the educational institutions' formal curriculum, the many other lessons they taught informally and the whole social experience of education helped introduce students to the values of the educated elites, or at least reinforced the appropriate values. The discussion now turns to an examination of the social experience of students in Austrian secondary and higher education.

CHAPTER

The Social Experience of Students

The Many Paths of Academic Education

Secondary and higher education help to select and prepare youth socially for learned pursuits as well as equip them intellectually. Advanced education in late-nineteenth-century Austria was expected, of course, to transmit the specific knowledge needed in various professions. Of equal importance, secondary and higher education were also to help develop character and a more general *Bildung,* the basic intellectual abilities and broader fund of knowledge in the humanities and sciences that were considered essential to cultivation. At the same time, whether graduates eventually had successful professional careers or not, simply completing secondary school, passing the *Matura,* and then going on to a university or technical college initiated youth into a small elite group, defined both intellectually and socially. Since even as late as 1910, less than 3.1 percent of all eleven- to eighteen-year-old boys and girls in Austria were studying in *Gymnasien* and *Realschulen* and only 1.7 percent of all nineteen- to twenty-two-year-olds were enrolled as matriculated students in universities and technical colleges, advanced education remained elitist in numerical terms, regardless of the students' diverse origins (see table 2/2 above).

Whatever students' social backgrounds, it is commonly assumed that secondary and higher education contribute significantly to socializing them. Surely formal education plays a part in transmitting social and political values, but the concept of socialization as often used in discussions of education simplifies what are, in fact, complex processes of social learning.[1] Social and political values are not created or imparted by any one agency. It is extremely difficult to isolate what instruction in secondary schools, universities, and technical colleges or students' whole experience in those institutions may contribute to developing such values as distinct from the students' early experiences in family, neighborhood, and a host of other influences. At the least, one can claim that advanced education in modern societies encourages and strengthens social and political values that are acquired from a range of sources. Here, then, it is important to try to describe what, in fact, characterized the social experience of students in Austrian secondary and higher education during the late nineteenth century and to suggest what distinguished such experience from that of other youth.

Study in the secondary schools, universities, and technical colleges set students apart in many ways from their contemporaries who remained at home or entered the work force without advanced education. Graduates were distinguished by various courtesies and privileges accorded them, whatever their actual professional or financial success. The high status of holders of doctoral degrees in medieval and early modern Austria had entitled them to be addressed as "Herr, Herr" and to march in processions behind counts but ahead of knights. By the eighteenth century they were addressed as "Excellenz" commonly enough for that courtesy to be banned as part of Empress Maria Theresa's rationalizing reforms.[2] Feudal salutations for the educated disappeared during the nineteenth century, but respect for academic degrees and titles remained a part of popular etiquette. During the early and mid-nineteenth century, even young *Gymnasium* students were treated as gentlemen by porters, servants, and carriage drivers. Those who studied in Vienna's Schottengymnasium in the 1860s later recalled wearing top hats when they went into the city streets.[3] Beyond qualifying individuals for certain occupations, academic education also carried with it significant social and political privileges throughout the late nineteenth century, most notably the "one-year, volunteer" military service for graduates of secondary schools and automatic voting rights in some municipal and provincial electoral systems.

It is tempting to portray the social experience of all who passed through secondary and higher education as an initiation into the privileged circle of the educated elite and the learning of that elite's mores. In this regard one could easily cite an array of Austria's most acute observers of society and culture between 1900 and 1914, ranging from Karl Kraus and Arthur Schnitzler to Bahr, Masaryk, and Jaroslav Hašek, who criticized the foibles of professionals and bureaucrats and blamed a number of their shortcomings on the educational system. A visible segment of the university and technical college students did enjoy the life of the playboy students who appear, for instance, in some of Schnitzler's works. Nonetheless, to focus on only a fraction of all students can obscure the social realities of educational institutions that served a range of functions for a variegated constituency. If, in fact, many more students enrolled in secondary and higher education than actually completed programs of study, then those who managed to graduate and enter professions shared much of their educational preparation with many youth who never attained such positions and perhaps never expected to.

A few of the *Gymnasien,* like that of the Theresianum in Vienna and several of the Catholic *Gymnasien* in the Alpine lands, earned reputations for the elitist recruitment of their students and their graduates' unusual professional success. The *Gymnasium* in Vienna's Theresianum drew its students strongly from the nobility, higher state officials, and the propertied middle class and sent a significant number of graduates into the army officers corps and the state bureaucracy.[4] The Benedictine Schottengymnasium in Vienna and the Jesuit *Gymnasien* in Feldkirch, Vorarlberg, and Kalksburg near Vienna apparently also recruited large segments of their students from privileged strata. Even the Schottengymnasium, however, enrolled a minority of students from humble origins. In 1899–1900, for instance, it exempted from tuition nearly 7 percent of its students.[5] Even among the most highly respected *Gymnasien* operated by Catholic orders in Austria, most schools served different social functions from those of the most prestigious English "public" schools.[6] Most of the highly regarded monastery schools in late-nineteenth-century Austria—like that in Kremsmünster, for instance—were much like state schools in recruiting the majority of their students from the lower middle classes and seeing their graduates go on to a wide range of careers. Alongside the most distinguished Catholic *Gymnasien,* a few state institutions like the Akademisches Gymnasium in Vienna's inner city and the Czech Akademické gymnasium in Prague also won reputations for the unusual success of their graduates; but they, like nearly all the state schools, had socially diverse student bodies with large lower-middle-class contingents and even a few laborers' children.[7]

It is best to view secondary and higher education in Austria, like that in much of Central and East-Central Europe in the period, as serving students from a range of upper-, middle-, and lower-middle-class backgrounds along with a few from the laboring class who had a wide range of aspirations. It is difficult then to speak of modal academic and social experiences shared by most students in the institutions. The variety of goals pursued by the students and the range of school experiences among them characterized the social processes of secondary and higher education perhaps as much as anything else, and that aspect of diversity merits closer examination.

The Many Purposes of Academic Secondary Education

Austria's mid-nineteenth-century educational reformers intended the curricula of the *Gymnasien* and *Realschulen* to be demanding. Taking up the model of the Prussian neohumanistic *Gymnasium,* they expected the Austrian schools to shape each student's character and intellect.[8] The *Gymnasium* curriculum emphasized the development of intellectual discipline, with intensive study of classical languages and literature at the core: eight years of Latin grammar, vocabulary, and literary texts and six years of Greek language and literature. After the completion of the reforms in the early 1870s, the *Gymnasien* also required in all eight forms the study of grammar and literature in the principal language of instruction, geography and history, mathematics, and religious instruction according to each student's faith. In addition, there was natural history for at least four years, physics for three or more years, and introductory philosophy and logic for two years. The required subjects amounted to twenty-four or twenty-five class hours per week. Nonrequired subjects, such as a second provincial language, drawing, gymnastics, and, around 1900 in some schools, a modern foreign language, might push the total to as high as twenty-nine hours per week.[9]

Within their shorter programs of study, the *Realschulen* and the girls' *Lyzeen* also developed challenging curricula as part of their efforts to attain equal status with the *Gymnasium*. The *Realschulen* exhibited more curricular variety than the *Gymnasien* because of the greater role of provincial authorities in operating those schools, but after the early 1870s they tended to require from twenty-eight to thirty-one hours of classes per week. The Austrian *Realschulen* generally required study during all seven years of the principal language of instruction, one modern foreign language, history and geography, mathematics, religion, geometric drawing, and gymnastics along with three or four years each of natural history, physics, chemistry, freehand drawing, a second modern foreign language, and perhaps a second provincial language. The girls' *Lyzeen* offered twenty-four to twenty-six hours of instruction per week, and their programs of typically six years tended to resemble those of the *Realschulen* with the addition of music and singing but less science and mathematics.[10]

Austrian secondary schools expected long hours of study, both in class and out. One inquiry claimed that the average work-day of secondary school students in Prague around 1900 extended to more than eleven hours, including classes, homework, and any independent activities such as music practice or tutoring.[11] The actual amount of home preparation varied with the individual student, of course. Homework ran to several hours a night for many, but Ludo M. Hartmann, an Austrian Social Democratic politician and historian, recalled that in Vienna's respected Wasagymnasium around 1880 a reasonably talented student could manage with as little as one hour per night most of the time.[12]

To guide the development of self-discipline and character, the Austrian secondary schools, like their German counterparts, had the authority to enforce general regulations on students' behavior both inside and outside the institutions. The schools commonly established rules for proper dress, cleanliness, general comportment, and punctuality; and they banned the frequenting of liquor establishments, joining associations, and sometimes even the use of lending libraries.[13] Many critics of Central European secondary education around 1900 complained that while the educators' vision of *Bildung* aimed to liberate the spirit and develop each student's highest abilities, the schools' methods were often blatantly authoritarian. Functioning primarily as day schools with little of their own recreational activities, the Austrian and German secondary schools, in fact, had only limited ability to control student behavior outside of classes.[14] Still, although many infractions slipped by, the schools could invoke penalties ranging from warnings to confinement in their own lock-ups, the issuing of failing grades, or expulsion.

An authoritarian approach characterized the pedagogy as well. In Reichsrat debates on secondary education in 1891, for instance, Masaryk joined other deputies in criticizing the authoritarian character of the teaching, excessive emphasis on memorization, and the resulting neglect of independent thinking. Masaryk allowed that the Austrian schools might be a little less rigidly bound to the traditional *Gymnasium* pedagogy in the classical languages than were schools in Germany, but he argued that Austrian *Gymnasien,* in fact, were preparing future university students just as poorly in Latin and Greek as in the natural sciences.[15] Secondary school teachers in Austria, like their German counterparts, relied heavily on regular graded recitation to assure mastery of the basic material and develop discipline. In Austria as in Germany, former students filled their memoirs with complaints about tyrannical *Gymnasium* instructors who tested them daily in class about difficult points of Latin and Greek grammar, vocabulary, and translations.[16] Students remembered with special affection teachers who offered a higher ratio of lecturing to recitation.[17]

The secondary schools' pedagogy complemented what were conservative curricula in many respects.[18] The state-mandated history textbooks, for instance, treated the modern era selectively and emphasized the triumphs and accomplishments of the Habsburg Monarchy.[19] The coverage of modern literature was also limited, and Darwinian evolution was virtually excluded from instruction in the sciences.[20]

The recollections of teaching reported by former students of *Realschulen, Realgymnasien,* and the girls' *Lyzeen* were more positive than those of *Gymnasium* graduates.[21] Students claimed that the *Realschulen, Realgymnasien,* and girls' schools offered freer, more enlightened pedagogy than did the classical *Gymnasien,* although there was doubtless an element of self-justification in such estimates insofar as these schools were still widely perceived as inferior in status.[22] At least, the *Realschulen, Realgymnasien,* and girls' schools did not share the special burdens and pedagogical traditions of teaching both Latin and Greek. Also, to the extent that many of these institutions were operated by provincial or municipal authorities or by voluntary associations, perhaps some of their teachers did not feel obliged to follow all the pedagogical conventions of the state *Gymnasien.*

The *Matura* examination added to the rigors of secondary education for those who managed to complete the seven or eight years of study. The Austrian educational authorities intended this as a measure of students' overall intellectual maturity rather than of their specific achievement in every subject. In the form established after the 1860s, the *Gymnasium Matura* was administered over several days and included written translations from Latin and Greek, a translation into Latin, mathematical problems, a written essay in the language of instruction, and an additional essay if a second provincial language was taught. After the written examinations, a panel of professors from the school chaired by the provincial school inspector or his deputy administered an oral examination that might touch on any subject included in the final years of the curriculum.[23] Students who failed might repeat the whole examination after six months or one year, but only in exceptional cases could the *Matura* be taken a third time. The *Matura* introduced in the *Realschulen* after the early 1870s generally followed the model of the *Gymnasium Matura*.[24]

By most accounts, Austrian students—and their parents as well—found the *Matura* a trying experience, and as we have seen, the ministerial authorities took major steps in 1908 to moderate the rigors.[25] Still, however much the *Matura* taxed Austrian students, they did not find passing it nearly as difficult as French students, for instance, found the *baccalauréat*. More than half the French students during this period might fail the first or second part of the *bac*, but, as was the case for the Prussian *Abitur*, 90 percent or more of Austrian secondary school students who took the *Matura* passed it.[26] Failure rates for the *Gymnasium Matura* in Austria were generally higher during the 1860s and 1870s than in the 1880s and early 1890s. Between 1867 and 1876, 12 to 18 percent failed the *Gymnasium Matura* each year. After a reform of the examinations in 1878, the failure rate dropped to 9.8 percent that year; but during the 1890s, as enrollments grew rapidly, failures increased a little in some crown lands. Typically, more than half of those who failed the *Gymnasium Matura* on the first attempt passed it on the second try. Failure rates for the *Realschule Matura* tended to be slightly higher than in the *Gymnasien* during the 1880s and 1890s.[27] In Austrian secondary schools, as in Germany, most of the weeding out of students took place not through the final examination but earlier during the studies.

Beyond the fundamental fact of not having to start full-time work as early as other youth, apparently what distinguished the experience of secondary school students most was the studies as such: the classroom instruction, home preparation, and the *Matura*. Otherwise, during the Austrian students' years in the secondary schools, the great majority continued to have close daily relationships with family and community. As elsewhere in Central Europe, the preponderance of Austrian secondary school students lived with parents or other relatives or as boarders in private homes. The state schools generally did not have dormitories, although most of the older schools operated by Catholic monasteries and the Theresianum housed students.[28] The religious orders, however, were educating only a small fraction of the total Austrian enrollments during the late nineteenth century; and even monastery *Gymnasien* enrolled many day students.

The great majority of students in the state *Gymnasien* and *Realschulen,* even those who came from the countryside to study in towns, still lived in some sort of family setting, either with relatives or in households that boarded students. In regional schooling centers such as Jičín in northeastern Bohemia, České Budějovice in southern Bohemia, or Krems in Lower Austria, a student from elsewhere might board in the same household as long as seven or eight years. Some of these towns had locally known "mothers of students" who took in students over decades.[29]

Secondary school students developed various forms of sociability, but much of this activity had some connection with the schooling itself. Throughout the second half of the century, students in most schools organized their own literary circles, musical groups, and chess clubs despite widespread prohibitions on student associations. They staged poetry recitations, put on dramatic and musical performances, and produced their own literary journals. These activities were nominally independent of the classroom work and often supposedly secret, but professors knew of them and sometimes assisted. While clubs and gatherings provided some recreation, the literary and musical productions self-consciously affirmed that these youth had intellectual accomplishments that set them apart from the unschooled part of the population. In the 1880s and 1890s producing literary magazines was virtually obligatory in the student culture. One student from the *reálné gymnasium* in Chrudim, Bohemia, for example, proudly recalled how his student cohort in the early and middle 1880s produced a literary magazine with the title *Čech* and donated the meager proceeds to the Czech nationalist school support society, the Ústřední matice školská.[30] Another former student from Chrudim in the early 1890s remembered with shame the inability of his class to produce any journal.[31] Less elevated forms of student group activity included minor mischief and visits to inns. Older students seem to have frequently violated the bans on visits to liquor establishments, and even the student memoirs published in anniversary volumes of the schools often included tales of evenings in local pubs.[32]

Secondary school teachers influenced their students in various ways, and one cannot easily generalize about the example they set for future members of the educated strata. *Gymnasium* and *Realschule* teachers were to be treated with respect. In Austria they had been commonly addressed as "professor" long before an imperial decree in February 1866 sanctioned that title.[33] Some of the professors had the rigid and forbidding demeanor that was often depicted in German and Austrian popular fiction of the late nineteenth and early twentieth centuries. Still, even Pavel Eisner, the Czech translator of Heinrich Mann, commented that he never encountered anyone like Professor Unrat in his own experience. The teachers in Eisner's own *reálné gymnasium* in Prague had been supportive and approachable.[34] Some of the secondary school teachers had doctoral degrees, although the certification standards did not explicitly require this; and some wrote scholarly studies during their teaching careers. A few of these professors eventually attained teaching positions in universities or technical colleges.[35] Outside of the largest cities, secondary school teachers might enjoy high prestige in their communities; and a number played important roles in local social and political affairs.[36]

The security and relative status of teaching in the *Gymnasien* and *Realschulen* were sufficient to attract many from humble origins who wanted upward social mobility. Samplings of the secondary school teachers in the Alpine lands during the late nineteenth century show that the majority came from the lower middle class and a few even from the laboring class.[37] The feminization of Austrian secondary school teaching began only after 1900, as secondary education for women expanded and the numbers of female students in the philosophical faculties increased. Secondary teaching in the more economically advanced crown lands attracted unusual numbers of migrants from within the monarchy or from foreign lands. In 1895, for instance, more than 40 percent of the regular full-time teachers in the *Gymnasien* and *Realschulen* of Lower Austria were born outside the territory of the present-day Austrian Republic, 29 percent in Bohemia and Moravia alone.[38] The recruitment of Jews into primary and secondary teaching in Lower Austria was sufficient to evoke complaints from anti-Semites after the early 1880s.

Senior *Gymnasium* and *Realschule* professors might attain high status in their communities, but the actual circumstances of their work were not always attractive. Because of large enrollments and understaffing, teaching loads might run up to thirty hours per week.[39] New teachers generally had to serve for a period as a supplementary or adjunct instructor, hired year by year until they secured regular, long-term appointments. Between the 1860s and the 1890s such supplementary instructors accounted for 35 to nearly 50 percent of all teachers in the *Gymnasien, Real-Gymnasien,* and *Realschulen* of what is now the

Austrian Republic.[40] In the periods of greatest oversupply of applicants for permanent appointments, such as the last years before 1914, service in these ill-paid temporary positions might last from five to ten years.[41] The regular *Gymnasium* and *Realschule* professors did not receive particularly high salaries either. At the end of the century, the professors stood in the ninth category (*Rangklasse*) of state officials, along with police commissars, postal savings controllers, and managers of state forests and domains. Around 1905–6, the base pay for professors during the first five years of service was 2,800 kr. per year. By comparison, a worker in Vienna's machine industry in 1907 earned on average 1,374 kr. per year.[42] Generally after ten years of service, secondary school professors became eligible for promotion into the eighth category, and after twenty years into the seventh category, where they ranked with district administrators (*Bezirkshauptmänner*), state prosecutors, and salaried associate (*außerordentliche*) professors in the universities and technical colleges.

Graduates of Austrian secondary schools had the strongest memories about their teachers, the daily recitation, course examinations, student activities, and, not least, the *Matura.* Simply passing together through the years of study seems to have done more than anything else to bind graduates together and distinguish them as a group. University and technical students, in contrast, had little identification with a class cohort, since most had some choice about when they took particular courses and how long they took to complete their programs of study. Judging from memoirs, identification with one's graduating class in the secondary schools seems to have been strong from the 1860s onward. Those bonds supported formal associations and class reunions. On the occasion of major anniversaries for the individual schools, the directors and professors appealed to such bonds by inviting graduates to celebrations and publishing commemorative volumes filled with graduates' reminiscences. All of this activity by and for graduates, of course, emphasized the shared experience of those who completed the whole seven- or eight-year program of studies and strengthened the ties among them. Easily overlooked were the larger numbers of former students who had participated in much of the same classroom experience but did not graduate.

Austrian secondary schools had high attrition rates throughout the period between the 1850s and World War I. The precise rates varied from one institution to the next, among types of schools, and among the various crown lands. Over the whole period, between 5 and 10 percent of new students left the schools before the end of the first year; and even among students who completed the final year, between around 5 and 10 percent failed to pass the *Matura*.[43] The first decades after the introduction of the new *Gymnasium* curriculum and the *Matura* saw the highest attrition rates: only 25 percent of all those who began *Gymnasium* studies in 1849–50, for instance, passed the *Matura* in 1857. In spring 1878, only 28 percent succeeded in passing the *Matura* of all those who had entered first-year classes in *Gymnasien* and *Realgymnasien* in 1870–71.[44] The persistence rates of secondary school students rose during the 1880s, but still a little less than half of all those admitted to the first form of the Moravian *Gymnasien* between 1887–88 and 1895, for instance, completed the fourth form, and only 22 percent eventually passed the *Matura*.[45] The *Realschulen,* which experienced significant declines in enrollments due to the poor economic conditions of the 1880s, had significantly higher attrition rates than the *Gymnasien* in that period: of all those who began the first form in Austrian *Realschulen* in autumn 1883, only 23 percent were enrolled in the seventh form in spring 1890, and only 19 percent of the original cohort passed the *Realschule Matura* in spring and summer 1890.[46]

Academic failure, economic pressures, and migration were only the most obvious reasons for high attrition rates in the secondary schools. Throughout the late nineteenth century, class enrollments showed a sharp falling off after the initial three or four forms. At the end of the 1884–85 school year, for instance, only one-third of all students in Austria's *Gymnasien* were enrolled in the upper four forms. At the same time, only one-sixth of all students in *Realschulen* were enrolled in their upper three forms. At the end of the 1909–10 school year, only 35 percent of all students in Austria's men's *Gymnasien* and *Realgymnasien,* 33 percent in the women's *Gymnasien,* and 29 percent in the *Realschulen* were enrolled in the upper forms of those schools.[47]

There are no systematic analyses of the students who dropped out of secondary schools, but many of those who left after the first three or four forms may not have ever intended to complete a full program of studies. In practice, the *Gymnasien, Realgymnasien,* and *Realschulen* served more varied educational purposes beyond developing academic *Bildung* and preparing youth for higher studies and professional careers. Many youth simply wanted to complete the last three or four years of the required basic education in a secondary school, if they could, rather than in a *Volksschule* or *Bürgerschule*.[48] As the director of the state *Gymnasium* in Opava (Troppau), Silesia, reported to the Ministry of Religion and Instruction in 1880, even if many students might not progress beyond the first four forms of a *Gymnasium* or *Realschule,* their parents preferred those schools because "one learns more there." That same year a report from the provincial governor's office in Trieste noted that where the majority of the local population spoke languages other than German, some parents wanted their children to attend the lower forms of an academic secondary school in order to learn proper German.[49] In many districts during the 1860s and 1870s and perhaps later, middle-class and lower-middle-class parents who sent their sons to secondary schools also had them begin learning trades in case their studies did not go well. Some parents sent children to the *Gymnasien* and *Realschulen* who were already destined for trades simply for them to learn a little more until they were older and physically strong enough to begin serious work.[50]

In many cases, youth enrolled in the lower forms of the academic secondary schools simply to gain qualifications for various white-collar jobs or admission to a vocational school. They might attend a *Gymnasium* or *Realschule* for several years only to go on to a military cadet school (*Kadettenschule*), higher commercial academy (*Handels-Akademie*), or advanced craft school (*Gewerbeschule*).[51] In some cases, by completing the lower forms of a *Gymnasium* or *Realschule* and then an advanced vocational school, one could qualify for "one-year, volunteer" military service just as did graduates of the academic secondary schools.[52] Many of the students enrolled in the lower forms of the secondary schools might have little interest or ability for some of the more demanding academic subjects, and professors might face pressure from parents to pass those students along so they might go on to vocational schools. One veteran Austrian educator commented that in those circumstances a *Gymnasium* teacher of Greek was "the unluckiest man in the world."[53]

With growth in the network of schools and the expansion of enrollments after the mid-nineteenth century, *Gymnasien* and *Realschulen* came to serve the functions of providing a general secondary education along with preparation for university and technical college studies. This, in part, motivated the calls by conservative politicians and officials after 1880 to restrict secondary school enrollments. At the turn of the century, observers like the sociologist Ehrlich saw this as reason to reaffirm the academic goals and standards of the *Gymnasien* and *Realschulen* and to increase the number of *Bürgerschulen*.[54] Others in Austria, as in Germany, concluded that the existing segmented system of secondary education represented a bad compromise between popular needs for general education and preparation for higher studies and called for a unified secondary school instead.[55]

The growing enrollments in Austrian *Gymnasien* and *Realschulen* during the late nineteenth century surely represented increases in the numbers of both students who hoped to go on to higher education and professional careers and those who had lesser ambitions. Many of the latter did not appear in the lists of graduates, and some may not have been invited to the schools' anniversary celebrations; but in most of the institutions they accounted for the majority of all who ever enrolled. Whatever the high academic goals for secondary education, in practice the *Gymnasien* and *Realschulen* had to serve these students as well as those who went on to higher education. Even while the secondary schools were supposed to be offering a demanding academic curriculum leading to advanced study in the universities or technical colleges, the lower forms also provided many students with only an extension of primary education and preparation for advanced vocational training. This multiplicity of purposes had to affect the instruction that all students received just as the diversity of students' social origins and goals had to affect the social experience of all who enrolled. Those who graduated and passed the *Matura* may have been a small elite in numerical terms, but less of their educational and social experience in the secondary schools than one might expect actually separated them from youth who were not going to join the privileged ranks of the learned professions or the higher public and private bureaucracy.

The Everyday Realities of Higher Education

The popular image of university and technical college students in late nineteenth-century Austria envisioned a privileged elite that enjoyed a comfortable life of dissipation and only occasional serious study while preparing for lives as respected professionals and officials. As young gentlemen destined to join the educated middle class, the male students enjoyed the relative comforts of one-year, volunteer military service instead of the normal conscription. Their adult lives would be graced, presumably, by academic and professional titles. Reality confirmed this image for a number of the students, but, in fact, most who entered the universities and technical colleges hardly enjoyed lives of comfort and gentility during their studies. Many did not complete doctoral degrees or all the state examinations in their programs. Large numbers of students stayed only a few years and went on to a range of semiprofessional or at best lesser professional careers that called for only some higher education. Certainly, many of the pioneering women students who wished to enter professions before World War I faced highly uncertain futures.

There are no systematic studies of attrition and graduation rates among students in Austrian higher education during the late nineteenth century, but a few soundings suggest that half or more of those who entered the most popular fields of university study did not complete final degrees.[56] In his May 1888 speech to the lower house of the Reichsrat, Minister of Religion and Instruction Gautsch lamented the flooding of secondary schools and universities with youth who did not finish programs of study and who, in his view, were wasting their resources and the state's by enrolling. The ministry's statistics showed that during the 1880s only 62 percent of those who began studies in the law faculties took the initial state examination in legal history, and then only 43 percent of the original number remained for the second state examination in jurisprudence. Allowing for the larger number of foreigners who studied in the medical faculties, Gautsch claimed similarly high attrition rates for medical students. Among the secular faculties, only in the philosophical faculties were a majority of the matriculated students taking all the state examinations and finishing their programs of study.[57]

Later, in the mid-1890s, several of Austria's largest medical faculties reported on completion rates for their students as part of the deliberations on the reform of medical education. In this period the majority of those who matriculated in the larger medical faculties eventually completed degrees, but many required extended periods to do so. In the Vienna medical faculty, out of a sample of 100 students who began studies in the middle and late 1870s, only 13 had managed to pass the first part of the doctoral examinations on schedule during the third year of study and only 37 had passed that section by the fifth year. Only around two-thirds of those who began medical studies in Vienna in the middle and late 1870s had completed the doctorate by the end of fifteen years after their initial matriculation.[58] In Prague, out of the 233 who began studies in the Czech medical faculty in 1884, only 31 percent had earned the doctorate by 1891; and in seven years' time fully 37 percent of the original cohort had not even passed the first part of the doctoral examinations.[59]

Some of the attrition from individual universities may have resulted from students simply transferring to other institutions. No comprehensive statistics are readily available on transfer rates, but it appears that such student "migration" was limited in late-nineteenth-century Austria. Distinctive Austrian requirements for state examinations and professional certification discouraged Austrian students from studying in other European countries or Hungary. Within Austria the relatively small number of institutions of higher learning gave students fewer choices than in Germany, for example; and Galician students who considered leaving Krakow or L'viv or Czech students who might leave Prague would have to accept education in their second or third language. The Vienna University, as the largest and most distinguished of the Austrian institutions, surely had some attraction for transfers by German-speaking students; but a survey of 968 matriculated and nonmatriculated students in the Vienna University's three secular faculties in 1910 showed that less than 10 percent had transferred from elsewhere, a little more than half of these from other Austrian institutions.[60]

Apparently, only a fraction of those who attended the Austrian universities and technical colleges intended to earn final degrees. Medical practice in the late nineteenth century required a doctorate, and law students had to complete the doctoral degree to become practicing attorneys or to qualify for certain higher state positions. Otherwise, simply passing one or several of the state examinations in law and public administration might qualify an individual for many lesser positions in governmental and private offices. Between 1859 and 1889 students might earn a doctorate of pharmacy in the Austrian medical faculties, but the great majority of students in this field took only a master's (*Magister*) degree, which required no more than four semesters' study of chemistry and botany in a philosophical faculty and sufficed for normal professional practice.[61] The preponderance of students in the philosophical faculties went on to careers in secondary school teaching, for which they needed to complete four years of university study and pass the state examinations for teacher certification.[62] Only a minority of the students in the philosophical faculties who were interested in research, teaching in higher education, or advancement as secondary school educators completed a doctorate.[63] Similarly, the majority of students in the various Catholic theological faculties and in the Eastern Orthodox theological faculty in Chernivtsi were preparing for careers as priests, for which they did not need a doctorate. To qualify for Catholic ordination, for instance, one needed merely to study in a theological faculty or seminary for four years and pass examinations. During the second half of the nineteenth century, only a small minority of the theology students in the Austrian universities earned the doctorate.[64]

It is difficult to assess attrition rates for the technical colleges in terms comparable to those for the universities. Technical college enrollments were more sensitive to economic downturns, and completing full programs of study conferred fewer advantages in many technical professions than in medicine, law, or state administration. Throughout Central Europe the processes and standards for professional certification in engineering and the applied sciences were still developing during the late nineteenth century. The Austrian technical colleges' comprehensive examinations and diplomas carried relatively little weight until the Ministry of Religion and Instruction approved a formal system of state examinations in 1878, and, as we have seen, the technical colleges only began to grant doctoral degrees after 1901.

University and technical college students' erratic study habits and irregular attendance of classes contributed much to the public image of them as carefree young gentlemen. During the late nineteenth century, lecture courses accounted for most of university instruction, except the latter stages of medical studies and advanced research training in the philosophical faculties. Lecture courses predominated in much of the technical college curriculum as well.[65] Student attendance of lectures was often poor, but efforts to compel students to attend might conflict with the traditions of freedom of study. Law students had the reputation for the worst attendance. In a 1910 survey of students in the three secular faculties of the Vienna University, just under half (49.7 percent) of the respondents from the law faculty claimed to attend lectures regularly. Medicine had the best attendance with 74 percent of the respondents claiming to attend regularly, but medical students faced greater pressures from the demanding curriculum and the supervision under which they worked in laboratory and clinical courses.[66]

Absence from lectures did not result simply from students' indolence or search for more entertaining pastimes. As enrollments grew, many lecture courses became terribly overcrowded. The law faculties faced the greatest problems in this respect, particularly those in Vienna and Prague, which had colossal enrollments after the mid-1890s. Law students found, however, that they could skip many of the lectures and still pass the examinations using textbooks and printed lecture notes.[67]

Beyond overcrowded lecture halls and calculations of what was required to pass, students' need to support themselves with part-time work ranked as the most common reason for poor class attendance.[68] The best available measures come from 1910, but they indicate the conditions among students as enrollments leaped up in the last years before World War I. Three-fifths of the surveyed students in the Vienna University's three secular faculties in 1910 reported that their parents fully supported them. One-fifth received only partial support; and one-eighth, nothing from their parents. Nearly 40 percent of the respondents had to work to help support themselves. Overall, parental support made up around two-thirds of the Viennese students' incomes, but the students' own work provided another one-fifth. The great majority of the students who worked, 27 percent of all the respondents in the survey, earned income by the method favored by Central European university students since the early modern era: tutoring younger students. There was much opportunity for such work in larger cities like Vienna and Prague, and the Vienna University students who tutored in 1910 worked for an average eleven hours per week.[69] Another 10 percent of the surveyed students in the Vienna University had various jobs in office work, translation, teaching classes, or occasionally manual labor.[70]

While tuition was relatively low, the total costs of a university or technical college education in Austria's larger cities presented a formidable burden for less well-to-do students. As we have seen, somewhat more of the Vienna University's students came from the propertied and educated elites than was the case among Prague's German and Czech university students or among technical college students in either city. The 1910 Vienna survey reported that the university students' average monthly income of 119 kr. slightly surpassed their average monthly expenses, and over 80 percent of the respondents indicated that they had no debts. Interestingly, though, among the Viennese university students with debts, those who were fully supported by their parents tended to owe more money than those whose parents supported them only partly. This suggests that some of the better-situated students may have been indulging in greater personal comforts or more numerous entertainments.[71] In contrast to the Vienna University students, a survey of Prague's German University and German Technical College in spring 1910 found that among those students who came from elsewhere to study in the city, 71 percent had monthly incomes of less than 100 kr., and fully 46 percent were below the threshold of 81 kr. that the director of the survey reckoned as a minimum subsistence level.[72] Average income levels among the Czech university and technical college students in Prague could only have been lower given the larger proportion of Czech students who came from modest commercial, craft, and farming backgrounds.

The 1910 surveys suggest that while many Austrian university and technical college students enjoyed some relative material comfort, a significant minority faced serious economic strain. The simplest way for students to economize, of course, was to live with family members, and 53 percent of the respondents to the 1910 survey of the Vienna University's secular faculties resided with parents or other relatives.[73] The institutions of higher learning in Prague apparently drew larger proportions of their students from outside the metropolis than did those in Vienna, and a smaller fraction of the students in Prague were able to live with parents or close relatives.[74] The costs of housing and food could weigh heavily on students living on their own. During the late medieval and early modern periods, various foundations and religious charities had provided poorer university students with housing and food; and in the late nineteenth century new foundations and independent associations arose that offered free meals to poor students.[75] There were few sources of subsidized housing, however. The Catholic dioceses and religious orders provided housing to few students beyond those in the theological faculties. The universities and technical colleges themselves generally had no dormitories during this period, and only after the 1890s did independent charities and foundations in Austria's various centers of higher education begin to operate some student residences.[76]

The great majority of university and technical college students who could not live with relatives had to rent rooms. The cost of lodgings could be high in Vienna and Prague, and the scattering of students' rooms around these cities could impede their contacts with other students and reduce further the attendance of lectures.[77] The quality of housing varied enormously, and respiratory maladies were rife among students throughout this era. With such living conditions, the social experience of students in Austria's larger cities could be alienating for many.

University and technical college students, in fact, quite often had only limited, distant relations with their professors. The full professors (*Ordinarien*) were figures of considerable distinction, appointed by the emperor from ranked lists of nominees that the individual faculties sent up to the Ministry of Religion and Instruction. During the late nineteenth century, the Austrian state classified full professors in the universities and technical colleges in the sixth category of the bureaucracy, which put them on a par with police directors in some larger cities, *Finanz-Räte* in the Finance Ministry, and senior inspectors in the tobacco and postal administrations. The full professors directed the various institutes in the universities and technical colleges, controlled the granting of doctoral degrees and the *Dozentur,* and elected the deans of faculties and the university rectors. The smaller number of salaried associate (*außerordentliche*) professors had much less authority and ranked in the seventh category of the state bureaucracy along with district administrators (*Bezirkshauptmänner*), *Polizei-Räte,* and *Ober-Kommissäre* in the Finance Ministry. The many unsalaried docents had no real authority in the granting of diplomas and degrees or in the governance of the universities and technical colleges. Until 1874 none of the docents received any salary beyond what they earned from students' instructional fees (*Kollegiengeld*). Thereafter, the Ministry of Religion and Instruction began to provide small salaries for a few docents in specialties where they were particularly needed.[78]

At the end of the century, the number of instructors in the Austrian universities and technical colleges was often low relative to the number of students and the range of subjects offered. In winter 1899–1900, for instance, a total of 96 full professors, 58 associate professors, 202 docents, and 142 other assistants, adjuncts, and teachers carried on all the teaching for the Vienna University's 6,320 matriculated and nonmatriculated students. The other universities had significantly smaller complements of professors: Prague's German University had only 58 full professors in winter 1899–1900; and the Czech University, only 59. At the same time, the Vienna Technical College with its 2,080 matriculated and nonmatriculated students had only 27 full professors, 25 associate professors, 27 docents, and 43 assistants and adjuncts.[79] The system of fees encouraged the professors to serve on many examinations and to have large enrollments in lectures. Between 1850 and 1898, when the ministry changed the regulations for instructional fees, those fees provided substantial supplementary income for the most popular lecturers, amounting to 1,600–1,800 kr. per year for some in the Vienna University.[80] Many full professors also earned moneys from the sale of their own textbooks.[81]

The organization of instruction and research in higher education often minimized direct dealings between students and the professors until students were far along in their studies. Students enrolled in large lecture courses might speak with their instructors only infrequently until they took course examinations. Seminars and medical clinics provided for closer contact, but depending on their specialty, students might take few, if any, seminars until late in their programs. At that stage, students who aspired to careers in research and scholarship might well develop closer relations with professors, but such students accounted for only a small fraction of the total enrolled. The rest were naturally less interested in current research than in broader education in their fields and preparation for professional practice. Even in seminars or clinics, students might find many full professors to be remote figures, preoccupied with their own research or service on governmental and academic commissions and perhaps surrounded by assistants. The conflict between the practical professional interests of many students and the scholarly goals of professors only increased as the Austrian universities and technical colleges followed the German institutions in becoming centers of specialized research. Indeed, the academic specialization of professors, docents, and assistants increased steadily in nearly all fields during the late nineteenth century. The full professors became more and more engaged in directing institutes, laboratories, and clinics that were devoted to narrowly focused research activity.[82] Outside the lecture halls, professorial offices, and laboratories, many of the larger student organizations tried to overcome the distance between students and instructors by inviting the participation of the latter, but the student associations had to compete with many other demands on the attention of the teaching personnel.

Full professors in Austrian higher education ranked as high state officials, and they expected to be treated with respect by both students and the general public. The central government and the emperor honored a number of the most distinguished university and technical college professors with appointment to the House of Lords in the Reichsrat.[83] The social origins of the university and technical college professors have not yet received thorough analysis. Apparently here, too, there was considerable diversity in socioeconomic background as well as in religion and ethnicity. Overall, though, a larger proportion of the teaching personnel in higher education than in the secondary schools seems to have come from the educated or propertied elites. A study of ninety-nine persons named as full professors in the Vienna medical faculty between 1848 and 1900, for instance, showed that fully 60 percent had fathers or guardians who were educated; 20 percent were public officials and military officers, 10 percent physicians, 10 percent Protestant clergy, and 10 percent teachers in secondary and higher education. The sons of craft producers accounted for 20 percent, and those of merchants/small business owners and of peasant farmers, only 10 percent each.[84] In Germany the offspring of educated professionals and higher officials accounted for a comparable share, as much as 65 percent, of all those appointed to teach in universities between 1864 and 1890, although German universities drew only around 20 percent of their instructors from lower-middle-class backgrounds.[85] Compared with Austrian secondary school teachers, the higher status and incomes of university and technical college professors may simply have attracted relatively more recruits from propertied or educated families; and for some, family resources helped through the extra years of study and often long apprenticeship required before a salaried position was attained in a university or technical college. On the other hand, the recruitment of instructors for higher education could not have been altogether different from that for the secondary schools because an appreciable portion of the professors in the philosophical faculties and technical colleges taught initially in secondary schools.[86]

Relative to their numbers in the total population, Protestants and Jews were strongly represented at the end of the century among professors in the technical colleges and the secular university faculties in

Vienna and Prague. Emperor Francis Joseph, for his part, was more willing to appoint as professors Protestants and Jews than nonbelievers of whatever origin. In 1911 Albert Einstein had to assuage such concerns about his religious beliefs in order to be appointed to a chair in the German University of Prague, and the determined nonbeliever Paul Ehrenfest could not be named to succeed Einstein after the latter left Prague in 1912.[87] Jewish professors were most numerous and most renowned in the Austrian medical faculties, which, as we have seen, also tended to have the largest share of the Jewish university students until after 1900. Around one-tenth of those named to be professors of medicine in Vienna between 1848 and 1900 were Jews who had not renounced their religious affiliation.[88] Smaller numbers of Jews were appointed in the faculties of philosophy and law. The German University of Prague also had significant numbers of Jewish professors and docents, although the numbers of Jewish instructors were lower in the other universities and technical colleges of the Alpine and Bohemian lands. Still, reaching the highest academic ranks remained more difficult for Jews than for Catholics; and, as in Germany, Jews were more numerous among Austria's associate professors and docents than among the full professors.[89] As in other areas of higher state service in Austria, some Jewish scholars found it advisable to convert in order to advance their teaching careers.[90] Conversion, though, did not spare them from the attacks of anti-Semitic politicians who complained about Jewish influence in higher education.

Taken together, students' living conditions and much of the instruction in higher education provided little basis for students to form close social bonds. Beyond the crowded lecture halls, only the seminars, laboratories, and clinical courses offered opportunities for students to form relationships among themselves as part of their academic work. With few other possibilities, students in Austrian higher education, as in Germany, had to look to their own organizations and informal relationships to provide for sociability and the articulation of group values.[91]

Student Organizations and Social Bonds in Higher Education

Allowing for the differences in Austrian political development, educational institutions, and the ethnic mix of the population, student organizations in Austria took many of the same forms as in Germany.

Around each university and technical college arose a myriad of student associations, ranging from large, inclusive reading societies, charitable groups, and religious associations to smaller bodies for particular academic disciplines and exclusive fraternities devoted to drinking and dueling. The large associations provided for conviviality and a sense of group belonging through a host of social activities and lectures. The smaller corporate fraternities (*Verbindungen*) offered their members a more intimate camaraderie supported by elaborate rituals, pledging and hazing, distinctively colored caps and sashes, group drinking, dueling, and lifetime connections through networks of "old boys" (*alte Herren*). Unfortunately, the social and political history of Austrian student corporations and societies during the late nineteenth century has received only limited scholarly attention in recent decades.[92] Here, one can only sketch the general evolution of student associations in order to suggest their significance in students' lives.

Modern student associations began to develop on a large scale in Austria during the mid-1840s as the old absolutist regime visibly weakened. Earlier in the nineteenth century, the government had prohibited student associations and forced underground any attempts to organize bodies like those existing in the German states.[93] Through encounters with German university students, Austrian students were acquainted with the student organizations being developed elsewhere in Central Europe; and they tended to follow German models when it became possible to establish their own associations in the middle and late 1840s. The Austrian government again banned student organizations after 1849, but with the weakening of controls in the late 1850s, such groups re-emerged. The Austrian student associations that developed thereafter took all the forms that were familiar in the German universities. Under the constitutional laws of 1867, Austrian university and technical college students won rights of association; but they were still barred from any formal political groups, and the rectors and academic senates had broad powers to regulate all organizations and meetings.[94]

By far the largest and most inclusive student organizations in Vienna and Prague during the late nineteenth century were various "reading and speech societies" (*Lese- und Redevereine*). These bodies ranged in size from several hundred students to over one thousand. Where both a university and technical college existed in the same city, the reading societies typically accepted students from both; and their members included students from the corporate fraternities as well as independent students. To signify the students' sharing in an academic community with their teachers, many of these societies also welcomed professors and docents as members. In the Alpine and Bohemian lands, the student reading societies accepted members of all religions until the emergence of radical German nationalism and anti-Semitism in Austrian student life after 1878. The reading societies provided for a broad range of individual and group activities. The largest of them built up sizable libraries and had comfortable facilities that were a welcome escape from students' often cramped and shabby lodgings. Members could go to the societies' rooms for reading, conversation, card games, music, and lecture programs.

The student reading societies had an obvious interest in maintaining large memberships and staying within the laws and academic codes, but they were easily drawn to politics. Inevitably, many of these organizations divided along ideological and ethnic or religious lines. When they strayed into political activity, they faced intervention by the academic authorities and the police. The first important student reading society in Vienna was the Akademischer Leseverein, founded in 1861. In subsequent decades divisions among the students and punitive actions by the authorities caused repeated schisms in the organization, changes of name, and dissolutions. By 1877 Vienna had separate student reading societies for German liberals, German nationalists, and the more conservative "German-Austrians." Later, the students of the Vienna Technical College developed their own organizations. The reading societies, like many student groups, may have exaggerated their claims of membership; in 1878 Vienna's three major organizations reported a total of nearly 1,560 student members along with a large representation of professors and docents.[95] In that year, the Vienna University and Technical College together had fewer than 5,100 matriculated and nonmatriculated students.[96]

Student organizations in Prague divided into separate German and Czech bodies during the latter phases of the 1848–49 upheavals: the German liberal students' Reading and Speech Hall (the Lese- und Redehalle der deutschen Studenten) and the Czech Academic Reading Society (Akademický čtenářský spolek).[97] The German students' Reading Hall grew to nearly 840 members in the mid-1880s, equal to around half of all matriculated and nonmatriculated students in the German University and German Technical College at the time. German liberal elements led the Reading Hall throughout the pre-1914 era, and the body lost about half its members between 1891 and 1892, when the anti-Semitic German nationalists seceded and founded their own reading society, the Germania.[98] The Czech Academic Reading Society at its peak in the mid-1870s drew the majority of the Czech university and technical college students in Prague, with a reported membership of more than 1,400 in 1873.[99] The Academic Reading Society supported the more conservative Old Czech Party during the 1860s and 1870s but came under the influence of the more democratic and militantly nationalist Young Czechs after 1887. The police dissolved the Academic Reading Society and seized its property in 1889 after it sent an allegedly provocative letter of congratulation to Parisian students on the opening of the Sorbonne's new building.[100] Other organizations, however, soon took the place of the Academic Reading Society.

Alongside the large and relatively inclusive reading societies, a number of small, more selective student fraternities developed in each center of higher education. German-speaking students in Vienna, Prague, Graz, and Innsbruck followed the established models of student corporations in the German states; and various *Landsmannschaften, Burschenschaften,* and *Corps* appeared in all those cities after the late 1850s. Initially, in Austria, as in Germany, the *Landsmannschaften* may have been dedicated primarily to simple sociability and maintaining ties of common regional origins, the *Burschenschaften* to German nationalism and libertarian traditions, and the *Corps* to a more conservative patriotism and elitist traditionalism.[101] Still, in Austria as in Germany, the forms and functions of most of these bodies came to resemble each other increasingly between the 1860s and 1880s. Each such group, counting between perhaps ten and thirty active members at any one time, offered members an intense camaraderie through the ritualized pledging of new members, upholding of honor codes, group singing, drinking fests, and, for many fraternities, corporately organized dueling with swords.

Initially during the 1860s and 1870s, most of the Austrian fraternities tended to draw members on the basis of common regional origins. Later, the shared rituals, group discipline, and carousing became the most important binding ties. Each fraternity had its favored pub where members gathered regularly. The costs of membership, sword instruction and equipment, drinking, and other entertainments could be significant. From an early date, critics of the student fraternities complained about their dissipation, debauchery, and violence. In their defense, Dumreicher, for instance, argued that, during his days in the Viennese *Burschenschaft* Silesia in the early 1860s, economic constraints and a distaste for engaging in very much dueling deterred many students from excessive carousing and fighting.[102] Other former students had more negative recollections about the fraternities, particularly in regard to the heavy drinking and neglect of studies.[103]

The number of corporate fraternities in each city varied greatly. In Vienna during the early 1870s, for example, eight student fraternities adhered to the local dueling code (*Paukkomment*): Silesia, Markomannia, Saxonia, Alemannia, Germania, Olympia, Liberta, and Bruna. By the late 1870s there were more than thirty fraternities in Vienna, counting both the dueling and nondueling bodies.[104] Just how many students from each institution of higher learning belonged to fraternities at any one time and which social strata were represented in the various groups still awaits systematic study.

The student fraternities in Austria's Alpine and Bohemian provinces took much from the model of associations in Germany, but Austria's distinct traditions, population, and politics caused the Austrian groups to develop some different customs. Many of the Austrian dueling fraternities, for instance, preferred different rules and weapons from those used in Germany. As in Germany, though, committed Austrian Catholics and some liberals objected to organized physical violence. During the 1860s liberal sentiments tended to dominate among Austrian university and technical college students, but avowedly Catholic groups grew stronger from the 1870s onward.[105] Catholic efforts to combat student dueling in Germany and Austria increased after 1891 when Pope Leo XIII addressed a letter to all German-speaking bishops condemning such practices.[106]

Competing national loyalties created sharp fissures in Austria's student associational life from the 1860s onward. At the outset in the late 1850s, some student fraternities in Prague, for instance, accepted Czech as well as German-speaking members. The division of public life in Prague into separate Czech and German spheres during the 1860s soon affected student associations.[107] In Vienna also, many of the first student fraternities in the late 1850s and early 1860s included Magyars, Czechs, and other ethnic groups along with German-speakers, and Protestants and Jews along with Catholics.[108] In that same period, a *großdeutsch* liberal German nationalism found considerable support among Austrian students. After the mid-1860s, however, German nationalist sentiment became a divisive factor in Austrian student organizations.

With the unification of Germany, German national loyalties became more problematic for German speakers in Austria. By the late 1870s many erstwhile liberal nationalist student associations had divided between moderately liberal or conservative German-Austrian bodies on the one hand and increasingly radical German nationalist groups on the other. By the middle or late 1880s, a number of the latter adopted an extreme Pan-German ideology based on racial nationalism. Some of these radical German nationalist groups resembled the Association of German Students (Verein deutscher Studenten) and other such bodies in Germany and had contact with them.[109] German nationalist students came into repeated conflict with students who supported the German liberals, the Catholic conservatives, the emerging Christian Socials, and the Social Democrats, and with students from Austria's other ethnic groups.

Beginning in the 1860s, students from Austria's other ethnic groups organized their own equivalents of the ethnic Germans' *Landsmannschaften* and fraternities. Czech students had a full array of associations in Prague by the early 1870s, and student organizations developed in Vienna representing most of the monarchy's major ethnic groups. In response to the growing exclusion of Jews from the ethnic German fraternities during the 1880s and 1890s, Jewish nationalist groups set up their own student associations.[110] The organizations of all the various ethnic groups adopted Latinate names, established rituals of pledging, wore distinctively colored caps and sashes, and indulged in a fair amount of carousing. Ethnic Polish and Magyar fraternities took up corporate dueling, and after the early 1880s Jewish dueling fraternities arose, such as Kadimah in Vienna and Barissia in Prague.[111] Czech student associations, however, tended to reject corporate dueling and some of the other customs that they identified with the hated ethnic German student fraternities.[112]

Whatever their ethnic, religious, or ideological stripe, student organizations provided their members with social networks and a sense of belonging that was often sorely lacking in the rest of their experience in higher education. Those social connections might engender lasting friendships and help to advance professional careers later on. Many leaders of student organizations also went on to play prominent roles in political parties across the spectrum in the monarchy and in the successor states.

At the end of the nineteenth century, Austrian student associations were notorious hotbeds of political radicalism, particularly for populist radical democracy and extreme nationalism. A number of historians have argued that for many students this expressed a generational revolt against the liberalism that was dominant among their parents between the late 1850s and the early 1880s.[113] Various individual biographies support the notion of generational conflict, but many Austrian students who gravitated to populist democracy and radical nationalism *after* the mid-1880s were only articulating what many in their parents' generation were already thinking and, within a few years, expressing at the ballot box as well.[114] Parents, police authorities, and professors often voiced their disapproval of student fraternities' mayhem, but far from expressing individual nonconformity, much of those groups' activity in Austria, as in Germany, demonstrated regulation and discipline, particularly in the dueling and even in the compulsory drinking.[115] Indeed, contemporary critics of the fraternities complained about their authoritarianism and the extreme conformity they expected of their members.

Obviously, the fraternities and other student associations could only provide group bonding and articulate group values for their own members. Student associational life could not give any one cast or direction to the social experience of university and technical college students or to the development of their values. The great reading societies often attracted large numbers of students, making up significant fractions of the total enrollments; but those large organizations by their nature generally could not impose much social or political uniformity on their members. Students might have more intimate and binding relationships with the fraternities or regional associations, but these were much smaller groups that apparently involved only limited segments of all the students. Moreover, an individual student could choose among a wide array of such organizations that competed with each other for members. Thus, the social and political experience of students in Austrian higher education during the late nineteenth century was characterized by much the same pluralism and diversity—in terms of academic discipline or professional interest, ethnicity, religion, and political ideology—that they would face during their adult lives.

Advanced Education and Nation-Building: The Case of the Czechs

Secondary and higher education had an important additional dimension for students from historically disadvantaged ethnic groups who rejected assimilation with the Germans in the Alpine and Bohemian lands or with the Poles in Galicia: contributing to nationalist efforts to overcome subjugation and build new, fully articulated social structures for their groups. During the late nineteenth century, leaders of nationalist movements among the Czechs, Slovenes, Ukrainians, Croatians, and Romanians were determined to end assimilation with the dominant nationalities of those who received advanced education and entered professional ranks. Many, if not most, of the nationalist leaders in this era had received advanced education themselves, even if it was often in a language other than their mother tongue. They treated secondary and higher education as critical mechanisms for forming their own national middle classes and for advancing the whole process of nation-building, and most agitated unceasingly for the expansion of education in their national languages.[116]

As we have seen, among the historically disadvantaged ethnic groups, Czechs had the greatest success during the late nineteenth century in winning a complete system of education in their mother tongue. Ukrainians and Romanians in the Carpathian lands and Slovenes, Croats, and Serbs in Carniola and the Adriatic provinces failed to achieve their own institutions of higher education before World War I, but all these groups used what secondary education they had in their mother tongues along with the higher education available in German, Czech, or Polish to build significant bodies of the educated who were committed to their national causes.[117] The Czech educational system in the Bohemian lands was much admired by the other Slavic groups, and nationally conscious Czech educators took pride in the fact that the other Slavic peoples sent students to Prague and Brno. The Czechs' attainments became a paradigm for the historically disadvantaged peoples of Austria and Hungary of what secondary and higher education could contribute to nation-building.

It was widely believed in Austria that advanced education aided nation-building processes not only by producing new professionals, higher officials, and educated employees, but also by shaping students' social and political consciousness. During political crises, German liberal and nationalist politicians pointed to the Czech educational institutions as centers of radical nationalist agitation. Indeed, many of the major initiatives in Czech nationalist politics found leadership and early support among professors and students in Prague's Czech University and Czech Technical College, and many of the nationalist disorders in Prague during the 1890s and after 1900 began with demonstrations involving Czech students along with their German counterparts.[118] Ethnic German political leaders frequently accused Czech teachers and professors of preaching nationalist ideology and inculcating anti-Habsburg and anti-German sentiments in their students. Fearing nationalist demonstrations, the Ministry of Religion and Instruction repeatedly banned observances in the Czech schools in honor of Czech national luminaries.[119] An authoritarian administrator such as Count Franz Thun-Hohenstein, who served as Bohemian governor in 1889–96 and 1911–15 and as Austrian minister-president in 1898–99, ordered tighter control and crackdowns on Czech nationalist activity among students.[120]

There can be no doubt that students and professors in Czech secondary schools and higher education articulated Czech national allegiances and helped propagate nationalist political beliefs. German-speaking students and professors did much the same, particularly in Bohemia, Moravia, and Styria, as did their Polish counterparts in Galicia. Within what were Austrian state schools with curricula and textbooks approved by the Ministry of Religion and Instruction, students and teachers were able to express national loyalties and nationalist political values. Austrian law prohibited students from participating in overtly political activities or organizations, but academic authorities and the police could not stop all political discussion by students or professors.

The state *Gymnasium* originally founded by Albrecht von Waldstein (Wallenstein) in 1622 in Jičín, northeastern Bohemia, offers many illustrations of Czech students' nationalist political engagement during the late nineteenth century. The Czech writer and politician Antal Stašek (1843–1931), for instance, recalled the strong Czech nationalism and anti-Austrian sentiments shared by students in Jičín in the late 1850s.[121] By then majorities of both the students and teachers were Czech, and in 1866–67 Czech was formally established as the principal language of instruction.[122] From the 1860s onward, students, particularly in the higher forms, were well informed of Czech nationalist cultural and political activities in the local region and in Prague. The students also knew what roles their professors played in various Czech nationalist organizations. In the early 1890s students in Jičín were eagerly reading the *Časopis českého studentstva* (Magazine of Czech students), published in Prague, despite official bans on its circulation in secondary schools. That and other lines of communication kept the Jičín students apprised of Czech politics and of the activities of Czech students and professors elsewhere.[123]

In the secondary schools that taught in Czech, obligatory demonstrations of Austrian patriotism competed with expressions of Czech national sentiment. Later, the dissolution of the monarchy and the founding of independent Czechoslovakia colored recollections of such matters; but throughout the late nineteenth century, many Czech students and their professors apparently had a strong sense of participating in the national movement and helping to build the Czech nation through their academic work. All students in state schools were required to intone the Austrian anthem in chapel services and on special occasions, but Czech students later remembered most vividly the lusty singing of favorite Czech religious hymns and national songs. They liked to claim that hardly any of them sang the Austrian anthem.[124]

At the beginning of the twentieth century, the Czech *reálné gymnasium* on Křemencová Street in Prague's New Town, for example, was known for its progressive curriculum and its support for Czech national causes. In 1908 the school celebrated in properly dignified fashion the sixtieth anniversary of Emperor Francis Joseph's coming to the throne, but the major speaker for the occasion chose to address the students and professors on "Czech Literature during the Reign of Emperor Francis Joseph." In the course of the speech, he did not even mention the monarch.[125]

Czech professors in secondary and higher education provided models for their students through their own engagement in Czech cultural and political activities. With the rapid advance of Czech-language instruction after the late 1850s, Czech textbooks were needed in many fields. Directors and students in Czech schools pointed proudly to their own professors who authored the first Czech textbooks in their specialties or defined new Czech terminology.[126] Czech students in both secondary and higher education inevitably shared in controversies about Czech history and literature that erupted among Czech scholars during the late nineteenth century. Many courses on Czech literature in the secondary schools, for instance, included the medieval Czech manuscripts purportedly discovered by the philologist Václav Hanka in 1817–18. Austrian German scholars had long questioned the authenticity of those manuscripts, but in 1886 a ferocious controversy broke out among Czech intellectuals on this question.[127] Judging from memoirs, not only Czech university students but also many secondary school students followed the debate closely, believing that it touched on the national honor.[128]

Throughout Austria's constitutional era, educators could be elected to town councils, provincial diets, and the Reichsrat. Particularly in the 1860s and 1870s, when there were not many Czech entrepreneurs and lawyers, a sizable number of Czech professors in secondary and higher education served as representatives. From Prague's first Czech *Realschule/reálka* alone, no fewer than five professors won seats in the Bohemian Diet in the first elections held in 1861.[129] Between the 1860s and the beginning of World War I, the emperor also named various senior Czech educators to the Reichsrat's House of Lords, along with a number of Czech artistic and political figures.

There can be little doubt that student organizations and the political activity of professors contributed significantly to the expression and propagation of national loyalties for all of Austria's nationalities. By providing advanced academic education to a relative few, the secondary schools and institutions of higher learning helped give their students a sense of belonging to a select elite that was expected to play a leadership role in society. For youth from the historically disadvantaged ethnic groups, the pursuit of advanced education involved them in efforts to emancipate themselves and their peoples from domination by other groups. Nonetheless, one should not overestimate the impact of secondary and higher education in propagandizing for the nationalist causes or in winning new supporters.

A thorough inquiry into how youth in late nineteenth-century Austria acquired their social and political values lies beyond the scope of this study, but some cautious generalizations can be offered. Advanced education was neither the sole nor, in all probability, a primary instrumentality for inculcating national loyalties and building support for nationalist politics among students. Students' experience in the educational institutions functioned only as part of a complex of social, economic, and political interactions, which all worked to encourage, shape, and articulate group identification and political allegiances. Social scientists generally believe that children in modern societies begin to develop basic group identities and political loyalties at early ages within the family and immediate community and continue to develop such concepts and values through a range of experiences and relationships during adolescence and early adult life. Formal education is seldom the principal instrumentality for transmitting social and political values to youth but works largely to supplement and reinforce the development of those values, which derive, in fact, from a variety of sources.[130] In late-nineteenth-century Austria, most children who came to a secondary school at age ten or eleven had probably already begun to define some sense of their place in society and a basic political orientation. What students learned in secondary and higher education surely helped them to strengthen and articulate further their basic commitments and develop more elaborate concepts of ideology and current issues. Nonetheless, the students' experiences in education worked along with many other influences in shaping their social and political values.

Youth in late-nineteenth-century Austria often made political commitments even before they attended a single class in a secondary school or higher education. The decision to attend an academic secondary school together with the choice of school was often laden with nationalist political freight in ethnically mixed regions where national loyalties were contested. For Czechs in the Bohemian lands or Slovenes in Carniola after the 1860s or 1870s, attending a German-language secondary school might no longer mean inevitable assimilation with German speakers. Nonetheless, where parallel educational tracks developed with different languages of instruction, parents had to make a decision of some nationalist political moment when they chose a school for their child. By the same token, when Czech community governments pushed to convert local schools to Czech-language instruction or they established new Czech schools, or when Slovenes tried to do similarly, those communities were also making commitments to use education in the service of nation-building even before a single class convened.

If secondary and higher education did transmit any political values, the educational experience probably served largely to elaborate and reinforce beliefs that were already held by students or were being propagated and developed simultaneously through their families, peer groups, and communities. Much of the communication of social and political values in schooling took place, in fact, between students themselves, whether in informal encounters, student associations, or student journals. As Jarausch has emphasized with regard to university education in imperial Germany, students were responsible for a significant portion of their own cultural, social, and political formation through the informal or "hidden" curriculum that was propagated through student group life.[131]

Commenting on the cultural and social functions of university education in modern France, the sociologists Pierre Bourdieu and Jean-Claude Passeron have also stressed the importance of the values that students bring with them from their previous experiences and commitments. In the view of Bourdieu and Passeron, even though universities are well equipped to transmit values and the ultimate function of higher education is to provide for the propagation of certain values, universities often do little directly to constrain the acceptance of cultural norms. Many of the students' basic values are already largely defined by their prior experience and their own aspirations to enter the ranks of the educated: "In reality, contrary to appearances, the university always preaches to the converted."[132] In the case of Czech students during the late nineteenth century, one can say that most of those who opted for Czech-language secondary and higher education rather than German-language institutions brought with them to the Czech schools commitments to a Czech identity and aspirations to join the ranks of educated Czechs already formed in their families and immediate communities.

Obviously, Austria differed from Germany or France in that Austria's ethnic and religious pluralism and inter-group competition added special dimensions to the social functions of secondary and higher education. In Austria, advanced education became segmented into parallel tracks, each operating with its own language of instruction, with complete systems of German, Czech, and Polish secondary and higher education and with secondary education provided in Slovene, Ukrainian, Romanian, Italian, and Serbo-Croatian as well. Those parallel educational systems served the formation of educated elites for their respective ethnic constituencies. In the crown lands with mixed populations, advanced education became an important instrument in the growing struggles for status and power among the developing national elites. The social product of Austrian secondary and higher education was thus a differentiated one in ethnic and national terms, but it was variegated in other ways as well.

As we have seen, students brought with them to the secondary schools, universities, and technical colleges a broad range of academic and career aspirations. In this regard, advanced academic education was probably no different in Austria from that in other Western societies during the late nineteenth century, but that heterogeneity in the purposes and functions served is often underestimated. Many studies of modern educational systems focus too narrowly on the production of *graduates* from secondary schools and institutions of higher learning. The curricula and comprehensive examinations are generally designed principally for students who will complete full programs of study. In fact, though, the majority of students who enrolled in Austrian secondary schools during the second half of the nineteenth century never completed the *Matura;* and German and French academic secondary education also had high attrition rates. In addition, large portions, a majority in many cases, of all who matriculated in the Austrian universities never earned final degrees but rather settled for passing one or several state examinations. These circumstances should not be dismissed simply as a matter of students' academic failure or as otherwise undefined "attrition." The low completion rates resulted to a great extent from the circumstances of students enrolling in the *Gymnasien, Realschulen,* universities, and technical colleges with a variety of educational and professional goals, many of which did not require a diploma or degree.

It is easy enough to point to the learned doctors in medicine, law, higher government offices, industrial research, and the higher academic ranks or to the engineering graduates in industry in Austria during the late nineteenth century and to talk about a narrow educated elite produced by secondary and higher education. In fact, though, the educational institutions that produced these individuals served a broad and diverse constituency that was not restricted to those who earned diplomas. Students who completed full programs of study shared much of their educational experience with many others who departed with more modest academic accomplishments to a range of less distinguished pursuits in commerce, industry, or public service. The educated professional and bureaucratic elites may have played important roles in society and government, but if secondary and higher education was responsible for a significant part of their recruitment and formation, even those educational processes, at least until the final stages, did much less than might be supposed to separate those who joined these elites from others who pursued less exalted goals. The youth who came to advanced education had such widely divergent aspirations and went on to such a range of careers in the highly stratified educated and semieducated segments of the workforce that we must conceive of the social product of advanced education as heterogeneous in this sense as well. The ethnic, national, and religious divisions among Austrian students only compounded the social and occupational heterogeneity in the product of secondary and higher education.

World War I interrupted the processes of development in Austrian education.[133] The government called to military service many university and technical college students, a number of their professors, and many secondary school teachers as well. As the war went on, growing numbers of older secondary school students volunteered for service. In some districts the government had to convert school facilities to use as hospitals, barracks, or supply depots. The loss of staff and facilities, budget cuts, and fuel shortages forced significant reductions in instruction. On an emergency basis the educational authorities cut requirements for examinations to enable students to complete their programs of study sooner.

The Ministry of Religion and Instruction put off consideration of any further reforms of secondary education during the war, although some educators and members of the public continued to criticize the classical *Gymnasium* curriculum and the persisting inferior status of *Realschulen*. Under popular pressure, additional *Gymnasien* converted to *Realgymnasien*. The coexistence of the various types of boys' and girls' academic secondary schools and calls to matriculate women in law faculties, technical colleges, and other institutions of higher learning were only a few of the many unresolved issues that imperial Austria's successor states had to face after 1918.

In Austria, as in much of Europe during the late nineteenth century, growth in the learned professions, in the educated public and private officialdom, and in a range of other semieducated occupations encouraged popular hopes for upward mobility through education. In Austria such aspirations for upward mobility worked along with the broader effects of economic development and the growing competition among the various ethnic groups to fuel sharply increasing popular demand for secondary and higher education. That growing popular appetite, the associated changing social recruitment of students, and changes in various academic disciplines and professions all challenged the highly regulated state educational system to transform itself rapidly. In Austria, the ministerial authorities and educators at times resisted the forces of change emanating from society and the economy, and the institutional structures and established culture of education aided such resistance. The relationship between the societal pressures for change and the schools' traditions and institutional structures in shaping the recruitment of the educated elites merits some concluding reflections.

CONCLUSION

Education, Society, and the State in the Late Nineteenth Century

As Austria modernized its secondary and higher education after 1848, enrollments grew remarkably, but that expansion paralleled developments in much of Western and Central Europe. In France the rate of secondary school attendance relative to the school-aged population increased by 53 percent between 1854 and 1911. Between 1876 and 1911, enrollments in French public higher education more than tripled relative to the population aged nineteen to twenty-two years.[1] In Prussia secondary school enrollments relative to the school-aged population increased by nearly 40 percent between 1870 and 1911. Throughout Germany, the number of matriculated university students relative to all twenty- to twenty-three-year-olds increased two and one-half times between 1870 and 1911.[2] The different structuring of British secondary education and spotty statistics make it difficult to draw direct comparisons with Britain for secondary education, but British higher education stood out as an exception to the pattern of strong growth in Western and Central Europe. Enrollments in British universities relative to the school-aged population lagged significantly behind the French and German levels throughout the late nineteenth century.[3] Attendance in Austrian academic secondary schools, in fact, grew faster than in the Prussian schools during much of the period, more than doubling relative to the eleven- to eighteen-year-old population between 1870 and 1910. The doubling of matriculated university students relative to all nineteen- to twenty-two-year-old youth in Austria between 1870 and 1910 more closely approximated the rate of growth for Germany's university enrollments, but the quadrupling of Austria's matriculated technical college students relative to the eighteen- to twenty-two-year-old population clearly exceeded the growth rate for technical colleges in Germany (see tables 2/1, 2/2, and 2/3 above).

The great expansion in enrollments in secondary and higher education during the half century before World War I represented a major transformation in European education. The numbers and size of institutions increased significantly, and curricula were renovated to meet the needs of changing professions, developing academic disciplines, and a widening audience for advanced education.[4] There was a basic alteration in the relationship of advanced education to society as new social elements gained access and the social product of the schools became larger and more highly differentiated in its training and subsequent occupations. Such multifaceted changes make it difficult to explain the precise causes and dynamics of the educational transformation.

In most Western societies the expansion and development of secondary and higher education resulted from complex processes involving population growth, economic development, advancing professionalization, changing government policies, and institutional factors within the educational systems themselves. Unprecedented demographic growth, the breakdown of the old corporate society, and the rise of market-based industrial economies and new state services increased the demand for educated professionals and for educated or semieducated administrators, managers, and employees. Heightened geographic and social mobility encouraged aspirations for secondary and higher education and for professional careers among segments of society that formerly lacked access to such pursuits. In addition, rising income levels enabled more people to meet the costs of advanced education.

The connection seems inescapable between modern demographic and economic development and the expansion of all modes of education. Nonetheless, in many Western countries, including Austria, the development of advanced education during the late nineteenth and early twentieth centuries often displayed an irregular rhythm that was not simply synchronous with the principal waves of demographic and economic growth. Swings in the balance between the supply of new graduates and demand for them in individual professions often had their own timing. In a sophisticated analysis of enrollments in German higher education from the mid-nineteenth century to World War II, Hartmut Titze has emphasized the irregularity of growth and argued for the importance of processes within the educational system itself in causing cycles of shortage, expansion, and oversupply of graduates for particular professions.[5] Ringer, C. Arnold Anderson, and some other historians of education have stressed the institutional, cultural, and political factors that they see as buffering the impact of demographic and economic forces on secondary and higher education and making possible, as Ringer puts it, a "degree of independence from the economy."[6] The experience of Austria and a number of other Western societies, however, suggests that, in the long term, population growth, economic development, and urbanization did foster increased demand for educated professionals, officials, and employees in general and expanding enrollments in secondary and higher education.[7] Over the short and medium terms, though, political mechanisms, popular values and customs, and institutional factors often mediated between demographic or economic forces and the educational systems. Insofar as central governments have had far-reaching authority to regulate and operate advanced education in most of continental Europe during the modern era, political mechanisms have been able to influence strongly educational development and expansion over shorter spans of time, moderating and sometimes countering the effects of demographic and economic change.

The principal waves of expansion in Austrian secondary and higher education between the 1850s and World War I generally coincided with periods of strong economic growth. Since this simultaneity was not accidental, one can hardly consider the growth processes in education as independent of the economy. Few good social and economic analyses are available for the various professions in Austria, but the boom conditions of the 1850s, 1860s, and early 1870s seem to have expanded employment opportunities in a range of industrial and commercial pursuits, the free professions, and government service and stimulated a broad increase in demand for advanced education among the upper and lower middle classes. The government strongly supported capitalist development in this period and aided the process by modernizing the systems of secondary and higher education. Although the central authorities were not eager to expand enrollments during the early 1850s, they contributed to growth later in that decade and more decidedly in the 1860s and 1870s by opening new secondary schools and adding to the numbers of programs and professors in higher education. While much of the impetus for educational development between the 1850s and 1870s came from the government and leading educators, pressure for change also came from society at large. The central government initiated the general modernization of the educational system and undertook institutional expansion, but increasing popular demand for advanced education drove much of the growth. That rising demand was manifested in rapidly swelling enrollments, which often outran the development of facilities. Community and provincial governments clearly responded to pressures from the populace and various economic interests when they established new secondary schools and expanded the technical colleges. Economic growth, of course, aided the expansion of education by increasing tax revenues and the popular ability to meet educational costs. Agricultural depression and a commercial and industrial slowdown between the mid-1870s and the early 1890s reduced the pace of educational expansion, but a new wave of economic growth began in the mid-1890s and with it an explosion in the numbers of students throughout secondary and higher education.

Still, if population growth and economic development alone had been the fundamental determinants of educational expansion, one would have difficulty in explaining the disjuncture between Austria's continued lagging behind Germany in relative population growth and in per capita national product and Austria's ability to catch up with the rates of secondary school attendance in Prussia by 1910–11 and to keep pace with the rising university enrollments relative to the school-aged population throughout Germany for much of the period between 1870 and World War I. The population in the territory of the German Empire increased by 83 percent between 1861 and 1910, compared with an increase of only 57 percent in the Austrian half of the Habsburg Monarchy between the censuses of 1857 and 1910. With 28.5 million inhabitants in 1910, Austria had less than half Germany's population.[8] The average annual percentage growth in Austria's gross national product may have matched Germany's after 1870, but the legacy of Germany's faster growth rates between 1830 and 1870 caused German per capita production to stay well ahead of Austria's. In 1913, the per capita Austrian gross national product stood at only 57 percent of Germany's; the figure for the territory of the later Austrian Republic was a little over 90 percent of Germany's in 1913.[9] In the last years before World War I, just over half of Austria's self-supporting population was still engaged in agriculture and forestry, with less than one-fourth in all areas of manufacture, while less than two-fifths of Germany's employed were in agriculture, forestry, and fishing.[10] For Austria to develop its systems of secondary and higher education so rapidly during the second half of the nineteenth century despite the slower rates of demographic and economic growth than in Germany, other factors must have also played important parts.

Indicative of this are the eddies one finds in the course of educational expansion that were at least partly autonomous from the broad economic trends. Those fluctuations showed the effects of political initiatives and changing popular values as well as the buffering of the educational system from short-term economic circumstances by the institutions and traditions of education itself. Poor economic conditions clearly retarded the expansion of education in the late 1870s and 1880s but could not stop it. After the financial crash of 1873, the founding of new secondary schools slowed; but total secondary school enrollments still managed to increase by one-seventh between 1875 and 1880. Relative to the growing eleven- to eighteen-year-old population, enrollments in secondary schools declined slightly between 1880 and 1890; but the total number of enrolled students still increased by 8 percent in the decade. While technical college enrollments declined because of the economic conditions in the 1880s, the numbers of university students increased substantially both in absolute terms and relative to the nineteen- to twenty-two-year-old age group (see table 2/3 above and table 2 in the appendix). Slowed industrial growth and depressed conditions in agriculture and commerce during the late 1870s and 1880s discouraged study in the *Realschulen* and technical colleges that would lead to careers in engineering, applied science, and technological fields; but those same conditions encouraged shifts to *Gymnasium* and university education that might lead to legal or medical practice, public or private bureaucracy, and teaching. Enrollments in the Austrian medical faculties, for instance, declined during the late 1870s in reaction to the overcrowding early in that decade but then rose strongly again in the 1880s despite the straitened business conditions (see table 2 in the appendix).[11]

Weak conditions in the general economy could slow the increase in total enrollments in the short run and cause shifts of students from one segment of secondary or higher education to another, but so also could excesses of new graduates seeking positions in various professions. Surpluses could occur during periods of general economic expansion as well as in economic downturns. In state service the supply of new candidates from the secondary schools and universities grew sufficiently between the 1850s and the 1880s to reduce sharply the numbers of uneducated persons in the lower bureaucratic ranks. Indeed, educational requirements for governmental employment tended to rise in tandem with the growing numbers of *Gymnasium* graduates and law students during the second half of the century, with some of the most significant moves toward higher qualifications coming in periods of economic recession and the greatest oversupply of educated job-seekers.[12] Between the 1890s and 1914, some regions saw cyclical swings as shortages of secondary school teachers gave rise to increased numbers of students in the philosophical faculties and led to surpluses of new candidates for teaching posts. Still, short-term surpluses of educated job-seekers could not reverse the stronger general trend during the late nineteenth century of rising popular aspirations for advanced education and for careers in the various educated and semi-educated callings.

In the face of persistent growth in popular demand for advanced education from the mid-nineteenth century onward, the Austrian central government found that it had diminishing powers to control the rising enrollments. The educational authorities were increasingly conscious of this after 1880. It was relatively easy for the central and provincial governments to help open the gates by expanding the institutional networks in the 1860s and 1870s, but official efforts to limit the opening of new secondary schools thereafter could not prevent the numbers of students from continuing to rise. Attempts during the 1880s and 1890s to stiffen admissions standards for the *Gymnasien* and *Realschulen* and to divert some youth to vocational education also failed to stem the growth in secondary school enrollments. The new wave of rapid growth in secondary and higher education after the mid-1890s forced the ministerial authorities to expand teaching staffs and existing facilities even if they were loath to open new institutions.

In Austria, as in Germany, the numbers of students relative to the school-aged population ballooned in both secondary and higher education after around 1895. That trend signified important qualitative changes in advanced education and in popular attitudes toward it that went beyond simple responses to economic growth and increased employment opportunities. As access broadened, the middle-class and lower-middle-class population and, more gradually, the responsible authorities changed their views about the purposes of secondary and higher education. The admission of women to the philosophical and medical faculties around 1900 and the efforts to raise girls' secondary schools toward equal status with the boys' schools, for example, represented changes in basic notions about the target audience for advanced education. As enrollments expanded, *Gymnasien* and *Realschulen* functioned even more than previously as multipurpose secondary schools, not merely as preparatory schools for students headed for the universities and technical colleges. Officials in the Ministry of Religion and Instruction might try to resist these tendencies, but between the mid-1890s and 1914 they increasingly bowed to public pressures by streamlining programs and requirements in secondary and higher education rather than stiffening them. Members of the public and some educators criticized the hallowed curriculum and pedagogy of the classical *Gymnasien* as outmoded and demanded greater equality of status for the different types of secondary schools. Austria's *Realschulen* did not gain an eighth form to win parity with the *Gymnasien* before World War I, but the new *Realgymnasium* that the ministry approved in 1908 could send graduates on to the universities with knowledge of Latin and a modern language in place of Greek. At the same time, the technical colleges moved toward more equal status with the universities; the ministry authorized them to grant their own doctoral degrees in 1901. The technical colleges attracted a flood of new students in the period after the mid-1890s so that their share of all enrollments in Austrian higher education grew rapidly, greatly surpassing the proportion in Germany.[13]

Economic development and each social group's specific economic circumstances surely contributed to the changes in representation of Austria's various ethnic and religious groups in advanced education during the late nineteenth century, but factors of popular culture, political mobilization, and simple geography were also at work. German speakers owed their continuing overrepresentation among students in secondary and higher education to their long-standing social, economic, and political advantages over the other ethnic groups. The Alpine and Bohemian lands, where the German population resided in greatest numbers, also had the oldest and densest networks of educational institutions; and those regions continued to enjoy significant institutional advantages through the late nineteenth century. Nonetheless, among German-speaking peasant and craft families in Upper Austria, Carinthia, and Styria, for instance, slower economic transformation, the survival of traditional social values, and greater distances to educational institutions than for residents of Lower Austria, Bohemia, or Moravia limited the enrollments.

The Czech population in Bohemia, Moravia, and Silesia greatly increased its representation in advanced education from the mid-nineteenth century onward, expressing a strong belief in education as a means for achieving individual advancement and the emancipation of the whole Czech nation from domination by German speakers. The

Czech national movement's mobilization of the Czech population for political and social action contributed directly to the efforts to expand Czech-language instruction at all levels and to increase Czech enrollments in secondary and higher education. Still, the strength of the national movement and the eagerness of the Czech public to pursue advanced education also owed much to the vigorous development of modern agriculture, industry, and commerce in the Bohemian lands, which dissolved traditional social relations more rapidly there than in many parts of the Alpine and Carpathian provinces.

The contrast was telling between the strong, rapid advance of Czechs in Austrian secondary and higher education and the slower progress of Slovenes and Ukrainians, for example. By 1870, the Czech share of all secondary school enrollments, measured by students' mother tongue, approximated the Czech share of the total Austrian population; but even as late as 1910 the enrollments of Slovene-speaking students in both secondary and higher education still stood far below the Slovene percentage of the Austrian population. The Slovene national movement had many goals similar to those of the Czechs, but until 1900 the Slovene movement remained much weaker. German-language instruction still predominated in Carniola's secondary schools in 1900 despite the Slovene majority in the local population and Slovene strength in the provincial diet. Slovenes faced continued control by German speakers over local government and secondary education in southern Carinthia and much of southern Styria and ethnic Italian control in many of the cities in the maritime lands of Görz, Istria, and Trieste. The Slovenes had smaller numbers than the Czechs, but their slower political and educational progress also resulted from poorer economic conditions and slower development in much of their territories and the Slovenes' persisting concentration in peasant agriculture, crafts, and wage labor.[14] Although Ukrainians greatly outnumbered the Slovene population in Austria, they faced many similar circumstances with regard to advanced education. Economic backwardness, the dominance of Polish-language instruction in eastern Galicia and German-language instruction in Bukovina, and the persistence of traditional social values all worked to keep Ukrainian enrollments in secondary and higher education well below the Ukrainian share of the total population until World War I.

Growth in the numbers of Polish-speaking students in Austrian secondary and higher education was second only to that of Czechs among the non-German nationalities during the second half of the nineteenth century. In 1910 Polish-speaking enrollments relative to total population surpassed the rates for German and Czech speakers. Here, though, segments of the Polish-speaking population in Galicia increased their demand for advanced education largely in the absence of significant economic development. Galicia had some of the worst poverty in all of Austria, and the province saw minimal industrialization until petroleum, mining, and textile production began to advance at the very end of the nineteenth century.[15] Between 1890 and 1914, more than two million emigrated from Galicia to escape the economic conditions. Through 1880 enrollments in Galician secondary schools relative to the school-aged population were among the lowest of any Austrian crown land, but they rose significantly at the turn of the century. Advanced technological education had little attraction given the province's economic circumstances, but Galician youth generated strong demand for university education, particularly those who reported Polish as their mother tongue in the registration records. In 1880 the number of Galician-born university students relative to the nineteen- to twenty-two-year-old population of the province already surpassed the rates for Silesia, Carniola, and Styria. In 1910, relative to school-aged population, Galicia and small Bukovina led all Austrian crown lands in the numbers of enrolled university students native to each province (see table 2/6).[16]

The numbers of Polish university students relative to the total Polish-speaking population grew with particular speed around 1900 (see table 4/3). By 1910 the Polish-speaking share of total Austrian enrollments significantly exceeded the Polish-speaking share of the total Austrian population, although around one-sixth of those Polish-speaking university students were Jewish and around one-eighth of the total were citizens of the Tsarist Empire. The Polish-speaking students also included some of Ukrainian origin who registered as Polish speakers. Still, enrollments of indigenous Polish Catholics were clearly growing at the turn of the century. Middle- and upper-class Polish Catholics faced the contradictory circumstances of a relatively good political position under the Habsburg crown but poor agriculture and commerce in Galicia, minimal industrial development, and gradually rising economic and social competition from the Jewish and Ukrainian populations. Under such conditions, university education, particularly preparation for traditionally esteemed careers in state service or legal practice, offered possibilities for protection of status to threatened upper-class Polish Catholics and security or upward mobility for those from intermediate and lower strata.[17]

Members of Austria's Jewish and Protestant religious minorities also looked to secondary and higher education during the late nineteenth century as a means of social advancement. Both these groups had suffered official persecution and social disadvantages during the early modern era. To a great extent both groups had survived by finding various economic niches, whether in petty commerce, services, and some minor crafts for Jews, or in craft production, entrepreneurial functions, and farming in isolated districts for the small Protestant population. In the 1780s Protestants won religious toleration and Jews, somewhat improved legal status; but the reform and expansion of secondary and higher education during the 1850s and 1860s came simultaneously with the granting of nearly full religious equality to Protestants and the lifting of the last restrictions on marriages, residence, and occupations for Jews. Austrian Jews were eager to escape the poverty and insecurity of small commerce and craft activity that dominated their old existence in the ghettos of the Alpine and Bohemian lands and in the Jewish towns and villages of the Carpathian provinces. Advanced education offered people who had only limited capital the possibility of white-collar employment and, for some, a learned profession in an era when economic development was increasing demand for office personnel and professional services and squeezing traditional petty commerce and craft activity. Jewish youth flocked to secondary schools and higher education as soon as they had the opportunity, and throughout the era up to World War I, Jews were significantly overrepresented in Austrian secondary and higher education relative to their share of the total population.

During the early nineteenth century Austria's Protestant minority tended to enjoy better economic conditions than did Jews, but Protestants' historic experience also motivated them to use education to achieve greater economic and social security. At the end of the 1850s Protestants had a share of university and technical college enrollments between two and three times larger than their portion of the total population, and they continued to be overrepresented in higher education throughout the late nineteenth century. The disproportionate presence of Protestants in the technical colleges and in the universities' medical and scientific programs probably derived to a great extent from Austrian Protestants' concentration in certain areas of craft manufacture and industrial entrepreneurship.

Compared with Protestants and Jews, Austria's Eastern Orthodox minority reaped fewer advantages from the expansion of secondary and higher education during the late nineteenth century. Up to World War I, indigenous Eastern Orthodox Christians remained underrepresented in academic secondary schools, universities, and technical colleges relative to their share of the population. Poverty, persisting traditional social values, greater distances to educational institutions, and often the lack of instruction in their native tongues all limited enrollments for the various Eastern Orthodox groups. Eastern Orthodox Christians were better represented in the educational institutions of Bukovina than elsewhere, perhaps because the authorities made special efforts to develop schooling in that small, remote territory, trying to make it an outpost of good Austrian administration and civilization. Enrollments of Ukrainians and Romanians, whether Uniate Catholics or Eastern Orthodox, increased in Bukovina's secondary and higher education at the end of the nineteenth century despite the predominance of German-language instruction. In 1909 the sociologist Ehrlich was moved to complain that local politicians were responding to the strong growth in the numbers of Bukovina's graduates from secondary and higher education in that province by creating new bureaucratic positions to employ them.[18]

Beyond trying to explain patterns of growth, studies of educational development in modern societies have been concerned with the degree to which various social elements have had access to education and whether formerly disadvantaged groups have won any greater representation as educational systems have developed. For Austria, the strong increases after the 1850s in the percentages of the school-aged population enrolled in secondary schools, universities, and technical colleges and the growing representation of the non-German ethnic groups and the Protestant and Jewish religious minorities offer compelling evidence of broadening opportunities. During the late eighteenth century and again in the 1820s, the Austrian government took steps to reduce enrollments in secondary and higher education. The Austrian reformers of the late 1840s and 1850s adopted much of the early-nineteenth-century German model of academic secondary and higher education, which presumed a limited target audience of the intellectually able and motivated. The new curricula were not designed for so-called *Brotstudenten,* who pursued advanced education mainly to prepare for an occupation. Such students, in fact, remained a significant presence in Germany's secondary and higher education throughout the nineteenth century as Austria's expanding systems of secondary and higher education took in large numbers of youth whose families lacked either education or wealth and were hoping for upward mobility through schooling.

During the late nineteenth century, Austria's *Gymnasien, Realgymnasien,* and *Realschulen* tended to recruit students broadly from the middle-class and lower-middle-class strata, particularly in the initial forms. Academic secondary schools in Germany during this era also drew large numbers of lower-middle-class students, and in Austria's Alpine and Bohemian lands two-thirds or more of the secondary school students came from families in small commerce, craft production, independent farming, teaching, and public or private white-collar employment. Some children of wageworkers made it to the Austrian secondary schools and even to higher education, but overall, children of laborers and of the poorest agricultural elements, particularly from more remote areas, remained weakly represented in the *Gymnasien, Realgymnasien,* and *Realschulen* relative to their population.

Offspring of the propertied and educated, of course, found it much easier than poorer youth to reach the secondary schools, universities, and technical colleges and to remain longer in those institutions. Despite broadening access during the late nineteenth century, advanced education in Austria, as throughout Central Europe, still helped to perpetuate social advantages for certain strata from one generation to the next. Sons and, after the turn of the century, a few daughters of well-to-do property-owners, large entrepreneurs, educated officials, and professionals accounted for larger shares of the Austrian university students than of the secondary school students. This was particularly true for matriculated German-speaking Catholic students in the Vienna and Prague universities, among whom children of the propertied and educated accounted for half or more between 1860 and 1910 (see table 9 in the appendix).[19]

At the same time, though, the expansion of Austrian education after the mid-nineteenth century offered increasing access to university and technical college education for youth who did not come from comfortable German-speaking Catholic families. The percentage of matriculated students from lower-middle-class origins remained strong in higher education in Vienna and Prague during the half century after 1860, while the share of the total school-aged population who were enrolled in Austrian universities more than doubled and that in the technical colleges quadrupled. Among all German-speaking Christian university students in Vienna and Prague during the period, between one-third and one-half of all the matriculated students came from the lower middle classes (see table 9 in the appendix). Much larger shares of the students from some of the other ethnic groups and the historically disadvantaged religious minorities came from lower-middle-class families: typically 60 to 70 percent of all the matriculated Czech Christian and Jewish university students in Vienna and Prague after 1860 derived from the lower-middle-class strata. Only between 4 and 10 percent of all matriculated students in the Vienna and Prague universities were children of wageworkers, but those figures still greatly exceeded the less than 1 percent of the total that was common in the Prussian universities during this period. Compared with university students, equal or even larger percentages of the matriculated technical college students in Vienna and Prague during the late nineteenth century, irrespective of ethnicity and religion, came from lower-middle-class and laboring-class families (see tables 11 and 12 in the appendix). To gauge any more precisely whether Austrian higher education was actually giving increased relative opportunities to students from poor lower-middle-class and working-class families requires further research on a wider array of the universities and technical colleges and some accurate measure of enrollments relative to the school-aged population for each major occupational and class grouping.

The differences between the socioeconomic origins of students in the Vienna and Prague universities and the recruitment of university students in Prussia at the beginning of the twentieth century seem to reflect more than anything Austria's lag behind northern Germany in overall economic development and in the accompanying transformation of class structures. The size of the propertied upper middle class grew appreciably in Germany with advancing industrialization, and offspring of the propertied surpassed those of the educated among Prussian university students in the 1890s. In the Prussian universities the numbers of students from the new lower middle class may not have kept up with the growth in their share of the school-aged population, but by 1911–12 they surpassed the numbers of students from the old lower middle class. In contrast, the Vienna and Prague universities in 1910 drew a smaller proportion of their matriculated students from propertied origins than did the Prussian universities overall and a significantly larger share (28 percent compared with 21 percent in Prussia) from the families of educated professionals and educated higher public and private officials. The matriculated university students in Vienna and Prague in 1910 still included a slightly larger percentage from the old lower middle class than from the new lower middle class, while the percentage of the latter was more than ten points lower in Vienna and Prague than in the Prussian universities. It was the stronger representation of the new lower middle class in the Prussian universities around 1900 that pushed the overall lower-middle-class share up even higher there than in Vienna and Prague. In 1911–12 more than 60 percent of the Prussian university students came from the lower middle class, compared with 51 percent of the Vienna and Prague university students in 1910. Although the expansion of Austria's secondary and higher education during the six decades after 1848 allowed Austria to catch up with Germany in approximate terms with respect to enrollments relative to the school-aged population, the socioeconomic origins of university students in Austria's core Alpine and Bohemian lands reflected an occupational structure that in 1910 still lagged behind that of Prussia or all northern Germany.

Determining just how much social mobility, upward or downward, resulted from the increasing inclusiveness of Austrian secondary and higher education requires study of students' career paths and the patterns of recruitment for the various professions.[20] Hopes for higher social status and better incomes surely motivated many youth who came to Austrian secondary schools and higher education from small business, craft, or peasant families and the smaller numbers who came from the laboring strata. Quantitative evidence is lacking regarding those students' subsequent careers, but it is clear that only a small portion of all who enrolled in the secondary schools matriculated in the universities and technical colleges, passed state examinations or earned degrees, and eventually entered a learned profession or the educated higher officialdom. Over the whole period, generally less than a third of those who began in the *Gymnasien* and *Realschulen* ultimately completed their programs of study and passed the *Matura*. In some sectors of higher education, half or fewer of the students who matriculated went on to complete full degree programs.

In simple numbers, anyone who had any secondary or higher education at all belonged to an elite group; but those who left before completing, along with many who passed the *Matura* or one of several state examinations in a university or technical college, went off to a wide range of pursuits. Many of those pursuits hardly represented professional careers in any real sense. Sensitive observers of society such as Masaryk and Ehrlich lamented the fate of the growing numbers of petty functionaries in public and private offices who were expected to have passed the *Matura* and perhaps also have some higher studies, but performed no more than menial clerical duties and received low salaries. In late-nineteenth-century Austria, as in Germany, to achieve any higher rank in most areas of state employment required meeting steadily rising educational qualifications and surviving at least a one-year internship without salary and then years of low-level positions.[21] Newly certified secondary school teachers often had to serve for several years in ill-paid temporary positions before finding a permanent appointment, which might then consign them to a modest middle-class life in a remote town. Understandably, educated and semieducated white-collar employees and teachers in Austria, as in much of Europe, around 1900 did much to vent their social and economic frustrations in their own organizations and political activity.

Those who graduated from the Austrian faculties of law and medicine but then had to struggle to make careers as lawyers and physicians may have been less eager to complain publicly of their disappointments, but they were also part of the expanded social landscape of the educated and semieducated at the beginning of the twentieth century. Many sons of Czech independent farmers and millers or of Jewish shop owners were able to graduate from the universities as attorneys and medical doctors, but their degrees and titles did not always guarantee escape from lower-middle-class economic circumstances. If some of these graduates had to work for insurance companies, banks, or the military to earn a livelihood, then they realized rather less economic improvement than they had probably expected.[22] Perhaps one needs to consider the emergence alongside the *Bildungsbürgertum* of a *Bildungskleinbürgertum,* as the historian Jiří Kořalka terms it, as advanced education became more inclusive and the educated and semieducated segments of the work force, more highly differentiated.[23]

It might seem surprising that the rates of enrollment in Austrian secondary and higher education relative to the school-aged population at the end of the nineteenth century approximated so closely those for Prussia or all of Germany and that Austrian students' socioeconomic origins did not vary more than they did from their Prussian or German counterparts. Austria and Germany differed significantly, after all, in levels of overall economic development, the ethnic and religious composition of their populations, their political structures, and many of their educational and social policies. In fact, though, there were broad parallels not only between Austria and Germany but across much of Europe between 1870 and 1914 in the portions of school-aged youth who enrolled in secondary and higher education and in the students' social recruitment. In explaining those similarities, the German historian Kaelble has suggested that in nearly all European countries the economic opportunities and challenges of industrialization increased the demand for advanced education by "traditional industrial, administrative, and educational elites," who wanted to protect and enhance their positions, and in the lower middle classes, old and new, whose members wanted to advance. Kaelble goes on to argue that while institutional developments varied from one country to another, they tended to have similar results in separating more sharply primary and secondary education and in distinguishing various tracks in secondary and higher education that differed in prestige, social access, and the career opportunities to which they led.[24] Austrian developments surely followed this general pattern, but the particularly strong similarities between Germany and Austria in the growth of enrollments and the broader parallels in the social recruitment of students also had more specific causes.

Germany and Austria, or at least Austria's Alpine and Bohemian lands, shared many common Central European traditions and social modes with regard to advanced education and the formation of educated elites. From the late medieval period, the institutional structures and social functions of secondary and higher education developed along much the same lines in the Alpine and Bohemian lands as in other parts of the Holy Roman Empire. The absolutist governments during the late seventeenth and eighteenth centuries increased some of the differences among the various German states and Austria with regard to institutional arrangements and growth patterns, but Austria's educational authorities in the 1850s and 1860s only reaffirmed the belief that Austria shared much the same academic culture with the German states when they modeled many of the reforms in the *Gymnasien* and universities after the most successful innovations of the preceding fifty years in northern Germany. During the early modern era, Austria's educated state officials, lawyers, physicians, and clergy had much the same training, functions, and status as their counterparts in the German states; and in the late nineteenth century professionals in Austria were generally eager to uphold standards comparable to those in Germany. Such thinking came naturally to educated German-speaking elements in Austria, and in the Alpine and Bohemian lands economic and social development did not lag so far behind Germany's as to challenge the assumptions about parity in the professional sphere. Inescapably, Czechs, Slovenes, and Italians in the Alpine and Bohemian lands also shared much the same academic and professional culture with the German-speaking population in Austria and the rest of Central Europe. In Galicia distinct Polish educational traditions and the poverty of the province left their marks on education and the professions there. In that region, also, however, Central European academic and professional values influenced the formation of the educated elements.

That broader Central European academic and professional culture imbued Austria's educational institutions and the laws and regulations that governed advanced education and the professions. During the late nineteenth century, the discourse of Austrian government officials and educators on such matters was much the same as that of their counterparts in Germany. The Austrians identified many of the same problems regarding curricula and the rapid growth in secondary and higher education as did their German counterparts. Those in the general Austrian public who were interested in advanced education or the professions were surely influenced by that common Central European academic and professional culture. In this light, it would be surprising indeed if the populace, educators, and state authorities in the Alpine and Bohemian lands had not held many views about the purposes of advanced education and access to it that were like those current in Germany.

The magnitude of growth in enrollments in secondary and higher education evoked much concern among conservative Austrian officials after 1880, but those who had labored in the late 1840s and 1850s or in the late 1860s and 1870s to establish modern educational institutions comparable to the best in Central Europe could be proud of the results. After 1900 Austria ranked high among European countries in enrollments in secondary and higher education relative to school-aged population.[25] At the end of the century, the quality of scholarship in the major Austrian universities and technical colleges was widely respected and attracted students from beyond the borders, especially from Eastern and Southeastern Europe but also some from Western Europe and North America. The universities and technical colleges in Vienna and Graz and the German institutions in Prague often competed with German and Swiss institutions for the services of the most talented scholars and scientists in Central Europe. This was a far cry from the period of Emperor Francis and Prince Metternich, when the Austrian authorities closely regulated teaching and scholarship in higher education and did not welcome foreign scholars. Inhabitants of many poorer and more remote rural areas did not benefit from the development of advanced education as much as did residents of Austria's more prosperous regions and larger urban centers, but that failing also afflicted many other Western countries in this period. The poorest and politically weakest of Austria's various ethnic groups won little state-supported advanced education in their native languages, but the expansion of education in other languages offered increased opportunities to some of their youth as well. Austrian secondary and higher education could be criticized for its overly centralized, bureaucratic administration; the tardiness of curricular reforms; and often for poor pedagogy, whether in the heavy reliance on lecture courses in higher education or the memorization and graded recitation practiced in secondary schools. Still, these, too, were common shortcomings in European education during the period.

The development of Austrian secondary and higher education between the 1850s and World War I left a manifold legacy to the monarchy's successor states. It is easy to underestimate the accomplishments of the Austrian state during the late nineteenth century in establishing effective, modern administration and public services in view of its well-known failures to develop viable, popularly based parliamentary government, to reconcile its contending nationalities, or even to maintain itself as a great European power without an ultimately fatal dependence on Germany. Here, historians of imperial Austria should take a cue from recent debates concerning what has and has not been unique about the course of Germany's modern development and not carry too far the notions of Austria's own political and social *Sonderweg*. Conflicts among the various popular political forces and between them and entrenched bureaucratic and propertied elites did paralyze Austrian cabinets and the Reichsrat repeatedly after the late 1890s, but after the 1880s the popular parties made steady advances in using municipal councils and many provincial diets for representational politics. Similarly, even though the Reichsrat exercised little effective control over the ministries at the turn of the century, the Austrian government ran modern systems of advanced education, civil administration, justice, public health, and transportation that functioned well by European standards.

At the beginning of the twentieth century, those state services were deeply rooted in law and popular custom; and many of them persisted in the successor states for years after 1918 with only limited changes. This was natural enough in the Austrian Republic, but Czechoslovakia's western lands—Bohemia, Moravia, and Silesia—also retained much of the Austrian law codes, administration, and educational system. Although proposals were made during the 1920s to consolidate the differing school systems in the various parts of Czechoslovakia, they were not enacted.[26] There were many similar Austrian survivals in law and public services in southern Poland and parts of Yugoslavia.

In the various new states of Central and East Central Europe after 1918, professionals, public officials, and private employees who were the products of Austrian secondary and higher education assumed important leadership roles as new national governments developed and the old political role of the aristocracy largely disappeared. Czechoslovakia found itself well supplied with educated Czech public officials, teachers, physicians, and lawyers; and they were responsible for much of the distinctive enlightened, relatively democratic but unabashedly bourgeois character of the new republic's politics and administration. Slovaks, in contrast, had no academic secondary or higher education in their own language during the last decades of rule from Budapest. Hungarian-language instruction had dominated advanced education in Slovakia, and before 1914 the territory had fewer than three hundred elementary schools teaching in Slovak. After 1918 Slovakia needed to develop a new class of educated state officials and professionals to replace the Magyar and Magyarized elements identified with the old regime. A crash program began under the new republic to create systems of Slovak secondary and higher education, but in the meantime nearly 22,000 Czech bureaucrats, educators, and professionals came to take up positions in Slovakia during the 1920s. Even as late as 1937, Slovak teachers still barely outnumbered Czechs in Slovakia's secondary schools; and Czechs made up the majority of the professors in Bratislava's university. The migration of Czech officials and educators to Slovakia along with Czech domination of the central government contributed much to the growing political friction between Czechs and Slovaks during the 1930s.[27]

Thanks to the legacy of Austrian education, Poland and Yugoslavia also showed some parallels to Czechoslovakia with respect to regional differences in the supply of educated professionals and public officials after 1918. Before World War I, Polish nationalists in the German- and Russian-held sectors of Poland made heroic efforts to compensate for the lack of public secondary and higher education in Polish with private, sometimes clandestine activities. They enjoyed considerable accomplishments, particularly in the Russian zone. Nonetheless, after 1918 the former Austrian sector provided educated personnel for public and private administration throughout Poland at least until the middle and late 1920s, when new Polish schools in the other regions began to produce significant numbers of graduates. Austrian education also left a valuable legacy to Slovenia and Dalmatia in the new Kingdom of the Serbs, Croats, and Slovenes. Although the Slovenes had not fared well under the Austrian regime in developing advanced education in their language, overall they still enjoyed higher levels of education than did the Serbians, Bosnians, Montenegrins, Albanians, and Macedonians in the new state. Because of this and the Slovene political leaders' negotiating skills, Slovenes were able to find positions in Yugoslavia's central bureaucracy during the interwar period far in excess of their small share of the population.[28]

The new Austrian Republic, of course, inherited in Vienna the old regime's central institutions of higher education and a huge concentration of trained bureaucrats and professionals. The large educational institutions and great numbers of educated persons had been appropriate for the nerve center of a large empire but were now marooned in the oversized capital of a largely agricultural country whose total population numbered only 6.5 million. Vienna swelled with immigrants during and just after World War I, and any former Habsburg state officials who migrated to the Austrian Republic from the other successor states only added to the country's social imbalances. In the Alpine lands at the end of the nineteenth century, cultural and political tensions were already apparent between conservative Catholic peasant farmers and craft producers in the villages and towns and the more cosmopolitan, better-educated, and often politically more radical populations in Vienna and the other large cities. After 1918 those differences contributed much to the political conflicts in the Austrian Republic that ultimately destroyed democratic government during the 1930s.[29]

Between the middle of the nineteenth century and the 1920s or 1930s, though, much had changed in the character, structure, and numbers of the educated middle classes in the lands of old Austria and throughout Europe. With the growth of modern industry, commerce, and government, a much greater range of occupations in both the public and private sectors came to require at least some advanced education. Attending academic secondary schools, universities, technical colleges, or other institutions of higher learning in the years just before or after World War I may have remained the privilege of a small percentage of the school-aged population, but in most European countries that percentage had increased substantially during the preceding five or six decades. In part, the expansion in enrollments in secondary and higher education was a response to growing demand for educated persons in private enterprises, state agencies, and the free professions, but the increasing flow of young people coming out of the educational institutions itself encouraged the raising of educational requirements for employment. One result was that the educated and semieducated segments of the middle classes became more highly differentiated, socially and economically, than they had been in the early and mid-nineteenth century.

Those processes of growth and differentiation caused many ironies. Advancing professionalization presumably raised the social status of many occupations along with the requisite qualifications, but diplomas and professional titles had carried much greater cachet and, for many, more certain economic and social benefits when they had belonged to a smaller elite of high officials, professors, physicians, lawyers, and clergy who were protected by the corporate privileges of early modern society. The changes that followed during the middle and late nineteenth century represented a great inflation of academic and professional honors that undercut their value in some ways. Much of that transformation was personally witnessed by the Social Democratic leader Karl Renner (1870–1950), who served as the first chancellor of the Austrian Republic after 1918 and as president of the restored republic after 1945. Born to a peasant family in Dolní Dunajovice (Untertannowitz), southern Moravia, Renner had been able to graduate from the Vienna University's law faculty. Writing in 1915, he captured well the contrasts between the new circumstances and those of the late 1860s for the educated segments of the middle classes:[30]

> One can conceive of the average administrative district [in 1869] thusly: Industry is still in its beginnings; the main railroad lines are just being built. . . . The great majority of village teachers have not come from a modern teacher training institute but are former subaltern army officers. The country doctor is usually an old surgeon, an assistant field medical officer gone into civilian life and no medical doctor. The administrators of the noble estates have not studied at a college of agriculture, but rather are experienced practical men who have worked their way up. . . . [In the towns] among craftsmen and small businessmen sit in isolation perhaps one lawyer, one notary, one physician. . . . Since then, society has quite unexpectedly grown in height and breadth; it has industrialized and intellectualized itself. . . .
>
> [Nowadays] the big farmers have attended agricultural middle schools and subscribe to agricultural newsletters. The tanner's son has become an engineer and calls himself a leather manufacturer. . . . On every corner in a small town resides an attorney, medical doctor, architect, or at least a midwife with a diploma on display. . . . All around everything has a title and dignity, a diploma and certificate, an office or at least a cashier's desk.

APPENDIX A

Supplementary Tables

TABLE 1
Enrollments in Austrian Secondary Schools, 1851–1910[*]

Academic yr.	Men's Gymn.	Realgymn.	Women's Gymn.	Total Gymn.	Realsch.	Total
1850–51	21,175			21,175	4,455	25,630
1855–56	19,958			19,958	6,662	26,620
1860–61	27,039			27,039	9,223	36,262
1865–66	31,969			31,969	11,866	43,835
1869–70	27,772	2,725		30,497	13,237	43,734
1874–75	22,686	11,451		34,137	21,552	55,689
1879–80	38,378	9,590		47,968	17,967	65,935
1884–85	43,775	9,459		53,234	16,327	69,561
1889–90	44,597	8,314		52,911	18,384	71,295
1894–95	49,842	6,310		56,152	23,600	79,752
1899–1900	59,649	4,998		64,647	31,267	95,914
1904–5	73,467	4,133	493	78,093	41,877	119,970
1909–10	--- 91,546	---	2,732	94,278	46,267	140,545

Sources: Schimmer 1858; Schimmer 1877; *Statistisches Jahrbuch für das Jahr 1874; Statistisches Jahrbuch für das Jahr 1879; Öster. Statistik* 2, no. 1 (1882); 16, no. 2 (1887); 28, no. 4 (1892); 61, no. 1 (1898); 68, no. 3 (1903); 79, no. 3 (1908); n.s., 7, no. 3 (1913).

[*] *Enrollments are the total number of matriculated ("public") and "private" students at the end of each academic year indicated.*

TABLE 2
Matriculated Students in Austrian Universities and Technical Colleges, 1857–1910

Winter sem.	Total univ.	Law	Med.	Phil.	Theol.	Total tech. col.
1856–57*	3,709	2,039	821	459	390	2,235
1864–65*	4,901	2,269	1,117	776	739	2,472
1869–70	7,904	3,038	2,376	1,515	975	1,699
1874–75	7,616	3,521	1,600	1,860	635	3,152
1879–80	8,114	4,364	1,544	1,384	822	2,988
1884–85	11,361	5,103	4,005	1,070	1,183	2,121
1889–90	12,421	4,922	5,234	939	1,326	1,608
1894–95	13,169	6,158	4,686	1,210	1,115	2,579
1899–1900	14,331	8,393	2,793	2,127	1,018	4,843
1904–5	17,613	8,621	2,214	5,581	1,197	7,656
1909–10	23,068	11,668	4,389	5,605	1,406	10,110

Sources: Schimmer 1858; *Statistisches Jahrbuch der öster. Monarchie für das Jahr 1865; Statistisches Jahrbuch für das Jahr 1869; Statistisches Jahrbuch für das Jahr 1874; Statistisches Jahrbuch für das Jahr 1879; Öster. Statistik* 2, no. 1 (1882); 16, no. 2 (1887); 28, no. 4 (1892); 61, no. 1 (1898); 68, no. 3 (1903); 79, no. 3 (1908); n.s., 7, no. 3 (1913).

* *The statistics for 1856–57 and 1864–65 do not include the universities of Pavia and Padua.*

TABLE 3
Mother Tongue of All Students in Austrian Academic Secondary Schools, 1857–1910[*]

Secondary Enrollments Analyzed in Percents

	End of Acad. Year	Total	German	Czech	Pol.	Ukra.	Slove./Serb./Cro.	Ital.	Rom.	Magy.	(Jewish)[†]
	1856–57†										
Gymnasien		21,002	42.6%	21.7	11.6	7.8	6.3	4.3	0.7	-	4.4
Realschulen		7,127	60.9%	11.2	4.3	0.27	2.2	1.4	-	1.3	7.8
Total		28,129	47.2%	19.0	9.7	5.9	5.3	3.6	0.5	0.6	5.3
	1869–70										
Gymn. & Realgymn.		30,497	43.8%	21.4	18.7	6.1	5.7	3.1	-	-	
Realschulen		13,237	60.6%	24.2	6.7	0.4	2.5	4.4	-	0.8	
Total		43,734	48.9%	22.3	15.0	4.4	4.7	3.5	0.6	0.5	

	End of Acad. Year	Total	German	Czech	Pol.	Ukra.	Slove.	Serb./Cro.	Ital.	Rom.	Magy.
	1879–80										
Gymn. & Realgymn.		47,968	43.8%	29.1	15.6	3.8	2.6	1.2	2.7	0.6	0.5
Realschulen		17,967	56.0%	27.7	7.8	0.6	1.0	0.6	4.9	-	0.9
Total		65,935	47.2%	28.7	13.5	2.9	2.2	1.0	3.3	0.5	0.6

[*] All enrollment statistics include all students, matriculated and "private."

[†] The Austrian government statistics on education for 1856–57 included the category of students' nationality, not mother tongue, and treated "Israelites" as a separate nationality.

	End of Acad. Year	Total	German	Czech	Pol.	Ukra.	Slove.	Serb./Cro.	Ital.	Rom.	Magy.
	1889–90										
Gymn. & Realgymn.		52,911	43.2%	26.6	17.4	4.1	3.2	1.2	3.1	0.6	0.3
Realschulen		18,384	61.3%	23.9	6.1	0.3	1.3	0.8	5.3	0.2	0.5
Total		71,295	47.9%	25.9	14.5	3.1	2.7	1.1	3.7	0.5	0.4
	1899–1900										
Gymn. & Realgymn.		64,647	41.3%	22.4	20.9	5.2	3.9	1.8	3.2	0.9	0.2
Realschulen		31,267	50.0%	34.4	8.2	0.7	1.2	1.0	3.9	0.2	0.2
Total		95,914	44.1%	26.4	16.7	3.7	3.0	1.5	3.4	0.7	0.2
	1909–10										
All Gym. & Realgymn.		94,278	37.4%	17.3	28.0	8.2	3.2	1.4	3.1	1.1	0.2
Realschulen		46,267	50.2%	34.4	7.8	0.7	1.8	1.0	3.6	0.2	0.2
Total		140,545	41.6%	22.9	21.4	5.7	2.7	1.3	3.3	0.8	0.2
(1910 census, language:			35.6%	23.0	17.8	12.6	4.5	2.8	2.8	1.0	0.04)

Sources: Schimmer 1858; *Statistisches Jahrbuch für das Jahr 1869; Statistisches Jahrbuch für das Jahr 1879; Öster. Statistik* 28, no. 4 (1892); 68, no. 3 (1903); n.s., 7, no. 3 (1913); and Urbanitsch 1980, 3, pt. 1: 38, table 1.

TABLE 4
Religion of All Students in Austrian Academic Secondary Schools, 1857–1910*

Secondary Enrollments Analyzed in Percents

END OF ACADEMIC YEAR 1856–57

	Total	R. Cath.	Gk. Cath	E. Orth.	Luth.	Calv.	Jewish
Gymnasien	100% = 21,002	87.0%	6.0	1.0	1.1	0.3	4.4
Realschulen	100% = 7,127	90.1%	0.3	0.2	1.4	0.2	7.8
Total	100% = 28,129	87.8%	4.5	0.8	1.2	0.3	5.3

END OF ACADEMIC YEAR 1869–70

	Total	R. Cath.	Gk. Cath	E. Orth.	Luth.	Calv.	Jewish
Gymn. & Realgymn.	100% = 30,497	80.8%	5.9	1.4	1.1	0.3	10.2
Realschulen	100% = 13,237	87.6%	0.4	0.5	1.4	0.3	9.4
Total	100% = 43,734	82.9%	4.3	1.2	1.2	0.3	10.0

	Total	All Cath.	E. Orth.	All Prot.	Jewish
END OF ACADEMIC YEAR 1879–80					
Gymn. & Realgymn.	100% = 47,968	81.8%	1.1	2.4	14.6
Realschulen	100% = 17,967	81.5%	0.5	3.4	14.6
Total	100% = 65,935	81.7%	1.0	2.7	14.6
END OF ACADEMIC YEAR 1889–90					
Gymn. & Realgymn.	100% = 52,911	81.9%	1.0	2.7	14.3
Realschulen	100% = 18,384	80.9%	0.4	4.4	14.1
Total	100% = 71,295	81.6%	0.9	3.3	14.3
END OF ACADEMIC YEAR 1899–1900					
Gymn. & Realgymn.	100% = 64,647	82.7%	1.6	2.2	13.4
Realschulen	100% = 31,267	82.4%	0.3	4.2	13.0
Total	100% = 95,914	82.6%	1.1	2.9	13.3
END OF ACADEMIC YEAR 1909–10					
All Gymn. & Realgymn.	100% = 94,278	78.6%	2.0	2.9	16.4
Realschulen	100% = 46,267	83.6%	0.3	4.6	11.3
Total	100% = 140,545	80.2%	1.5	3.5	14.7
(1910 census:		90.8%	2.3	2.1	4.6)

Sources: Schimmer 1858; *Statistisches Jahrbuch für das Jahr 1869; Statistisches Jahrbuch für das Jahr 1879; Öster. Statistik* 28, no. 4 (1892); 32, no. 1 (1892); 63, no. 1 (1902); 68, no. 3 (1903); n.s., 7, no. 3 (1913); and Urbanitsch 1980, 3, pt. 1: 54, table 5.

* *The enrollment totals include all students, matriculated and "private."*

TABLE 5
Religion and Mother Tongue of Austrian University Students, 1857–1910

Percentages of Total Matriculated and Nonmatriculated Students

RELIGION

Winter Sem.	Total Enroll.	Cath.	Jew.	Prot.	E. Orth.
1856–57*	5,340	83.3%	9.4	5.7	1.4
1869–70	8,992	79.7	12.6	3.7	1.8

NATIONALITY/MOTHER TONGUE

Winter Sem.	Total Enroll.	Ger.	Cze.	Pol.	Ukra.	Slove./Serb./Cro.	Magy.	Isra.*
1856–57*	5,340	38.1%	19.9	8.9	5.6	6.3	7.3	9.4
1869–70	8,992	45.6	20.2	14.6	5.8	5.4	4.8	

RELIGION

Winter Sem.	Total Enroll.	Cath.	Jew.	Prot.	E. Orth.
1879–80	9,561	78.1%	15.2	3.4	2.8
1889–90	15,121	71.8	20.1	4.0	3.3
1899–1900	17,209	76.7	16.7	3.3	2.9
1909–10	27,531	75.0	17.5	3.4	3.1
(Pop.-1910 census:		90.8%	4.6	2.1	2.3)

MOTHER TONGUE

Winter Sem.	Total Enroll.	Ger.	Cze.	Pol.	Ukra.	Slove.	Serb./Cro.	Magy.	Ital.
1879–80	9,561	47.5%	16.0	16.6	5.0	2.0	2.8	4.2	3.4
1889–90	15,121	45.4	21.4	15.4	3.8	1.0	3.0	3.1	3.0
1899–1900	17,209	46.5	20.5	17.3	3.8	2.2	3.6	0.8	3.0
1909–10	27,531	40.5	16.4	24.4	5.4	2.0	3.0	0.6	2.4
(Pop.- 1910 census:		35.6%	23.0	17.8	12.6	4.5	2.8	0.04	2.8)

Sources: Schimmer 1858; *Statistisches Jahrbuch für das Jahr 1869; Statistisches Jahrbuch für das Jahr 1879; Öster. Statistik* 28, no. 4 (1892); 32, no. 1 (1892); 63, no. 1 (1902); 68, no. 3 (1903); n.s., 7, no. 3 (1913); and Urbanitsch 1980, 3, pt. 1: 38 (table 1), 54 (table 5).

* *The enrollment totals for 1856–57 are for the universities located in territory included in the Austrian half of the monarchy after 1867. In this year, but not in the subsequent years selected, the government statistics on education analyzed the students according to nationality, not mother tongue, and "Israelites" were counted separately from the other nationalities.*

TABLE 6
Religion and Mother Tongue of Austrian Technical College Students, 1857–1910

Percentages of Total Matriculated and Nonmatriculated Students

RELIGION

Winter Sem.	Total Enroll.	Cath.	Jew.	Prot.	E. Orth.
1856–57*	2,475	79.6%	12.3	6.2	1.9
1869–70	2,317	84.1	9.7	3.9	1.2

NATIONALITY/MOTHER TONGUE

Winter Sem.	Total Enroll.	Ger.	Cze.	Pol.	Ukra.	Slove./Serb./Cro.	Magy.	Isra.*
1856–57*	2,475	37.2%	19.1	15.4	0.7	3.2	10.3	12.3
1869–70	2,317	41.9	14.5	26.0	1.1	5.0	4.2	--

RELIGION

Winter Sem.	Total Enroll.	Cath.	Jew.	Prot.	E. Orth.
1879–80	3,236	76.6%	16.8	4.6	1.7
1889–90	1,798	75.2	15.9	6.0	2.7
1899–1900	5,334	74.9	17.8	6.0	1.0
1909–10	10,805	77.2	14.2	5.1	1.7
(Pop.- 1910 census:		90.8%	4.6	2.1	2.3)

MOTHER TONGUE

Winter Sem.	Total Enroll.	Ger.	Cze.	Pol.	Ukra.	Slove.	Serb./Cro.	Magy.	Ital.
1879–80	3,236	48.5%	28.8	11.1	0.3	1.0	2.1	5.0	1.9
1889–90	1,798	52.6	23.6	12.8	0.6	1.0	2.1	2.7	2.3
1899–1900	5,334	50.6	27.1	14.9	0.8	0.5	2.0	0.9	1.9
1909–10	10,805	43.0	30.8	16.5	0.8	0.9	2.2	0.2	1.9
(Pop.- 1910 census:		35.6%	23.0	17.8	12.6	4.5	2.8	0.04	2.8)

Sources: Schimmer 1858; *Statistisches Jahrbuch für das Jahr 1869; Statistisches Jahrbuch für das Jahr 1879; Öster. Statistik* 28, no. 4 (1892), 32, no. 1 (1892); 63, no. 1 (1902); 68, no. 3 (1903); n.s., 7, no. 3 (1913); and Urbanitsch 1980, 3, pt. 1: 38, (table 1), 54 (table 5).

* *The enrollment totals for 1856–57 are for the technical colleges located in territory included in the Austrian half of the monarchy after 1867. In this year, but not in the subsequent years selected, the government statistics on education analyzed the students according to nationality, not mother tongue, and "Israelites" were counted separately from the other nationalities.*

TABLE 7
Social Origins of Matriculated University Students in Vienna and Prague, 1860–1910

University/ Winter Sem.	Propertied (in %)	Educated (in %)	Lower middle class Old + New = Sum (in %)	Laborers (in %)
		Vienna University		
1859–60 (n=510/456)*	13.8	34.4	30.9 + 11.6 = 42.5	9.0
1879–80 (n=651/559)	18.6	30.7	32.7 + 13.0 = 45.7	4.8
1899–1900 (n=678/564)	16.1	29.8	28.7 + 18.4 = 47.1	6.6
1909–10 (n=1061/908)	17.7	32.6	26.9 + 18.3 = 45.2	4.4
		Prague University		
1859–60 (n=704/646)	8.0	25.4	49.1 + 11.9 = 61.0	4.2
1879–80 (n=885/790)	10.5	24.6	46.5 + 10.6 = 57.1	7.6
		Czech University of Prague		
1899–1900 (n=525/481)	7.1	20.4	43.2 + 19.8 = 63.0	8.9
1909–10 (n=549/505)	7.9	19.4	41.0 + 23.0 = 64.0	8.5
		German University of Prague		
1899–1900 (n=1035/958)	15.8	26.5	36.6 + 17.1 = 53.7	3.3
1909–10 (n=795/725)	10.3	27.2	30.6 + 24.6 = 55.2	6.6
		Vienna and Prague Universities—weighted averages†		
1859–60	11.9	31.5	36.7 + 11.7 = 48.4	7.5
1879–80	15.9	28.7	37.3 + 12.2 = 49.5	5.7
1899–1900	13.4	26.6	34.0 + 18.7 = 52.7	6.9
1909–10	14.2	28.4	31.1 + 20.3 = 51.4	5.8

Sources: Samples of the registration records in the *Katalogen der Hörer, Katalogy posluchačů, Nationalen,* and *Nationaly* for the respective winter semesters, Archiv der Universität Wien, Vienna, and Archiv Univerzity Karlovy, Prague.

Confidence Intervals: largest—all lower-middle-class students in the Vienna Univ., w. 1859–60: 42.5% ± 4.5%; smallest—laboring-class students in the German Univ. of Prague, w. 1899–1900: 3.3% ± 1.1%

* *"n" equals the total number of matriculated students in the sample for each semester/the number who listed an occupation for his or her father or guardian.*

† *In calculating the weighted averages from the samples for the separate institutions, the percentages for each university have been weighted according to the total number of matriculated students in each institution.*

TABLE 8
Distribution by University Faculty in Vienna and Prague of Matriculated Students from Various Social Origins, 1880–1910

	Law	Medicine	Philosophy	Theology	Total*
Vienna Univ. - 1880 *German Christians (and without relig.)†*					
Propertied (n=47)‡	53.2%	12.8	31.9	2.1	100%
Educated (n=106)	61.3%	17.0	21.7	—	100%
Old low. mid. class (n=51)	37.3%	13.7	41.2	7.8	100%
New low. mid. class (n=36)	50.0%	5.6	41.7	2.8	100%
Laborers (n=9)	11.1%	—	66.7	22.2	100%
Total (n=249)	51.4%	13.3	32.1	3.2	100%
Vienna Univ. - 1900 *German Christians (and without relig.)*					
Propertied (n=44)	54.5%	22.7	18.2	4.5	100%
Educated (n=111)	72.1%	16.2	11.7	0	100%
Old low. mid. class (n=60)	60.0%	16.7	20.0	3.3	100%
New low. mid. class (n=59)	59.3%	22.0	15.2	3.4	100%
Laborers (n=25)	64.0%	8.0	28.0	—	100%
Total (n=299)	63.9%	17.7	16.4	2.0	100%
Vienna Univ. - 1910 *German Christians (and without relig.)*					
Propertied (n=85)	52.9%	23.5	23.5	—	100%
Educated (n=196)	52.0%	16.3	29.1	2.0	100%
Old low. mid. class (n=90)	37.8%	18.9	34.4	8.9	100%
New low. mid. class (n=101)	40.6%	16.8	38.6	4.0	100%
Laborers (n=29)	41.4%	6.9	48.3	3.4	100%
Total (n=501)	46.7%	17.6	32.1	3.4	100%

* *Total equals the number of matriculated students with reported father's or guardian's occupation in each sample for the particular ethnic, religious, and class category for the whole university.*
† *For simplicity, "German Christians (and without relig.)" includes all matriculated students in each sample who reported their father's or guardian's occupation, had German mother tongue, and were not Jewish.*
‡ *"n" equals the number of matriculated students in the sample from the particular social category who listed an occupation for the father or guardian.*

	Law	Medicine	Philosophy	Theology	Total*
Prague Univ. - 1880 *German Christians (and without relig.)*					
Propertied (n=29)	75.9%	6.9	13.8	3.4	100%
Educated (n=76)	64.5%	14.5	21.0	0	100%
Old low. mid. class (n=50)	42.0%	26.0	16.0	16.0	100%
New low. mid. class (n=22)	54.6%	4.6	40.9	—	100%
Laborers (n=10)	40.0%	0	40.0	20.0	100%
Total (n=188)	54.0%	15.8	22.3	7.9	100%
German Univ. - 1900 *German Christians (and without relig.)*					
Propertied (n=101)	62.4%	25.7	10.9	1.0	100%
Educated (n=183)	56.8%	25.7	16.9	1.1	100%
Old low. mid. class (n=181)	51.9%	16.6	22.1	9.4	100%
New low. mid. class (n=118)	61.0%	15.2	21.2	2.5	100%
Laborers (n=28)	60.7%	3.6	21.4	14.3	100%
Total (n=613)	57.4%	19.7	18.4	4.4	100%
German Univ. - 1910 *German Christians (and without relig.)*					
Propertied (n=49)	55.1%	20.4	20.4	4.1	100%
Educated (n=150)	48.0%	24.0	27.3	0.7	100%
Old low. mid. class (n=150)	38.7%	24.7	30.7	6.0	100%
New low. mid. class (n=146)	51.4%	17.1	30.1	1.4	100%
Laborers (n=41)	31.7%	22.0	31.7	14.6	100%
Total (n=541)	45.5%	22.0	28.8	3.7	100%
Prague Univ. - 1880 *Czech Christians (and without relig.)§*					
Propertied (n=36)	61.1%	8.3	19.4	11.1	100%
Educated (n=95)	65.3%	22.1	10.5	2.1	100%
Old low. mid. class (n=254)	50.0%	11.8	25.6	12.6	100%
New low. mid. class (n=47)	55.3%	6.4	25.5	12.8	100%
Laborers (n=46)	50.0%	6.5	23.9	19.6	100%
Total (n=479)	54%	13	22	11	100%

§ For simplicity, "Czech Christians (and without relig.)" includes all matriculated students in each sample who had Czech mother tongue, reported their father's or guardian's occupation, and were not Jewish.

	Law	Medicine	Philosophy	Theology	Total*
Czech Univ. - 1900 *Czech Christians (and without relig.)*					
Propertied (n=34)	73.5%	23.5	2.9	—	100%
Educated (n=91)	68.1%	15.4	16.5	—	100%
Old low. mid. class (n=193)	57.5%	16.6	19.2	6.7	100%
New low. mid. class (n=92)	59.8%	15.2	19.6	5.4	100%
Laborers (n=43)	39.5%	11.6	34.9	14.0	100%
Total (n=456)	59.6%	16.2	18.9	5.3	100%
Czech Univ. - 1910 *Czech Christians (and without relig.)*					
Propertied (n=32)	56.2%	15.6	18.8	9.4	100%
Educated (n=95)	62.1%	21.1	14.7	2.1	100%
Old low. mid. class (n=178)	38.8%	22.5	32.0	6.7	100%
New low. mid. class (n=110)	46.4%	16.4	35.5	1.8	100%
Laborers (n=42)	54.8%	11.9	28.6	4.8	100%
Total (n=458)	48.2%	19.2	28.0	4.6	100%
Vienna Univ. - 1880 *Jewish Students#*					
Propertied (n=26)	53.8%	34.6	11.5	—	100%
Educated (n=18)	22.2%	61.1	16.7	—	100%
Old low. mid. class (n=88)	48.9%	39.8	11.4	—	100%
New low. mid. class (n=20)	50.0%	30.0	20.0	—	100%
Laborers (n=8)	25.0%	62.5	12.5	—	100%
Total (n=160)	45.6%	41.3	13.1	—	100%

 # "Jewish students" includes all matriculated students with reported father's or guardian's occupation who indicated Judaism as their religion in the registration records. Analysis of the Jewish students matriculated in the Czech University of Prague in 1900 and 1910 is omitted because of their small numbers compared to the Jewish enrollments in the German University.

	Law	Medicine	Philosophy	Theology	Total*
Vienna Univ. - 1900 *Jewish Students*					
Propertied (n=26)	46.2%	38.5	15.4	—	100%
Educated (n=23)	56.5%	30.4	13.0	—	100%
Old low. mid. class (n=74)	47.3%	43.2	9.5	—	100%
New low. mid. class (n=23)	56.5%	30.4	13.0	—	100%
Laborers (n=2)	50.0%	50.0	—	—	100%
Total (n=150)	50.0%	38.0	12.0	—	100%
Vienna Univ. - 1910 *Jewish Students*					
Propertied (n=33)	48.5%	18.2	33.3	—	100%
Educated (n=45)	44.4%	35.6	20.0	—	100%
Old low. mid. class (n=106)	43.4%	32.1	24.5	—	100%
New low. mid. class (n=41)	39.0%	41.5	19.5	—	100%
Laborers (n=2)	50.0%	50.0	—	—	100%
Total (n=228)	43.9%	32.5	23.7	—	100%
Prague Univ. - 1880 *Jewish Students*					
Propertied (n=10)	40.0%	40.0	20.0	—	100%
Educated (n=15)	73.3%	20.0	6.7	—	100%
Old low. mid. class (n=51)	52.9%	33.3	13.7	—	100%
New low. mid. class (n=13)	61.5%	7.7	30.8	—	100%
Laborers (n=3)	33.3%	33.3	33.3	—	100%
Total (n=92)	55.4%	28.3	16.3		100%
German Univ. - 1900 *Jewish Students*					
Propertied (n=43)	46.5%	44.2	9.3	—	100%
Educated (n=53)	54.7%	37.7	7.6	—	100%
Old low. mid. class (n=162)	48.8%	50.6	0.6	—	100%
New low. mid. class (n=34)	52.9%	41.2	5.9	—	100%
Laborers (n=1)	—	100	—	—	100%
Total (n=295)	49.8%	46.4	3.7	—	100%

	Law	Medicine	Philosophy	Theology	Total*
		German Univ. - 1910 *Jewish Students*			
Propertied (n=23)	52.2%	21.7	26.1	—	100%
Educated (n=36)	36.1%	41.7	22.2	—	100%
Old low. mid. class (n=66)	45.5%	39.4	15.2	—	100%
New low. mid. class (n=26)	57.7%	26.9	15.4	—	100%
Laborers (n=1)	—	—	100%	—	100%
Total (n=152)	46.1%	34.9	19.1	—	100%

Sources: Samples of the registration records in the *Katalogen der Hörer, Katalogy posluchačů, Nationalen*, and *Nationaly* for the respective winter semesters, Archiv der Universität Wien, Vienna, and Archiv Univerzity Karlovy, Prague.

Confidence Intervals: largest—German Christian laboring-class students in the phil. faculty of the Vienna Univ., w. 1879-80: 66.7% ± 30.8%; and Jewish laboring-class students in the law or medical faculty of the Vienna Univ., w. 1899–1900: 50% ± 69.3%; narrowest—all German Christian students in the theological faculty of the German Univ. of Prague, w. 1899–1900: 4.4% ± 1.6%.

TABLE 9
Social Origins of Matriculated German Christian, Czech Christian, Jewish, and Women Students in the Vienna and Prague Universities, 1880–1910

University/ Winter sem.	Propertied (in %)	Educated (in %)	Lower middle class Old + New = Sum (in %)	Laborers (in %)
		Vienna University*		
		CZECH CHRISTIANS (& WITHOUT RELIG.)		
1879–80 (n=39)	15.4	15.4	46.2 + 10.3 = 56.5	12.8
1899–1900 (n=22)	13.6	18.2	36.4 + 27.3 = 63.7	4.6
1909–10 (n=26)	15.4	26.9	42.3 + 15.4 = 57.7	0
		GERMAN CHRISTIANS (& WITHOUT RELIG.)		
1879–80 (n=249)	18.9	42.6	20.5 + 14.5 = 35.0	3.6
1899–1900 (n=299)	14.7	37.1	20.1 + 19.7 = 39.8	8.4
1909–10 (n=362)	17.0	39.1	18.0 + 20.2 = 38.2	5.8
		JEWS		
1879–80 (n=160)	16.2	11.2	55.0 + 12.5 = 67.5	5.0
1899–1900 (n=150)	17.3	15.3	49.3 + 15.3 = 64.6	1.3
1909–10 (n=228)	14.5	19.7	46.5 + 18.0 = 64.5	0.9
		WOMEN		
1899–1900 (n=28) (phil. fac.)	14.3	50.0	17.9 + 17.9 = 35.8	0
1909–10 (n=33) (phil. & med. fac.)	18.2	39.4	24.2 + 18.2 = 42.4	0

* *"n" equals the number of matriculated students in each sample with reported occupations for their fathers or guardians for each ethnic/religious or gender group. For women in the Vienna philosophical faculty in 1899–1900, "n" equals all matriculated women students.*

University/ Winter sem.	Propertied (in %)	Educated (in %)	Lower middle class Old + New = Sum (in %)	Laborers (in %)
		Prague†		
		CZECH CHRISTIANS (& WITHOUT RELIG.)		
Prague Univ./ 1859–60 (n=328)	8.8	17.4	58.2 + 9.8 = 68.0	4.9
Prague Univ./ 1879–80 (n=479)	7.5	19.8	53.0 + 9.8 = 62.8	9.6
Czech Univ./ 1899–1900 (n=456)	7.5	20.2	42.3 + 20.0 = 62.3	9.4
Czech Univ./ 1909–10 (n=458)	7.0	20.7	38.9 + 24.0 = 62.9	9.2
		GERMAN CHRISTIANS (& WITHOUT RELIG.)		
Prague Univ./ 1859–60 (n=239)	5.9	37.7	34.3 + 15.5 = 49.8	4.6
Prague Univ./ 1879–80 (n=188)	15.4	40.4	26.6 + 11.7 = 38.3	5.3
German Univ./ 1899–1900 (n=613)	16.5	29.9	29.5 + 19.2 = 48.7	4.6
German Univ./ 1909–10 (n=541)	9.1	27.7	27.7 + 27.0 = 54.7	7.6

† *"n" equals the total number of matriculated students for the particular ethnic/religious group with reported occupations for their fathers or guardians in each sample. Jewish students are analyzed for the German University after 1882 but not for the Czech University because of the low Jewish enrollments there.*

University/ Winter sem.	**Propertied (in %)**	**Educated (in %)**	**Lower middle class Old + New = Sum (in %)**	**Laborers (in %)**
		JEWS		
Prague Univ/ 1859–60 (n=54)	7.4	9.3	72.2 + 9.3 = 81.5	0
Prague Univ/ 1879–80 (n=92)	10.9	16.3	55.4 + 14.1 = 69.5	3.3
German Univ/ 1899–1900 (n=295)	14.6	18.0	54.9 + 11.5 = 66.4	0.34
German Univ/ 1909–10 (n=152)	15.1	23.7	43.4 + 17.1 = 60.5	0.66

Sources: Samples of the registration records in the *Katalogen der Hörer, Katalogy posluchačů, Nationalen,* and *Nationaly* for the respective winter semesters, Archiv der Universität Wien, Vienna, and Archiv Univerzity Karlovy, Prague.

Confidence intervals: largest—Czech Christian students from the old lower middle class in the Vienna Univ., w. 1899–1900: 36.4% ± 20.1%; and women students from the educated strata in Vienna phil. and med. faculties, w. 1909–10: 39.4% ± 16.7%; narrowest—German Christian students from the laboring strata in the German Univ. of Prague, w. 1899–1900: 4.6% ± 1.7%

TABLE 10
Occupational Stratification of the Austrian Population, 1910

	German everyday language		Czech everyday language		Total population	
			ALL ECONOMIC SECTORS			
Independents/ self-employed	1,921,250	19.3%	1,146,430	17.8%	5,410,271	18.9%
Qualified employees	335,830	3.4	122,992	1.9	620,493	2.2
Workers/ laborers/apprentices	2,634,785	26.5	1,695,743	26.4	5,833,852	20.4
Assisting family members	729,916	7.3	550,383	8.6	4,155,789	14.5
All employed/ self-supporting	5,621,781	56.5	3,515,548	54.6	16,020,405	56.1
Servants	217,049	2.2	98,876	1.5	470,072	1.6
Dependents without employment	4,111,848	41.3	2,821,108	43.8	12,080,323	42.3
Total	9,950,678	100.0%	6,435,532	100.0%	28,570,800	100.0%
			DISTRIBUTION OF POPULATION BY ECONOMIC SECTOR			
Agriculture and forestry	2,988,596	30.0%	2,478,203	38.5%	13,842,707	48.4%
Industry and crafts	3,621,335	36.4	2,388,128	37.1	7,562,508	26.5
Commerce and transport.	1,638,797	16.5	730,170	11.4	3,539,448	12.4
Public service, free prof., other, and without occup.	1,701,950	17.1	839.031	13.0	3,626,137	12.7
Total	9,950,678	100.0%	6,435,532	100.0%	28,570,800	100.0%

Source: *Öster. Statistik*, n.s., 3, no. 1: 52–54, table 5; cited in Urbanitsch 1980, 3, pt. 1: 138, table 16.

TABLE 11
Social Origins of Matriculated Technical College Students in Vienna and Prague, 1860–1910

Technical college/ Winter sem.	Propertied (in %)	Educated (in %)	Lower middle class Old + New = Sum (in %)	Laborers (in %)
		Vienna Technical College		
1859–60 (n=427/423)*	16.8	24.8	32.4 + 11.6 = 44.0	13.5
1879–80 (n=706/622)	19.0	19.0	38.1 + 16.9 = 55.0	6.4
1899–1900 (n=468/422)	17.1	14.9	31.8 + 27.5 = 59.3	8.3
		Bohemian Polytechnic Institute, Prague		
1859–60 (n=324/294)	11.9	16.0	48.0 + 11.9 = 59.9	10.2
		Czech Technical College, Prague		
1879–80 (n=254/237)	7.2	9.3	61.6 + 13.9 = 75.5	8.0
1899–1900 (n=278/252)	6.0	11.1	49.6 + 23.8 = 73.4	9.5
1909–10 (n=295/264)	6.8	12.5	38.6 + 31.1 = 69.7	11.0
		German Technical College, Prague		
1899–1900 (n=214/198)	20.7	11.6	36.4 + 24.8 = 61.2	5.0
1909–10 (n=303/285)	16.8	11.2	37.5 + 27.7 = 65.2	6.7
		Vienna and Prague Tech. Colleges - weighted averages†		
1859–60	16.9	20.0	32.1 + 19.2 = 51.3	11.0
1899–1900	14.1	13.2	38.1 + 25.9 = 64.0	8.2

Sources: Samples of the *Katalogen der Hörer, Katalogy posluchačů* for the respective winter semesters in the Archiv der Technischen Universität Wien, Vienna, and the Archiv Českého vysokého učení technického, Prague.

Confidence intervals: largest—all students from the lower middle classes in the German Technical College, w. 1899–1900: 61.2% ± 6.8%; narrowest—students from the laboring strata in the Vienna Technical College, w. 1879–80: 6.4% ± 1.9%.

* *"n" equals the total number of matriculated students in each sample/the number with reported occupations for their fathers or guardians.*

† *In calculating the weighted averages, the percentages for each technical college were weighted according to the total number of matriculated students in each institution. No averages are presented for winter 1879–80 because of the lack of data for the German Technical College in Prague, or for 1909–10 because of the lack of appropriate data for the Vienna Technical College.*

TABLE 12
Social Origins of Matriculated German Christian, Czech Christian, and Jewish Students in the Vienna and Prague Technical Colleges, 1880–1910

Technical college/ Winter sem.	Propertied (in %)	Educated (in %)	Lower middle class Old + New = Sum (in %)	Laborers (in %)
		Vienna*		
		CZECH CHRISTIANS (& WITHOUT RELIG.)		
Vienna Tech./ 1879–80 (n=35)†	17.1	2.9	60 + 8.6 = 68.6	11.4
		GERMAN CHRISTIANS (& WITHOUT RELIG.)		
Vienna Tech./ 1879–80 (n=315)	19.7	23.2	26.0 + 23.5 = 49.5	7.6
Vienna Tech./ 1899–1900 (n=234)	16.2	17.1	21.4 + 32.5 = 53.9	12.4
		JEWS		
Vienna Tech./ 1859–60 (n=61)	16.4	14.8	57.4 + 8.2 = 65.6	3.3
Vienna Tech./ 1879–80 (n=158)	16.5	7.6	62.0 + 8.9 = 70.9	4.4
Vienna Tech./ 1899–1900 (n=129)	17.8	5.4	51.9 + 21.7 = 73.6	2.3

* *The Katalogen der Hörer for 1859–60 included no information on the mother tongue of the students. Statistics for the winter semester 1909–10 are not presented here due to problems with the source materials. Data on the Czech students are presented for winter 1879–80 but not for winter 1899–1900 because of the very small number of students with Czech mother tongue, only five, in the sample for the latter semester.*

† *"n" equals the total number of matriculated students for the particular ethnic/religious group with reported occupations for their fathers or guardians in each sample.*

Technical college/ Winter sem.	Propertied (in %)	Educated (in %)	Lower middle class Old + New = Sum (in %)	Laborers (in %)
		Prague		
		CZECH CHRISTIANS (& WITHOUT RELIG.)		
Bohem. Tech./ 1859–60 (n=145)	10.3	14.5	49.7 + 13.1 = 62.8	9.7
Czech Tech./ 1879–80 (n=234)	6.8	9.4	62.0 + 13.7 = 75.7	8.1
Czech Tech./ 1899–1900 (n=244)	5.3	10.7	50.0 + 24.2 = 74.2	9.8
Czech Tech./ 1909–10 (n=244)	6.6	12.3	38.5 + 31.1 = 69.6	11.5
		GERMAN CHRISTIANS (& WITHOUT RELIG.)‡		
Bohem. Tech./ 1859–60 (n=77)	11.7	15.6	46.8 + 11.7 = 58.5	14.3
Ger. Tech./ 1899–1900 (n=125)	25.6	17.6	21.6 + 26.4 = 48.0	7.2
Ger. Tech./ 1909–10 (n=194)	18.6	13.4	27.3 + 30.9 = 58.2	9.8
		JEWS‡		
Bohem. Tech./ 1859–60 (n=12)	0	0	75.0 + 16.7 = 91.7	8.3
Ger. Tech./ 1899–1900 (n=59)	13.6	1.7	67.8 + 15.3 = 83.1	0
Ger. Tech./ 1909–10 (n=82)	13.4	3.7	62.2 + 20.7 = 82.9	0

Sources: Samples of the registration records in the *Katalogen der Hörer, Katalogy posluchačů* for the respective winter semesters in the Archiv der Technischen Universität Wien, Vienna, and the Archiv Českého vysokého učení technického, Prague.

Confidence intervals: largest—Jewish students from the old lower middle class in the Bohemian Polytechnical Institute, w. 1859–60: 75% ± 24.5%; and Czech Christian students from the old lower middle class in the Vienna Technical College, w. 1879–80: 60% ± 16.2%; narrowest—German Christian students from the laboring class in the Vienna Technical College, w. 1879–80: 7.6% ± 2.9%.

‡ *The Katalog der Hörer for the German Technical College in 1879–80 could not be located.*

APPENDIX B

Statistical Methods

Sampling Methods

The data on occupational and class origins for the matriculated university and technical colleges students in Vienna and Prague derive from samples of the manuscript registration records preserved in the archives of the individual institutions (see Sources for a listing). Where the institutions used catalogs, they recorded the individual student registrations in volumes in alphabetical order by the student's last name. Where they used individual registration forms (*Nationalen*), those forms were bound together in alphabetical order by the student's last name. Samples large enough for statistical analysis with reasonable confidence intervals have been drawn systematically by taking every nth (second, third, fourth, etc.) page in each catalog or every nth *Nationale* in the bound volumes, extending all the way through the alphabet. Nonmatriculated students have been excluded, since they were not subject to all the normal admissions requirements and were not eligible to take the principal state examinations or degrees. Strictly speaking, the samples of student registrations from the catalogs are "cluster samples" since each page in a catalog included a number of individual registrations. Nonetheless, for statistical purposes the samples from the catalogs and *Nationalen* have all been treated as direct random samples since for both kinds of records a student with a last name beginning with any letter in the alphabet had an equal chance of inclusion and, with respect to the registrations recorded in the catalogs, listing on a particular page had no connection with any of the variables being measured.

Many scholars prefer to draw samples from a run of records covering a period of years in order to avoid the possibility of temporary circumstances that might skew the data for a particular year or semester. Konrad H. Jarausch, for instance, drew a systematic sample from the Bonn University records for the whole period 1865–1914 (see Jarausch 1979, 1982). That approach, however, makes it difficult to develop any reliable time series analysis unless one draws a very large sample running through the whole period and/or presents temporal comparisons for whole decades, as Jarausch does. In this study limitations on access to the manuscript registrations and the sheer volume of the materials dictated selecting the four discrete semesters. Within their respective eras, the years 1879–80, 1899–1900, and 1909–10 do not appear to have been atypical for Austrian demography or the educational system over the whole period. Austrian university enrollments in the 1850s, however, were erratic. Winter 1859–60 may show some of the aftereffects of the "Hungry Forties," the economic conjuncture of 1857–58, and the Austrian mobilization for the war in northern Italy that occurred in the spring of 1859.

John E. Craig points out that students who studied longer and thus registered more often during their academic careers than did others can introduce a bias into social analyses based on registration records (Craig 1983, 226–27). Craig argues that analyses should be based on the total numbers of matriculations during any given period of time rather than the number of registrations so as to correct for the effects of some students remaining in school longer or changes in the length of academic programs. Statistics on the number of matriculations for each occupational or class category, however, cannot be easily derived from the records of registrations for each semester found in the catalogs and *Nationalen* of the Austrian institutions. Any attempt to adjust mathematically the number of registrations in order to derive statistics on matriculations might produce an approximation that is no more reliable than the uncorrected registration statistics. Uncorrected registration statistics have therefore been used throughout this study.

Occupational and Class Categories

The classifications used here generally follow the occupational and class categories for nineteenth-century Germany and Austria offered in Hubbard 1977 and Hubbard and Jarausch 1979. As in census returns, the occupations of fathers or guardians reported in the student registration records were often vague, but no alternative source is readily available that would offer more precise information. One cannot be sure of how large an enterprise or property was held by someone described as a business owners (*Kaufmann* in German or *obchodník* in Czech) or a farmer/peasant (*Landwirt* or *Bauer* in German, *sedlák* or *rolník* in Czech). Also, the status and general qualifications are often unclear for many described as employees and "private officials." For practical purposes in this study, owners of businesses have been classified as "large merchants" in the propertied category only if there is some indication in the registration records that they owned a large business. Otherwise, it has been assumed that the vast majority of fathers or guardians reported simply as business owners were really proprietors of small or intermediate-sized businesses and belonged to the old lower middle class. Similarly, craft producers and small manufacturers such as bakers, furniture makers, or builders have been classified as independent craft producers; and agricultural proprietors have been classified as peasant farmers in the category of the old lower middle class unless there was some indication in the registration records that they were proprietors of large enterprises.

For convenience, the rankings of government employees and military personnel that were current in the late 1890s have been used in all coding here (see *Niederösterreichisches Amts-Kalendar 1898* [1898], 97–99, 167–73, for a listing of all governmental employment categories). "Government officials" who have been counted in the educated category here include all salaried state, provincial, and municipal employees who were generally expected to have at least some higher education. In the schedule of bureaucratic ranks adopted by the Austrian state in 1873, this would include all the officials in ranks 1 to 9 inclusive. In coding the original data, these were divided between the "higher government officials" in the first through the seventh ranks and the "lower government officials" in the eighth and ninth ranks. One study of the Austrian state officialdom in 1893 showed that only 2,338 of the 15,098 state employees with higher education (*Hochschulbildung*) were in the tenth and eleventh ranks, while the ninth rank had the largest single number, 6,406, including the vast majority of the secondary school professors (cited in Megner 1985, 345–46). For purposes of this current study, the lowest government clerks, bookkeepers, and unskilled salaried employees in ranks ten and eleven have been counted among the clerks, bookkeepers, and unskilled salaried personnel in the new lower middle class.

All the higher commissioned army officers from field marshal down to lieutenant colonel (bureaucratic ranks 1 through 7) have been included here in the category of educated professionals. For the higher officers, education in the military academies and/or various advanced army schools like the *Kriegsschule* was a form of higher education; and their professional experience and official bureaucratic rank gave them a social status that was at least equal to the civilian state employees with university education who were in the same numbered categories. During the late nineteenth century, however, graduates of the military academy in Wiener Neustadt accounted for only one out of every eight infantry officers and only half of all the cavalry officers in the joint army of the Habsburg Monarchy. Large numbers of graduates of cadet schools, whose curriculum hardly went beyond the level of academic secondary schools, were commissioned as lieutenants after one or two years' service as ensigns (see Deák 1990, 85–92). It seems inappropriate then to classify as educated professionals the lower-ranking commissioned officers whose education did not extend beyond the cadet schools. Accordingly, "lower military officers" from major down to lieutenant (ranks 8 through 11) have been included here in the new lower middle class. Navy officers from admiral (rank 3) down to *Fregarten-Capitän* (rank 7) have been included among the educated professionals along with "higher military officers." The lower naval officers from *Corvetten-Capitän* (rank 8) down to ensign (rank 10) have been included among the "new lower middle class." In practice, the number of lower army and navy officers found among the parents and guardians of the sampled university and technical college students was extremely small.

Confidence Intervals

Any findings based on sampled data, like those presented here for the occupational and class origins of university and technical students in Vienna and Prague, are only accurate within a certain confidence interval. Confidence intervals have been calculated here according to standard statistical procedures using conservative assumptions. The samples have been treated as simple, direct random samples assuming normal distributions of the population. No finite population corrections have been made in the calculations, but in most cases the samples are sufficiently large that such a correction would have only a minute effect on the confidence interval. In the interests of economy, for each of the tables based on sampled data, confidence intervals have been presented for only one or two of the statistics that have the greatest possible error and for the one or two statistics that have the smallest possible error. This at least suggests the range of confidence intervals for all the statistics in each table. The formula used here for calculating the confidence intervals with a 95 percent level of certainty is:

$$\rho \pm 1.96 \sqrt{\frac{\rho\ (1-\rho)}{N}}$$

where ρ equals the percentage in a particular cell in a table converted to a proportion, and N equals the number of observations in the respective sample. Unless otherwise indicated, the totals for the samples include only those matriculated students who reported an occupation for their fathers or guardians. The confidence intervals for each reported percentage based on sampled data must be kept in mind in analyzing any changes over time. The differences between percentages over time can be measured by standard significance tests for proportions based on normal approximations of the binomial.

Students from Unidentified Occupational Origins

There is a potential for bias in the findings presented here on the occupational and class origins of university and technical college students due to the number of students who did not report the occupation of their father or guardian in the registration records. Nearly all students reported their birth date, birthplace, religion, and mother tongue; but significant numbers reported that they were adults independent of their parents or simply left blank the item for the father's or guardian's occupation. The father's or guardian's occupation and whether a student was still considered dependent on the parents, of course, directly affected eligibility for stipends and exemptions from the hourly tuition fees. The percentages of students in the samples used here who did not identify their father's or guardian's occupation ranged typically between 7 percent and 14 percent, with the lowest being 0.9 percent for the Vienna Polytechnical Institute in 1859–60 and 5.9 percent for the German Technical College in Prague in 1909–10, and the highest being 16.8 percent for the Vienna University in 1899–1900 and 14.4 percent for the Vienna University in 1909–10 (see the listing of sample sizes in tables 7 and 11 in the appendix). While students with unidentified occupational origins represent appreciable shares of these samples, those percentages are lower than for samples from similar sources used in many other historical studies of education.

If the students with unidentified occupational origins consistently had a significantly different profile from those with identified occupational origins with regard to the other measured variables—province/country of birth, religion, mother tongue, and age—that might cast doubt on the representativeness of the students in the samples who did report their father's or guardian's occupation. Not surprisingly, the most consistent difference found between the students with identified occupational origins and the unidentified was in age, with the latter being on average older. In the samples for the Vienna and Prague universities, the unidentified tended to have a median age of twenty-three or twenty-four years compared with the twenty-one that was typical for the identified. The students with unidentified occupational origins in the samples for the technical colleges also tended to be slightly older than the identified, although there was greater variability in the differences of the medians in those samples. In the majority of all the samples, many of the variances with respect to province of birth, religion, or mother tongue between the students with identified occupational origins and the unidentified were small enough to fall within the range of the sampling error. Where the variances were larger than the sampling error, the students with unidentified occupational origins tended to have larger percentages born outside the immediate recruitment area of the particular educational institution and larger percentages drawn from religious and linguistic minorities than among the students with identified occupational origins. For example, in the sample for the Vienna University in winter 1899–1900, which had the largest percentage of students with unidentified occupational origins (114 unidentified compared with 564 identified), the variances were as follows:

	Students with identified occup. origins	**Unidentified occup.**
	Birthplace	
Lo. Austria (w. Vienna)	36 %	26 %
Moravia	20	13
Bohemia	8.7	7.9
Galicia	4.8	10.5
Hungary	4.1	3.5

	Students with identified occup. origins	Unidentified occup.
	Mother tongue	
German	76 %	66 %
Croatian	3.9	3.5
Czech	4.3	2.6
Italian	2.7	6.1
Polish	2.0	6.1
	Religion	
Rom. Catholic	65 %	60 %
Jewish	27	18
Protestant	4.0	8.8
Eastern Orthodox	2.1	8.8

If higher age tended to be the most important factor in causing the university and technical college students to fail to identify their father's or guardian's occupation, then it might be expected that somewhat larger percentages of these students also were born in more remote provinces or foreign countries and belonged to what were linguistic and religious minorities in the Alpine and Bohemian lands than was the case among the students with identified occupational origins. Members of minority groups and individuals from more remote places might well tend to be older than the other students when they entered the institutions of higher learning and/or might take longer to complete their studies there. Being slightly older would result in a greater tendency not to report the father's or guardian's occupation. One can only guess what differences there might actually have been between the occupational origins of the identified and unidentified groups in the samples. That the unidentified tended to be older and more strongly recruited from minority linguistic and religious groups might mean that they also tended to come from humbler occupational backgrounds than the identified. On the other hand, if a larger share of the unidentified were born in more remote places than among the identified, some of these could also have come from relatively prosperous families who wanted their children to receive advanced education in Vienna or Prague.

Including only the students who reported their father's or guardian's occupation in the registration records for the occupational and class analysis of university and technical college students presented in this study involves some bias then against older students and, by extension, some small bias against students who were born in more remote provinces or who belonged to smaller ethnic and religious groups and might be older than other students when they registered. Nonetheless, insofar as the percentage with unidentified occupational origins was less than 15 percent in all samples but one and many of the variances in province/country of birth, mother tongue, or religion between those with identified occupational origins and the unidentified fell within the sampling error, the analysis of the students' occupational and class origins presented here can be taken as reasonably fair for each university or technical college in toto and for the largest ethnic and religious groups among the students. It should be remembered, though, that all discussions in this study of the recruitment of students by province of birth, mother tongue, and religion *apart* from the analysis of occupational and class origins for the universities and technical colleges are based on the published official statistics for *all* students in each institution.

NOTES

INTRODUCTION
Social Development and Austria's Modern Educated Elites

1. See, for example, the interpretation in Gross 1973, 11–12. On historical interpretations of the failings of bourgeois liberalism among Austrian Germans, see Ritter 1984.
2. Until 1993 the two most important published studies of Austria's German liberal movement both dated back to 1955: Eder 1955; and Franz 1955. Representative of recent research on the German liberals are Höbelt 1993; Judson 1987; and Ritter 1984. On Czech liberal politics, see Garver 1978; Malíř 1975–79, 1985, 1988; and Vojtěch 1980.
3. See Blackbourn and Eley 1984; and Boyer 1995, xii–xiii, 452–60.
4. Lhotsky 1962 is a standard older work on Habsburg and Austrian historiography. For more recent discussions of particular historiographical issues, see Fichtner 1971; Good 1984, 4–10; and Rath 1991. On Czech historiography, see Kutnar 1973–77; G. Cohen 1979; Plaschka 1955; and Rossos 1982.
5. See, for example, the treatment of the modern middle class and its politics in survey histories such as Alexander Gieysztor et al. 1968; Macek et al. 1958; Říha and Mésároš 1960; and the later, less orthodox Pamlényi 1973.
6. For examples, see Urban 1978, 1982; and the collections of essays from the 1970s and 1980s by Péter Hanák (1984) and Jiří Kořalka (1991).
7. For revisionist studies that offer a higher estimation of economic development in the Habsburg Monarchy during the nineteenth century, see Good 1984; Berend and Ránki 1974; and Rudolph 1975. For some counterarguments, see Gerschenkron 1977.
8. Schorske 1980. For discussions of Schorske's contribution and of the recent interest in turn-of-the-century Viennese culture, see Roth 1994 and Steinberg 1991.
9. On nineteenth-century Austrian entrepreneurship, see Klima 1977; Matis 1969; Mentschl 1973; Mentschl and Otruba 1965; and Michel 1976.
10. For examples, see Hának 1984; Kořalka 1991; Malíř 1975–79, 1985, 1988; Urban 1978, 1982; and the collective volumes, Bruckmüller, Döcker, Stekl, and Urbanitsch 1990; and Stekl, Urbanitsch, Bruckmüller; and Heiss 1992. The *Beiträge zur historischen Sozialkunde,* published by the Verein für Geschichte und Sozialkunde in Vienna and the Vienna University's Institut für Wirtschafts- und Sozialgeschichte since 1970 for secondary school teachers of history, and the *Newsletter: Geschichte des Bürgertums in der Habsburgermonarchie,* published by Peter Urbanitsch and Hans Peter Hye of the Austrian Academy of Sciences in Vienna since 1992, have been barometers for the rising interest in the modern middle classes among Austrian historians.
11. On the state officials, see Heindl 1990; and Megner 1985.

12. Lundgreen, Kraul, and Ditt 1988, 11–12.

13. For examples, see, in general, Ringer 1979; and Müller, Ringer, and Simon 1987; on Britain, Banks 1955; and Floud, Halsey, and Martin 1957; on France, Bourdieu and Passeron 1979; Gerbod 1965; Harrigan with Neglia 1979; and Harrigan 1980; on the United States, Jencks and Riesman 1969; and Veysey 1965; and on Germany, Berg 1991; Jarausch 1982; McClelland 1980; and Müller 1977.

14. On the historiography of Austrian education through the mid-1970s, see Engelbrecht 1977. Strakosch-Graßmann 1905 offers a generally sound discussion of institutional and political developments, marked by some German liberal, centralist biases and with little on social dynamics. The older general studies by Czech scholars—Kádner 1931; and Šafránek 1913–18—have virtues similar to those of Strakosch-Graßmann, complemented by Czech nationalist biases. The essays in Lechner, Rumpler, and Zdarzil 1992 are representative of recent work by Austrian historians. Engelbrecht 1982–88 is a masterful synthesis on institutional, political, and pedagogical developments in all sectors of education but focuses primarily on the territory of the current Austrian Republic. On social dynamics, Engelbrecht offers what he can from the limited studies available. Höflechner 1988 focuses on the political history of Austrian higher education with only limited treatment of the late nineteenth century. On the history of Czech education, Kopáč 1968 offers a broad survey, while Kuzmin 1981, also broad in approach, is more sensitive to social issues.

15. See the methodological and conceptual discussions in Craig 1983; Lundgreen, Kraul, and Ditt 1988, 15–20; and McClelland 1986; and Ringer 1979, 1–31.

16. Ringer 1979, 22–25.

17. Some, like J. Maillet and Victor Karady, have questioned whether analyzing the size and social composition of enrollments in secondary and higher education relative to the total population reveals anything important about the social dynamics of advanced education or the professions, since such education has typically served small, very specific social groups in any case. In practice, though, historians have need for absolute measures of the social composition of students in advanced education and the membership of various professions *as well as* measures of access to education and the professions relative to the numbers of the school-aged and the total population. See the comments on this debate in Ringer 1979, 25; and further discussion in chapter 5 below.

18. See, for example, the multicausal explanation for the growth of enrollments in Germany's secondary and higher education during the nineteenth century in Jarausch 1982, 72–76.

19. For reviews of the literature and methodology of the history of education, see S. Cohen 1973; Jarausch 1986; and Talbott 1971.

20. "Austria" will be used here to denote all the non-Hungarian lands and territories that were represented after 1867 in the Vienna parliament, the Reichsrat, even though the imperial government did not officially adopt that designation until World War I. The term *Cisleithania,* often used to denote all the territories on the Austrian side of the Leitha river, the old boundary between Lower Austria and the Kingdom of Hungary, is somewhat obscure and clumsy. See Zöllner 1965, 1980.

1
CHAPTER ONE
Education and the Modernization of Austria in the Mid-nineteenth Century

1. See Good 1984, 45–46; and Wrigley 1969, 153, 185. Good notes that in the period between 1830 and 1845, Britain's industrial output per capita increased by 1.9 percent per annum, although one must add that Britain's per capita industrial base at the time was larger than Austria's.
2. Statistics on numbers of *Gymnasien* and their enrollments derive from Ficker 1873, 130–38.
3. See Engelbrecht 1982–88, 3:261–62; and Šafránek 1898, 30.
4. See discussion of the institutional developments in chapter 2.
5. See Engelbrecht 1982–88, 3:280–81; and Lesky 1976, 16–22, 96–117.
6. Engelbrecht 1982–88, 3:270. Engelbrecht notes difficulties in tracing enrollment trends for the Vienna University because of the inclusion in the university registries until 1848–49 of students from the Vienna *Gymnasien* and until 1842–43 of external students, *Privatstudierenden.* On the growth in the law faculty's enrollments, see Heindl 1990, 181–82.
7. Petráň 1983, 126–27. On the 1824 reform of the philosophical faculties' curriculum, see Engelbrecht 1982–88, 3:277–79.
8. On the academies in eighteenth-century Austria, see Engelbrecht 1982–88, 3:181–86. On the Theresianum, see the literature cited by Engelbrecht 1982–88, 3:362n. 6. On the training of Austrian military officers in the nineteenth century, see Deák 1990, 78–94. The standard work on the military academy in Wiener Neustadt is Svoboda 1894–97. On the military engineering academy and other technical training for army officers, see Brunner and Kerchnawe 1942; and Gatti and Obermayr 1942. On the Josephs-Akademie, see Neuburger 1935.
9. See Engelbrecht 1982–88, 4:252; and Jílek and Lomič 1973, passim.
10. Jílek and Lomič 1973, 275–76.
11. Strakosch-Graßmann 1905, 115–17; Ficker 1873, 137.
12. On educational reforms in Central Europe under enlightened absolutism, see McClelland 1980, 69–93; and Engelbrecht 1982–88, 3:68–120, 146–64, 189–201.

13. Windt 1879a, 225–29; Kammerer 1951, 162–63; Engelbrecht 1982–88, 3:149–50.
14. Engelbrecht 1982–88, 3:162–63.
15. See Šafránek 1910, 5–6.
16. See the critical descriptions by late-nineteenth-century liberal educational historians, Frankfurter 1893, 53–54; and Wolf 1883, 82–83; and the more recent and balanced treatment in Lentze 1962, 19–22.
17. See Kammerer 1951, 175–76; A. Hübl 1907, 142–46; Engelbrecht 1982–88, 3:255–57.
18. On the oversupply of the educated in Britain, France, and Germany during the first half of the century, see O'Boyle 1970.
19. Lentze 1962, 71–72; Engelbrecht 1982–88, 3:279–80.
20. See the discussion in McClelland 1980, 97–132.
21. Hasner 1892, 17. Molisch 1939, 1, also attributes this statement to Francis I, and cites as a source the *Augsburger Allgemeine Zeitung* (1821), 152.
22. See Sked 1989, 79–80.
23. Hasner 1892, 16–18.
24. L. Frankl 1910, 78.
25. Pichler 1905, 93–97.
26. Hanslick 1894, 34.
27. Hanslick 1894, 35.
28. For standard English-language accounts of the European crisis of the 1840s, see Langer 1969; Sperber 1994; and Stearns 1974. For English-language works on Austria's Alpine and Bohemian lands, see Pech 1969; and Rath 1957. More recent Central European scholarship is represented by Häusler 1979; Niederhauser 1990; and Štaif 1990.
29. See Heindl 1990, 187–90.
30. Boyer 1981, 4–7. See also the discussion of the Austrian police before 1848 in Sked 1989, 44–52, 82–83.
31. On the emergence of liberal sentiment among Austrian university professors before the 1848 upheavals, see Lentze 1962, 113–14.
32. See Engelbrecht 1982–88, 3:257–59; Ficker 1873, 135–36; and Hartel 1889, 7–8.
33. On *Gymnasium* curricula in the German states before 1848, see Kraul 1984, 52–56.
34. Engelbrecht 1982–88, 3:278–79; Meister 1963, 1:111.
35. Meister 1963, 1:69.
36. "Entwurf der Grundzüge des öffentlichen Unterrichtswesens in Österreich," originally published in the *Wiener Zeitung,* 11–21 July 1848; reprinted in full in Meister 1963, 2:241–44; introduction reprinted in Engelbrecht 1982–88, 4:517–20.
37. From "Entwurf der Grundzüge," no. 62; quoted in Meister 1963, 1:72; text reprinted in full in Meister 1963, 2:241–44.

38. On the progressive, innovative aspects of state policy in the 1850s, see Boyer 1981, 17–19; Brandt 1978, 1:246–69, 995–1028; Rumpler 1970, 41, 74; and Stölzl 1971, 248–74. Contrast with these interpretations the emphasis on the reactionary aspects in Walter 1970, 96–97, cited in Boyer 1981, 51.
39. On Schwarzenberg, Bruck, and Austria's competition with Prussia, see Good 1984, 78–84; Böhme 1974, passim; and Macartney 1969, 433–37.
40. On Count Leo Thun, see Lentze 1962; Meister 1963, 1:79–91; and Thienen-Alderflycht 1967. Frankfurter 1893 emphasizes Thun's liberal commitment to freedom of teaching and learning, while underestimating the importance of his conservative Catholic goals. Kann 1991, 315–17, describes Count Thun fairly as a "broadminded" and "enlightened" conservative but without mentioning his commitment to Catholic restoration thinking.
41. A. Dumreicher 1909, 20.
42. See Prinz 1969, 53.
43. To date the most thorough treatment of Thun's policies in this regard is in Lentze 1962, 86–210, 235–36.
44. Count Thun's memorandum to the ministerial conference, 8 October 1853, quoted in Lentze 1962, 202–03.
45. See Lentze 1962, 91–92.
46. See Engelbrecht 1982–88, 4:223–27; Lentze 1962, 35–42; and Meister 1963, 1:77–111.
47. On Count Thun's personnel policies, see Lentze 1962, 113–48, 172.
48. On the technical institutes in 1848 and during the 1850s, see Engelbrecht 1982–88, 4:252–54; Jílek and Lomič 1973, 363–406; Neuwirth 1915, 225–54; and Wurzer 1965–67, 28–38.
49. On the charters and other changes in the technical institutes in the 1860s, see Engelbrecht 1982–88, 4:253–54; Jílek and Lomič 1973, 463–72; and Wurzer 1965–67, 29–37.
50. On the Exner-Bonitz "Organizational Proposal" and the associated curricular changes, see Strakosch-Graßmann 1905, 201–4; Engelbrecht 1982–88, 4:147–52; and Meister 1963, 1:90–102.
51. See Engelbrecht 1982–88, 4:147–48.
52. On the *Matura* examination, see Ficker 1873, 171–73; and further discussion in chapter 6 below.
53. Quoted in Engelbrecht 1982–88, 4:153.
54. See Egger 1874, 19; Ficker 1873, 185–87; Engelbrecht 1975, 17–18; and Engelbrecht 1982–88, 4:153–54.
55. See Hartel 1889, 4–5, 18–19; and Engelbrecht 1975, 16–17.
56. See the critique by an Austrian liberal historian in Strakosch-Graßmann 1905, 330.
57. Engelbrecht 1976, 22–23.
58. Engelbrecht 1976, 23–24.
59. On the growth patterns, see chapter 2 below.

60. See Meister 1963, 1:83, 110–11; and Engelbrecht 1982–88, 4:225.
61. Widmann 1974, 202–4. Another imperial decree in 1868 closed the Josephs-Akademie again. The existing literature on the learned professions in nineteenth-century Austria does not permit a more precise analysis of the balance between supply and demand for new physicians and surgeons in the 1850s and 1860s.
62. Count Thun's memorandum of 8 October 1853, quoted in Lentze 1962, 204–6.
63. Megner 1985, 22–23.
64. Wolf 1883, 122. On the educational experience of students in the Austrian universities, see chapter 6 below.
65. See Meister 1963, 1:79–87.
66. See Lentze 1962, 97–102.
67. See Lentze 1962, 77–78, 213–15, 232–50; and Engelbrecht 1982–88, 4:228.
68. On the theological faculties, see the critical discussion in Strakosch-Graßmann 1905, 193–94; and the more balanced treatment in Engelbrecht 1982–88, 4:169, 265–68. One sign of the different standards for the theological faculties in the 1850s was the ordinance of the Ministry of Religion and Instruction issued on 26 May 1851, Z. 5123, allowing admission to theological studies on an exceptional basis of students who had completed the eighth year of a *Gymnasium* but had not passed the *Matura*. Another decree of 16 September 1851, Z. 6165, stipulated, however, that anyone admitted to a theological faculty on those terms must be treated as a nonmatriculated (*außerordentliche*) student and would not be eligible to take the doctoral examinations. See Schweickhardt 1885, 1:266–68.
69. On the Concordat of 1855, see the brief comments in Boyer 1981, 20–21; and Boyer 1994, 25:13–14. See also the larger studies, Weinzierl-Fischer 1960; and Mayer 1989.
70. On the role of the Catholic Church in Austrian education during the 1850s, see Strakosch-Graßmann 1905, 204–7; Engelbrecht 1982–88, 4:108–11, 150–51; and Lentze 1962, 235–36, 260.
71. Hartel 1889, 19; Strakosch-Graßmann 1905, 204–6.
72. See Lentze 1962, 190, 202–3.
73. Lentze 1962, 268.
74. See G. Cohen 1988, 34–36; Kuzmin 1981, 84–88; and Prinz 1969, 52–53.
75. See Lentze 1962, 190–91; G. Cohen 1988, 34; and Kuzmin 1981, 85–86.
76. Kavka 1964, 195–96.
77. On political and constitutional developments in the late 1850s and the early 1860s, see Kann 1974, 325–30; and Macartney 1969, 486–516.
78. Count Thun remained an important figure among the conservative great landowners in the Bohemian Diet through the 1860s. Exner died in 1853, but Bonitz continued as a professor in the Vienna philosophical faculty until

1867, when he returned to Prussia. On his work as head of the department of secondary education in the Prussian Ministry of Education between 1875 and 1888, see Albisetti 1983, passim.

79. See Engelbrecht 1982–88, 4:10–12, 227; Kann 1991; and Stourzh 1985, 53–188, passim.

80. Strakosch-Graßmann 1905, 244–45.

81. On these legislative and administrative changes, see Boyer 1994, 25:15–20; Engelbrecht 1982–88, 4:10–11, 111–13; Ficker 1873, 12–13; and Strakosch-Graßmann 1905, 244–63.

82. *Statistisches Jahrbuch 1869* (1871), 366–97; and Ficker 1873, 148. See also Engelbrecht 1976, 17–18; and Engelbrecht 1982–88, 4:65, 150–52, 164–66.

83. On the expansion of secondary and higher education throughout Europe in the 1860s and 1870s, see Ringer 1979, 52–54, 135–39, 146–47; Jarausch 1983, 12–14; Jarausch 1984, 71–75; and Kaelble 1986b, 35–53.

84. See the summary of these developments in Engelbrecht 1982–88, 4:86–91.

85. Badeni 1900, 281–82; Strakosch-Graßmann 1905, 270. See the discussion of primary school attendance in the various crown lands in chapter 2 below.

86. See the charts of the curricula in Engelbrecht 1982–88, 4:484–93.

87. See Engelbrecht 1982–88, 4:112–14.

88. See Stourzh 1985, 166–89; and Engelbrecht 1982–88, 4:297–300.

89. See Engelbrecht 1982–88, 4:214–18.

90. On the evolution of the curriculum for the *Realschulen,* see A. Dumreicher 1881, 5–7; Ficker 1873, 186–91, 194–97; and Engelbrecht 1982–88, 4:153–55. On the growth of the *Realschulen,* see chapter 2 below.

91. See Megner 1985, 23–35.

92. On the "one-year, volunteer" right in Austria, see Engelbrecht 1982–88, 4:13–16, 206–8, 216. On the practice in Germany, see Albisetti 1983, 26–27, 90–91; and Kraul 1984, 40.

93. On the *Real-Gymnasium,* see Šafránek 1913; and Engelbrecht 1982–88, 4:155–56.

94. On these developments, see chapter 3 below. On the Prussian *Realgymnasium,* see Albisetti 1983, 77, 230–37, 262–68; and Jarausch 1982, 36, 38–39, 103–9.

95. See, for example, the memorandum of 8 August 1870 to the minister of religion and instruction by Adolf Ficker, the director of administrative statistics for the ministry, included in *Verhandlungen der Gymnasial-Enquête* 1871, 3–14.

96. "Verordnung des Ministers für Cultus und Unterricht vom 14. März 1870," Z. 2370, in Ministerium für Kultus und Unterricht [hereafter, KUM], *Ministerial-Verordnungsblatt* (hereafter, MVB) 1870, 173, 230–31. A modification issued on 7 April 1878 (Z. 5416) provided for merely an oral examination in religion, which would be waived if the student presented a grade of "good" or better in religion from the *Volksschule.*

97. A search of the original indices for the general and presidial papers of the ministry for 1870 and of the relevant surviving files in the Allgemeines Verwaltungsarchiv, Vienna (hereafter, AVA Wien), produced little on the preparation of the ordinance on admission requirements for secondary schools, AVA Wien KUM PNr. 2370/15 March 1870.

98. Ficker 1873, 148.

99. KUM ministerial decree, 3 September 1870, Z. 420 praes., to all provincial school authorities, reprinted in *Verhandlungen der Gymnasial-Enquête* 1871, 15–16. Both Engelbrecht 1982–88, 4:159, and the earlier Malfertheiner 1897, 10, reverse the order of events, claiming that the advisory commission's deliberations, in the autumn of 1870, led to the introduction of the admissions examinations in the ordinance of 14 March 1870.

100. *Verhandlungen der Gymnasial-Enquête* 1871, 27–54.

101. *Verhandlungen der Gymnasial-Enquête* 1871, 179–180.

102. *Verhandlungen der Gymnasial-Enquête* 1871, 152–53, 176–261.

103. See Engelbrecht 1982–88, 4:152.

104. For a similar interpretation, see Engelbrecht 1982–88, 4:159.

105. The minutes of the Austrian ministerial council from this period are only partly preserved in AVA Wien, but the agenda (*Tagesordnungen*) for the meetings from 1 November 1869 to the end of May 1870, ten weeks after the issuing of the ordinance on secondary school admissions, include no mention of this subject or of the *Gymnasial-Enquête*.

106. Schimmer 1879.

107. *Statistisches Jahrbuch 1869* (1871), 366–87; *Statistisches Jahrbuch 1874* (1877), 25–45.

108. See G. Cohen 1988, 34–35; and Kuzmin 1981, 86–87.

109. Strakosch-Graßmann 1905, 234–40; Ficker 1873, 146–47, 153–54; Ficker 1875, 109; *Statistisches Jahrbuch 1874* (1877), 24–45. See further discussion of the developing educational patterns for the various ethnic groups in Austria in chapters 2 and 4 below.

110. See Jílek and Lomič 1973, 467–71.

111. Strakosch-Graßmann 1905, 235.

112. Kavka 1964, 207–13.

113. See Strakosch-Graßmann 1905, 283–84; Otruba 1975, 99; and Urbanitsch 1980, 100–101.

114. KUM ministerial decree, 12 October 1868, praes. Z. 606. On Bohemia's so-called *Sprachenzwanggesetz* of 1863, see Prinz 1969, 53.

115. See Ficker 1873, 48–49; and Strakosch-Graßmann 1905, 281–86. For an example of the German liberal criticism of governmental support for the "school industry of Austria's Slavic peoples," as some termed it, see Egger 1874, 35–36.

116. See Strakosch-Graßmann 1905, 286–88.

117. Ordinance of 5 April 1878; see Strakosch-Graßmann 1905, 286.

118. Census statistics cited in Urbanitsch 1980, 38, table 1.

119. Stremayr 1899, quoted in Kann 1991, 327.
120. On this series of reforms, see Wolf 1883, 174–76; and Engelbrecht 1982–88, 4:227–28. On the *Universitäts-Organisationsgesetz* of 27 April 1873, see Mischler 1905–9, passim. On the doctors' colleges, see the sympathetic treatment of them in Gall 1965, 23–25, 169–71; and Gall 1975b.
121. See Engelbrecht 1982–88, 4:228–29; Ficker 1873, 245–53; and Widmann 1974, 79–82, 174–77, 189–91, 204–9.
122. See Huerkamp 1980, 355–59; and Huerkamp 1990, 66–70. Prussia recognized in a law of 8 October 1852 the formal unification of medical, surgical, and obstetrical practice by university-educated doctors, who would henceforth bear the title of "practicing physician, surgeon, and obstetrician" (*Praktischer Arzt, Wundarzt, und Geburtshelfer*).
123. See Windt 1881, 446; and [Oppenheimer] 1882, 197–98.
124. See Lesky 1976, 101.
125. See Lesky 1976, 100–101; and Widmann 1974, 202–9. On the parallel developments in the German states, see Huerkamp 1980, 358–61; and McClelland 1991, 38–40, 54–57.
126. See chapter 3 below.
127. KUM ministerial decree, 21 January 1869; discussed in Wolf 1883, 186. See also Engelbrecht 1982–88, 4:266–67; and Widmann 1974, 174–75.
128. See Wurzer 1965–67, 38–45; Engelbrecht 1982–88, 4:254; Lomič and Horská 1978, 22–32, 67; and Neuwirth 1915, 295–305.
129. See Strakosch-Graßmann 1905, 292; Engelbrecht 1982–88, 4:253–54; and Lomič and Horská 1978, 2:24–27.
130. See Lomič and Horská 1978, 269–73; and Wurzer 1965–67, 45–47.

2
CHAPTER TWO
Opening the Gates

1. Schimmer 1858, 7, no. 4:20–21, 78–79; *Statistisches Jahrbuch 1879* (1882), 84–117; *Öster. Statistik,* n.s., 7, no. 3 (1913): 40–87. All totals for secondary enrollments include the *Privatisten,* who studied privately but took all the course examinations, as well as the *ordentliche* students. Schimmer's statistics are apparently from the end of the summer semester for each year. All statistics reported here on secondary school enrollments after 1870 are from the end of the summer semester of the year in question.
2. Schimmer 1858, 7, no. 1:32–33, 128–29; *Öster. Statistik,* n.s., 7, no. 3 (1913): 2, 14. The 1856–57 statistics do not include the theological faculty at Olomouc, the only faculty then remaining of the former university there, or the universities of Pavia and Padua, which were lost to the new kingdom of Italy during the next decade.
3. The Austrian enrollment statistics derive from the sources listed in notes 1 and 2 above and from *Öster. Statistik* 28, no. 4 (1892): 2–17, 30–43; 68, no.

3 (1903): 2–19, 32–49; n.s., 7, no. 3 (1913): 2–17, 40–87. The population totals derive from Urbanitsch 1980, 38, table 1. Some historians of nineteenth-century education report per capita enrollments for secondary and higher education based only on the male population, arguing that women were generally excluded from such education. All relative rates of enrollment reported here will be based on the total male and female population or the total school-aged male and female population, since women were admitted to Austrian secondary and higher education at the end of the nineteenth century and since, in any case, women were always part of the population.

4. See the methodological discussions in Craig 1983, 219–20; Lundgreen 1981; and McClelland 1986, 182–83. On the question of using numbers of students registered or numbers of matriculations, see the appendix on statistical methods.

5. Statistics on the age stratification of the population derive from *Bevölkerung und Viehstand* 1871, 14–461; and *Öster. Statistik* 2, no. 2 (1882): 530–65; 32, no. 1 (1892): 178–83; 63, no. 3 (1903): 14–33; and n.s., 1, no. 3 (1914): 2–39.

6. See sources in notes 1, 2, 3, and 5 above. Nineteen- to twenty-two-year-olds are taken as the prime age group for the Austrian universities in this period, since in the period from 1860 to 1910 between 60 and 70 percent of the matriculated students in the Vienna and Prague universities at any time belonged to that age group. Nineteen- to twenty-two-year-olds accounted for 59 to 68 percent of four large samples taken from winter semesters between 1859–60 and 1909–10 (see the appendix for discussion of the samples). Since the seven-year program of studies in the Austrian *Realschulen* in the late nineteenth century was one year shorter than that for the *Gymnasien,* eighteen to twenty-two years of age is taken here as the prime age for technical college students. Eighteen- to twenty-two-year-olds accounted for between 73 and 84 percent of the matriculated technical college students in Vienna and Prague sampled from four semesters between 1860 and 1910. The rate of enrollment in the technical colleges relative to all nineteen- to twenty-two-year-olds is also provided in the table to facilitate comparisons with the enrollments in the universities.

7. Prussian statistics from Ringer 1979, 272–73. The Austrian statistics derive from the sources cited in notes 1, 2, 3, and 5.

8. Kaelble 1986b, 40–41. For comparisons of secondary education in Germany, France, Britain, and the United States see Ringer 1979, passim.

9. Statistics for Germany derive from Titze 1987, 27, 70, for 1856–57 and from Ringer 1979, 291–92, for later years; the sources for Austria are cited in notes 1, 2, and 3 above.

10. The comparison with Germany here is based on Fritz Ringer's calculations of total matriculated enrollments relative to the total numbers of twenty- to twenty-three-year-olds, male and female, in the population. In measuring enrollments in German higher education, Konrad Jarausch prefers to use

nineteen- to twenty-three-year-olds; Hartmut Kaelble, twenty- to twenty-four-year-olds; and Hartmut Titze, either eighteen- to twenty-five-year-olds or nineteen- to twenty-three-year-olds. See Jarausch 1983, 12–17; and Titze 1987, 66, 72–73. Each scholar has a rationale for his definition of the prime age group for university studies or all higher education. I have used Ringer's statistics in this discussion, since they can be compared more readily to my statistics for the Austrian universities, which are also based on a four-year age cohort, the nineteen- to twenty-two-year-olds in Austria. Nineteen- to twenty-two-year-olds represented the prime age group for Austrian university study because Austria had an eight-year *Gymnasium* program compared with the nine years that was standard in Germany in the late nineteenth century.

11. Enrollment and population statistics for Germany derive from Titze 1987, 27–29, 70–71. The statistics on enrollments for technical institutes in Germany in Ringer 1979, 291–92, include nonmatriculated students and special students up to 1905 and appear to be based on a different group of institutions from Titze's.

12. Kaelble 1986b, 42–45. Kaelble's figure for Austria in 1910 refers only to the territory included later in the Austrian Republic. See Ringer 1979, passim, for comparisons of growth in German, French, British, and American higher education during the nineteenth and twentieth centuries. Jarausch 1983 compares trends in Britain, Germany, Russia, and the United States.

13. Haan 1917, 157, 169. Haan drew no international comparisons of enrollments in higher education relative to school-aged populations. Any effort to present more precise comparisons between Austria and European countries other than Germany with regard to enrollments in various segments of higher education would not be particularly meaningful here because of the greater institutional differences between Austrian higher education and the other national systems.

14. Engelbrecht 1982–88, 4:164, 166–68.

15. *Statistisches Jahrbuch 1874* (1877), 25–45; *Statistisches Jahrbuch 1879* (1882), 84–117.

16. Schimmer 1877, 3:55; *Öster. Statistik,* n.s., 7, no. 3 (1913): 40–86. These totals include all institutions whether or not they offered the full program of studies and excludes the schools in the Italian provinces that the Habsburg Monarchy lost in the late 1850s and 1860s.

17. See, for example, Ficker 1873, especially 129–52; 1875, 97–118. See also Schimmer 1877.

18. See, for examples, Šafránek 1913–18, passim; "Pravda o poměrech německého obecného školství" 1896. See also Wotawa 1905; 1918.

19. See the evaluation in Glettler 1980, 479.

20. Strakosch-Graßmann 1905, 273.

21. Firnberg and Otruba 1951, 33. All statistics on the portion of the school-aged population that attended primary schools in the nineteenth century

should be taken as approximations because of under-reporting to the state authorities of the numbers of children, particularly in rural areas and among the poorest segments of the population.

22. Engelbrecht 1982–88, 4:117.

23. See Strakosch-Graßmann 1905, 270–733; and the statistics on literacy cited in Kuzmin 1981, 98.

24. From statistics cited in Kuzmin 1981, 101.

25. Rom 1914, 591–92.

26. Statistics on the number of *Volksschulen* derive from *Statistisches Jahrbuch 1880* (1883), 420–21; and *Öster. Statistik* 68, no. 3 (1903): 244–45. Statistics on the age stratification of the population derive from *Bevölkerung und Viehstand* 1871, no. 3: 14–461; and *Öster. Statistik* 2, no. 2 (1882): 530–65; 32, no. 1 (1892): 178–83; 63, no. 3 (1903): 14–33; and n.s., 1, no. 3 (1914): 2–39.

27. *Statistisches Jahrbuch 1880* (1883), 420–21; and *Öster. Statistik* 68, no. 3 (1903): 244–45.

28. This was particularly true for Bohemia and Moravia, where after 1900 the provincial governments were paying more than half the cost of primary schools. See Strakosch-Graßmann 1905, 270; and Wotawa 1918, 13.

29. Megner 1985, 26–29, 364–65.

30. See the discussion in chapter 3 below.

31. Schimmer 1858, 7, no. 4: 20–21, 78–81.

32. Schimmer 1858, 7, no. 4: 20–21, 78–81. Calculations of numbers of *Gymnasien* relative to territory for 1817, 1847, and 1873 are reported in Ficker 1873, 130, 137, 151.

33. See Brandt 1978, vol. 2, passim.

34. See Engelbrecht 1982–88, 4:111–12.

35. See Engelbrecht 1982–88, 4:28–29, 150–51, 165–66; and Strakosch-Graßmann 1905, 204–8, 253–74.

36. Schimmer 1877, 55.

37. Gerstendörfer 1896.

38. Herrmann 1913, 29–30.

39. Honza 1926, 8–9.

40. Lewinsky 1868, 5.

41. See the critical comments on the efforts of many small towns to start new secondary schools and their motives for preferring *Realschulen* by a prominent ministerial official in A. Dumreicher 1881, 7.

42. It is difficult to establish an accurate count of how many secondary schools at any one time were funded by the central state, how many by the provincial governments, and how many by communities or of what the relative shares were when sponsorship was shared. These arrangements evolved for each institution, and *Gymnasien* and *Realschulen* that were nominally

communal or provincial institutions might be receiving significant subsidies from the Ministry of Religion and Instruction, while schools taken into central state administration might still receive some funding from local communities or provincial governments.

43. *Statistisches Jahrbuch 1865* (1867), 342–63; *Statistisches Jahrbuch 1874* (1877), 24–45. The 1865 statistics are used here because those from 1866 used in table 1 in the appendix, derived from Schimmer 1877, 60, do not analyze separately the students in the *Real-Gymnasien*.

44. See discussion of the trends in Pliwa 1910, 2–10.

45. See the discussion of attrition during the course of studies in secondary and higher education in chapters 3 and 6.

46. These densities are reported in terms of *Quadratmeilen* in Ficker 1875, 99.

47. Calculated from the enrollment statistics in table 2/5 and the age distributions of the population for each province from the 1880 census, in *Öster. Statistik* 2, no. 1 (1882): 530–65.

48. See discussion of these policies in chapter 3.

49. See Strakosch-Graßmann 1905, 293; Engelbrecht 1976, 44; and Malfertheiner 1897, 6.

50. See the comments by an anonymous contemporary observer in *Die vor- und nachmärzliche Mittelschule* 1889, 29–30.

51. See the descriptions of the development of the *Real-Gymnasien* in the third, ninth, and seventeenth districts of Vienna in Loos 1896, 10–11; and of those in Tábor, Plzeň, Litomyšl, Kutná hora, and Přerov, Bohemia, in Zenkl 1892, 41–46.

52. See discussion of the ministerial policies in chapter 3.

53. See Engelbrecht 1982–88, 4:21–31, passim.

54. From a 1910 study by Rudolph Laemmel, cited in Engelbrecht 1982–88, 4:53.

55. See sources in notes 1 and 3 above.

56. Calculated from enrollment statistics in table 2/5 and the age stratification of the population by province from the 1910 census, in *Öster. Statistik*, n.s., 1, no. 3 (1914): 2–39.

57. See sources in notes 1 and 3 above. All statistics for secondary school enrollments refer to the total, at the end of each school year, of all matriculated students and *Privatisten*.

58. Ehrlich 1909, 17. See also Ehrlich's remarks in Scheu 1908, 286.

59. Albisetti 1994, 22; Engelbrecht 1982–88, 4:281, 290; Lind 1961, 42–47. In an ordinance of 6 May 1878 (KUM MVB 1878, no. 15), the ministry stipulated that passing a *Matura* examination did not entitle a woman to a *Matura* certificate or matriculation in a university.

60. Wurzer 1965–67, 102.

61. *Öster. Statistik,* n.s., 7, no. 3 (1913): 14.
62. On the development of advanced education for women, see Engelbrecht 1982–88, 4:278–94; Forkl and Koffmahn 1968; Heindl and Tichy 1990; and Lind 1961.
63. On "Minerva," see Honzáková 1930. Contemporary developments in Germany are described in Jarausch 1982, 109–13; and Ringer 1979, 41–42.
64. *Öster. Statistik,* n.s., 7, no. 3 (1913): 68–71.
65. See further discussion of the early women students in chapter 5.
66. Statistics derive from Schimmer 1858, 7, no. 1: 26–27, 125; Schimmer 1877, 59, 65; *Statistisches Jahrbuch 1869* (1871), 334–35, 354–55; *Statistisches Jahrbuch 1874* (1877), 8–9, 14–15; *Statistisches Jahrbuch 1879* (1882), 10–21, 36–47; *Öster. Statistik,* 16, no. 2 (1887): 2–5, 14–17; 28, no. 4 (1892): 2–5, 14–17; 51, no. 1 (1898): 2–5, 15–17; 68, no. 3 (1903): 2–5, 16–19; 79, no. 3 (1908): 2–5; 14–17; and n.s., 7, no. 3 (1913): 2–5, 14–17.
67. See discussion of the social origins of university and technical college students in chapter 5 below. Ringer 1979, passim, emphasizes the social differentiation of the various segments of secondary and higher education in late-nineteenth-century Germany, but others, such as Lundgreen 1981, point out that the sons of all occupational groups in Germany preferred the classical *Gymnasien* over other secondary schools. In Lundgreen's view only the universities and technical colleges in Germany showed the social segmentation that Ringer claims.
68. See Schimmer 1877, 61; Otruba 1975, 77; Prinz 1969, 60; and Jílek and Lomič 1973, 444.
69. Megner 1985, 77.
70. See Stark 1906, 193–94; and Lomič and Horská 1978, 168–71.
71. On the introduction of doctoral degrees in the technical colleges, see Engelbrecht 1982–88, 4:254; and Lomič and Horská 1978, 269. On the limitation of enrollments, see Wurzer 1965–67, 48; and the ordinances reprinted in Jähnl 1916, 433–37. See further discussion of these emergency measures in chapter 3 below.
72. Forman, Heilbron, and Weart 1975, 6–8.
73. Calculated from statistics in Haan 1917, 161; and Titze 1987, 28–32, 70–71.
74. The primacy here of Lower Austria, including Vienna, was not simply the result of migration to Vienna by students, since the statistics on education published by the Austrian Statistical Central Commission analyzed students on the basis of birthplace or legal home residence (*Heimatrecht*), not current residence. The published statistics on the geographical origins of students did not distinguish between the matriculated students, who were pursuing diplomas and degrees, and nonmatriculated students.
75. See further discussion of the recruitment of students in secondary and higher education in chapters 4 and 5.

76. The Germanizing tendencies of the neo-absolutist regime during the 1850s led even to the introduction of German-language instruction in the University of Krakow after 1853, but reduced central control in the early 1860s allowed the Galician provincial authorities to begin the gradual establishment of Polish as the language of instruction in the universities of Krakow and L'viv, a process that was essentially complete by 1871. See Strakosch-Graßmann 1905, 283–84; and Urbanitsch 1980, 100–101.

77. See further discussion in chapter 4.

78. Haan 1917, 183, 189.

79. On the division of the Prague University, see Goll 1908; and Skilling 1949, 430–49. On the attempt to open an Italian law faculty in Innsbruck in 1904, see chapter 3.

80. See Haan 1917, 165; and Engelbrecht 1982–88, 4:256–59, 274–76.

81. See O. Frankl 1905–9; and Engelbrecht 1982–88, 4:263–65.

82. Engelbrecht 1982–88, 4:255–56.

83. Statistics in Schimmer 1858, 7, no. 1:26–27, 125; Schimmer 1877, 59, 65; *Statistisches Jahrbuch 1869* (1871), 334–35, 354–55; *Statistisches Jahrbuch 1874* (1877), 8–9, 14–15; *Statistisches Jahrbuch 1879* (1882), 10–21, 36–47; *Öster. Statistik,* 16, no. 2 (1887): 2–5, 14–17; 28, no. 4 (1892): 2–5, 14–17; 51, no. 1 (1898): 2–5, 15–17; 68, no. 3 (1903): 2–5, 16–19; 79, no. 3 (1908): 2–5; 14–17; and n.s., 7, no. 3 (1913): 2–5, 14–17.

84. See Haan 1917, 162, 167.

85. *Öster. Statistik,* n.s., 7, no. 3 (1913): 2–5, 14–17.

86. See Haan 1917, 170–73. In winter 1910–11 the largest technical colleges in Germany, in Munich and Berlin, had 2,452 and 2,150 matriculated students respectively. In the same semester the Berlin law faculty had 2,835 matriculated students and the Munich law faculty 1,625.

87. See, for example, the complaints from students in the Vienna University medical faculty in 1869, reported in Lesky 1976, 262. See further discussion of student experiences in the educational institutions in chapter 6 below.

88. See Lentze 1962, 31, 113–48.

89. Engelbrecht 1982–88, 4:235.

90. Ficker 1873, 245.

91. See Strakosch-Graßmann 1905, 315–18.

92. See Engelbrecht 1982–88, 4:227–38.

93. See Juraschek 1876, 333; and Schimmer 1877, 72–73.

94. Statistics calculated from table 2 in the appendix and from data on Germany in Haan 1917, 161; and Ringer 1979, 291.

95. See Widmann 1974, 202–17.

96. Pliwa 1908, 9–10.

97. Titze 1984, 104–5.

98. On the development of the reforms in the medical curriculum, see Lesky 1976, 261–73.
99. *Öster. Statistik* 16, no. 2 (1887): 2–3. See discussion of the trends in medical enrollments in Lesky 1976, 261.
100. AVA Wien KUM Praes. 1891, no. 13447, "Promemoria des Vereins der Ärzte des I. Bezirkes in Wien in Angelegenheit der Reformfrage der medicinischen Studienordnung," 20 June 1891.
101. See Titze 1984, 105–6.
102. On enrollment trends in Germany, see Jarausch 1982, 38–49, 145–48.
103. On the trends in Germany, see Titze 1984, 105–6.
104. See the statistics in Jarausch 1982, 136.
105. See discussion in chapter 5.
106. Late in life, Sigmund Freud reminisced about choosing during his *Gymnasium* years between future study of law or medicine, although he asserted he decided more on intellectual than professional grounds. See Freud [1935] 1950, 13–15.
107. Jarausch 1982, 136.
108. On these developments in Germany, see Jarausch 1982, 134–59.
109. See statistics in Jarausch 1982, 136.
110. See table 2 in the appendix for the Austrian statistics and for Germany, Jarausch 1982, 136.
111. *Öster. Statistik* 79, no. 3 (1908): 26–29. During the late nineteenth century Austria's traditional orthodox rabbis were trained in various yeshivas in Galicia and Hungary. Future rabbis from the Alpine and Bohemian lands who wanted more modern education typically studied first in a philosophical faculty and then completed their training in a rabbinical seminary in Germany or Hungary. A small Jewish theological institute was founded in Vienna in 1893. On Austria's seminaries and church-run theological schools, see Engelbrecht 1982–88, 4:265–68.
112. On general enrollment trends in the Austrian technical colleges, see Wurzer 1965–67, 60–66; and for Prague, Lomič and Horská 1978, 170–71, 380–88.
113. See chapter 3.
114. See chapter 3.
115. Prinz 1969, 50. Prinz balances this by placing the factor of national competition in the context of economic and social development in the Bohemian lands (pp. 49–66, passim). Turn-of-the-century commentators on Czech education tended to portray the rise of Czech secondary and higher education as part of the struggle for national rights. For examples, see Šafránek 1913–18; Šafránek 1898; and from an Austrian German perspective, Wotawa 1918.
116. On ethnic identification and nationalistic political mobilization in the Bohemian lands, see G. Cohen 1981; Stölzl 1971; and the somewhat more schematic interpretation in Urban 1978, 179–256, passim.

117. *Die vor- und nachmärzliche Mittelschule* 1889, 31–32; also quoted in Engelbrecht 1976, 45.

3

CHAPTER THREE
Guarding the Gates

1. A. Dumreicher 1881, 11–12.
2. Quoted in Wotawa 1918, 41.
3. See Jenks 1965, 51–70; and Macartney 1969, 611–15.
4. On the Taaffe government's educational policies, see Engelbrecht 1982–88, 4:29.
5. See Jenks 1965, 55–56.
6. See Kolmer 1972–80, 3:101–6; Boyer 1981, 150; and Jenks 1965, 124–25.
7. See Jenks 1965, 127–29; and Kolmer 1972–80, 3:103–6. Strakosch-Graßmann 1905, 301, contradicts Jenks and Kolmer by asserting that the Taaffe cabinet supported the Lienbacher bill against the recommendations of Conrad-Eybesfeld. It seems more likely that the cabinet wanted to avoid being caught in a direct confrontation between its Catholic conservative supporters and the German liberals.
8. On the 1883 school legislation, see Boyer 1981, 150; Engelbrecht 1982–88, 4:118–19; Jenks 1965, 130–40; and Kolmer 1972–80, 3:287–301.
9. KUM ministerial decree, 20 August 1880, Z. 12050; in *Wiener Zeitung,* 28 August 1880.
10. KUM ministerial decree, 20 August 1880, Z. 12050; in *Wiener Zeitung,* 28 August 1880.
11. AVA Wien KUM in gen., Z. 12050/28 July 1880, Dept. no. 9, Heinrich Schramm, "Der Gewerbliche Unterricht im Verhältnis zum Mittelschulwesen."
12. AVA Wien KUM in gen., Z. 12050/1880, drafts of the ministerial decree of 20 August 1880, with comments and suggestions by Sections-Rat Armand von Dumreicher and Ministerial-Rat Eduard Krischek. On Dumreicher, see Bilger 1928. It is difficult to determine which other high-level ministerial officials or ministers may have been involved in issuing this decree. The *Tagesordnungen* for the Austrian ministerial council during the period from November 1879 to December 1880 that are preserved in AVA Wien include no items relating to admissions procedures for the secondary schools.
13. A. Dumreicher 1881.
14. A. Dumreicher 1881, 46–47.
15. On the debates over "school ballast" in Prussia between the late 1870s and 1884, see Albisetti 1983, 87–98; Jarausch 1982, 52–61; and Müller 1977, 274–97.
16. AVA Wien KUM in gen., Z. 17460/1880, Z. 17623/1880, and Z. 19575/1880 contain extensive reports from all the provincial school boards in response to the August 1880 decree, most of them including copies of reports from individual school directors to the boards.

17. These points were made repeatedly in reports from the provincial governor's office in Trieste and from secondary school directors in Innsbruck, Tirol; Bielitz and Opava (Troppau), Silesia; Graz, Styria; and Prague, Bohemia (the Czech Akademické Gymnasium); in AVA Wien KUM in gen., Z. 17460/1880, Z. 17623/1880.

18. AVA Wien KUM in gen., Z. 17460/1880, director of the K. K. Staatsgymnasium Villach to the Carinthinian Provincial School Board, 12 October 1880.

19. AVA Wien KUM in gen., Z. 19575/1880, report by the Moravian Governor to the Minister of Religion and Instruction on secondary school enrollments, 4 December 1880. Baron Korb-Weidenheim was an estate owner with German liberal connections who served briefly as minister of commerce in Count Taaffe's cabinet during late 1879 and the first half of 1880.

20. Kolmer 1972–80, 4:6–7; and Kazbunda 1934, 88, 95.

21. KUM ministerial decree, 3 June 1887; discussed in Malfertheiner 1897, 23.

22. Kazbunda 1934, 88–89, 94–96.

23. Kazbunda 1934, 94–96.

24. Austria, Reichsrat, *Stenog. Protokolle des Hauses der Abgeordneten,* 10th session, 228th sitting (8 May 1888): 8322–24, 8347–51.

25. Austria, Reichsrat, *Stenog. Protokolle des Hauses der Abgeordneten,* 10th session, 228th sitting (8 May 1888): 8350. See further discussion of student attrition in chap. 6 below.

26. Austria, Reichsrat, *Stenog. Protokolle des Hauses der Abgeordneten,* 10th session, 228th sitting (8 May 1888): 8350–51.

27. On Austrian vocational education during the late nineteenth century, see Engelbrecht 1982–88, 4:193–206, 210–14.

28. Fuchs 1946, 85.

29. On Austria, see Engelbrecht 1982–88, 4:170–85, 232–34; for Germany, see Albisetti 1983, 158–291, passim; and Jarausch 1982, 100–113.

30. See Engelbrecht 1982–88, 4:171.

31. AVA Wien KUM 10 D_1 in gen., Z. 30011/1895, 16 December 1895.

32. Engelbrecht 1982–88, 4:177–78.

33. Engelbrecht 1982–88, 4:30. As for many issues of Austrian domestic politics and administration between 1897 and World War I, there is limited historical literature on educational affairs during that period. The following discussion must rely heavily on the synthesis provided by Engelbrecht.

34. Boyer 1994, 32–36.

35. See the overview in Engelbrecht 1982–88, 4:16–18, 29–31, 177–78.

36. On Christian Social educational politics, see Boyer 1981, 149–54; and Boyer 1994. Educational policies are hardly mentioned in Knoll 1973.

37. See Engelbrecht 1982–88, 4:16–18. On the Social Democrats' educational policies, see K. Rothschild 1974, 339–41; and Weidenholzer 1981, 40–51.

38. See Boyer 1994, 37–45.

39. Kann 1991, 322–24. On the Wahrmund affair, see also Engelbrecht 1982–88, 4:249–50; Höttinger 1949, cited in Engelbrecht 1982–88; and Kavka 1964, 246–47.
40. On the Celje affair, see Radzyner 1983, 140–61; and Sutter 1960–65, 1:108–27.
41. On Italian-language higher education in Austria, see Engelbrecht 1982–88, 4:317–18; Kostner 1972; Schusser 1972; and Sutter 1980, 274–75.
42. For an example of the Czech nationalist agitation for a second Czech university, see the speech of Prof. Gabriel Blažek in the Chamber of Deputies of the Reichsrat in July 1891, Austria, Reichsrat, *Stenog. Protokolle des Hauses der Abgeordneten,* 10th session, 35th sitting (1 July 1891): 1437.
43. See Engelbrecht 1982–88, 4:232–34; and Kavka 1964, 222–42, 248–52, passim. On Theodor Billroth's proposals in the 1880s to limit admission to the Vienna medical faculty to students with an Austrian *Matura,* see G. Cohen 1994; and Lesky 1976, 265–67.
44. See the summary of these university reforms in Engelbrecht 1982–88, 4:232–34.
45. See Lesky 1976, 261–73.
46. This was most apparent when the ministerial authorities insisted on some residual German-language instruction and examinations in the law faculties of Krakow and L'viv after they adopted Polish instruction in the 1860s and stipulated that competence in the German language be tested in the state examinations of Prague's Czech law faculty after the division of the Prague University in 1882. On Krakow and L'viv, see Otruba 1975, 99–100; and on the Prague University, see Jenks 1965, 71–89; Kavka 1964, 221–23, 235; and Skilling 1949.
47. See Lesky 1976, 266–67.
48. See the arguments in this vein from 1894 by the eminent professor of neurology in Vienna, Moriz Benedikt, in *Gutachten und Anträge zur Reform* 1894, 92–94. In winter 1879–80, for instance, more than half of all matriculated and nonmatriculated students in the Vienna faculty came from outside of Austria [*Statistisches Jahrbuch 1879* (1882), 40–41].
49. *Gutachten und Anträge zur Reform* 1894.
50. *Wiener Medizinische Wochenschrift,* 21 December 1895: 2194–95.
51. AVA Wien KUM praes., Z. 740/1895, minutes for the sittings of the *Enquête* on the reform of the medical curriculum and examination, 1st sitting (19 December 1895).
52. Lesky 1976, 268–69.
53. See Engelbrecht 1982–88, 4:233; Lesky 1976, 268–69; and Beck von Mannagetta and Kelle 1906, 884–96. The tumultuous parliamentary politics in these years may have helped delay issuing the new regulations for the medical degree. Count Badeni's cabinet had a stormy career due primarily to the Czech-German conflict in Bohemia. After Badeni fell in late November 1897,

Gautsch served as minister-president for three months while retaining the portfolio for religion and instruction. When Count Franz Thun-Hohenstein became minister-president in early March 1898, Arthur Bylandt replaced Gautsch as Minister of Religion and Instruction.

54. AVA Wien KUM praes. Z. 740/1895, minutes for the sittings of the *Enquête* on the reform of the medical curriculum, 4th sitting (21 December 1895).

55. The new ordinance adopted for the technical colleges in March 1900 continued the requirement of four semesters of study for the first state examination and reduced from six to five the minimum number of additional semesters required for the second examination in general engineering or civil engineering. The new ordinance continued the former required minimum of four additional semesters for the second examination in mechanical or chemical engineering. See Lomič and Horská 1978, 262–66; and Stark 1906, 236–41, 257.

56. Wurzer 1965–67, 85–86. Apparently, no adjustments were made in these cost estimates for changes in the general price index.

57. For the ministerial ordinances, see Jähnl 1916, 433–37. See the discussion of them in Wurzer 1965–67, 48–66, 78, 83–87. Wurzer does not describe the academic and ministerial machinations that led to the limits on enrollments. These extraordinary steps merit further study.

58. See Lomič and Horská 1978, 267–68, 275–82, 330–31.

59. Lomič and Horská 1978, 268–69.

60. Jähnl 1916, 436–37.

61. Engelbrecht 1982–88, 4:30–31.

62. See Engelbrecht 1982–88, 4:172–74; and the reports on the Berlin school reform conference of December 1890 by Salomon Frankfurter in the *Zeitschrift für die öster. Gymnasien* 41, nos. 7–9 (1891); the comments by Hartel, K. Schenkl, and Frankfurter in *Zeitschrift für die öster. Gymnasien* 42 (1891): 255, 264, 841; and Höfler 1891, 106; all cited by Engelbrecht.

63. See Albisetti 1983, 190–226; and Jarausch 1982, 100–107.

64. See Albisetti 1983, 263–91.

65. On Scheu, see Boyer 1978, 82–84.

66. Scheu 1898, 52–53, 79–109. On Jodl, see Schorske 1980, 232–34.

67. Scheu 1898, passim. On the 1898 *Mittelschul-Enquête,* see also Engelbrecht 1982–88, 4:173–74.

68. See Engelbrecht 1982–88, 4:174–76.

69. See Boyer 1978, 84–85; and Scheu's introductory remarks in Scheu 1908, vi–vii.

70. Scheu 1908, 17–18. On this conference, see Engelbrecht 1982–88, 4:176.

71. Scheu 1907.

72. For a more detailed discussion of the ministry's policies on secondary education between 1887 and 1907, see Engelbrecht 1982–88, 4:177–82. See also the briefer discussion in Šafránek 1910, 13–15.

73. Engelbrecht 1982–88, 4:182–83.

74. See the detailed discussion of the 1908 *Mittelschul-Enquête* in Engelbrecht 1982–88, 4:182–86; and accounts of the proceedings in Frankfurter 1910 and Drtina 1908, cited by Engelbrecht.

75. KUM ministerial ordinance, 8 August 1908, Z. 34180. See discussion of this in Šafránek 1913, 3–4.

76. KUM MVB 1908, nos. 18, 19, 23, 28, and 36; 1909, no. 10 and no. 11, cited and discussed in Engelbrecht 1982–88, 4:186–88. See also Šafránek 1910, 16–20; and Prinz 1969, 55.

77. See Engelbrecht 1982–88, 4:185–88.

78. AVA Wien KUM 10 D_1 in gen. Z. 17460/1880, Governor of Styria as chair of the Provincial School Board, Graz, no. 6877, 12 November 1880; report of the Second Gymnasium in Graz to the Provincial School Board, no. 5935, 4 October 1880.

4
CHAPTER FOUR
The Changing Ethnic and Religious Recruitment of Students

1. AVA Wien KUM 10 D_1 in gen. Z. 17460/1880 (17623/1880), Director of the Staatsgymnasium Bielitz to the Silesian Provincial School Board, 11 October 1880.

2. See Ringer 1979, 81–97; Jarausch 1982, 78–159, passim; and Craig 1983, 228–39.

3. On imperial Germany, see Jarausch 1982, 157–59.

4. See Engelbrecht 1982–88, 3: 162, 198.

5. Because of this lack of data, there are no analyses of the ethnic composition of students in Austrian secondary and higher education during the eighteenth and early nineteenth centuries in works such as Engelbrecht 1982–88, Kavka 1964, Kuzmin 1981, and Petráň 1983.

6. A nominally free republic administered the city of Krakow with its university and the immediately surrounding territory from the Congress of Vienna until 1836, when it fell under Habsburg authority.

7. See Strakosch-Graßmann 1905, 84–98; and Engelbrecht 1982–88, 3:73–76, 121–22, 197. Jews were barred from earning diplomas in the philosophical faculties until later in the first half of the nineteenth century, since in official thinking Jews had no need for them as long as they could not be appointed as regular secondary school teachers or university professors.

8. See Engelbrecht 1982–88, 3:160–64, 189–92, 197–201, 252–54, 283–84; and Kavka 1964, 167–76.

9. Statistics from Mitterstöger 1979, 215–17; and Engelbrecht 1967, 146, cited in Engelbrecht 1982–88, 3:257. Few statistics are available on the social origins of secondary school students in other parts of Austria during the early nineteenth century.

10. See Kraul 1976, 509–19; 1980, 142–44. Kraul contradicts somewhat Müller 1977, 44–45, 188–90, who sees German *Gymnasium* students in the early nineteenth century as more broadly recruited from all social strata.

11. See Strnadová 1973, 146–47. These broad occupational designations, based on the registration records, offer no indication of precise social status or of actual wealth or income.

12. On the patterns in Vienna, see Firnberg and Otruba 1951, 50–51. On the general European trend, see Kaelble 1986b, 33–69.

13. Kudlich 1873, 1:138, quoted in Firnberg and Otruba 1951, 53.

14. Data for the Prague Polytechnic Institute derive from a study of students enrolled in basic mathematics courses, Klepl 1957, 153, cited in Jílek and Lomič 1973, 321–22. These occupational categories provide no indication of actual wealth or precise social status.

15. Jílek and Lomič 1973, 322.

16. Reliable aggregate statistics on enrollments in Austrian higher education are not readily available for the early nineteenth century. In 1856–57, Austria had 0.20 matriculated students per thousand people in the total population, compared with 0.34 per thousand people in the German states (statistics from Schimmer 1858, 7, no. 1:32–35; and Titze 1987, vol. 1, part 1:70). See discussion of this comparison in chapter 2 above.

17. Cf. Heindl 1990, 184–85.

18. See Jarausch 1982, 85–87; and McClelland 1980, 151–61, 198–99.

19. See the statistics for Erlangen, Göttingen, Heidelberg, Kiel, and Tübingen analyzed in Jarausch 1981; 1982, 84–87. See also McClelland 1980, 198–200. Ringer 1979, 81–89, reports statistics generally similar to Jarausch's but concludes that it was surprising that German higher education was as progressive as it was in the early nineteenth century. None of these studies treats students in Germany's technical institutes in this period.

20. Heindl 1990, 139–40.

21. On the Austrian bureaucracy in the early nineteenth century, see Heindl 1982a and 1990. There is no study, though, of relations between the Austrian state and society comparable to the work on Prussia in Koselleck 1967; and Gillis 1968, 1971.

22. See Bihl 1980a, 884–85, 908–10; and Rozenblit 1983, 132–46. In the same period, Jews in Prague apparently faced less pressure to convert than did those in Vienna; see G. Cohen 1977, 39–40; 1981, 78–80.

23. *Öster. Statistik,* n.s., 7, no. 3 (1913): 2–5, 64–67. Statistics on the religious composition of the Austrian population derive from Urbanitsch 1980, 54, table 5.

24. Rozenblit 1983, 138–39.

25. See the discussion in Haan 1917, 192.

26. On the controversies regarding the Austrian census statistics on everyday language, see Brix 1982, passim; and Rauchberg 1905, 1:13–18.

27. See Brix 1982, 19–66; and Stourzh 1985, 25, 53–83, 114–21.
28. See the lucid discussion in Bihl 1980a, 894–96, 904–8.
29. On the Czech-Jewish movement in Bohemia and Czech Jews' continued preference for German-language education, see Kieval 1988, 36–63; and G. Cohen 1981, 221–26.
30. See Brix 1982, 367–89.
31. On the issues of assimilation and ethnic identity for Austrian Jews, see Bihl 1980a; G. Cohen 1977; Kieval 1988; McCagg 1989; Rozenblit 1983; and Stölzl 1973–74.
32. *Statistisches Jahrbuch 1879* (1882), 16–17, 42–43; and *Öster. Statistik,* n.s., 7, no. 3 (1913): 2–5, 14–17. The statistics on Austrian education published in the *Mittheilungen aus dem Gebiete der Statistik* for the late 1850s and in the *Statistisches Jahrbuch* for the 1860s and 1870s included no data on the citizenship of secondary school students.
33. See the methodological comments in the introduction above and the argument in Craig 1983, 219–44, for measuring the representation of various segments of the population relative to the numbers of their school-aged youth. Craig in his own study is forced at several points to use extrapolations where he lacks adequate statistics on age stratification for each subgroup in the population. In contrast, Jarausch 1979, 1982, in analyzing the socioeconomic origins of German university students, has not tried to measure the representation of each class or occupational group relative to its school-aged population.
34. The statistical sources for the following discussions of secondary and higher education are: Schimmer 1858; *Statistisches Jahrbuch 1869* (1871), 334–87; *Statistisches Jahrbuch 1879* (1882), 11–117; *Öster. Statistik* 28, no. 4 (1892): 2–43; 68, no. 3 (1903): 2–49; and n.s., 7, no. 3 (1913): 2–87. Comparisons with the ethnic composition of the total Austrian population are based on the census statistics reported in Urbanitsch 1980, 38–39, and 54–55, tables 1 and 5; and *Öster. Statistik* 32, no. 1 (1892): xvii–xix; and 63, no. 1 (1902): xxxii–xxxiii.
35. The Austrian census of 1869 included no formal measure of nationality or language, but from 1880 to the end of the monarchy, Austrian censuses included a question about the "language of everyday use," which was popularly considered a measure of ethnic or national loyalties. Heads of household filled out the census questionnaires and anyone with minimal competence in a language was free to report it as his/her "language of everyday use" regardless of the individual's origins. On *Umgangssprache,* see G. Cohen 1981, 88–91; and Brix 1982, passim.
36. See the statistical sources cited in n. 34 above. On Czech-speaking enrollments in *Realschulen,* see also Urbanitsch 1980, 88–89.
37. The Austrian government statisticians published only aggregate statistics on the citizenship of secondary school students in the late nineteenth century, but it appears that the great majority of those registered with Italian

mother tongue were Austrian citizens. At the end of the 1881–82 school year, for instance, the Austrian *Gymnasien* had 1,512 students with Italian, Romansh, or Friulian mother tongue, compared with a total of only 1,128 foreign students altogether. At the end of the 1909–10 school year, 2,934 students with Italian, Romansh, or Friulian mother tongue were enrolled in Austria's men's *Gymnasien,* while only a total of 1,302 students were citizens of any country other than Austria, Hungary, or Bosnia-Herzegovina (*Öster. Statistik* 3, no. 2 [1884]: 38–39; n.s., 7, no. 3 [1913]: 64–65).

38. See Corsini 1980; Ara 1974, 9–140; Kostner 1972; and Schusser 1972.

39. Urbanitsch 1980, 56, table 6.

40. *Statistisches Jahrbuch 1869* (1871), 366–87.

41. *Öster. Statistik,* n.s., 7, no. 3 (1913): 62–63, 68–69, 86–87. The secondary school students in Galicia at the end of the 1909–10 school year included 19,791 Latin-rite Catholics, 7,265 Uniate Catholics, and 236 Protestants. Only 669 of the secondary school students in Galicia reported German as their mother tongue, while the great majority of the Uniate Catholic students reported Ukrainian as their mother tongue.

42. Census statistics for 1910 derive from Urbanitsch 1980, 38, table 1; and Bihl 1980a, 905, table 92. Cross-tabulations of everyday language and religion are not readily available from earlier Austrian censuses.

43. On Ukrainian social patterns under the Habsburg Monarchy, see Bihl 1980b; Himka 1988; and Rudnytsky 1982.

44. One cannot determine from the published official educational statistics how many of the Austrian secondary school students who were registered with Romanian as their mother tongue were not Austrian citizens.

45. On the Slovenes, see Pleterski 1980; Zwitter 1967; and for the city of Trieste, Cattaruzza 1991.

46. As discussed above, the measure of Jewish representation includes only those students who reported their religion as Jewish on their registration forms. The statistics on enrollments derive from the sources cited in n. 34 above. Statistics on the religious composition of the total population derive from *Öster. Statistik* 32, no. 1 (1892): xvii–xix, 130–31; 63, no. 1 (1902): xxxii–xxxv; and Urbanitsch 1980, 54, table 5.

47. *Öster. Statistik,* n.s., 7, no. 3 (1913): 66, 70, 86; and Urbanitsch 1980, 54, table 5.

48. For a summary of statistics on natural increase in Austria by province between 1871 and 1913, see Urbanitsch 1980, 42–43, table 3.

49. For examples of contemporary discussions, see [Oppenheimer] 1882, 197–99, 231–32; Ficker 1875, 102; Windt 1881; Haan 1917, 174–75, 179–80; and Adámek 1900. On the agitation for quotas, see Höflechner 1988, 37–38; Molisch 1939, 133–37; Whiteside 1975, 117–19; and the March 1885 interpellation in the Reichsrat by the Tirolean deputy Joseph Greuter, discussed in

Kolmer 1972–80, 3:303. For further discussion of Jewish educational patterns in late-nineteenth-century Austria, see G. Cohen 1990a.

50. *Öster. Statistik* 3, no. 2 (1884): 32–45, and n.s., 7, no. 3 (1913): 40–85.

51. See the statistical sources cited in n. 34 above.

52. On the growth of Vienna's Jewish population and of Jewish secondary school enrollments there, see Rozenblit 1983, 13–45, 99–108.

53. See the statistical sources cited in n. 34 above.

54. See the statistical sources cited in n. 34 above.

55. In winter 1879–80, for instance, of the 9,561 matriculated and nonmatriculated students enrolled in Austrian universities, 969 were citizens of Hungary and Transylvania, 161 of Croatia-Slavonia, but only 191 of Germany and 25 of Switzerland. Of the 3,236 students in all the Austrian technical colleges that semester, 316 were citizens of Hungary, 59 of Croatia-Slavonia, only 27 of Germany, and 2 of Switzerland (*Statistisches Jahrbuch 1879* [1882], 18–19, 44–45). In winter 1909–10, of the 27,531 matriculated and nonmatriculated university students in Austria, only 499 were citizens of Hungary, 312 of Croatia-Slavonia, 280 of Germany, and 39 of Switzerland. Of the 10,805 students in the technical colleges in that same semester, only 144 were citizens of Hungary, 116 of Croatia-Slavonia, 26 of Germany, and 9 of Switzerland (*Öster. Statistik,* n.s., 7, no. 3 [1913]: 2–4, 14–16). The published statistics on enrollments provide no cross-tabulations of citizenship with mother tongue or religion, and they analyze citizenship, mother tongue, and religion only for all matriculated and nonmatriculated students combined.

56. In analyzing the recruitment of students in German higher education, Jarausch 1979, 1982, 1983 does not raise the methodological problem of the distorting effects of including foreign students. The percentage of foreign students in the German universities (only 8.7 percent of all university students in 1905–6), was generally smaller than in Austria during this period. Germany's technical colleges, in contrast, had larger percentages of foreign students at the turn of the century than did the Austrian institutions. This problem is raised in more general terms in Craig 1983, 227–28, where Craig argues for considering only the students from whichever state is under discussion and then all such students, wherever they studied.

57. No corrections can be made for the presence of foreign students in these statistics, which are based on the published aggregate enrollments. The inclusion of German-speaking students from outside Austria or of Slovaks from Hungary, who may have registered as Czech speakers, should have little effect on calculations for the representation of Austria's German-speaking and Czech populations in winter 1909–10, given the low foreign enrollments in that semester. See the statistics on foreign enrollments in n. 55 above.

58. The statistics for the Czech University and Czech Technical College in Prague from winter 1889–90 derive from *Öster. Statistik* 28, no. 4 (1892): 2–5,

14–17. The statistics for the Vienna University in winter 1889–90 derive from the author's sample of the *Catalogen der Studirenden* in the Archiv der Universität Wien (on the sampling methods, see the appendix). In winter 1909–10, the Czech University in Prague had 4,329 registered students, but only 4 who were citizens of Hungary, while the Czech Technical Colleges in Prague and Brno had only 19 students from Hungary out of a total of 3,514 (*Öster. Statistik,* n.s., 7, no. 3 [1913]: 2–5, 14–17).

59. In winter 1879–80, for instance, the University of L'viv had 14 students who were citizens of the Russian Empire out of its 1,057 matriculated and nonmatriculated students, and the University of Krakow, 30 from Russia and 13 from Germany out of its total of 707 (*Statistisches Jahrbuch 1879* [1882], 18–19). In winter 1909–10, the University of L'viv had 15 students from Germany and 174 from Russia out of its 4,710 matriculated and nonmatriculated students, while the University of Krakow had 37 from Germany and 639 from Russia out of its total of 3,250 (*Öster. Statistik,* n.s., 7, no. 3 [1913]: 2–5). Neither of these universities had more than a handful of students who reported their mother tongue as German, so one can safely assume that the great majority of the students from Germany and Russia were Polish Catholics, Ukrainians, and Jews with perhaps a few ethnic Russians. The published Austrian statistics did not include totals for students with Russian mother tongue.

60. *Öster. Statistik,* n.s., 7, no. 3 (1913): 2–5. The published statistics reported mother tongue, religion, and country of citizenship separately with no cross-tabulations, so that without using manuscript registration records one can only approximate the totals for the religion or citizenship of the Polish-speaking students. There were a total of 1,645 matriculated and nonmatriculated Jewish students that semester in the universities of Krakow and L'viv, but only a total of 19 students there (of all religions) declared German as their mother tongue. Of the 1,223 Jewish students in the University of L'viv that semester, 495 reported Hebrew as their mother tongue. Presumably, the great majority of the other Jewish students in Krakow and L'viv registered Polish as their mother tongue.

61. In the winter semester 1909–10, for instance, when few students from the Hungarian crown lands were enrolled in the Austrian universities, only 837 of all matriculated and nonmatriculated students in the Austrian universities were registered with Serbian or Croatian as their mother tongue. Probably more than half of these were foreign citizens. Among all university students that semester, 312 were citizens of Croatia-Slavonia, 145 of Bosnia-Herzegovina, and 127 of Serbia, although we cannot assume that all of these students listed Croatian or Serbian as their mother tongue. In the Austrian technical colleges in winter 1909–10, a total of 238 matriculated and nonmatriculated students were enrolled who reported Serbian or Croatian as their mother tongue. In that same semester, 116 of all the technical college students were citizens of Croatia-

Slavonia, 31 of Bosnia-Herzegovina, and 10 of Serbia (*Öster. Statistik,* n.s., 7, no. 3 [1913]: 2–4, 14–16).

62. *Statistisches Jahrbuch 1869* (1871), 334–35, 354–55, 366–87.

63. These statistics derive from the author's samples of the registration records of the Vienna University in the *Catalogen der Studirenden* and the *Nationalen* for the winter semesters 1879–80 and 1909–10 in the Archiv der Universität Wien and the *Catalogen der Studirenden* for the same semesters in the Archiv der Technischen Universität Wien (see the appendix for discussion of the sampling methods). Of all the matriculated Latin-rite and Uniate Catholic students in the sample for the Vienna University in winter 1879–80, 16 percent were born in Hungarian crown lands, 3 percent in other foreign countries, and 81 percent in Austria. In that same semester, 14 percent of the matriculated Catholic students in the sample for the Vienna Technical College were born in Hungary and Croatia, 2 percent in other foreign countries, and 84 percent in Austria. In winter 1899–1900, 92 percent of the matriculated Catholic students in the sample for the Vienna University were native to Austria, and only 8 percent born in the Hungarian crown lands or other foreign countries. In the sample for the Vienna Technical College in winter 1899–1900, 92 percent of the matriculated Catholic students were born in Austria. Beyond the university and technical college in Vienna and the University of Innsbruck, or at least its theological faculty, the other universities and technical colleges in the Alpine and Bohemian lands during the late nineteenth century generally had much lower percentages of foreign students.

64. The statistics used here are based on samples of the manuscript registration records from the universities and technical colleges in Vienna and Prague (see the appendix). No adjustments can be made here for the small discrepancies between the data on the *country of birth* for matriculated students derived from the sampled registration records and the published official statistics on the *citizenship* for all students, matriculated and nonmatriculated. Nonmatriculated students in the late nineteenth century typically accounted for over 15 percent of all Austrian university enrollments and between 6 and 8 percent of all Austrian technical college students. Compared with the matriculated students, individuals with foreign citizenship were probably more numerous among the nonmatriculated students, who were not pursuing diplomas and were not subject to the normal admission requirements, although no precise statistics are available. If the statistics based on the samples of the registration records for the matriculated students underestimate somewhat the percentage of foreigners among the total number of students by excluding the nonmatriculated, they also overestimate slightly the percentage of foreign students by using the category of birthplace rather than citizenship. Some of the students born in foreign lands might have become Austrian citizens by the time they registered in a university or technical college. Given the difficulties that immigrants faced

in gaining Austrian citizenship during the late nineteenth century, though, it is assumed here that the great majority of the foreign-born students in Austrian higher education were not citizens. On naturalization in Austria, see Ulbrich 1905–9, 312–14.

65. In winter 1899–1900, 92 percent of the matriculated Catholic students in the sampled registration records for the Vienna University and 92 percent of the matriculated Catholics in the sample for the Vienna Technical College were born in Austria (see the appendix on the samples).

66. Jarausch 1979, 619–20; 1982, 96–100. Jarausch offers no statistics on Jewish enrollments in Prussian or German technical colleges. Prussia was not only the largest among the various states in the German Empire, but it also published some of the most detailed educational statistics.

67. This is an estimate, since the numbers of Eastern Orthodox students in the author's samples of the registration records for the universities and technical colleges in Vienna and Prague are generally too small to be statistically reliable. In a sample of 908 matriculated students in the Vienna University in winter 1909–10, for instance, there were only 23 Eastern Orthodox students, only one of whom was born in Austria (on the samples, see the appendix).

68. *Öster. Statistik,* n.s., 7, no. 3 (1913): 2–5. Only 58 out of all 1,054 matriculated and nonmatriculated students in the University of Chernivtsi that semester were not citizens of Austria.

69. Based on the statistics in tables 4/3 and 4/4 above and tables 5 and 6 in the appendix, these ratios refer to the combined totals of matriculated and nonmatriculated students.

70. *Öster. Statistik,* n.s., 7, no. 3 (1913): 2–5, 14–17. These ratios refer to the combined totals of matriculated and nonmatriculated students.

71. These statistics are based on the sources cited in n. 34 above.

72. On the ethnic and religious composition of Austrian public officials in the late nineteenth century, see Megner 1985, 250–85, passim; and Rozenblit 1983, 49–53.

73. On Protestant students in Austrian higher education, see Haan 1917, 177. On the Protestant minority's social and economic patterns, see the brief discussion in Gottas 1985, 4:591–93.

74. On the emancipation of Austrian Jews, see Scherer 1905–9; and Bihl 1980a, 890–96.

75. On the social and economic experience of Austrian Jews during the second half of the nineteenth century, see McCagg 1989, 65–158, passim; Kestenberg-Gladstein 1968–84; Kieval 1988, 3–17; and Rozenblit 1983, 13–70.

76. On the employment of Jews in the state officialdom, see Megner 1985, 283–85; and Bihl 1980a, 940–48.

77. Statistics from Rozenblit 1983, 62–68. Compare this with Beller 1989, 34–35, who speaks in sweeping terms about the exclusion of Jews from the higher official ranks and the teaching profession in late-nineteenth-century

Austria. In 1910, 5.3 percent of the total male and female self-supporting (*berufstätig*) population in Vienna I–XIX were in civilian governmental employment, excluding educators (*Öster. Statistik*, n.s., 3, no. 1 [1916]: 138–39).

78. See discussion of Jews' prominent role in the legal profession in Vienna in Beller 1989, 137–38; and the more cautious assessment in Rozenblit 1983, 52–53.

79. See Engelbrecht 1982–88, 4:108–11, 118–19, 150–51.

80. Bihl 1980a, 922–27. Statistics on the numbers of Jews who served as professors in Austrian secondary schools are hard to find, and Bihl offers none.

81. See the comments on Jewish preferences among the various faculties in Haan 1917, 176. On Jewish docents and professors in Austrian higher education, see chapter 6 below.

82. See the discussion of Moritz Frühling's statistics on Jewish career officers in the Austro-Hungarian army in Deák 1990, 176–77. Beller 1989, 37–38, notes that Jewish physicians in Vienna at the end of the century faced discrimination against them when they sought higher positions in hospitals and some felt pressured to convert. Data on the occupations of the fathers or guardians of Jewish students who enrolled in the universities and technical colleges of Vienna and Prague and on the participation of Jews in civic life in Prague suggest, however, that a number of Jewish physicians who had not converted to Christianity held important positions in public health and in hospitals in some cities other than Vienna and in some rural districts.

83. See contemporary discussions of the motivations of Jewish university students in Austria in [Oppenheimer] 1882, 197; and Windt 1881, 445–47. For comparisons of Jewish representation in Austrian higher education during this period with that of other ethnic and religious groups in Austria, see G. Cohen 1990a.

84. See the persuasive argument in Slater 1969.

85. See G. Cohen 1994, 83–98; and McClelland 1980, 119–40.

86. On the importance of education in Czech nationalist ideology, see Garver 1978, 112–14, 181; Kádner 1931, passim; and Šafránek 1913–18, passim.

87. See further discussion in chapter 5 below and in G. Cohen 1990a, 152–54.

88. Statistics on medical enrollments derive from the sources cited in n. 34 above and *Öster. Statistik* 16, no. 2 (1887): 2–5.

89. On Theodor Billroth's thinking regarding the medical curriculum and admissions, see Engelbrecht 1982–88, 4:245; Lesky 1976, 261–73; and G. Cohen 1994, 84.

5
CHAPTER FIVE
The Limits of Opportunity

1. See further discussion of the methodology for analyzing the social origins of students in the appendix. On general problems of analyzing students' social origins, see Jarausch 1979, 620–24; and McClelland 1986, 182–83.

2. Ringer 1979, 71.

3. KUM ministerial decree, *Wiener Zeitung,* 28 August 1880.

4. Engelbrecht 1976, 40 n.

5. Stollenmayer 1950, 24–26. On the Kremsmünster *Gymnasium,* see also Krinzinger 1981, 40–48.

6. For occupational statistics from 1910, see Urbanitsch 1980, 108–11, table 13.

7. Rozenblit 1983, 110–13.

8. *Almanach stát. reál. gymnasia v Praze, Ječná ulice,* 100–101.

9. AVA Wien KUM 10 D_1 in gen. Z. 17460/1880, Styrian Provincial Oberrealschule, Graz, to the Styrian Provincial School Board, 11 October 1880.

10. Ulbrich 1905, 109.

11. "Die Aufnahmsprüfungen" 1883, 441.

12. Wegs 1989, 75–97, stresses the widespread sense of alienation and exclusion from academic secondary education in the Viennese working class between 1890 and the late 1930s. The recollections about schooling of members of Austria's urban and rural lower classes in the late nineteenth and early twentieth centuries in Tesar 1985 and Weber 1984 include hardly any mention of experiences in secondary or higher education.

13. See F. Hübl 1878, 152–53.

14. Austrian government statistics cited in Megner 1985, 186.

15. Marenzeller 1884–89, 2:291–92.

16. See F. Hübl 1878, 152–53; and Marenzeller 1884–89, 2:292–93.

17. F. Hübl 1878, 152–53.

18. *Öster. Statistik* 79, no. 3 (1908): 38–39, 46–47; and n.s., 7, no. 3 (1913): 66–67, 86–87.

19. See the comments of Minister of Religion and Instruction Gautsch to the Reichsrat in May 1888, Austria, Reichsrat, *Stenog. Protokolle des Hauses der Abgeordneten,* 10th session, 228 sitting (8 May 1888): 8349.

20. Ficker 1875, 112; Pliwa 1910, 15.

21. Pliwa 1910, 15.

22. Pliwa 1910, 15.

23. *Alldeutsches Tagblatt,* 1906, no. 234, cited in Megner 1985, 267–68.

24. Statistics prepared by the Austrian Statistical Central Commission, cited in Scheindler 1910, 179. See further discussion of student attrition in chapter 6 below.

25. On the German universities, see Jarausch 1982, 40–41.

26. See Thaa 1871, 6, 41–42; and Beck von Mannagetta and Kelle 1906, 500–502, 531–33.

27. Jähnl 1916, 475–78.

28. Thaa 1876, 44.

29. Jähnl 1916, 476–77.

30. Windt 1879b, 580; *Statistisches Jahrbuch 1869* (1871), 334–35, 354–55; *Statistisches Jahrbuch 1879* (1882), 14–17, 40–47; and *Öster. Statistik* 28, no. 4 (1892): 2–5, 14–17; 68, no. 3 (1903): 2–5, 16–19; and n.s., 7, no. 3 (1913): 2–5, 14–17. On financial aid for students in Germany's universities, see Jarausch 1982, 40–41, 60–61.

31. Pliwa 1908, 9, emphasizes the students' more difficult material circumstances in Austria's "Slavic universities."

32. See sources in n. 30 above and Lomič and Horská 1978, 175, 323.

33. Jarausch 1982, 40.

34. See sources in n. 30 above.

35. See sources in n. 30 above.

36. See the discussion in chapter 6 below.

37. This may be the main reason for the paucity of scholarly studies on the socioeconomic origins of university and technical college students in nineteenth-century Austria, compared with the richer literature on higher education in Germany. The analyses of women students in the Vienna University in Heindl and Tichy 1990 and of technical college students in Prague in Lomič and Horská 1978 are based on manuscript registration records.

38. See the statistics in Schimmer 1858, no. 1:32–33, no. 4:32–37; *Statistisches Jahrbuch 1869* (1871), 334–87; *Statistisches Jahrbuch 1879* (1882), 11–117; and *Öster. Statistik* 28, no. 4 (1892): 2–43; 68, no. 3 (1903): 2–49; and n.s., 7, no. 3 (1913): 2–87.

39. Engelbrecht 1982–88, 4:226, 236; *Öster. Statistik,* n.s., 7, no. 3 (1913): 2.

40. *Statistisches Jahrbuch 1879* (1882), 37–43; *Öster. Statistik,* n.s., 7, no. 3 (1913): 14.

41. The samples of the registration records were drawn from the alphabetic runs of the *Katalogen der Hörer/Katalogy posluchačů* or *Nationalen/Nationaly* from the Archiv der Universität Wien, the Archiv der Technischen Universität Wien, the Archiv Univerzity Karlovy, and the Archiv Českého vysokého učení technického, Prague. See the appendix for further discussion of these sources and the sampling techniques used here. Registration records could not be located for the German Technical College in Prague in 1879–80, and the use of a different format from that previously used for recording registrations in the Vienna Technical College for 1909–10 preclude the presentation of any data from that year.

42. See the discussion of the occupational and class categories used here in the appendix. Owners of businesses have been classified as "large merchants" in the propertied category only if there was some indication in the registration records that it was a large business. Similarly, craft producers and small manufacturers such as bakers, builders, or master brewers are classified as independent craft producers in the category of old lower middle class unless there was some indication that they were proprietors of large industrial

concerns. All the higher commissioned army officers from field marshal down to lieutenant colonel (bureaucratic ranks 1–7) are included here in the category of educated professions.

43. See the descriptions of the occupational categories in *Öster. Statistik* 1, no. 3 (1882); 33, no. 1 (1894); 66, no. 1 (1904); and n.s., 3, no. 1 (1916). On the difficulties of using these categories for analyzing social stratification, see Horská-Vrbová 1972.

44. Findings from a survey of the three secular faculties of the Vienna University in 1909–10 offer some confirmation of this. Of all the responding matriculated and nonmatriculated students, 28 percent had parents with at least some higher education; 37 percent had parents who had complete secondary school educations (see Engliš 1915, 285).

45. Petersilie 1910, 182–91; 1913, 140–46; and Jarausch 1982, 122–23.

46. See Deák 1990, 183–87.

47. See the discussions in Jarausch 1982, 122–23; 1979, 624–27. Using Jarausch's social categories, I have made my own calculation of the percentages of Prussian university students from each social class in 1911–12 based on data in Petersilie 1913, 147.

48. On the attitudes of the Austrian nobility toward higher education, see Engelbrecht 1982–88, 4:22–23. On the representation of the nobility in Germany's universities, see Jarausch 1979, 620–21; 1982, 120–21; and Ringer 1979, 81–94.

49. See sources cited in n. 41 above.

50. Engliš 1915, 283–84.

51. Statistics derive from the Austrian census of 1910, as cited by Urbanitsch 1980, 138, table 16.

52. Petersilie 1913, 147. On this trend, see also Jarausch 1982, 125–26, which offers slightly different statistics.

53. Since these findings are based on samples of all students registered in each selected semester, the percentages in each social category reported here are subject to possible error. For each table or figure based on the sampled registration records, confidence intervals have been calculated, at the 95 percent certainty level, for the reported percentage with the widest margin of error and for that with the narrowest margin of error to provide some sense of the range for all the percentages. Those confidence intervals are presented in the annotations for each table or figure. See the appendix for further discussion of methodology.

54. Jarausch 1982, 123–31; Petersilie 1913, 147.

55. See sources cited in n. 41 above. Because of the possible skewing of the 1860 enrollments and constraints of space, table 8 in the appendix does not include any analysis of enrollments by religious and national groups for 1860. The numbers of Protestant and Eastern Orthodox Christians included in the sampled registration records were too small to analyze separately. For

simplicity in making the cross-tabulations, all the Christian students and those recorded as without religion have been grouped together.

56. For further discussion of the students in the various faculties of the Vienna University, see G. Cohen 1987, 299–312.

57. Jarausch 1982, 134–55, 316–23.

58. The statistics on the socioeconomic recruitment of the students in the various faculties are calculated from table 8 in the appendix and derive from the sampled registration records for the Vienna and Prague universities in winter 1859–60, 1879–80, 1899–1900, and 1909–10.

59. Statistics for winter 1899–1900 and 1909–10 derive from the sources cited in n. 41 above. Similar findings for the Vienna University, using a different occupational scheme, are reported by M. Tichy in Heindl and Tichy 1990, 94–95. The numbers of women in my samples for the Prague University are insufficient to permit an equivalent analysis.

60. See M. Tichy, in Heindl and Tichy 1990, 95–96.

61. See sources for the Vienna University cited in n. 41 above. For further discussion of the religious composition of the women students in the Vienna University, 1900–1914, see W. Heindl, in Heindl and Tichy 1990, 139–50.

62. On Germany, see Jarausch 1979, 618–19.

63. Cf. Engelbrecht 1982–88, 4:289.

64. See sources cited in n. 41 above.

65. All statistics on the occupational and class composition of students in the universities and technical colleges of Vienna and Prague presented in this section are based on the samples of manuscript registration records from the winter semesters 1859–60, 1879–80, 1899–1900, and 1909–10 (see the appendix on the sampling methods).

66. *Öster. Statistik,* n.s., 7, no. 3 (1913): 4–5, 16–17.

67. Confidence intervals: 28% ± 4.1% for students from the propertied and educated strata among Czech-speaking Christians in the Czech University in 1909–10, 24% ± 3.9% for those from the new lower middle class, and 8% ± 2.5% for the offspring of independent craft producers. See also the social analysis of Czech university and technical college students in Prague for 1889, in Freeze 1974, 38–39, which is mostly consistent with the findings presented here.

68. Confidence intervals: 40% ± 7.8% for the offspring of small or intermediate business owners among Jewish students in the German University in Prague in 1909–10, 17% ± 6% for the Jewish students from the new lower middle class.

69. The numbers of Jewish laboring-class students in the samples are too small to permit statistically reliable comparisons.

70. Austrian census statistics as cited in Urbanitsch 1980, 138, table 16. The 1900 and 1910 census statistics included cross-tabulations between occupation and everyday language and between occupation and religion but no cross-tabulation of occupation with everyday language *and* religion.

71. Confidence intervals: 20.3% ± 3.7% for Czech-speaking Christian students in the Czech University in 1909–10, 18% ± 4.8% for their counterparts in the Czech Technical College in Prague.

72. See the discussion in Kavka 1964, 201.

73. No comparable data could be prepared for the Vienna Technical College in 1909–10. Confidence intervals: 5.8% ± 2.4% for German-speaking Christian students in the Vienna University in 1909–10, 7.2% ± 2.2% for their counterparts in the German University in Prague, and 7.2% ± 3.6% for the German Technical College.

74. Confidence intervals: 7.7% ± 2.4% for Czech-speaking Christian students in the Czech University in 1909–10, 13.1% ± 4.2% for their counterparts in the Czech Technical College. See also the analysis of the social recruitment of Czech technical college students in Prague in Lomič and Horská 1978, 173, which stresses the strong representation of the "intermediate petty bourgeois strata," primarily craft producers and small manufacturers, and then of officials and educated persons in the free professions. The occupational composition of the Czech-speaking population derives from census statistics as cited in Urbanitsch 1980, 138, table 16.

75. Confidence intervals: 4.2% ± 2.1% for German-speaking Christian students in the Vienna University in 1909–10, 5.6% ± 2.9% for their counterparts in the Vienna Technical College in 1899–1900.

76. Confidence intervals: 9.8% ± 2.5% for German-speaking Christian students in the German University in Prague in 1909–10, and 7.7% ± 3.8% for their counterparts in the German Technical College in 1909–10. On the circumstances of craft manufacture in German Bohemia and its long-term decline, see Whiteside 1962, passim.

77. *Öster. Statistik* n.s., 7, no. 3 (1913): 5, 17.

78. *Öster. Statistik* 66, no. 1 (1904): clxvii; and Urbanitsch 1980, 138, table 16.

79. Confidence intervals: 43% ± 7.9% for Jewish students in the Vienna University in 1899–1900, 45% ± 8.6% for their counterparts in the Vienna Technical College, 51.1% ± 5.7% for the German University in Prague, 54.4% ± 12.7% for the German Technical College.

80. On this issue, see also G. Cohen 1990a; Rozenblit 1983, 99–126; and the more provocative but also more problematic treatment in Beller 1989, 43–70, 88–105.

81. Austrian census statistics as cited in Urbanitsch 1980, 138, table 16.

82. *Öster. Statistik* 66, no. 1 (1904): clxvii.

83. On the rise of the Czech agricultural middle class, see Heumos 1979; Stölzl 1971, 25–55; and Urban 1978, 134–54.

84. On the social structures and popular culture of peasants in Lower Austria and the Alpine lands in general at the end of the nineteenth century, see Bruckmüller 1977; and Lewis 1978.

85. Rozenblit 1983, 108–9. Rozenblit bases her argument on an analysis of the students in several Viennese *Gymnasien*. My findings suggest that German-speaking Catholic small and intermediate business owners were not as underrepresented in higher education relative to their population as were the German-speaking Catholic peasant farmers and craft producers.
86. Using the published occupational statistics from the Austrian censuses, the best rough approximation for the numbers of the new lower middle class would be the total of white-collar employees (*Angestellter*) in the manufacturing, commercial, and governmental-professional sectors, although this aggregate figure includes educated high-level employees. In this discussion, estate managers are classified in the old lower middle class.
87. See Ringer 1979, 22–27.
88. See the discussions in Jarausch 1986, 227–30; Kraul 1984, 97–98, 118–19; Lundgreen, Kraul, and Ditt 1988, 68–72; Kaelble 1986b, 41; and Müller 1977, 37–60, 287–97, 521–24.
89. Ringer 1979, 90–97.
90. Jarausch 1982, 122–31, 155–59.
91. Craig 1983, 231–44. Although generally rigorous, Craig's work involves some approximations and extrapolations at several crucial points where he lacked sufficiently detailed statistics on the age stratification of the various occupational groupings in the population. Jarausch 1979 and 1982 attempted no such analysis relative to the school-age population for each socioeconomic grouping.
92. See Craig 1983, 225. Craig's discussion of the Karlsruhe Technical College is based on Cron 1897, 73–78. The comparison of university and technical college students in Germany in Ringer 1979, 100–104, avoids any specific discussion of the late nineteenth century.
93. Düwell 1989.
94. See discussion of various examples in Firnberg and Otruba 1951, 77–80, 107–9.
95. Austria, Reichsrat, *Stenog. Protokolle des Hauses der Abgeordneten,* 11th session, 34 sitting (30 June 1891): 1397. On this issue in Germany, see Jarausch 1982, 158–59.
96. See discussion of the findings of K. Vondung and J. Henning in Jarausch 1982, 157–58.
97. Quoted in Megner 1985, 78.
98. Megner 1985, 78–80.
99. Statistics on the mean and median ages of matriculated university and technical college students in Vienna and Prague are based on the samples from the registration records for the winter semesters 1859–60, 1879–80, 1899–1900, and 1909–10 (see the appendix).
100. Engliš 1915, 287–88, however, found that the matriculated women in the medical and philosophical faculties of the Vienna University in 1909–10 had a slightly higher mean age than male students.

101. For further analysis of median ages for various segments of the student body in the Vienna University and comparisons for different provinces of birth, see G. Cohen 1987, 314–15.

6

CHAPTER SIX
The Social Experience of Students

1. See the discussions in Jarausch 1982, 237–38; and Lundgreen 1977.
2. Firnberg and Otruba 1951, 97.
3. Fuchs 1946, 27–28.
4. See Johnston 1972, 67.
5. *Öster. Statistik* 68, no. 3 (1903): 32–33. See also A. Hübl 1907, 202–8. More than 10 percent of the students in the Schottengymnasium at this time were not Catholic. The Jesuits' *Gymnasien* in Feldkirch and Kalksburg were apparently more exclusive. At the turn of the century, the great majority of the students in these two institutions boarded in the schools, and neither school awarded more than a handful of stipends each year (*Öster. Statistik* 68, no. 3 [1903]: 32–35; and n.s., 7, no. 3 [1913]: 42–43, 50–51).
6. See the comparative discussions of European secondary education in Ringer 1979; and Müller, Ringer, and Simon 1987. On British secondary education, see Banks 1955; and Floud, Halsey, and Martin 1957. On France, see Harrigan with Neglia 1979; and Harrigan 1980.
7. On Vienna's Akademisches Gymnasium, see the comments in Johnston 1972, 67.
8. See the quotation from the October 1849 disciplinary ordinance for Austrian higher education in Molisch 1939, 18.
9. See the charts in Ficker 1873, 151; and Engelbrecht 1982–88, 4:494–505.
10. Ficker 1873, 197; and Engelbrecht 1982–88, 4:500–504.
11. Quoted by L. Bürgerstein in Scheu 1908, 205–6.
12. L. M. Hartmann in Seligmann 1921, 47–48. On Hartmann, see Johnston 1972, 72; and Bauer 1926.
13. On the schools' disciplinary functions, see Engelbrecht 1976, 41; Engelbrecht 1982–88, 4:36; Martinak 1905–9a; and Martinak 1905–9b.
14. See the comparisons between German secondary schools and English boarding schools in Gillis 1981, 115–18.
15. See the speeches of Masaryk in Austria, Reichsrat, *Stenog. Protokolle des Hauses der Abgeord.*, 11th session, 34th sitting (30 June 1891): 1400–1401; and of Masaryk and August Fournier in *Stenog. Protokolle des Hauses der Abgeord.*, 11th session, 61th sitting (30 October 1891): 2827, 2838.
16. See, for example, the recollections of J. Roubal in *Památník stát. čs. gymnasia F. Lepaře v Jičíně* 1933, 240–41; of F. Mareš, R. Bílek, and J. Bartoš in *1868–1928: Šedesát Let Jirsíkova Gymnasia v Č. Budějovicích* 1928, 46,

127–33, and 136–37; Fuchs 1946, 28; and the accounts by various Austrian students in Scheu 1907, pt. 2, passim.

17. See, for example, the account of V. Kebrle in *Památník k 60. roč. založení měst. střední školy na malé straně* 1926, 32–33; and Pavel Eisner's recollections in *Almanach stát. reál. gymnasia v Praze, Ječná ul.* 1948, 97–100.

18. See the critiques in Malfertheiner 1897, 58; Scheu 1898, 8–9, 19–22, 39–41, 46–47; and by Marianne Hainisch in Scheu 1908, 139–41.

19. On some of the Austrian history textbooks, see Langer 1980.

20. For complaints about the *Gymnasium* curriculum in the natural sciences, see Scheu 1908, 72–73.

21. See, for example, the recollections of the Czech sociologist Břetislav Foustka from the 1870s in *Sborník Masaryková stát. reál. gymnasia v Praze II, Křemencová ul.* 1948, 21–22; and of various former students of the Minerva women's school in Prague, in Honzáková 1930, passim.

22. For example, see J. Dvořák in *Památník k 60. roč. založení měst. střední školy na malé straně* 1926, 43–45.

23. See the description from the early 1870s in Ficker 1873, 171–72.

24. Ficker 1873, 202.

25. For a sampling of common complaints about the *Matura* examinations at the turn of the century, see Scheu 1908, 68–75. On the changes in the *Matura* examinations made in 1908, see Šafránek 1910, 16–19.

26. On failure rates for the *bac* in France and the *Abitur* in Germany, see Ringer 1979, 57, 121.

27. Statistics on failure rates for the *Gymnasium* and *Realschule Matura* derive from Windt 1879a; Engelbrecht 1976, 42; Malfertheiner 1897, 41; and Scheindler 1905, 76.

28. See, for example, the recollections about the Benedictine *Gymnasium* in Kremsmünster from the late 1850s and early 1860s in Krachowiczer 1879.

29. See, for example, the various recollections about Jičín in *Památník stát. čs. gymnasia F. Lepaře v Jičíně* 1933, 240–41, 247–49, 274–75.

30. F. Procházka in Burket 1913, 282–84.

31. V. Novák in Burket 1913, 299–300. See other recollections about student literary journals and clubs in Houška, Klecanda, and Tiller 1893, 77, 99–100; L. Winter in *Památník na oslavu šedesát. trvání reál. gymnasia v Táboře* 1922, 18–20; and Winter 1946, 20–21.

32. See, for example, Burket 1913, 275–76; *Padesát let čes. gymnasia v Opavě* 1933, 81–82; and Sáňka 1927, 87.

33. Engelbrecht 1976, 37; and A. Hübl 1907, 183.

34. P. Eisner in *Almanach stát. reál. gymnasia v Praze, Ječná ul.* 1948, 97–98.

35. See the recollections of former secondary school students about such teachers in *Památník k 60. roč. založení měst. střední školy na malé straně* 1926, 13–14; and *Almanach stát. reál. gymnasia v Praze, Ječná ul.* 1948, 78–79.

36. On Austrian secondary school teachers, see Engelbrecht 1976, 32–38; and Engelbrecht 1982–88, 4:63–72.
37. Engelbrecht 1976, 34–35; and Engelbrecht 1982–88, 4:69. On secondary school teaching in early-twentieth-century Austria, see Tribl 1966.
38. Statistics derive from the *Jahrbuch des höheren Unterrichtswesens in Österreich* 1895, vol. 8, cited in Engelbrecht 1976, 34.
39. Ficker 1873, 193–94; H. Mitteis, in *Verhandlungen der Gymnasial-Enquête-Commission* 1871, 217–18.
40. Engelbrecht 1976, 34–35.
41. On the waiting periods for regular teaching appointments in Czech secondary schools in 1914, see Beringer 1914; and Havránek 1987, 114–15. On the compensation of supplementary instructors in 1905–6, see Martinak 1905–9a, 611.
42. On the professors' salaries in 1905–6, see Martinak 1905–9a, 611. Data on Viennese machine workers derive from Reden 1984, 165, as cited in Deák 1990, 119. On the ranking of civilian and military positions in Austrian state service at the end of the nineteenth century, see the *Niederösterreichisches Amts-Kalendar für das Jahr 1898* (1898), 167–73.
43. See the estimates in Engelbrecht 1982–88, 4:167–68.
44. Schimmer 1879, 351, 356–58. This reckoning is based on a comparison of the total number of students who passed the *Matura* in all Austrian *Gymnasien* at the end of eight years with the total number of first-year students at the beginning. Students who graduated from Austrian schools other than those where they began are therefore still included.
45. Malfertheiner 1897, 11.
46. "Die Aufnahmsprüfungen" 1883, 440; *Öster. Statistik* 28, no. 4 (1892): 36–39, 42–43, 49.
47. *Öster. Statistik* 16, no. 2 (1887): 34–43; and n.s., 7, no. 3 (1913): 40–87. The aggregate statistics for secondary schools published by the Austrian Central Statistical Commission before the early 1880s did not analyze enrollments by students' year of study. On enrollment trends in the lower and upper forms of the Austrian *Gymnasien* in the 1880s and 1890s, see Malfertheiner 1897, 6–9.
48. The phenomenon of youth choosing to complete their required schooling in academic secondary schools is described in AVA Wien KUM in gen., Z. 17460/1880, Governor of Styria as chair of the Provincial School Board, Graz, 12 November 1880, no. 6877, Report of the Director of the Provincial Secondary School in Leoben to the Styrian Provincial School Board, 4 October 1880; and Provincial School Board for Bohemia, no. 28035, 28 November 1880, Report of the Realschule Director in Trutnov (Trautenau) to the Bohemian Provincial School Board in Prague, 31 October 1880.
49. AVA Wien KUM in gen., Z. 17460/1880, Director of the State Gymnasium in Opava (Troppau) to the Silesian Provincial School Board, 8 October 1880; and Governor's Office in Trieste, Z. 15057, 29 November 1880.

50. Fuchs 1946, 29; J. Španihel in Štětina, Pösl, and Kaska 1907, 183–90; and AVA Wien KUM 10 D_1 in gen., 17460/1880, Director, Higher Real-Gymnasium in Tábor, 29 October 1880.

51. See the comments by Dr. K. Kreipner in Scheindler 1910, 190.

52. These motivations are described in AVA Wien KUM in gen., Z. 17460/1880, Governor of Styria as chair of the Provincial School Board, Graz, 12 November 1880, no. 6877, Report of the Styrian Provincial Oberrealschule to the Styrian Provincial School Board, 11 October 1880; and by Doz. Dr. H. V. Heller of the Vienna Technical College, in Scheu 1908, 2, 254–55.

53. Malfertheiner 1897, 36–37.

54. E. Ehrlich in Scheu 1908, 287–90.

55. See, for example, the arguments of Otakar Hostinský, a professor of philosophy and esthetics in the Czech University of Prague, quoted in Šafránek 1913, 15. On the movement for the reform of Austrian secondary education around 1900, see Engelbrecht 1982–88, 4:172–89. On the contemporary debate in Germany, see Albisetti 1983, passim.

56. No good statistics are available regarding the attrition of students in the technical colleges. For the Czech Technical College in Prague, Václav Lomič estimated dropout rates of 5.5 to 10 percent, presumably per annum, for the years 1873–76, in Lomič and Horská 1978, 52. Pavla Horská does not discuss attrition rates in the later chapters dealing with the turn-of-the-century period.

57. Austria, Reichsrat, *Stenog. Protokolle des Hauses der Abgeord.*, 10th session, 228th sitting (8 May 1888): 8350. The students in the theological faculties were not directly comparable, since the great majority were exempted from tuition, the Catholic Church provided many with free housing, and some were already in minor orders.

58. *Gutachten und Anträge zur Reform der med. Studien* 1894, 6–7.

59. *Gutachten und Anträge zur Reform der med. Studien* 1894, 132–44.

60. Engliš 1915, 337.

61. See the brief comments on pharmaceutical training in Kavka 1964, 234; and Engelbrecht 1982–88, 4:228–29.

62. Between 1849 and 1884 it was possible to complete the requirements for secondary school teaching in exceptional cases with only three years of university studies. The revised requirements issued in 1884 stipulated eight semesters at a university. See Engelbrecht 1976, 35; Engelbrecht 1982–88, 4:64–65; and Petráň 1983, 149, 220.

63. See, for example, the discussion of the Czech philosophical faculty in Prague in Petráň 1983, 220; and the listing of dissertations completed in the Czech and German philosophical faculties between 1882 and 1913–14, in Havránek and Kučera 1965.

64. In the early 1890s, for instance, the theological faculty of the Vienna University had enrollments of 210 to 230 matriculated students each semester, but no more than 10 to 12 completed the doctorate there each year

(Zschokke 1894, 156). On the functions of the theological faculties during the late nineteenth century, see also Wappler 1884.

65. See Kavka 1964, 223–43, passim.

66. Engliš 1915, 338–40. Responding to this survey were 868 students out of the 9,279 matriculated and nonmatriculated students in the three secular faculties in the academic year 1909–10.

67. Wolf 1883, 209–10.

68. Engliš 1915, 339–40.

69. Engliš 1915, 315–19. See also the recollections in Stockert-Meynert 1930, 78–79, about tutoring by Engelbert Pernerstorfer, a future Austrian Social Democratic leader, in the household of Theodor Meynert, a professor of psychiatry and neurology in Vienna.

70. Engliš 1915, 308–11.

71. Engliš 1915, 291–308.

72. Winkler 1912, 35–36, 94. Winkler's survey drew responses from 95 percent of the matriculated and nonmatriculated students of the German University and from 81 percent of the German Technical College's students.

73. Engliš 1915, 300.

74. Only 25.8 percent of the respondents to Wilhelm Winkler's survey of the German University and German Technical College in Prague in 1909–10 reported that their parents resided in Prague (Winkler 1912, 23). According to an analysis of students in the Czech University and the Czech Technical College for winter 1889–90, only 15 percent of the Czech students were born in Prague or came from families that had moved there before or during their studies (Freeze 1974, 38–39).

75. On such assistance for technical college students in Prague, see Lomič and Horská 1978, 179–80; and for university students in Prague, Kavka 1964, 244.

76. See Gall 1965, 121; and Kavka 1964, 244.

77. Wolf 1883, 209–10.

78. On the classification and remuneration of professors and docents in Austrian higher education, see Engelbrecht 1982–88, 4:72.

79. *Öster. Statistik* 68, no. 3 (1903): 2, 16. For a discussion of trends in student-faculty ratios in Germany, see Ringer 1992, 257–59. For all universities in Germany, Ringer calculated an overall ratio of 14 students per each "regular faculty member," excluding emeriti and "auxiliary personnel with short term or irregular appointments in special capacities." In winter 1899–1900, the ratio of all matriculated and nonmatriculated students in the Vienna University to all teaching personnel there except the various short-term instructors and teachers (*Supplenten* and *Lehrer im engeren Sinne*) was 13.2 to 1; for all Austrian universities in that semester, the ratio was 11.9 to 1. These statistics include the adjunct lecturers (*Adjuncten*) among the university teaching personnel, since the official statistics counted them together with the *Assistenten*.

80. The law of 19 September 1898, RGB Nr. 167, MVB Nr. 48, took the *Kollegiengeld* away from the full and associate professors and adjusted their salaries so that the new beginning base salary for full professors in all institutions of higher learning was 6,400 kr. and for salaried associate professors, 3,600 kr., with various supplementary emoluments. The associate professors and docents who were not salaried would still receive the *Kollegiengeld* paid by the students. See Beck von Mannagetta and Kelle 1906, 93–97.
81. See Engelbrecht 1982–88, 4:72. On Viennese professors' incomes, see the recollections in Benedikt 1906, 1:56–58; and Fuchs 1946, 33, 88–89.
82. On the tensions in Austrian higher education during the late nineteenth century between broad educational principles and increasing specialization and between teaching and research, see G. Cohen 1994; and Haan 1917, 156–57.
83. Between 1861 and World War I, the emperor appointed to the House of Lords forty-six professors from the Vienna University alone. The majority of these came from the law faculty, with the second-largest number from medicine. See Heinrich 1947, 208–9.
84. Gall 1975a, 63–74.
85. On the social origins of new *ordentliche* and *außerordentliche* professors and unsalaried docents appointed in the German universities between 1864 and 1890, see Ringer 1992, 263–70. Ringer notes that information on the father's occupation is lacking for more than 40 percent of the personnel for each contingent in the time series for the late nineteenth century, and as a result the findings may be skewed in favor of those from educated or propertied backgrounds.
86. According to the career profiles included in Stark 1906 and Birk 1931, 18 percent of all the individuals who were appointed as full professors, salaried associate professors, and salaried docents to the Bohemian Technical College between 1850 and 1869 and to the German Technical College in Prague between 1869 and 1918 had taught previously in academic secondary schools or advanced vocational schools.
87. See Clark 1972, 173–76, 193–94; and Engelbrecht 1982–88, 4:8–9.
88. Gall 1975a, 69.
89. On the religious composition of the teaching personnel in Germany's universities, 1864–1938, and in the technical colleges, 1900–1938, see Ringer 1992, 276–79.
90. Beller 1989, 35–36, reports that at least 51 percent of those teaching in the Vienna University's medical faculty in 1910 and at least 39 percent of those teaching in all three secular faculties were Jews or of Jewish descent.
91. Cf. Jarausch 1982, 236–38, 329–31; and Rassem 1968, 15–33, cited in Jarausch 1982.
92. Among older works, see Scheuer 1910 for a sound, generally balanced narrative of general developments for Austria's German student groups. For a briefer work on Vienna alone, see Beurle 1893. On Czech student groups in

Prague, see the early publications, Slavík 1874 and Wellner 1895. Molisch 1939 and Wolmar 1943 reflect German nationalist and Nazi influences. Since World War II, a number of dissertations and diploma theses have been produced in Prague and Vienna on various aspects of student political and organizational life.

93. See Scheuer 1910, 128–30; and Engelbrecht 1982–88, 3:283–84.

94. See the summary in Freeze 1974, 16–21.

95. Statistics for 1878 derive from Scheuer 1910, 228. On student reading societies in Vienna from the early 1870s to the 1890s, see also Quidam 1895.

96. *Öster. Statistik* 3, no. 2 (1884): iii, ix.

97. On the Lese- und Redehalle, see Slavíček 1973. On the Czech Academic Reading Society, see Slavík 1869, and Wellner 1895.

98. Slavíček 1973, 57–62. In the winter semester 1884–85, the German University had a total of 1,458 matriculated and nonmatriculated students, and the German Technical College, a total of 260 (*Öster. Statistik* 6, no. 2 [1887]: 2, 14). On the political development of German student organizations in Prague, see G. Cohen 1981, 209–14.

99. Kavka 1964, 202–3. The statistics on 1874–75 enrollments derive from *Statistisches Jahrbuch 1874* (1877), 8–9, 14–15.

100. Kavka 1964, 202–3, 245; Lomič and Horská 1978, 185–86; and Freeze 1974, 60–64.

101. See Jarausch 1982, 239–332, for the best recent English-language synthesis on student corporations in imperial Germany. On fraternities and corporations among ethnic German students in Austria, see Scheuer 1910, passim; Beurle 1893; Gall 1965, 172–89; and Whiteside 1975, 43–52, 247–49.

102. A. Dumreicher 1909, 3–4.

103. Fuchs 1946, 44.

104. Scheuer 1910, 187–219, 229–31; Beurle 1893, 5–29; and Whiteside 1975, 45.

105. On Catholic student organizations in Vienna, for instance, see Scheuer 1910, passim; and Stich 1899.

106. On opposition to dueling among Catholic student groups in Germany, see Jarausch 1982, 255–56.

107. See Kavka 1964, 202–5; and G. Cohen 1981, 33, 45–51, 63–72.

108. Gall 1965, 176–77.

109. On support for liberal and radical nationalist politics among German-speaking students in Austria, see Molisch 1939, 68–118; Harrington-Müller 1972, 14–26; Höbelt 1993, passim; McGrath 1971, 33–52; and Whiteside 1975, 49–52, 68–74, 81–106.

110. On Prague, see Borman 1972; and Kieval 1988, 93–123. On Vienna, see Rozenblit 1983, 159–69, 206–7.

111. See Gall 1965, 179; Rozenblit 1983, 161–66; and Kieval 1988, 116–19, 124–26.

112. On Czech antipathy toward German student fraternities in Prague, see, for example, the novelistic treatment in Dyk 1906.

113. See, for example, McGrath 1971; Schorske 1980, 120–33; Whiteside 1975, 57–58; and Wandruszka 1954, 376–77.

114. See the discussion of this for Bohemian Germans in G. Cohen 1981, 211–12.

115. On student fraternities in Germany, see Jarausch 1982, 260–62, 329–31. See also the comments on the conservative role of student fraternities in modern youth culture in Gillis 1981, 24–26.

116. On nation-building among the Slavic peoples of Austria, see Wandruszka and Urbanitsch 1980, passim; G. Cohen 1979; Kořalka 1991, 23–125; Urban 1978; Kann and David 1984; and Markovits and Sysyn 1982.

117. See the overview of social, economic, and political development among the peoples of the eastern Habsburg lands in Kann and David 1984, 392–447, 471–75. On the Ukrainians in Galicia, see Rudnytsky 1982, 35–37, 62–63; and on Slovene students in Vienna, see Petritsch 1972.

118. On the political roles of professors and students from the Czech University and Czech Technical College in Prague, see Freeze 1974, passim; and Prinz 1969, 60. On the nationalistic street disorders in Prague at the turn of the century, see G. Cohen 1981, 233–44; and Kieval 1988, 71–74.

119. In 1892, for instance, Minister of Religion and Instruction Gautsch banned celebrations of the three hundredth anniversary of the birth of Jan Amos Komenský; but in Jičín some *Gymnasium* students still managed to observe the occasion. See the recollections of A. Seifert in *Památník stát. čs. gymnasia F. Lepaře v Jičíně* 1933, 257.

120. Governor Franz Thun declared a state of emergency in Prague in September 1893 to deal with Czech nationalist demonstrations and then mounted a mass trial of Czech young men based on false charges of a conspiracy, the *Omladina* affair. See Garver 1978, 182–89; and Freeze 1974, 233–76. In spring 1895, a year after the *Omladina* trial, Franz Thun issued special orders regarding discipline and control in the Bohemian secondary schools (AVA Wien KUM Praes. 915/1895, 30 April 1895, Bohemian Governor's Office, Presidium, to the Minister for Religion and Instruction, Dr. Stanislaus Ritter von Madeyski).

121. Stašek 1925, 29.

122. V. Buchar in *Památník stát. čs. gymnasia F. Lepaře v Jičíně* 1933, 65–69.

123. *Památník stát. čs. gymnasia F. Lepaře v Jičíně* 1933, 243, 256–57.

124. See, for example, the recollections of V. Švejcar from around 1868 and of J. Dvořák for 1895, in *Památník k 60. roč. založení měst. střední školy na malé straně* 1926, 30, 43–44; the recollections from after 1900 of E. Konrád and V. Příhoda in *Sborník Masarykova stát. reál. gymnasia v Praze II* 1948,

63–64, 66; and the account of the annual spring excursions of the Jičín *Gymnasium* by Z. Lepař in Štětina, Pösl, and Kaska 1907, 195–98.

125. V. Příhoda in *Sborník Masaryková stát. reál. gymnasia v Praze II* 1948, 66.

126. For examples, see the recollections of Doc. dr. Jiří Klíma for the years 1884–92, in *Sborník Masaryková stát. reál. gymnasia v Praze II* 1948, 48; and the biographical sketches and obituaries of Czech university and technical college professors published in the *Kalendář českého studentstva* 1871–94.

127. See Schmidt-Hartmann 1984, 89–90; and Otáhal 1986.

128. For former secondary school students' recollections about Hanka's manuscripts and the controversy over their authenticity, see V. Novotný (from the early and middle 1880s) and R. Bílek (1895–1903) in *1868–1928: Šedesát Let Jirsíkova Gymnasia v Č. Budějovicích* 1928, 104, 127–28; F. Cvetler (middle and late 1880s) in Burket 1913, 278–80; and B. Novák (late 1870s) and Z. Foustka (1885–93) in *Sborník Masaryková stát. reál. gymnasia v Praze II* 1948, 19, 38. For examples of secondary school students' awareness of their professors' stances on political issues, see J. Horák (from 1855–62) in Štětina, Pösl, and Kaska 1907, 174–75; and V. Švejcar (late 1860s) in *Památník k 60. roč. založení měst. střední školy na malé straně* 1926, 29–31.

129. J. Bartoš in *Almanach stát. reál. gymnasia v Praze, Ječná ul.* 1948, 33–34.

130. For examples of discussions in the social sciences about political socialization and the role of education, see Greenstein 1968, 551–55; Merelman 1980; Jennings 1980; Ramirez and Meyer 1980; and as applied to the study of German secondary and higher education in the late nineteenth century, Jarausch 1978, 609–30. For criticisms of socialization theory, see Prewitt 1975; and Meyer 1977.

131. Jarausch 1982, 329–32. In part, Jarausch follows the interpretation of the role of student organizations in the "self-education" of students advanced in Paulsen 1919–21.

132. Bourdieu and Passeron 1979, 43.

133. See the discussions of the war's impact on Austrian secondary and higher education in Engelbrecht 1982–88, 4:189–92, 250–51; and Höflechner 1988, 84–105.

CONCLUSION
Education, Society, and the State in the Late Nineteenth Century

1. Ringer 1979, 316–17, 335. On the broad parallels in the expansion of secondary and higher education and the social recruitment of students across Europe, see Kaelble 1986b, 32–41, 65–69.

2. Ringer 1979, 291–92. Jarausch has faulted Ringer's methodology for calculating these statistics and uses the nineteen- to twenty-three-year-old age group for German university students. Nonetheless, his calculations show

only slightly higher growth in rates of enrollment in German universities between 1870–71 and 1910–11. See Jarausch 1983, 16.

3. Ringer 1979, 220–31. See also the comparisons of Britain, Germany, Russia, and the United States in Jarausch 1983, 12–18.

4. Jarausch 1982, 32, calls the growth in enrollments a "seismic shift," a designation that apparently originated with Lawrence Stone, in Stone 1974, 1:vii. On this conceptualization, see also Eley 1986, 290.

5. Titze 1981, 1983, 1984.

6. See Ringer 1979, 3–4; Anderson 1961, 253–55; and McClelland 1986, 183–93. For analyses of the possible effects of educational expansion on economic development in modern Germany, see Lundgreen 1975, 1976.

7. Compare with this the arguments for economic growth and development as a causal factor for the expansion of higher education and the recruitment of students in modern Germany in Craig 1983, and the broader discussions in Craig 1981b, and Craig and Spear 1982. Jarausch 1983 argues for an ambiguous "partial modernization" approach in explaining the relationship between the development of higher education and broader social and economic changes in Europe and America during the late nineteenth and early twentieth centuries.

8. Population statistics derive from Mitchell 1978, 3–4.

9. See statistics based on work of A. Kausel and P. Bairoch in Good 1984, 240–41.

10. Austrian statistics derive from *Öster. Statistik,* n.s., 3, no. 1 (1916): 52–54, as cited in Urbanitsch 1980, 138, table 16; statistics for Germany derive from Mitchell 1978, 54.

11. On trends in medical enrollments in Germany, see Titze 1984, 104–6.

12. See Megner 1985, 25–28.

13. For enrollments in Germany's technical colleges, see Titze 1987, 28–29.

14. See Barker with Moritsch 1984; Moritsch 1991; and Pleterski 1980.

15. On economic and social conditions in Austrian Galicia, see the grim assessment in Davies 1984, 2:139–62; the more balanced account in Wandycz 1974, 214–28; and the treatment of economic development in Good 1984, 146–48.

16. Here one would much like to have statistics on age stratification for Austria's various ethnic groups in each crown land.

17. At the turn of the century the law faculties in Krakow and L'viv had disproportionately larger enrollments compared with medicine and philosophy than in any of the universities of the Alpine and Bohemian lands except the Czech University of Prague. In winter 1909–10, the law faculty of the University of L'viv had 2,822 matriculated students compared with only 362 in medicine and 359 in philosophy; in Krakow the law faculty had 1,344 matriculated students, medicine 515, and philosophy 913 (*Öster. Statistik,* n.s., 7, no. 3 [1913]: 2).

18. Ehrlich 1909, 14–17.

19. In table 9 in the appendix, "German Christians" include all students with German mother tongue who were Catholic, as well as those who belonged to any other Christian denomination, or *konfessionslos;* but Catholics account for the great majority in this category.

20. For examples of the small existing literature on social mobility for late-nineteenth-century Austria, see Dokoupil 1973; and Hubbard 1984. See Kaelble 1986b, for a bibliography of studies for modern Europe and North America.

21. See Megner 1985, 80–82.

22. On Jewish physicians in the Habsburg army, see Deák 1990, 173, 177. Just as Czech civil servants became common in many intermediate and lower levels of the Austrian bureaucracy, the Jewish doctor became a stock figure in Austrian military life. Joseph Roth's famous novel, *The Radetzky March,* for example, includes a Jewish *Regimentsarzt* who dies in a duel.

23. On the stratification of the educated elements in late-nineteenth-century Austria, see Kořalka 1992, 210–21; and Bruckmüller 1990, 14–15. On Germany, see Jarausch 1982, 157–59.

24. Kaelble 1986b, 35–69. See also Kaelble 1975.

25. See Haan 1917, 159, 169.

26. See the brief general discussions in Korbel 1977, 63–84, passim; Mamatey and Luža, 1973, 78–79, 121, 134–36; Sládek 1990; and J. Rothschild 1974, 113–14. Just what remained of Austrian regulations in primary and secondary education in Czechoslovakia during the mid-1930s can be seen in Placht and Havelka 1934.

27. On the development of Slovak education in the 1920s and 1930s, see Johnson 1985. On Czech-Slovak frictions in the interwar period, see J. Rothschild 1974, 117–21, 132–35; Leff 1988, 45–85; Mamatey and Luža 1973, 114–26, 148–52; and from a decidedly Czech perspective, Korbel 1977, 85–111.

28. See J. Rothschild 1974, 29–30, 208.

29. For general treatments of the social and political conflicts in the first Austrian Republic, see Benedikt 1954; Carsten 1986; Diamant 1960; Goldinger and Binder 1992; Gulick 1948; Rabinbach 1983, 1985.

30. Renner 1916–17, 1:87–88; also quoted in part in Megner 1985, 25.

Archival Sources

Archiv českého vysokého učení technického (Archive of the Czech Technical College) [AČVUT], Prague

STUDENT REGISTRATION RECORDS, 1859/60–1909/10

Haupt-Katalog über die Studierenden am ständischen polytechnischen Institute zu Prag im Schuljahre 1859–60

C. k. česká vysoká škola technická v Praze, *Katalogy posluchačů, 1879–1880, 1899–1900, 1909–10* (Imperial-Royal Czech Technical College in Prague, Catalogs of Students, 1879–80, 1899–1900, 1909–10)

Haupt-Katalog über die ordentlichen und außerordentlichen Hörer der k. k. deutschen technischen Hochschule im Studienjahre 1899–1900

K. K. deutsche technische Hochschule in Prag. *Haupt-Katalog über die ordentlichen und außerordentlichen Hörer im Studienjahre 1909–10*

(Registration records for the German Technical College in Prague for 1879–80 could not be located.)

Archiv der Technischen Universität Wien, Vienna

STUDENT REGISTRATION RECORDS, 1859/60–1909/10

K. K. Polytechnisches Institut in Wien. *Katalog über die Studenten der tech. Abteilung im Jahr 1859–60*

K. K. technische Hochschule in Wien. *Haupt-Catalog der ordentlichen und außerordentlichen Hörer, sowie der Hörer der Bodencultur im Studienjahr 1879–80*

K. K. technische Hochschule in Wien. *Haupt-Katalog der ordentlichen und außerordentlichen Hörer im Studienjahr 1899–1900*

Archiv der Universität Wien, Vienna

STUDENT REGISTRATION RECORDS, 1859/60–1909/10

Catalog der Studirenden, winter semester 1859–60

Nationalen, winter semesters 1879–80, 1899–1900, 1909–10

Archiv Univerzity Karlovy (Archive of the Charles University) (AUK), Prague

STUDENT REGISTRATION RECORDS, 1859/60–1909/10

Hauptkatalog der Hörer im Wintersemester 1859–60

Katalog der Studirenden im Wintersemester 1879–80

Nationaly posluchačů české university (Individual student registrations of the Czech University), winter semester 1899–1900, winter semester 1909–10

Nationalen (German University), winter semesters 1899–1900, 1909–10

VŠESTUDENTSKY ARCHIV (ARCHIVE FOR ALL STUDENT GROUPS)

Papers of the Lese- und Redehalle der deutschen Studenten

Okresní archiv Ustí nad Labem (District Archive Ustí nad Labem), Czech Republic

Pozůstalost Franz Josef Umlauft (Papers of Franz Josef Umlauft)

F. J. Umlauft, "Geschichte des deutschen Gymnasiums in Aussig von 1893–1943," ms., no. 1270.

F. J. Umlauft, "Geschichte meines Lebens," ms., no. 1274.

Österreichisches Staatsarchiv: Allgemeines Verwaltungsarchiv, Vienna [AVA], Wien

Ministerium für Cultus und Unterricht [KUM], praesidium papers and in genere

Ministerratspräsidium, Ministerratsprotokolle—Tagesordnungen 1878–81

Austrian Governmental Periodicals

Bevölkerung und Viehstand der im Reichsrathe vertretenen Königsreiche und Länder nach der Zählung vom 31. December 1869. No. 3, *Bevölkerung nach dem Alter.* 1871. Vienna: K. K. Hof- und Staatsdruckerei.

K. K. Ministerium für Cultus und Unterricht. *Verhandlungen der Gymnasial-Enquête-Commission im Herbste 1870.* 1871. Vienna: K. K. Ministerium für Cultus und Unterricht.

K. K. Ministerium für Cultus und Unterricht. *Verordnungsblatt für den Dienstbereich des Ministeriums für Cultus und Unterricht Jahrgang 1870.* 1870. Vienna: K. K. Hof- und Staatsdruckerei.

Mittheilungen aus dem Gebiete der Statistik. 1852–74.

Niederösterreichisches Amts-Kalendar. 1866–1918.

Österreichische Statistik. 1882–1910; n.s., 1910–18.

Reichsrat. *Stenographische Protokolle des Hauses der Abgeordneten.* 1862–1918.

Statistisches Jahrbuch der österreichischen Monarchie für das Jahr 1863 et seq. 1864–68; after 1867, *Statistisches Jahrbuch für das Jahr 1867* et seq. 1869–84.

Statistische Monatsschrift. 1875–95; n.s., 1896–1917.

Tafeln zur Statistik der Österreichischen Monarchie. 1859–71.

Daily and Weekly Newspapers

Neue freie Presse (daily, Vienna).

Wiener medizinische Wochenschrift (weekly, Vienna).

Wiener Zeitung (daily, Vienna).

Other printed sources

Adámek, Karel. 1900. *Slovo o židech* (A word on the Jews). 2d ed. Chrudim.

Albert, Eduard. 1880. *Über Theorie und Praxis im Universitäts-Studium.* Innsbruck.

Albisetti, James C. 1983. *Secondary School Reform in Imperial Germany.* Princeton: Princeton University Press.

______. 1994. "Mädchenerziehung im deutschsprachigen Österreich, im Deutschen Reich und in der Schweiz, 1866–1914." In *Frauen in Österreich: Beiträge zu ihrer Situation im 19. und 20. Jahrhundert,* edited by David Good, Margarete Grandner, and Mary Jo Maynes, 15–31. Vienna: Böhlau.

Almanach chrudimského studentstva na "Majales" roku 1919 (Commemorative volume of the Chrudim students, "Majales," 1919). 1919. Chrudim.

Almanach státního reálního gymnasia v Praze, Ječná ulice: Na pamět století I. české reálky (Commemorative volume of the state Realgymnasium in Prague, Ječná Street: In memory of one hundred years of the first Czech *Realschule*). 1948. Prague.

Almanach vydáný k oslavě padesátileté působnosti státního gymnasia v Domažlicích 1871–1921 (Commemorative volume published for the celebration of fifty years of operation of the State Gymnasium in Domažlice, 1871–1921). 1921. Domažlice: E. Prunar.

Anderson, C. Arnold. 1961. "Access to Higher Education and Economic Development." In *Education, Economy and Society,* edited by A. H. Halsey, J. E. Floud, and C. A. Anderson, 252–65. New York: Macmillan.

Ara, Angelo. 1974. *Ricerche sugli auto-italiani e l'ultima Austria.* Rome: Elia.

"Die Aufnahmsprüfungen an den österreichischen Mittelschulen für das Schuljahr 1882–1883." 1883. *Statistische Monatsschrift* 9:435–49.

Badeni, Graf Stanislaw H. 1900. "Schulpflicht und Schulbesuch in Oesterreich." *Statistische Monatsschrift,* n.s., 5:281–309.

Banks, Olive. 1955. *Parity and Prestige in English Secondary Education.* London: Routledge and Kegan Paul.

Barker, Thomas M., with Andreas Moritsch. 1984. *The Slovene Minority of Carinthia.* Boulder, Colo.: East European Monographs.

Bauer, Stephan. 1926. "Ludo Moritz Hartmann." *Neue Österreichische Biographie, 1815–1918,* 3:197–209. Vienna: Öster. Akademie der Wissenschaften.

Bauernfeld, Eduard von. 1923. *Aus Alt- und Neu-Wien.* Vienna: Öster. Schulbuchverlag.

Beck von Mannagetta, Leo Ritter, and Carl von Kelle, eds. 1906. *Die österreichischen Universitätsgesetze.* Vienna: Manz.

Beller, Steven. 1989. *Vienna and the Jews, 1867–1938: A Cultural History.* Cambridge: Cambridge University Press.

Benedikt, Heinrich, ed. 1954. *Geschichte der Republik Österreich.* Munich: R. Oldenbourg.

Benedikt, Moriz. 1906. *Aus meinem Leben: Erinnerungen und Erörterungen.* 3 vols. Vienna: C. Konegen.

Berend, Iván, and György Ránki. 1974. *Economic Development in East-Central Europe in the Nineteenth and Twentieth Centuries.* New York: Columbia University Press.

Berg, Christa, ed. 1991. *Handbuch der deutschen Bildungsgeschichte.* Vol. 4, *1870–1918.* Munich: C. H. Beck.

Beringer, Antonín. 1914. "Naděje profesorského dorostu" (The prospects for future *Gymnasium* professors). *Všestudentský kalendář Svazu Československého studentstva v Praze, 1914–1915* (All-student calendar of the League of Czecho-Slav Students in Prague, 1914–1915), 115–24.

Beurle, Carl. 1893. *Beiträge zur Geschichte der deutschen Studentenschaft Wiens.* Vienna: Lesk und Schwidernoch.

Bihl, Wolfdieter. 1980a. "Die Juden." In *Die Habsburgermonarchie, 1848–1918,* edited by Adam Wandruszka and Peter Urbanitsch, vol. 3, pt. 2:880–948. Vienna: Öster. Akademie der Wissenschaften.

______. 1980b. "Die Ruthenen." In *Die Habsburgermonarchie, 1848–1918,* edited by Adam Wandruszka and Peter Urbanitsch, vol. 3, pt. 1:555–84. Vienna: Öster. Akademie der Wissenschaften.

Bilger, Ferdinand. 1928. "Armand Freiherr von Dumreicher." *Neue Österreichische Biographie 1815–1918,* 5:114–29. Vienna: Amalthea Verlag.

Billroth, Theodor. 1876. *Über das Lehren und Lernen der medicinischen Wissenschaften an den Universitäten der Deutschen Nation nebst allgemeinen Bemerkungen über Universitäten: Eine culturhistorische Studie.* Vienna: C. Gerold.

______. 1886. *Aphorismen zum "Lehren und Lernen der medicinischen Wissenschaften."* 2d ed. Vienna: C. Gerold.

______. 1888. "Wünsche und Hoffnungen für unsere medicinische Facultät." *Wiener klinische Wochenschrift* 1, no. 36: 733–36.

Binder, Dieter A. 1981. "Duell und Duellverweigerung: Zur Frühgeschichte des CV in Österreich." *Blätter für Heimatkunde* (Historischer Verein für Steiermark) 55, no. 2:42–52.

Birk, Alfred. 1931. *Die deutsche Technische Hochschule in Prag 1806–1931.* Prague: J. Calvé.

Blackbourn, David, and Geoff Eley. 1984. *The Peculiarities of German History.* Oxford and New York: Oxford University Press.

Bloch, Joseph S. 1922. *Erinnerungen aus meinem Leben.* 2 vols. Vienna and Leipzig: R. Löwit Verlag.

Böhme, Helmut. 1974. *Deutschlands Weg zur Grossmacht: Studien zum Verhältnis von Wirtschaft und Staat während der Reichsgründungszeit, 1848–1881.* 3d ed. Cologne: Kiepenheuer & Witsch.

Borman, Stuart. 1972. "The Prague Student Zionist Movement, 1896–1914." Ph.D. diss., University of Chicago.

Bourdieu, Pierre, and Jean-Claude Passeron. 1979. *The Inheritors: French Students and Their Relation to Culture.* Translated by Richard Nice. Chicago: University of Chicago Press.

Boyer, John W. 1978. "Freud, Marriage, and Late Viennese Liberalism: A Commentary from 1905." *Journal of Modern History* 50:82–84.

______. 1981. *Political Radicalism in Late Imperial Vienna: Origins of the Christian Social Movement 1848–1897.* Chicago: University of Chicago Press.

______. 1994. "Religion and Political Development in Central Europe around 1900: A View from Vienna." *Austrian History Yearbook* 25:13–57.

______. 1995. *Culture and Political Crisis in Vienna: Christian Socialism in Power, 1897–1918.* Chicago: University of Chicago Press.

Brandt, Harm-Hinrich. 1978. *Der österreichische Neoabsolutismus: Staatsfinanzen und Politik, 1848–1860.* 2 vols. Göttingen: Vandenhoeck & Ruprecht.

Brix, Emil. 1982. *Die Umgangssprachen in Altösterreich zwischen Agitation und Assimilation.* Vienna, Cologne, and Graz: Böhlau.

Bruckmüller, Ernst. 1977. *Landwirtschaftliche Organisation und gesellschaftliche Modernisierung: Vereine, Genossenschaften und politische Mobilisierung der Landwirtschaft Österreichs vom Vormärz bis 1914.* Salzburg: W. Neugebauer.

______. 1990. "Herkunft und Selbstverständnis bürgerlicher Gruppierungen in der Habsburgermonarchie: Eine Einführung." In *Bürgertum in der Habsburgermonarchie,* edited by E. Bruckmüller et al., 1:13–20. Vienna and Cologne: Böhlau.

Bruckmüller, Ernst, Ulrike Döcker, Hannes Stekl, and Peter Urbanitsch, eds. 1990. *Bürgertum in der Habsburgermonarchie.* Vienna and Cologne: Böhlau.

Brunner, Moritz Ritter von, and Hugo Kerchnawe. 1942. *225 Jahre Technische Militärakademie 1717 bis 1942.* Vienna.

Burket, Josef et al., eds. 1913. *Almanach vydáný k oslavě padesátileté působnosti c. k. reálného a vyššího gymnasia v Chrudimi a spolu ke sjezdu všech bývalých žáků chrudimského gymnasia ve dnech 27.–29. září 1913* (Commemorative volume published in celebration of fifty years of the Imp.-Royal *Real-* and *Obergymnasium* in Chrudim and the assembly of all former students of the Chrudim Gymnasium, 27–29 September 1913). Chrudim.

Carsten, Francis L. 1986. *The First Austrian Republic 1918–1938.* Aldershot: Gower Publ. Co.

Cassidy, David. 1983. "Recent Perspectives on German Technical Education." *Historical Studies in the Physical Sciences* 14:187–200.

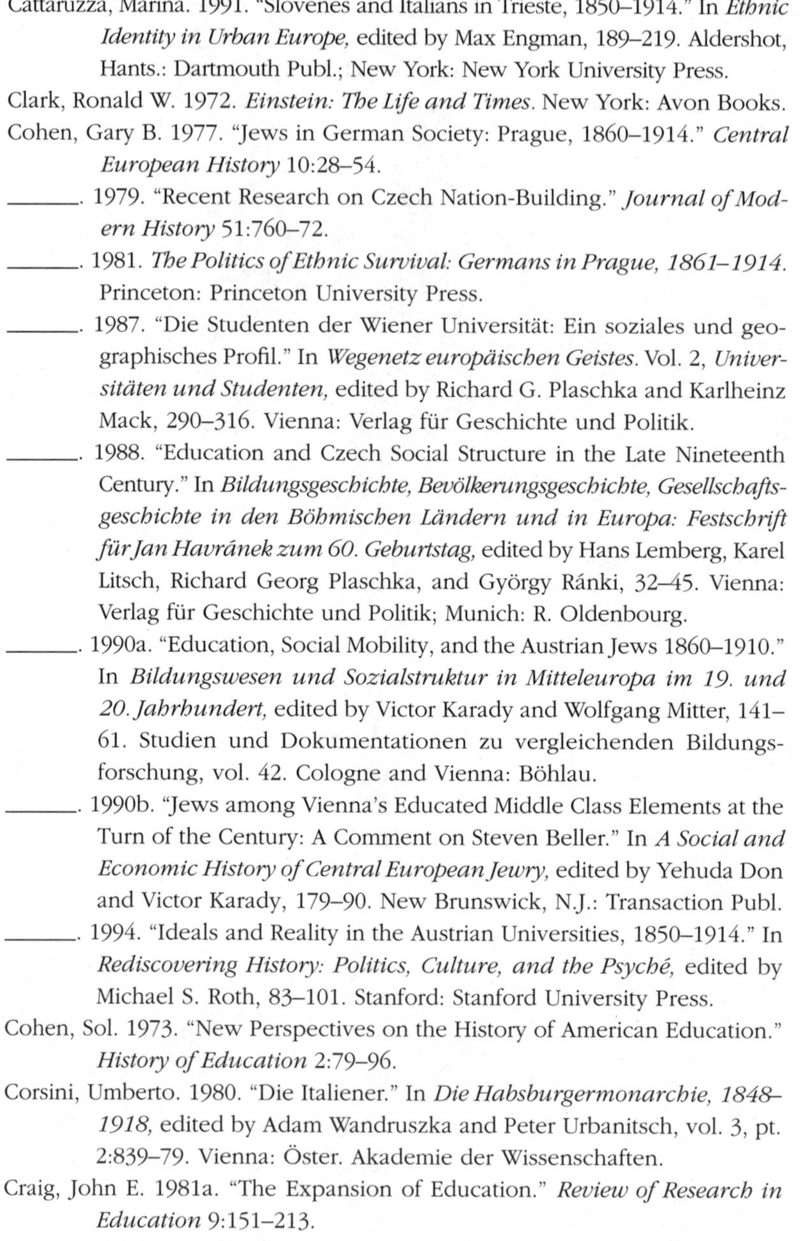

Cattaruzza, Marina. 1991. "Slovenes and Italians in Trieste, 1850–1914." In *Ethnic Identity in Urban Europe,* edited by Max Engman, 189–219. Aldershot, Hants.: Dartmouth Publ.; New York: New York University Press.

Clark, Ronald W. 1972. *Einstein: The Life and Times.* New York: Avon Books.

Cohen, Gary B. 1977. "Jews in German Society: Prague, 1860–1914." *Central European History* 10:28–54.

———. 1979. "Recent Research on Czech Nation-Building." *Journal of Modern History* 51:760–72.

———. 1981. *The Politics of Ethnic Survival: Germans in Prague, 1861–1914.* Princeton: Princeton University Press.

———. 1987. "Die Studenten der Wiener Universität: Ein soziales und geographisches Profil." In *Wegenetz europäischen Geistes.* Vol. 2, *Universitäten und Studenten,* edited by Richard G. Plaschka and Karlheinz Mack, 290–316. Vienna: Verlag für Geschichte und Politik.

———. 1988. "Education and Czech Social Structure in the Late Nineteenth Century." In *Bildungsgeschichte, Bevölkerungsgeschichte, Gesellschaftsgeschichte in den Böhmischen Ländern und in Europa: Festschrift für Jan Havránek zum 60. Geburtstag,* edited by Hans Lemberg, Karel Litsch, Richard Georg Plaschka, and György Ránki, 32–45. Vienna: Verlag für Geschichte und Politik; Munich: R. Oldenbourg.

———. 1990a. "Education, Social Mobility, and the Austrian Jews 1860–1910." In *Bildungswesen und Sozialstruktur in Mitteleuropa im 19. und 20. Jahrhundert,* edited by Victor Karady and Wolfgang Mitter, 141–61. Studien und Dokumentationen zu vergleichenden Bildungsforschung, vol. 42. Cologne and Vienna: Böhlau.

———. 1990b. "Jews among Vienna's Educated Middle Class Elements at the Turn of the Century: A Comment on Steven Beller." In *A Social and Economic History of Central European Jewry,* edited by Yehuda Don and Victor Karady, 179–90. New Brunswick, N.J.: Transaction Publ.

———. 1994. "Ideals and Reality in the Austrian Universities, 1850–1914." In *Rediscovering History: Politics, Culture, and the Psyché,* edited by Michael S. Roth, 83–101. Stanford: Stanford University Press.

Cohen, Sol. 1973. "New Perspectives on the History of American Education." *History of Education* 2:79–96.

Corsini, Umberto. 1980. "Die Italiener." In *Die Habsburgermonarchie, 1848–1918,* edited by Adam Wandruszka and Peter Urbanitsch, vol. 3, pt. 2:839–79. Vienna: Öster. Akademie der Wissenschaften.

Craig, John E. 1981a. "The Expansion of Education." *Review of Research in Education* 9:151–213.

———. 1981b. "On the Development of Educational Systems." *American Journal of Education* 89:189–211.

______. 1983. "Higher Education and Social Mobility in Germany." In *The Transformation of Higher Learning,* 1860–1930, edited by Konrad H. Jarausch, 219–44. Stuttgart: Klett-Cotta; Chicago: University of Chicago Press.

Craig, John E., and Norman Spear. 1982. "Explaining Educational Expansion: An Agenda for Historical and Comparative Research." In *The Sociology of Educational Expansion: Take-off, Growth, and Inflation in Educational Systems,* edited by Margaret S. Archer, 133–57. London and Beverly Hills: Sage.

Cron, Ludwig. 1897. "Der Zugang der Badener zu den badenischen Universitäten und zur technischen Hochschule Karlsruhe in den Jahren 1869 bis 1893." Ph.D. diss., Universität Heidelberg.

Davies, Norman. 1984. *God's Playground: A History of Poland.* 2 vols. New York: Columbia University Press.

Deák, István. 1990. *Beyond Nationalism: A Social and Political History of the Habsburg Officer Corps, 1848–1918.* New York and Oxford: Oxford University Press.

Diamant, Alfred. 1960. *Austrian Catholics and the First Republic.* Princeton: Princeton University Press.

Dobretsberger, Josef. 1947. "Die soziale Herkunft unserer Intelligenz." *Die Furche* 3, no. 1:5.

Dokoupil, Lumír. 1973. "Territorialní a socialní mobilita populace ostravské průmyslové oblasti v období její geneze a počátečního rozvoje" (Geographical and social mobility of the populace of the Ostrava industrial region in the period of its genesis and initial development). *Československý časopis historický* 21:355–68.

Drtina, Franz [František]. 1908. *Aus der Mittelschulenquête (Separatabdruck aus der "Čechischen Revue").* Prague: E. Leschinger.

Dumreicher, Armand Freiherr von. 1881. *Ueber die Aufgaben der Unterrichtspolitik im Industriestaate Oesterreich.* Vienna: A. Hölder.

______. 1909. *Aus meiner Studentenzeit.* Vienna: Manz.

Dumreicher, Johann von. 1878. *Über die Notwendigkeit von Reformen des Unterrichtes an den Medicinischen Facultäten Österreichs.* Vienna.

Düwell, Kurt. 1989. "Die Sozialstruktur der Studierenden an deutschen Technischen Hochschulen (1870–1920): Die soziale Herkunft am Beispiel Aachens." Paper presented to the German Studies Association Annual Conference, Milwaukee.

Dyk, Viktor. 1906. *Prosinec* (December). Prague: J. Otto.

Eder, Karl. 1955. *Der Liberalismus in Altösterreich.* Vienna: Herold.

Egger, Alois. 1874. *Industrie und Schule in Österreich: Eine culturpolitische Studie.* Volksbildung und Schulwesen, edited by A. Egger, no. 1. Vienna: A. Hölder.

Ehalt, Hubert C. 1978. "Das Wiener Schulwesen in der liberaler Ära: Determinanten des österreichischen Schulwesens im 19. Jahrhundert." *Forschungen und Beiträge zur Wiener Stadtgeschichte* 1:120–47.

Ehrlich, Eugen. 1909. *Die Aufgaben der Sozialpolitik im österreichischen Osten, insbesonder in der Bukowina mit besonderer Beleuchtung der Juden- und Bauernfrages*. Chernivtsi: Sozialwissenschaftlicher akademischer Verein.

Eley, Geoff. 1986. "Educating the Bourgeoisie: Students and the Culture of 'Illiberalism' in Imperial Germany." *History of Education Quarterly* 26:287–300.

Engelbrecht, Helmut. 1967. "Die Philosophische Lehranstalt zu Krems unter der Direktion Vincenz Eduard Mildes." *Mitteilungen des Kremser Stadtarchivs* 7:131–76.

______. 1975. "Zur österreichischen Bildungspolitik im Sekundarschulbereich in der zweiten Hälfte des 19. Jahrhunderts." *Jahresbericht des Bundesgymnasiums Krems am Schlusse des Schuljahres 1974/75*, 14–33. Krems a. D.: Bundesgymnasium Krems.

______. 1976. "Zur Organisation der österreichischen Sekundarschulen in der zweiten Hälfte des 19. Jahrhunderts." *Jahresbericht des Bundesgymnasiums Krems am Schlusse des Schuljahres 1975/76*, 5–46. Krems a. D.: Bundesgymnasium Krems.

______. 1977. "Zur Geschichte der pädagogischen Historiographie im Österreich." *Jahresbericht des Bundesgymnasiums Krems am Schlusse des Schuljahres 1976/77*, 5–33. Krems a. D.: Bundesgymnasium Krems.

______. 1982–88. *Geschichte des österreichischen Bildungswesens*. 5 vols. Vienna: Öster. Bundesverlag.

Engliš, Karl. 1915. "Eine Erhebung über die Lebensverhältnisse der Wiener Studenten." *Statistische Monatsschrift*, n.s., 20:273–354.

Festschrift des n.-ö. Landes-Real- und Obergymnasiums in St. Pölten 1863–1913. 1913. St. Pölten: Landes-Obergymnasium St. Pölten.

Festschrift zur Erinnerung an das fünfundzwanzighährige Bestehen der Communal-Ober-Realschule in Leitmeritz. 1890. Litoměřice: Verlag der Communal-Oberrealschule.

Festschrift zur Erinnerung an die Feier des Fünfzigjährigen Bestandes der deutschen Staatsrealschule in Mährisch-Ostrau, 1877–1927. 1927. Moravská ostrava: Deutsche Staatsrealschule Mährisch-Ostrau.

Festschrift zur Feier des dreihundertjährigen Bestandes des deutschen Staatsgymnasiums in Troppau, Juni 1930. 1930. Opava: T. Heinz.

Festschrift zur Feier des hundertjährigen Bestandes des k. k. Staatsgymnasiums in Mährisch-Trübau. 1903. Třebíč: Verlag des k. k. Staatsgymnasiums.

Festschrift zur Gedenkfeier des fünfundzwanzigjährigen Bestandes des k.k. Staatsgymnasiums in Krumau. 1896. Český krumlov: Verlag des Festausschusses.

Fichtner, Paula Sutter. 1971. "History, Religion, and Politics in the Austrian *Vormärz.*" *History and Theory* 10:33–48.

Ficker, Adolf. 1873. "Geschichte, Organisation und Statistik des öster. Unterrichtswesens." In *Bericht über österreichisches Unterrichtswesen aus Anlaß der Weltaustellung 1873,* vol. 1. Vienna: A. Hölder.

______. 1875. "Die österreichischen Mittleschulen in dem Vierteljahrhundert von 1850 bis 1874." *Statistische Monatsschrift* 1:97–118.

Firnberg, Hertha, and Gustav Otruba. 1951. *Die Soziale Herkunft der niederösterreichischen Studierenden an Wiener Hochschulen.* Der Niederösterreichischen Arbeiter: Studien zur Sozial- und Wirtschaftsstruktur Niederösterreichs in Vergangenheit und Gegenwart, no. 3. Vienna: Kammer für Arbeiter und Angestellte in Niederösterreich.

Flich, Renate. 1992. *Wider die Natur der Frau? Entstehungsgeschichte der höheren Mädchenschulen in Österreich.* Vienna: Bundesministerium für Unterricht und Kunst.

Floud, Jean E., A. H. Halsey, and F. M. Martin. 1957. *Social Class and Educational Opportunity.* London: Heinemann.

Forkl, Martha, and Elisabeth Koffmahn, eds. 1968. *Frauenstudium und akademische Frauenarbeit in Österreich.* Vienna and Stuttgart: W. Braumüller.

Forman, Paul, John Heilbron, and Spencer Weart, eds. 1975. *Physics circa 1900.* Supplement to *Historical Studies in the Physical Sciences,* vol. 5. Princeton: Princeton University Press.

Fournier, August. 1923. *Erinnerungen.* Munich: Drei Masken Verlag.

Frankfurter, Salomon. 1893. *Graf Leo Thun-Hohenstein, Franz Exner, und Hermann Bonitz: Beiträge zur Geschichte der österreichischen Unterrichtsreform.* Vienna: A. Hölder.

______. 1910. *Verlauf und Ergebnisse der Mittelschulenquete des Unterrichtsministeriums 21.–25. Jänner 1908 und andere Beiträge zur Geschichte der österreichischen Mittelschulreform.* Vienna: C. Fromme.

Frankl, Ludwig August. 1910. *Erinnerungen,* edited by Stefan Hock. Prague: J. Calvé.

Frankl, Otto. 1905–9. "Bergbaulehranstalten." In *Österreichisches Staatswörterbuch,* edited by Ernst Mischler and Josef Ulbrich, 1:484. 2d ed. rev. Vienna: Hölder.

Franz, Georg. 1955. *Die Deutschliberale Bewegung in der habsburgischen Monarchie.* Munich: G. D. W. Callwey.

Freeze, Karen Johnson. 1974. "The Young Progressives: The Czech Student Movement, 1887–1897." Ph.D. diss., Columbia University.

Freud, Sigmund. [1935] 1950. *An Autobiographical Study*. Translated by James Strachey. London: Hogarth Press.

Fuchs, Ernst. 1946. *Wie ein Augenarzt die Welt sah: Selbsbiographie und Tagebuchblätter,* edited by Adalbert Fuchs. Vienna: Urban & Schwarzenberg.

Gall, Franz. 1965. *Alma Mater Rudolphina 1365–1965: Die Wiener Universität und ihre Studenten*. Vienna: Verlag Austria.

______. 1975a. "Akademische Laufbahnen an der Universität Wien in der zweiten Hälfte des neunzehnten Jahrhunderts unter besonderer Berücksichtigung der medizinischen Fakultät." In *Student und Hochschule im 19. Jahrhundert,* edited by Christian Helfer and Mohammed Rassem, 63–74. Göttingen: Vandenhoeck & Ruprecht.

______. 1975b. "Die Doktorenkollegien der vier Fakultäten an der Wiener Universität, 1849–1873." In *Student und Hochschule im 19. Jahrhundert,* edited by Christian Helfer and Mohammed Rassem, 47–62. Göttingen: Vandenhoeck & Ruprecht.

Garver, Bruce M. 1978. *The Young Czech Party 1874–1901 and the Emergence of a Multi-Party System*. New Haven: Yale University Press.

Gatti, Ferdinand, and A. Obermayr. 1942. *Geschichte der k. u. k. Technischen Militärakademie 1717 bis 1942*. Vienna: W. Braumüller.

Gerbod, Paul. 1965. La condition universitaire en France au XIXe siècle. Paris: Presses Universitaires de France.

Gerschenkron, Alexander. 1977. *An Economic Spurt That Failed*. Princeton: Princeton University Press.

Gerstendörfer, Josef. 1896. "Geschichte des Gymnasiums in Krumau." In *Festschrift zur Gedenkfeier des fünfundzwanzigjährigen Bestandes des k. k. Staatsgymnasiums in Krumau,* 1–44. Český krumlov: Verlag des Festausschusses.

Gieysztor, Alexander, et al. 1968. *History of Poland*. Warsaw: PWN.

Gillis, John R. 1968. "Aristocracy and Bureaucracy in Nineteenth-Century Prussia." *Past and Present,* no. 41: 105–29.

______. 1971. *The Prussian Bureaucracy in Crisis, 1840–1860*. Stanford: Stanford University Press.

______. 1981. Youth and History: Tradition and Change in European Age Relations, 1770–Present. Expd. ed. New York: Academic Press.

Glettler, Monika. 1980. "Erziehungswesen, Schule, und Gesellschaftsstruktur seit der Aufklärung." In *Deutschland und Österreich: Ein bilaterales Geschichtsbuch,* edited by Robert A. Kann and Friedrich Prinz, 450–89. Vienna and Munich: Jugend und Volk.

Goldinger, Walter, and Dieter A. Binder. 1992. *Geschichte der Republik Österreich 1918–1938*. Vienna: Verlag für Geschichte und Politik; Munich: R. Oldenbourg.

Goll, Jaroslav. 1908. *Rozdělení pražské university Karlo-Ferdinandovy roku 1882 a počátek samostatné university české* (The Division of the Charles-Ferdinand University of Prague and the Beginning of the Independent Czech University). Prague: Nakl. Klubu historického.

Good, David F. 1984. *The Economic Rise of the Habsburg Empire, 1750–1914*. Berkeley and Los Angeles: University of California Press.

Gottas, Friedrich. 1985. "Die Geschichte des Protestantismus in der Habsburgermonarchie." In *Die Habsburgermonarchie, 1848–1918*. Vol. 4, *Die Konfessionen,* edited by Adam Wandruszka and Peter Urbanitsch, 489–595. Vienna: Öster. Akademie der Wissenschaften.

Greenstein, Fred I. 1968. "Political Socialization." *International Encyclopedia of the Social Sciences* 14:551–55. New York: Macmillan.

Gross, Nachum T. 1973. "Die Stellung der Habsburgermonarchie in der Weltwirtschaft." In *Die Habsburgermonarchie, 1848–1918*. Vol. 1, *Die Wirtschaftliche Entwicklung,* edited by Adam Wandruszka, Peter Urbanitsch, and Alois Brusatti, 1–28. Vienna: Öster. Akademie der Wissenschaften.

Gulick, Charles A. 1948. *From Habsburg to Hitler*. 2 vols. Berkeley and Los Angeles: University of California Press.

Gutachten und Anträge zur Reform der medicinischen Studien und Rigorosen-Ordnung: Erstattet von den medicinischen Facultäten der österreichischen Uniersitäten. 1894. Vienna: Karl Gorischek.

Haan, Hugo Freiherr von. 1917. "Statistische Streiflichter zur österreichischen Hochschulfrequenz." *Statistische Monatsschrift,* n.s., 22:155–208.

Halma, Adalbert, and Gustav Schilling. 1912. *Die Mittelschulen Österreichs (Sammlung der Vorschriften)*. Vienna and Prague: K. K. Schulbücherverlag.

Hanák, Péter. 1984. *Ungarn in der Donaumonarchie: Problem der bürgerlichen Umgestaltung eines Vielvölkerstaates*. Vienna: Verlag für Geschichte und Politik; Munich: Oldenbourg; and Budapest: Akadémiai Kiadó.

Handbuch der allgemeinbildenen höheren Schulen Österreichs 1981. 1981. Vienna.

Hanslick, Eduard. 1894. *Aus meinem Leben: Erstes Buch —Jugend und Studentenzeit in Prag, 1825–1845*. Berlin: Allgemeiner Verein für Deutsche Literatur.

Harrigan, Patrick J. 1980. *Mobility, Elites, and Education in Second Empire France*. Waterloo, Ont.: Wilfrid Laurier University Press.

Harrigan, Patrick J., with Victor Neglia. 1979. *Lycéens et collégiens sous le Second Empire: Etude statistique sur les fonctions sociales de l'enseignement secondaire publiée d'après l'enquête de Victor Duruy 1864–1865*. Paris: Editions de la Maison des Sciences de l'Homme.

Harrington-Müller, Diethild. 1972. *Der Fortschrittsklub im Abgeordnetenhaus des österreichischen Reichsrats 1873–1910*. Vienna, Cologne, and Graz: Böhlau.

Hartel, Wilhelm von. 1874. "Die Universitäten." Group 26, Sect. 5. In *Officieller Ausstellungs–Bericht,* edited by Carl T. Richter. Vienna: n.p.

______. 1889. *Bonitz und sein Wirken in Oesterreich.* Lecture given on 15 December 1888 to the society "Mittelschule." Linz: Privately published.

Hasner, Leopold von. 1892. *Denkwürdigkeiten: Autobiographisches und Aphorismen.* Stuttgart: J. G. Cotta.

Häusler, Wolfgang. 1979. *Von der Massenarmut zur Arbeiterbewegung: Demokratie und soziale Frage in der Wiener Revolution von 1848.* Vienna: Jugend und Volk.

Havránek, Jan. 1987. "Die Rolle der Universitäten und der modernen 'pergrinatio academica' für den sozialen Aufstieg der Studenten." In *Wegenetz europäischen Geistes.* Vol. 2, *Universitäten und Studenten,* edited by Richard G. Plaschka and Karlheinz Mack, 114–17. Vienna: Verlag für Geschichte und Politik.

Havránek, Jan, and Karel Kučera, eds. 1965. *Disertace pražské university* (Dissertations of the Prague University). 2 vols. Sbírka pramenů a příruček k dějinám University Karlovy, no. 2. Prague: Universita Karlova.

Heindl, Waltraud. 1982a. "Die österreichische Bürokratie: Zwischen deutscher Vorherrschaft und österreichischer Staatsidee (Vormärz und Neoabsolutismus)." In *Österreich und die deutsche Frage im 19. und 20. Jahrhundert,* edited by Heinrich Lutz and Helmut Rumpler, 73–91. Vienna: Verlag für Geschichte und Politik.

______. 1982b. "Universitätsreform—Gesellschaftsreform: Bemerkungen zum Plan eines 'Universitätsorganisationsgesetzes' in den Jahren 1854/55." *Mitteilungen des österreichischen Staatsarchivs* 35: 134–49.

______. 1990. *Gehorsame Rebellen: Bürokratie und Beamte in Österreich 1780–1848.* Vienna, Cologne, and Graz: Böhlau.

Heindl, Waltraud, and Marina Tichy, eds. 1990. *"Durch Erkenntnis zu Freiheit und Glück . . .": Frauen an der Universität Wien (ab 1897).* Schriftenreihe des Universitätsarchivs Universität Wien, vol. 5. Vienna: WUV-Universitätsverlag.

Heinrich, Edith. 1947. "Die Lehrkörper der Wiener Universität in den öffentlichen Vertretungskörpern Österreichs 1861–1918 mit besonderer Berücksichtigung der Tätigkeit der Wiener Universitätsprofessoren im Herrenhaus des österreichischen Reichsrates zur Zeit der liberalen Ära 1861–1879." Ph.D. diss., Universität Wien.

Herrmann, August. 1913. "Die St. Pöltner Mittelschule." In *Festschrift des n.-ö. Landes-Real- und Obergymnasiums in St. Pölten 1863–1913,* 1–40. St. Pölten: Privately printed.

Heumos, Peter. 1979. *Agrarische Interessen und nationale Politik in Böhmen 1848–1889.* Wiesbaden: Franz Steiner.

Himka, John-Paul. 1988. *Galician Villagers and the Ukrainian National Movement in the Nineteenth Century.* New York: St. Martin's Press.

Höbelt, Lothar. 1993. *Kornblume und Kaiseradler: Die deutschfreiheitlichen Parteien Altösterreichs 1882–1918*. Vienna: Verlag für Geschichte und Politik; Munich: R. Oldenbourg.

Höflechner, Walter. 1988. *Die Baumeister des künftigen Glücks: Fragment einer Geschichte des Hochschulwesens in Österreich vom Ausgang des 19. Jahrhunderts bis in das Jahr 1938*. Graz: Akademische Druck und Verlagsanstalt.

Höfler, Alois. 1891. "Bemerkungen zu den Berliner Verhandlungen über Fragen des höheren Unterrichtes." *Österreichische Mittelschule* 5:106.

Honza, J. 1926. "Městská střední škola v Praze na Malé straně" (The municipal secondary school in Malá strana, Prague). In *Památník k 60. ročnici založení městské. střední školy na malé straně v Praze a z ní vzešlých ústavů 1866–1926* (Commemorative volume for the sixtieth anniversary of the founding of the municipal secondary school in Malá strana, Prague, and of the successor institutions), 7–15. Prague: n.p.

Honzáková, Albina. 1930. *Československé Studentky Let 1890–1930: Almanach na oslavu čtyřicátého výročí založení ženského studia Eliškou Krásnohorskou* (Czechoslovak women students, 1890–1930: Commemorative volume for the fortieth anniversary of the founding of a women's program by Eliška Krásnohorská). Prague: Ženská národní rada a spolek Minerva.

Horská, Pavla. 1990. "Stadt und Land in der Entstehung und Abgrenzung bürgerlicher Schichten im 18. und 19. Jahrhundert in den böhmischen Ländern." In *Bürgertum in der Habsburgermonarchie,* edited by Ernst Bruckmüller et al., 1:43–56. Vienna and Cologne: Böhlau.

Horská-Vrbová, Pavla. 1972. "Pokus o využiti rakouských statistik pro studium společenských rozvrstvení českých zemí v 2. polovině 19. století" (An attempt to use Austrian statistics for the study of social stratification in the Bohemian lands during the second half of the nineteenth century). *Československý časopis historický* 20:648–76.

Höttinger, Matthias. 1949. "Der Fall Wahrmund." Ph.D. diss., Universität Wien.

Houška, František, Jan Klecanda, and Karel Tiller, eds. 1893. *Almanach bývalých žáků české reálky pražské* (Almanac of former students of the Czech Realschule in Prague). Prague: Privately published.

Hubbard, William H. 1977. "Forschungen zur städtischen Haushaltsstruktur am Ende des 19. Jahrhunderts: Das Grazhaus-Projekt." In *Sozialgeschichte der Familie in der Neuzeit Europas,* edited by Werner Conze, 283–91. Stuttgart: Klett.

———. 1984. "Social Mobility and Social Structure in Graz, 1857–1910." *Journal of Social History* 17:453–62.

Hubbard, William H., and Konrad H. Jarausch. 1979. "Occupation and Social Structure in Modern Central Europe: Some Reflections on Coding Professions." *Quantum Information,* no. 11:10–19.

Hübl, Albert. 1907. *Geschichte des Unterrichts im Stifte Schotten in Wien.* Vienna: K.u.K. Hof-Buchdruckerei & C. Fromme.

Hübl, Franz. 1878. *Handbuch für Direktoren, Professoren und Lehramtskandidaten der österreichischen Gymnasien, Realschulen und Verwandten Anstalten.* 2d ed. Prague: H. Mercy.

______. 1888. *Normalien-Index für die österreichischen Mittelschulen.* Most.

Huerkamp, Claudia. 1980. "Ärzte und Professionalisierung in Deutschland: Überlegungen zum Wandel des Arztberufs im 19. Jahrhundert." *Geschichte und Gesellschaft* 6:349–83.

______. 1990. "The Making of the Modern Medical Profession, 1800–1914: Prussian Doctors in the Nineteenth Century." In *German Professions, 1800–1950,* edited by Geoffrey Cocks and Konrad H. Jarausch, 66–84. New York and Oxford: Oxford University Press.

Jähnl, Wilhelm. 1916. *Vorschriften für die Technischen Hochschulen Österreichs.* Vienna: K. K. Schulbücherverlag.

Jarausch, Konrad H. 1978. "Liberal Education as Illiberal Socialization: The Case of Students in Imperial Germany." *Journal of Modern History* 50:609–30.

______. 1979. "The Social Transformation of the University: The Case of Prussia, 1865–1914." *Journal of Social History* 12:609–36.

______. 1981. "Die neuhumanistische Universität und die bürgerliche Gesellschaft 1800–1860." *Darstellungen und Quellen zur Geschichte der Deutschen Einheitsbewegung im 19. und 20. Jahrhundert* 11:11–58.

______. 1982. *Students, Society, and Politics in Imperial Germany.* Princeton: Princeton University Press, 1982.

______. 1983. "Higher Education and Social Change: Some Comparative Perspectives." In *The Transformation of Higher Learning,* edited by K. H. Jarausch, 9–36. Stuttgart: Klett–Cotta; Chicago: University of Chicago Press.

______. 1984. *Deutsche Studenten 1800–1970.* Frankfurt a. M.: Suhrkamp.

______. 1986. "The Old 'New History of Education': A German Reconsideration." *History of Education Quarterly* 26:225–41.

Jaroš, Karel, and Jan Job. 1961. *Rozvoj československého školství v číslech* (The advance of Czechoslovak education in statistics). Prague: SEVT.

Jencks, Christopher, and David Riesman. 1969. *The Academic Revolution.* New York: Doubleday.

Jenks, William A. 1965. *Austria under the Iron Ring, 1879–1893.* Charlottesville: University Press of Virginia.

Jennings, M. Kent. 1980. "Comment on Richard Merelman's 'Democratic Politics and the Culture of American Education.'" *American Political Science Review* 74:333–37.

Jílek, František, and Václav Lomič. 1973. *Dějiny českého vysokého učení technického* (History of the Czech Technical College). Vol. 1, pt. 1. Prague: České vysoké učení technické.

Johnson, Owen V. 1985. *Slovakia 1918–1938: Education and the Making of a Nation*. East European Monographs, no. 180. Boulder, Colo.: East European Monographs.

Johnston, William M. 1972. *The Austrian Mind: An Intellectual and Social History 1848–1938*. Berkeley and Los Angeles: University of California Press.

Judson, Pieter M. 1987. "German Liberalism in Nineteenth-Century Austria: Clubs, Parties, and the Rise of Bourgeois Politics." Ph.D. diss., Columbia University.

Juraschek, Franz. 1876. "Der Besuch der österreichischen Universitäten in den Jahren 1861–1875." *Statistische Monatsschrift* 2:303–37.

Kádner, Otakar. 1931. "Školství v republice Československé" (Education in the Czechoslovak Republic). In *Československá vlastivěda,* vol. 10, *Osvěta* (Czechoslovak National Encyclopedia, vol. 10, Enlightenment), 7–222. Prague: "Sfinx"-Bohumil Janda.

Kaelble, Hartmut. 1975. "Chancenungleichheit und akademische Ausbildung in Deutschland 1910–1960." *Geschichte und Gesellschaft* 1:41–71.

______. 1983. *Soziale Mobilität und Chancenungleichheit im 19. und 20. Jahrhundert*. Göttingen: Vandenhoeck & Ruprecht.

______. 1986a. *Industrialization and Social Inequality in Nineteenth-Century Europe*. New York: St. Martin's Press.

______. 1986b. *Social Mobility in the Nineteenth and Twentieth Centuries: Europe and America in Comparative Perspective*. New York: St. Martin's Press.

Kalendář českého studentstva (Almanac of Czech students). 1871–94.

Kalendář českych professorů 1911–1912 (Almanac of Czech professors, 1911–1912). 1911-1912. Prague: Ústřední spolek čes. professorů.

Kammerer, Wilhelm. 1951. "Die Wiener Gymnasien von 1740 bis 1848." Ph.D. diss., Universität Wien.

Kann, Robert A. 1974. *A History of the Habsburg Empire, 1526–1918*. Berkeley and Los Angeles: University of California Press.

______. 1991. "Higher Education and Politics in the Austrian Constitutional Monarchy (1867–1918)." In *Dynasty, Politics and Culture: Selected Essays,* by Robert A. Kann, edited by Stanley B. Winters, 311–32. Boulder, Colo.: Social Science Monographs.

Kann, Robert A., and Zdeněk V. David. 1984. *The Peoples of the Eastern Habsburg Lands, 1526–1918*. Seattle: University of Washington Press.

Kavka, František, ed. 1964. *Stručné dějiny University Karlovy* (Outline history of the Charles University). Prague: Universita Karlova.

Kazbunda, Karel. 1934. "Krise české politiky a vídeňská jednání o t. zv. punktace roku 1890" (The crisis of Czech politics and the Vienna negotiations for the so-called *Punctation* of 1890). *Český časopis historický* 40:80–108.

Kestenberg-Gladstein, Ruth. 1968–84. "The Jews between Czechs and Germans in the Historic Lands, 1848–1918." In *The Jews of Czechoslovakia,* edited by Avigdor Dagan, 1:21–71. Philadelphia: Jewish Publication Society.

Kieval, Hillel J. 1988. *The Making of Czech Jewry: National Conflict and Jewish Society in Bohemia, 1870–1918.* New York and Oxford: Oxford University Press.

Klepl, Jan. 1957. "Pražská technika před březnem 1848" (The Prague Technical Institute before March 1848). *Sborník Národního technického muzea* 3:140–56.

Klíma, Arnošt. 1977. "Industrial Growth and Entrepreneurship in the Early Stages of Industrialization in the Czech Lands." *Journal of European Economic History* 6:549–74.

Knoll, Reinhold. 1973. *Zur Tradition der Christlich-Sozialen Partei: Ihre Früh- und Entwicklungsgeschichte bis zu den Reichsratswahlen.* Studien zur Geschichte der Österreichisch-ungarischen Monarchie, vol. 13. Vienna, Cologne, and Graz: Böhlau.

Kodedová, Oldřiška, and Zdeněk Uherek. 1972. *Kapitoly z dějin českého učitelství 1890–1938* (Chapters from the history of the Czech teaching profession). Prague: SPN.

Kolmer, Gustav. [1902–14] 1972–80. *Parlament und Verfassung in Österreich.* 8 vols. Reprint, Graz: Akademische Druck- und Verlagsanstalt.

Kopáč, Jaroslav. 1968. *Dějiny české školy a pedagogiky v letech 1867–1914* (History of Czech schools and pedagogy, 1867–1914). Spisy Pedagogické fakulty University J. E. Purkyně v Brně (Publications of the Pedagogical Faculty of J. E Purkyně University in Brno), no. 5. Brno: Universita J. E. Purkyně.

Kořalka, Jiří. 1991. *Tschechen im Habsburgerreich und in Europa 1815–1914.* Vienna: Verlag für Geschichte und Politik; Munich: Oldenbourg.

______. 1992. "Tschechische Bildungsbürger und Bildungskleinbürger um 1900 (am Beispiel der südböhmischen Stadt Tábor)." In *Bürgertum in der Habsburgermonarchie.* Vol. 2, *"Durch Arbeit, Besitz, Wissen und Gerechtigkeit,"* edited by Hannes Stekl, Peter Urbanitsch, and Hans Heiss, 210–21. Vienna, Cologne, and Weimar: Böhlau.

Korbel, Josef. 1977. *Twentieth-Century Czechoslovakia: The Meanings of Its History.* New York: Columbia University Press.

Koselleck, Reinhart. 1967. *Preussen zwischen Reform und Revolution.* Stuttgart: Klett.

Kostner, Maria. 1972. "Die Geschichte der italienischen Universitätsfrage in der österreichisch-ungarischen Monarchie 1864–1914." Ph.D. diss., Universität Innsbruck.

Krachowiczer, Ferdinand. 1879. *Im Convict: Erinnerungen an Kremsmünster.* Linz: Privately published.

Kraul, Margret, 1976. "Untersuchungen zur sozialen Struktur der Schülerschaft des preussischen Gymnasiums im Vormärz." *Bildung und Erziehung* 29:509–19.

______. 1980. *Gymnasium und Gesellschaft im Vormärz: Neuhumanistische Einheitsschule, städtische Gesellschaft und soziale Herkunft der Schüler.* Göttingen: Vandenhoeck & Ruprecht.

______. 1984. *Das deutsche Gymnasium, 1780–1980.* Frankfurt a. M.: Suhrkamp.

Krinzinger, P. Jakob. 1981. "Materialien zum Studentenleben früherer Zeit." In *Öffentliches Stiftsgymnasium Kremsmünster 124. Jahresbericht 1981,* 40–59. Wels: Verlag Welsermühl.

Kudlich, Hans. 1873. *Rückblicke und Erinnerungen.* 3 vols. Vienna, Pest, and Leipzig: A. Hartleben.

Kussmaul, Adolf. 1902. *Jugenderinnerungen eines alten Arztes.* 5th ed. Stuttgart: A. Bonz.

Kutnar, František. 1973–77. *Přehledné dějiny českého a slovenského dějepisectví* (An outline history of Czech and Slovak historiography). 2 vols. Prague: Státní pedagogické nakladatelství.

Kuzmin, Michail N. 1981. *Vývoj školství a vzdělání v Československu* (The development of schools and education in Czechoslovakia). Prague: Academia. Originally published in Russian as *Shkola i obrazovanije v Tschechoslovakii* (Moscow: Nauka, 1971).

Langer, Adalbert. 1980. "Böhmen in den Geschichtslehrbüchern des alten Österreich." In *Deutschtschechische Beziehungen in der Schulliteratur und im populären Geschichtsbild,* edited by Hans Lemberg and Ferdinand Seibt, 69–77. Studien zur Internationalen Schulbuchforschung, Schriftenreihe des Georg-Eckert-Instituts, vol. 28. Braunschweig: Limbach.

Langer, William L. 1969. *Political and Social Upheaval, 1832–1852.* New York: Harper and Row.

Lechner, Elmar, Helmut Rumpler, and Herbert Zdarzil, eds. 1992. *Zur Geschichte des österreichischen Bildungswesens: Probleme und Perspektiven der Forschung.* Vienna: Österreichische Akademie der Wissenschaften.

Leff, Carol Skalnik. 1988. *National Conflict in Czechoslovakia: The Making and Remaking of a State, 1918–1987.* Princeton: Princeton University Press.

Lemberg, Hans. 1980. "Ein Geschichtsbuch unter drei Staatssystemen: Josef Pekařs Oberklassenlehrbuch von 1914–1945." In *Deutschtschechische Beziehungen in der Schulliteratur und im populären Geschichtsbild,* edited by Hans Lemberg and Ferdinand Seibt, 78–88. Studien zur Internationalen Schulbuchforschung, Schriftenreihe des Georg-Eckert-Instituts, vol. 28. Braunschweig: Limbach.

Lentze, Hans. 1962. *Die Universitätsreform des Ministers Graf Leo Thun-Hohenstein*. Österreichische Akademie der Wissenschaften, Philosophisch-Historische Klasse, Sitzungsberichte, vol. 239, no. 2. Vienna: Böhlau.

Lesky, Erna. 1976. *The Vienna Medical School of the Nineteenth Century*. Translated by L. Williams and I. S. Levij. Baltimore: Johns Hopkins University Press.

______. 1978. *Die Wiener Medizinische Schule im 19. Jahrhundert*. 2d ed. Graz and Cologne: Böhlau.

Lewinsky, Heinrich. 1868. *Beiträge zur Statistik der Gymnasien Wiens*. Vienna.

Lewis, Gavin. 1978. "The Peasantry, Rural Change and Conservative Agrarianism: Lower Austria at the Turn of the Century." *Past and Present,* no. 81:119–43.

Lhotsky, Alfons. 1962. *Österreichische Historiographie*. Vienna: Verlag für Geschichte und Politik.

Lind, Anna. 1961. "Das Frauenstudium im Österreich, Deutschland und in der Schweiz." Dissertation der Rechts- und Staatswiss. Fakultät, Universität Wien.

Lomič, Václav, and Pavla Horská. 1978. *Dějiny českého vysokého učení technického* (History of the Czech Technical College). Vol. 1, pt. 2. Prague: České vysoké učení technické.

Loos, Joseph. 1896. "Ein Rückblick auf die ersten 25 Jahre (1871–1896)." In *Jahres-Bericht des k. k. Maximilians-Gymnasium in Wien für das Schuljahr 1895/96,* 1–58. Vienna.

Lundgreen, Peter. 1975. "Industrialization and the Educational Formation of Manpower in Germany." *Journal of Social History* 9:64–80.

______. 1976. "Educational Expansion and Economic Growth in Nineteenth-Century Germany: A Quantitative Study." In *Schooling in Society: Studies in the History of Education,* edited by Lawrence Stone, 20–66. Baltimore: Johns Hopkins University Press.

______. 1977. "Historische Bildungsforschung." In *Historische Sozialwissenschaft: Beiträge zur Einführung in die Forschungspraxis,* edited by Reinhard Rürup, 96–125. Göttingen: Vandenhoeck & Ruprecht.

______. 1981. "Bildung und Besitz—Einheit oder Inkongruenz in der europäischen Sozialgeschichte?" *Geschichte und Gesellschaft* 7:262–75.

Lundgreen, Peter, Margret Kraul, and Karl Ditt. 1988. *Bildungschancen und soziale Mobilität in der städtischen Gesellschaft des 19. Jahrhunderts*. Göttingen: Vandenhoeck & Ruprecht.

Macartney, Carlisle A. 1969. *The Habsburg Empire, 1790–1918*. New York: Macmillan.

Macek, Josef, et al., eds. 1958. *Přehled československých dějin*. Pt. 1, *Do roku 1848* (Survey of Czechoslovak history. Pt. 1, To 1848). Prague: Československá akademie věd.

Magocsi, Paul R. 1978. *The Shaping of a National Identity: Subcarpathian Rus' 1848–1918*. Cambridge: Harvard University Press.

Malfertheiner, Anton. 1897. *Vergleichende Statistik des Unterrichtserfolges der österreichischen Gymnasien*. Vienna: A. Pichler.

Malíř, Jiří. 1975–79. "Pokrokové hnutí na Moravě" (The Progressive Movement in Moravia). Parts 1 and 2. *Sborník prací filozofické fakulty brněnské univerzity* 23–24, no. 21–22 (1975–76): 101–22; 27–28, no. 25–26 (1978–79): 99–129.

______. 1985. *Vývoj liberálního proudu české politiky na Moravě: Lidová strana na Moravě do roku 1909* (The development of the liberal current in Czech politics in Moravia to 1909). Spisy Univerzity J. E. Purkyně v Brně, Filozofická Fakulta, no. 258 (Publications of the Philosophical Faculty, J. E. Purkyně University in Brno, no. 258). Brno: University J. E. Purkyně.

______. 1988. "Zu einigen Entwicklungszügen der tschechischen liberalen Parteien vor 1914." *Sborník prací filozofické fakulty brněnské univerzity* 37, no. 35:49–69.

Mamatey, Victor S., and Radomír Luža, eds. 1973. *A History of the Czechoslovak Republic, 1918–1948*. Princeton: Princeton University Press.

Marenzeller, Edmund Edler von. 1884–89. *Normalien für die Gymnasien und Realschulen in Österreich*. 2 parts. Vienna: K. K. Schulbücher Verlag.

Markovits, Andrei S., and Frank E. Sysyn, eds. 1982. *Nationbuilding and the Politics of Nationalism: Essays on Austrian Galicia*. Cambridge.: Harvard University Press.

Martinak, Eduard. 1905–9a. "Gymnasien." In *Österreichisches Staatswörterbuch,* edited by Ernst Mischler and Josef Ulbrich, 2:610–13. 2d rev. ed. 4 vols. Vienna: A. Hölder.

______. 1905–9b. "Realschulen." In *Österreichisches Staatswörterbuch,* edited by Ernst Mischler and Josef Ulbrich, 4:6–8. 2nd rev. ed. 4 vols.Vienna: A. Hölder.

Matis, Herbert. 1969. "Der österreichische Unternehmer." In *Wissenschaft, Wirtschaft und Technik,* edited by Karl-Heinz Manegold, 286–98. Munich: Bruckmann.

Mayer, Gottfried. 1989. *Österreich als "katholische Grossmacht": Ein Traum zwischen Revolution und liberaler Ära*. Vienna: Öster. Akademie der Wissenschaften.

McCagg, William O., Jr. 1989. *A History of Habsburg Jews, 1670–1918*. Bloomington and Indianapolis: Indiana University Press.

McClelland, Charles E. 1980. *State, Society and University in Germany, 1700–1914*. Cambridge: Cambridge University Press.

______. 1986. "Structural Change and Social Reproduction in German Universities, 1870–1920." *History of Education* 15:177–93.

McClelland, Charles E. 1988. "'To Live for Science': Ideals and Realities at the University of Berlin." In *The University and the City: From Medieval Origins to the Present,* edited by Thomas Bender, 181–97. New York: Oxford University Press.

______. 1991. *The German Experience of Professionalization: Modern Learned Professsions and Their Organizations from the Early Nineteenth Century to the Hitler Era.* Cambridge: Cambridge University Press.

McGrath, William J. 1971. *Dionysian Art and Populist Politics in Austria.* New Haven: Yale University Press.

Der medicinische Unterricht an der Wiener Hochschule und seine Gebrechen. 1869. Vienna: Manz.

Megner, Karl. 1985. *Beamte: Wirtschafts- und sozialgeschichtliche Aspekte des k. k. Beamtentums.* Studien zur Geschichte der Österreichisch-ungarischen Monarchie, vol. 21. Vienna: Öster Akademie der Wissenschaften.

Meister, Richard. 1963. *Entwicklung und Reformen des österreichischen Studienwesens.* 2 vols. Öster. Akademie der Wissenschaften, Philosophisch-Historische Klasse, Sitzungsberichte. Vol. 239. pt. 1. 2 vols. Vienna: Böhlau.

Mentschl, Josef. 1973. "Das österreichische Unternehmertum." In *Die Habsburgermonarchie, 1848–1918,* edited by Adam Wandruszka, Peter Urbanitsch, and Alois Brusatti, 1:250–77. Vienna: Öster. Akademie der Wissenschaften.

Mentschl, Josef, and Gustav Otruba. 1965. *Österreichische Industrielle und Bankiers.* Vienna: Bergland.

Merelman, Richard M. 1980. "Democratic Politics and the Culture of American Education." *American Political Science Review* 74:319–32.

Meyer, John W. 1977. "The Effects of Education as an Institution." *American Journal of Sociology* 83:55–77.

Michel, Bernard. 1976. *Banques et banquiers en Autriche au début du 20e siècle.* Paris: Presses de la Fondation Nationale des Sciences Politiques.

Mischler, Ernst. 1905–9. "Universitäten: Allgemeine Universitätsverfassung." In *Österreichisches Staatswörterbuch,* edited by Ernst Mischler and Josef Ulbrich, 4:652–60. 2d rev. ed. Vienna: A. Hölder.

Mitchell, B. R. 1978. *European Historical Statistics, 1750–1970.* Abgd. ed. New York: Columbia University Press.

Mitterstöger, Sabrina. 1979. "Zum vormärzlichen Gymnasialstudienwesen Österreichs: Aus den Archivalien des Klosterneuburger Propstes Jakob Ruttenstock in seiner Funktion als Gymnasialstudiendirektor und Referent der k. k. Studienhofkommission (1832–1842)." Ph.D. diss., Universität Wien.

Molisch, Paul. 1939. *Politische Geschichte der deutschen Hochschulen in Österreich von 1848 bis 1918.* 2d rev. ed. Vienna and Leipzig: W. Braumüller.

Moritsch, Andreas, ed. 1991. *Vom Ethnos zur Nationalität: Der nationale Differenzierungsprozess am Beispiel ausgewählter Orte in Kärnten und im Burgenland.* Vienna: Verlag für Geschichte und Politik.

Müller, Detlef K. 1977. *Sozialstruktur und Schulsystem: Aspekte zum Strukturwandel des Schulwesens im 19. Jahrhundert.* Studien zum Wandel von Gesellschaft und Bildung im Neunzehnten Jahrhundert, vol. 7. Göttingen: Vandenhoeck & Ruprecht.

Müller, Detlef K., Fritz Ringer, and Brian Simon, eds. 1987. *The Rise of the Modern Educational System.* Cambridge: Cambridge University Press.

Neuburger, Max. 1935. *Die Josephinische medizinisch-chirurgische Akademie (1785–1874).* Offprint from the *Wiener Medizinische Wochenschrift,* nos. 51 & 52.

Neuwirth, Joseph, ed. 1915. *Die k. k. Technische Hochschule in Wien 1815–1915: Gedenkschrift.* Vienna: K. K. Technische Hochschule in Wien.

Niebauer, Anton Freiherr von. 1898. "1848: Erinnerungen eines Schülers des Schottengymnasiums in Wien." *Neue Freie Presse,* 13 March 1898, 25–27.

Niederhauser, Emil. 1990. *1848—Sturm im Habsburgerreich.* Vienna: Kremayr und Scheriau.

O'Boyle, Lenore. 1970. "The Problem of an Excess of Educated Men in Western Europe, 1800–1850." *Journal of Modern History* 42:471–95.

[Oppenheimer, Ludwig Freiherr von]. 1882. *Austriaca: Betrachtungen und Streiflichter.* Leipzig: Duncker und Humblot.

Otáhal, Milan. 1986. "The Manuscript Controversy in the Czech National Revival." *Cross Currents* 5:419–38.

Otruba, Gustav. 1965. *Österreichische Industrielle und Bankiers.* Vienna: Bergland.

______. 1975. "Die Universitäten in der Hochschulorganisation der Donau-Monarchie: Nationale Erziehungsstätten im Vielvölkerreich 1850 bis 1914." In *Student und Hochschule im 19. Jahrhundert,* edited by Christian Helfer and Mohammed Rassem, 75–155. Göttingen: Vandenhoeck & Ruprecht.

Padesát let českého gymnasia v Opavě (Fifty years of the Czech Gymnasium in Opava). 1933. Opava: Výbor pro oslavy padesátiletí českého gymnasia v Opavě.

Památník k 60. ročnici založení městské střední školy na malé straně v Praze a z ní vzešlých ústavů 1866–1926 (Commemomrative volume for the sixtieth anniversary of the foundation of the municipal secondary school in Malá strana, Prague, and of the successor institutions). 1926. Prague: n.p.

Památník na oslavu šedesátiletého trvání reálného gymnasia v Táboře a padesátiletého trvání akademického spolku "Štítný" (Commemorative volume in celebration of the sixtieth anniversary of the *Realgymnasium* in Tábor and the fiftieth anniversary of the academic society "Štítný"). 1922. Tábor: Akademický spolek "Štítný."

Památník státního čs. gymnasia Františka Lepaře v Jičině (Commemorative volume of the Czechoslovak František Lepař Gymnasium in Jičín). 1933. Jičín: F. Šmejc.

Památník státního reálného gymnasia v Chrudimi 1863–1948 (Commemorative volume of the State Reálné Gymnasium in Chrudim, 1863–1948). 1948. Chrudim: Fr. Slavík.

Pamlényi, Ervin, ed. 1973. *A History of Hungary*. Budapest: Corvina.

Pauley, Bruce F. 1992. *From Prejudice to Persecution: A History of Austrian Anti-Semitism*. Chapel Hill: University of North Carolina Press.

Paulsen, Friedrich. 1919–21. *Geschichte des gelehrten Unterrichts auf den deutschen Schulen und Universitäten vom Ausgang des Mittelalters bis zur Gegenwart*. 3d expd. ed. 2 vols. Leipzig: Veit.

Pech, Stanley Z. 1969. *The Czech Revolution of 1848*. Chapel Hill: University of North Carolina Press.

Petersilie, Albert. 1910. "Statistik der preußischen Landesuniversitäten für das Studienjahr Ostern 1908/09." *Preußische Statistik* 223.

———. 1913. "Statistik der Landesuniversitäten für das Studienjahr Ostern 1911/12." *Preußische Statistik* 236.

Petráň, Josef. 1983. *Nástin dějin filozofické fakulty Univerzity Karlovy (do roku 1948)* (Outline of the history of the philosophical faculty of the Charles University—to 1948). Prague: Univerzita Karlova.

Petritsch, Wolfgang. 1972. "Die Slovenischen Studenten an der Universität Wien (1848–1890)." 2 vols. Ph.D. diss., Universität Wien.

Petschl, Oskar. 1947. "Soziale Herkunft und Studium: Eine Erhebung an den Linzer Mittelschulen." *Die Furche* 3, no. 25: 5.

Pichler, Adolf. 1905. *Zu meiner Zeit: Schattenbilder aus der Vergangenheit*. 2d ed. rev. Munich and Leipzig: G. Müller.

Placht, Otto, ed. 1914. *Všestudentský Kalendář svazu Československého studentstva na rok 1914–1915* (All-student almanac of the Society of Czech Students for 1914–1915). Prague: Svaz českosl. studentstva.

Placht, Otto, and František Havelka, eds. 1934. *Příručka školské a osvětové správy pro potřebu služby školské a osvětových úřadů a orgánů* (Handbook of school and educational administration for use in school and education offices and agencies). Prague: Státní nakladatelství.

Plaschka, Richard Georg. 1955. *Von Palacký bis Pekař*. Graz and Cologne: Böhlau.

Pleterski, Janko. 1980. "Die Slowenen." In *Die Habsburgermonarchie 1848–1918,* edited by Adam Wandruszka and Peter Urbanitsch, vol. 3, pt. 2:801–38. Vienna: Öster. Akademie der Wissenschaften.

Pliwa, Ernst. 1908. *Österreichs Universitäten 1863/4–1902/3: Statistisch-Graphische Studie*. Vienna: F. Tempsky.

———. 1910. *Österreichs Mittelschulen (Gymnasien, Realgymnasien, Realschulen), 1865/66 bis 1905/6: Statistisch-graphische Studie*. Vienna: A. Hölder.

Pollak, Ernst, ed. 1933. *Die Nikolander Realschule in Prag, 1833–1933*. Prague: H. Mercy.

Pravda o poměrech německého obecného školství v Praze (The truth about conditions in the German public schools of Prague). 1896. Pamphlet. Prague: A. Wiesner.

Pražák, Alois. 1926–27. *Paměti a Listář Dra. Aloise Pražáka* (Memoirs and letters of Dr. Alois Pražák), ed. Dr. František Kameníček. Vols. 1 & 2. Prague: Česká akademie věd a umění.

Prewitt, Kenneth. 1975. "Some Doubts about Political Socialization Research." *Comparative Education Review* 19:105–14.

Prinz, Friedrich. 1968. *Prag und Wien 1848: Probleme der nationalen und sozialen Revolution im Spiegel der Wiener Ministerratsprotokolle*. Munich: R. Lerche Verlag.

______. 1969. "Das Schulwesen der Böhmischen Länder von 1848 bis 1939: Ein Überblick." In *Aktuelle Forschungsprobleme um die Erste Tschechoslowakische Republik*, edited by Karl Bosl, 49–66. Munich and Vienna: R. Oldenbourg.

______. 1974. "Nation und Gesellschaft in den Böhmischen Ländern im 19. und 20. Jahrhundert." In *Geschichte in der Gesellschaft: Festschrift für Karl Bosl zum 65. Geburtstag*, edited by Friedrich Prinz, Franz-Josef Schmale, and Ferdinand Seibt, 333–49. Stuttgart: A. Hiersemann.

Quidam. 1895. *Ein Rückblick auf die Lesevereine deutscher Hochschüler in Wien seit dem Jahre 1870*. Vienna: W. Beiglböck.

Rabinbach, Anson G. 1983. *The Crisis of Austrian Socialism: From Red Vienna to Civil War, 1927–1934*. Chicago: University of Chicago Press.

______. 1985. *The Austrian Socialist Experiment: Social Democracy and Austromarxism, 1918–1934*. Boulder, Colo.: Westview Press.

Radzyner, Joanna. 1983. *Stanislaw Madeyski 1841–1910: Ein austro-polnischer Staatsmann im Spannungsfeld der Nationalitätenfrage in der Habsburgermonarchie*. Studien zur Geschichte der Öster.-ungarischen Monarchie, vol. 20. Vienna: Österreichische Akademie der Wissenschaften.

Ramirez, Francisco O., and John W. Meyer. 1980. "Comparative Education: The Social Construction of the Modern World System." In *Annual Review of Sociology*, edited by Alex Inkeles, 6:369–99.

Ramminger, Johann. 1981. "Nationalismus und Universität: Die Geneze des Nationalismus und die cisleithanischen Universitäten 1859–1900." Dissertation der geisteswiss. Fakultät, Universität Wien.

Rappold, Jacob. 1893–1913. *Die Vorbereitung für die Aufnahmsprüfung der Gymnasien und Realschulen aus der deutschen Sprache und dem Rechnen*. Vienna: A. Pichler, 1893, and subsequent editions through the seventh, 1913.

Rassem, Mohammed. 1968. "Die problematische Stellung der Studenten im sogenannten Humboldtschen System." *Studien und Berichte der katholischen Akademie in Bayern* 44:15–33.

Rath, R. John. 1957. *The Viennese Revolution of 1848*. Austin: University of Texas Press.

———. 1991. "Three Score and Fifteen Years of Habsburg and Austrian Historiography and a Quarter-Century of Editing the Austrian History Yearbook." *Austrian History Yearbook* 22:1–21.

Rauchberg, Heinrich. 1905. *Der nationale Besitzstand in Böhmen*. 3 vols. Leipzig: Duncker & Humblot.

Reden, Alexander Sixtus von. 1984. *Österreich-Ungarn. Die Donaumonarchie in historischen Dokumenten*. Salzburg: Nonntal Bücherdienst.

Renner, Karl. 1916–17. *Österreichs Erneuerung*. 3 vols. in 1. Vienna: Ignaz Brand.

Říha, Oldřich, and Július Mésároš, eds. 1960. *Přehled československých dějin*. Part 2, *1848–1918* (Survey of Czechoslovak history. Part 2, 1848–1918). Prague: Československá akademie věd.

Ringer, Fritz K. 1977. "Problems in the History of Higher Education: A Review Article." *Comparative Studies in Society and History* 19:239–55.

———. 1978. "The Education of Elites in Modern Europe." *History of Education Quarterly* 18:159–72.

———. 1979. *Education and Society in Modern Europe*. Bloomington: Indiana University Press.

———. 1992. "A Sociography of German Academics, 1863–1938." *Central European History* 25:251–80.

Ritter, Harry. 1984. "Austro-German Liberalism and the Modern Liberal Tradition." *German Studies Review* 7:227–48.

Rom, Adalbert. 1913. "Der Bildungsgrad der Bevölkerung in den öster. Alpen- und Karstländern nach den Ergebnissen der letzten vier Volkszählungen, 1880–1910." *Statistische Monatsschrift,* n.s., 18:769–814.

———. 1914. "Der Bildungsgrad der Bevölkerung Österreichs und seine Entwicklung seit 1880 mit besonderer Berücksichtigung der Sudeten- und Karpathenländer." *Statistische Monatsschrift,* n.s., 19:589–642.

Rossos, Andrew. 1982. "Czech Historiography." *Canadian Slavonic Papers/ Revue Canadienne des Slavistes* 24:245–60, 359–85.

Roth, Michael S. 1994. "Performing History: Modernist Contextualism in Carl Schorske's *Fin-de-Siècle Vienna*." *American Historical Review* 99:729–45.

Rothschild, Joseph. 1974. *East Central Europe between the Two World Wars*. Seattle: University of Washington Press.

Rothschild, Kurt W. 1974. "Bildung, Bildungspolitik, und Arbeiterbewegung." In *Geschichte und Gesellschaft: Festschrift für Karl R. Stadler,* edited by Gerhard Botz, Hans Hautmann, and Helmut Konrad, 339–41. Vienna: Europaverlag.

Rozenblit, Marsha L. 1983. *The Jews of Vienna, 1867–1914: Assimilation and Identity*. Albany: State University of New York Press.

Rudnytsky, Ivan L. 1982. "The Ukrainians in Galicia under Austrian Rule." In *Nationbuilding and the Politics of Nationalism: Essays on Austrian Galicia,* edited by Andrei S. Markovits and Frank E. Sysyn, 23–67. Cambridge: Harvard University Press.

Rudolph, Richard. 1975. "The Pattern of Austrian Industrial Growth from the Eighteenth to the Early Twentieth Century." *Austrian History Yearbook* 11:3–25.

Rumpler, Helmut, ed. 1970. *Die Protokolle des österreichischen Ministerrates, 1848–1867: Einleitungsband: Ministerrat und Ministerratsprotokolle, 1848–1867.* Vienna: Öster. Bundesverlag.

Šafránek, Jan. 1898. *Rozvoj českého školství: Památník na oslavu Padesatiletého Jubilea Františka Josefa I* (The development of Czech schooling: Commemorative volume for the Fiftieth Jubilee of Francis Joseph I). Prague.

______. 1907. "Otázka reformy středoškolské: Některé myšlenky pro širší veřejnost" (The question of secondary school reform: Some thoughts for the broader public). *Osvěta,* no. 12: 1026–33, 1053–61.

______. 1910. "Ústav náš ve vývoji školských oprav" (Our school in the development of educational reforms). In *Zpráva c. k. vyššího (humanitního) gymnasia v Praze v Křemencově ulici 1910* (Report of the k. k. higher (humanistic) Gymnasium in Prague, Křemencová Street), 1–24.

______. 1913. *Reálné gymnasium: Obraz jeho vzniku, vývoje a osudů: Přehled jeho učebných osnov* (The *Realgymnasium:* A portrait of its origin, development, and fate: A survey of its curricula). Prague: I. Kober.

______. 1913–18. *Školy české: Obraz jejich vývoje a osudů* (Czech schools: A portrait of their development and trials). 2 vols. Prague: Nakl. Matice česká.

______. 1924. *Vzpomínky na Kolín* (Recollections of Kolín). Prague: Ústřední Matice Školská.

Sáňka, Hugo, ed. 1927. *Šedesát let českého gymnasia v Brně 1867–1927* (Sixty years of the Czech *Gymnasium* in Brno). Brno: Privately published.

Sborník Masaryková státního reálného gymnasia v Praze II, Křemencová ulice (Commemorative Collection on the Masaryk State Realgymnasium in Prague II, Křemencová ulice). 1948. Prague: n.p.

Scheindler, August, ed. 1905. *Verhandlungen der II. Konferenz der Direktoren der Mittelschulen im Erzherzogtum Österreich unter der Enns im Auftrage des K.K. nö. Landesschulrates.* Verhandlungen der nö. Mittelschuldirektoren-Konferenzen, 1. Vienna: A. Hölder.

______, ed. 1910. *Verhandlungen der IV. Konferenz der Direktoren der Mittelschulen (Gymnasien, Realgymnasien und Realschulen) im Erzherzogtum Österreich unter der Enns.* Verhandlungen der nö. Mittelschuldirektoren-Konferenzen, 3. Vienna: A. Hölder.

Scherer, Johann. 1905–9. "Juden: Geschichtlich." In *Österreichisches Staatswörterbuch,* edited by Ernst Mischler and Josef Ulbrich, 2:946–71. 2d rev. ed. Vienna: A. Hölder.

Scheu, Robert, ed. 1898. *Mittelschul-Enquête der "Wage."* Vol. 1, *Was leistet die Mittelschule.* Vienna: Gesellschaft für graphische Industrie.

______. 1901. *Culturpolitik.* Vienna: Wiener Verlag.

______, ed. 1907. *Die Mittelschulenquête der Kulturpolitischen Gesellschaft.* Vol. 2, pt. 2, *Schülerbriefe über die Mittelschule.* Vienna: M. Perles.

______, ed. 1908. *Protokolle der Mittelschulenquête der Kulturpolitischen Gesellschaft.* Vol. 2, pt. 1. Vienna: M. Perles.

Scheuer, Oskar. 1910. *Die geschichtliche Entwicklung des deutschen Studententums in Österreich mit besonderer Berücksichtigung der Universität Wien von ihrer Gründung bis zur Gegenwart.* Vienna and Leipzig: Ed. Beyer Nachf.

Schimmer, Gustav A. 1858. "Statistik der Lehranstalten des österreichischen Kaiserstaates für die Studienjahre 1851–1857." Parts 1 and 2. *Mittheilungen aus dem Gebiete der Statistik* 7, no. 1; no. 4.

______. 1877. "Frequenz der Lehranstalten Oesterreichs von 1841 bis 1876, in Vergleichung zur Bevölkerung." *Statistische Monatsschrift* 3:53–74.

______. 1879. "Der Gymnasial-Besuch in Vergleichung zu den Jahres-Generationen und den Maturitäts-Prüfungen." *Statistische Monatsschrift* 5:345–58.

______. 1884. "Aufnahmsprüfungen für die 1. Classe des österreichischen Mittelschulen zu Beginn des Schuljahres 1883/84." *Statistische Monatsschrift* 10:359–62.

Schmidt-Hartmann, Eva. 1984. *Thomas G. Masaryk's Realism: Origins of a Czech Political Concept.* Munich: R. Oldenbourg.

Schorske, Carl E. 1980. *Fin-de-Siècle Vienna: Politics and Culture.* New York: Alfred Knopf.

Schusser, Adalbert. 1972. "Zur Entwicklung der italienischen Universitätsfrage in Österreich 1861–1918: Untersuchungen über das Verhalten von Regierung und Parlament zur Schaffung einer italienischen Rechtsfakultät." Ph.D. diss., Universität Wien.

Schweickhardt, Friedrich Frh. von, ed. 1885. *Sammlung der für die öster. Universitäten giltigen Gesetze und Verordnungen.* 2d ed. rev. 2 vols. Vienna: K. K. Schulbuchverlag.

Seligmann, Adalbert F., et al., ed. 1921. *Das Wasagymnasium: 50 Jahre einer Wiener Mittelschule.* Vienna.

Siegrist, Hannes. 1990. "Public Office or Free Profession? German Attorneys in the Nineteenth and Early Twentieth Centuries." In *German Professions,* ed. Geoffrey Cocks and Konrad H. Jarausch, 46–65. New York and Oxford: Oxford University Press.

Sked, Alan. 1989. *The Decline and Fall of the Habsburg Empire 1815–1918.* London: Longman.

Skilling, H. Gordon. 1949. "The Partition of the University of Prague." *Slavonic Review* 27:430–49.

______. 1967. "The Czech-German Conflict in Bohemia, 1867–1914." Unpubl. revision of 1940 Ph.D. diss., University of London.

Sládek, Zdeněk. 1990. "Das tschechoslowakische Grund- und Mittelschulwesen nach 1918: Kontinuität und Diskontinuität." In *Bildungswesen und Sozialstruktur in Mitteleuropa im 19. und 20. Jahrhundert,* edited by Victor Karady and Wolfgang Mitter, 27–40. Studien und Dokumentationen zu vergleichenden Bildungsforschung, vol. 42. Cologne and Vienna: Böhlau.

Slater, Mariam K. 1969. "My Son the Doctor: Aspects of Mobility among American Jews." *American Sociological Review* 34, no. 3:359–73.

Slavíček, Antonín. 1973. "Dějiny a archiv spolku Lese- und Redehalle der Deutschen Studenten in Prag" (The history and archive of the association Lese- und Redehalle der Deutschen Studenten in Prag). Diploma thesis, Phil. Faculty, Univerzita Karlova, Prague.

Slavík, František A. 1869. *Stručný dějepis Akademického čtenářského spolku v Praze* (Outline history of the Academic Reading Society in Prague). Prague: Akad. čtenářský spolek.

______. 1874. *Dějiny českého studentstva* (History of Czech students). 2d ed. Prague: Akad. čtenářský spolek.

Sperber, Jonathan. 1994. *The European Revolutions, 1848–1851.* Cambridge: Cambridge University Press.

Springer, Anton. 1892. *Aus meinem Leben.* Berlin: G. Grote.

Štaif, Jiří. 1990. *Revoluční léta 1848–1849 a české země* (The revolutionary years 1848–1849 and the Bohemian lands). In Opera Instituti Historici Pragae—Práce Historického ústavu ČAV, Řada A-Monographia (Works of the Historical Institute of the Czech Academy of Sciences, Series A-Monographs), vol. 3. Prague: Historický ústav ČSAV.

Stark, Franz, ed. 1906. *Die k. k. deutsche technische Hochschule in Prag 1806–1906.* Prague: Selbstverlag.

Stašek, Antal [Antonín Zeman]. 1925. *Vzpomínky* (Memoirs). Prague: F. Borový.

Stearns, Peter N. 1974. *1848: The Revolutionary Tide in Europe.* New York: W. W. Norton.

Steinberg, Michael P. 1990. *The Meaning of the Salzburg Festival: Austria as Theater and Ideology, 1890–1938.* Ithaca, N.Y.: Cornell University Press.

______. 1991. "'Fin-de-Siècle Vienna' Ten Years Later: 'Viel Traum, Wenig Wirklichkeit.'" *Austrian History Yearbook* 22:151–62.

Stekl, Hannes, P. Urbanitsch, E. Bruckmüller, and G. Heiss, eds. 1992. *Bürgertum in der Habsburgermonarchie.* Vol. 2, *Durch Arbeit, Besitz, Wissen, und Gerechtigkeit.* Vienna, Cologne, and Weimar: Böhlau.

Štětina, Karel, František Pösl, and František Kaska, eds. 1907. *Jubilejní Památník c. k. vyššího gymnasia v Jičíně* (Jubilee commemorative volume of the imperial-royal higher Gymnasium in Jičín). Jičín: B. Outrata.

Stich, Ignaz. 1899. *Die katholisch-österreichischen Studenten-Verbindungen "Austria" und "Rudolfina" in Wien: Ihr Wesen und ihre Ziele.* Vienna: Franz Doll.

Stockert-Meynert, Dora. 1930. *Theodor Meynert und seine Zeit: Zur Geistesgeschichte Österreichs in der 2. Hälfte des 19. Jahrhunderts.* Vienna and Leipzig: Österreichischer Bundesverlag.

Stölzl, Christoph. 1971. *Die Ära Bach in Böhmen: Sozialgeschichtliche Studien zum Neoabsolutismus 1849–1859.* Munich and Vienna: R. Oldenbourg.

______. 1973–74. "Zur Geschichte der böhmischen Juden in der Epoche des modernen Nationalismus." *Bohemia: Jahrbuch des Collegium Carolinum* 14:179–221; 15:129–57.

Stollenmayer, P. Pankraz. 1950. "Zum Kampf um das humanistische Gymnasium: Ein Beitrag aus der Geschichte des Gymnasiums Kremsmünster." In *93. Jahresbericht des Obergymnasiums der Benediktiner zu Kremsmünster: Schuljahr 1950,* 3–35. Kremsmünster: n.p.

Stone, Lawrence, ed. 1974. *The University in Society.* 2 vols. Princeton: Princeton University Press.

Stourzh, Gerald. 1985. *Die Gleichberechtigung der Nationalitäten in der Verfassung und Verwaltung Österreichs 1948–1918.* Vienna: Öster. Akademie der Wissenschaften.

Strakosch-Graßmann, Gustav. 1905. *Geschichte des österreichischen Unterrichtswesens.* Vienna: A. Pichler.

Streeruwitz, Ernst Streer Ritter von. 1934. *Wie es war: Erinnerungen und Erlebnisse eines alten Österreichers.* Vienna: Steyrermühl-Verlag.

Stremayr, Carl von. 1899. *Erinnerungen aus dem Leben.* Vienna.

Strnadová, Věra. 1973. "Posluchači filosofickeho studia na Universitě Karlově v první polovině 19. století" (Students in philosophical studies at the Charles University in the first half of the nineteenth century). *Acta Universitatis Carolinae—Historia Universitatis Carolinae Pragensis* 13, fasc. 1–2:137–48.

Strogoň, Tomáš, Josef Cach, Jozef Mátej, and Jozef Schubert. 1981. *Dějiny školstva a pedagogiky* (A history of education and pedagogy). Bratislava: Slovenské Pedagogické Nakladatelštvo.

Sutter, Berthold. 1960–65. *Die Badenischen Sprachenverordnungen.* 2 vols. Graz and Cologne: Böhlau.

______. 1980. "Die politische und rechtliche Stellung der Deutschen in Österreich 1848 bis 1918." In *Die Habsburgermonarchie, 1848–1918,* edited by Adam Wandruszka and Peter Urbanitsch. Vol. 3, pt. 1:154–339. Vienna: Öster. Akademie der Wissenschaften.

Svoboda, Johann. 1894–97. *Die Theresianische Militär-Akademie zur Wiener Neustadt und ihre Zöglinge von der Gründung der Anstalt bis auf unsere Tage*. 3 vols. Vienna: K. K. Hof- und Staatsdruckerei.

Talbott, John E. 1971. "The History of Education." *Daedalus* 100:133–50.

Tesar, Eva, ed. 1985. *Hände auf die Bank: Erinnerungen an den Schulalltag*. Vienna, Cologne, and Graz: Böhlau.

Thaa, Georg, ed. 1871. *Sammlung der für die österreichischen Universitäten gilten Gesetze und Verordnungen*. Vienna: Manz.

Thaa, Georg, ed. 1876. *Sammlung der für die österreichischen Universitäten gilten Gesetze und Verordnungen*. Supplement no. 1. Vienna: Manz.

Thienen-Alderflycht, Christoph. 1967. *Graf Leo Thun im Vormärz: Grundlage des böhmischen Konservatismus im Kaisertum Österreich*. Graz, Vienna, and Cologne: Styria Verlag.

Titze, Hartmut. 1981. "Überfüllungskrisen in akademischen Karrieren: Eine Zyklustheorie." *Zeitschrift für Pädagogik* 27:187–224.

______. 1983. "Enrollment Expansion and Academic Overcrowding in Germany." In *The Transformation of Higher Learning*, 1860–1930, edited by K. H. Jarausch, 57–88. Stuttgart: Klett-Cotta; Chicago: University of Chicago Press.

______. 1984. "Die zyklische Überproduktion von Akademikern im 19. und 20. Jahrhundert." *Geschichte und Gesellschaft* 10:92–121.

______. 1987. *Das Hochschulstudium in Preußen und Deutschland 1820–1944: Datenhandbuch zur deutschen Bildungsgeschichte*. Vol. 1, pt. 1. Göttingen: Vandenhoeck & Ruprecht.

Tribl, Erich. 1966. "Aspekte des Lehrerseins in der Fachliteratur seit der Jahrhundertwende." Ph.D. diss., Universität Wien.

Uhl, Friedrich. 1908. *Aus meinem Leben*. Stuttgart and Berlin: J. Cott Nachf.

Ulbrich, Josef. 1905–9. "Staatsbürgerschaft." In *Öster. Staatswörterbuch*, edited by Ernst Mischler and Josef Ulbrich, 4:312–14. 2d rev. ed. Vienna: A. Hölder.

Ulbrich, Karl, ed. 1905. *Festschrift zur Erinnerung an die Feier des Fünfzigjährigen Bestandes der K. K. Staats-Realschule im IV. Bezirk in Wien (vormals Wiedner Kommunal-Oberrealschule)*. Vienna: Privately printed.

Umlauft, Franz Josef, ed. 1924. *Festschrift des Aussiger Gymnasiums anläßlich des 30-jährigen Bestandes von 1893–1923*. Ustí nad Labem.

Urban, Otto. 1978. *Kapitalismus a česká společnost: K otázkám formování české společnosti v 19. století* (Capitalism and Czech society: On the questions of the formation of Czech society in the nineteenth century). Prague: Svoboda.

______. 1982. *Česká společnost 1848–1918* (Czech society, 1848–1918). Prague: Svoboda.

Urbanitsch, Peter. 1980. "Die Deutschen in Österreich: Statistisch-deskriptiver Überblick." In *Die Habsburgermonarchie, 1848–1918,* edited by Adam Wandruszka and Peter Urbanitsch, vol. 3, pt. 1:33–410. Vienna: Öster. Akademie der Wissenschaften.

———. 1990. "Bürgertum und Politik in der Habsburgermonarchie: Eine Einführung." In *Bürgertum in der Habsburgermonarchie,* edited by Ernst Bruckmüller et al., 1:165–75. Vienna and Cologne: Böhlau.

Vaníček, Alois, ed. 1860. *Schematismus der österreichischen Gymnasien und Realschulen für das Schuljahr 1859–1860.* Prague: F. Tempsky.

Veysey, Laurence R. 1965. *The Emergence of the American University.* Chicago: University of Chicago Press.

Vojtěch, Tomáš. 1980. *Mladočeši a boj o politickou moc v Čechách* (The young Czechs and the struggle for political power in Bohemia). Prague: Academia.

Die vor- und nachmärzliche Mittelschule Österreichs. 1889. Vienna: A. Pichler.

Walter, Friedrich. 1970. *Die österreichische Zentralverwaltung.* Vol. 3, pt. 3, *Die Geschichte der Ministerien vom Durchbruch des Absolutismus bis zum Ausgleich mit Ungarn und zur Konstitutionalisierung der österreichischen Länder, 1852 bis 1867.* Vienna: A. Holzhausens Nachf.

Wandruszka, Adam. 1954. "Österreichs Politische Struktur." In *Geschichte der Republik Österreich,* edited by Heinrich Benedikt, 289–486. Munich: R. Oldenbourg.

Wandruszka, Adam, and Peter Urbanitsch, eds. 1980. *Die Habsburgermonarchie, 1848–1918.* Vol. 3, *Die Völker des Reiches.* 2 pts. Vienna: Öster. Akademie der Wissenschaften.

Wandycz, Piotr S. 1974. *The Lands of Partitioned Poland, 1795–1918.* Seattle: University of Washington Press.

Wappler, Anton. 1884. *Geschichte der Theologischen Fakultät der k. und k. Universität zu Wien.* Vienna: W. Braumüller.

Weber, Therese. 1984. *Häuslerkindheit: Autobiographische Erzählungen.* Vienna, Cologne, and Graz: Böhlau.

Wegs, J. Robert. 1989. *Growing Up Working Class: Continuity and Change among Viennese Youth, 1890–1938.* University Park: Pennsylvania State University Press.

Weidenholzer, Josef. 1981. *Auf dem Weg zum "Neuen Menschen": Bildungs- und Kulturarbeit der österreichischen Sozialdemokratie in der Ersten Republik.* Schriftenreihe des Ludwig Boltzmann Instituts für Geschichte der Arbeiterbewegung, vol. 12. Vienna, Munich, and Zürich: Europaverlag.

Weinzierl-Fischer, Erika. 1960. *Die österreichischen Konkordate von 1855 und 1933.* Vienna: Verlag für Geschichte und Politik.

Wellner, Max, ed. 1895. *Průvodce akademickým životem* (Guide to academic life). Prague: Akademický odbor národopisný.

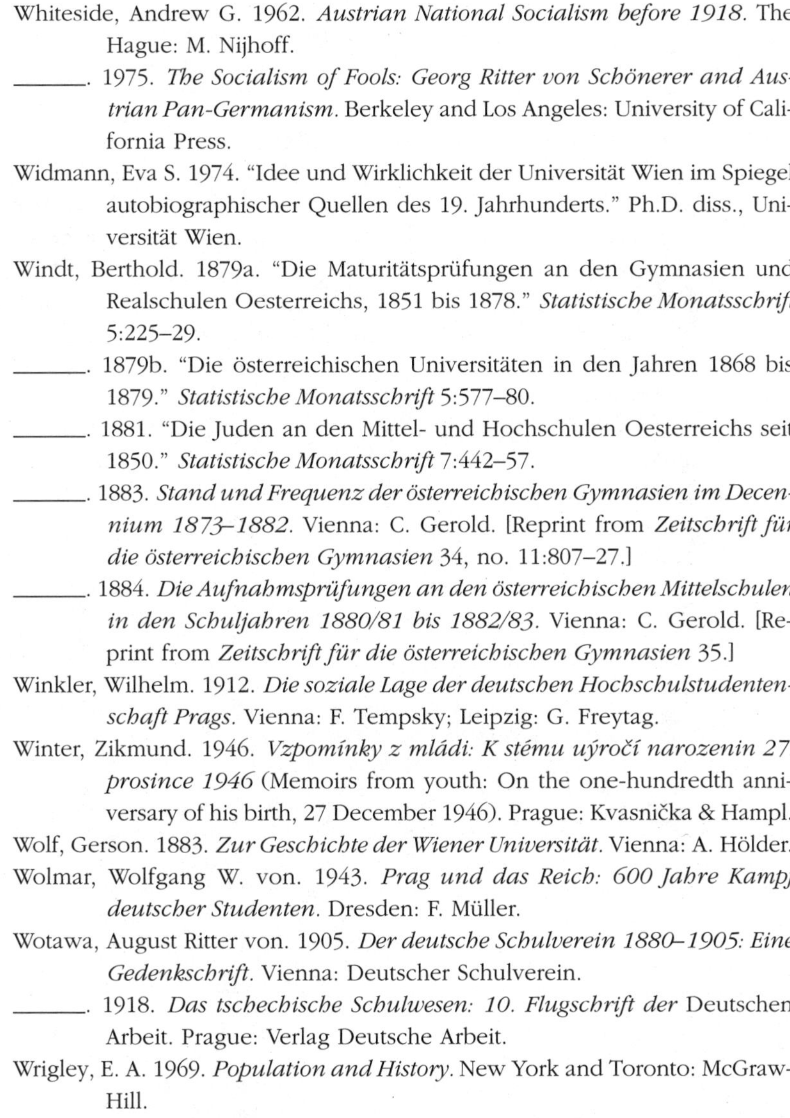

Whiteside, Andrew G. 1962. *Austrian National Socialism before 1918*. The Hague: M. Nijhoff.

______. 1975. *The Socialism of Fools: Georg Ritter von Schönerer and Austrian Pan-Germanism*. Berkeley and Los Angeles: University of California Press.

Widmann, Eva S. 1974. "Idee und Wirklichkeit der Universität Wien im Spiegel autobiographischer Quellen des 19. Jahrhunderts." Ph.D. diss., Universität Wien.

Windt, Berthold. 1879a. "Die Maturitätsprüfungen an den Gymnasien und Realschulen Oesterreichs, 1851 bis 1878." *Statistische Monatsschrift* 5:225–29.

______. 1879b. "Die österreichischen Universitäten in den Jahren 1868 bis 1879." *Statistische Monatsschrift* 5:577–80.

______. 1881. "Die Juden an den Mittel- und Hochschulen Oesterreichs seit 1850." *Statistische Monatsschrift* 7:442–57.

______. 1883. *Stand und Frequenz der österreichischen Gymnasien im Decennium 1873–1882*. Vienna: C. Gerold. [Reprint from *Zeitschrift für die österreichischen Gymnasien* 34, no. 11:807–27.]

______. 1884. *Die Aufnahmsprüfungen an den österreichischen Mittelschulen in den Schuljahren 1880/81 bis 1882/83*. Vienna: C. Gerold. [Reprint from *Zeitschrift für die österreichischen Gymnasien* 35.]

Winkler, Wilhelm. 1912. *Die soziale Lage der deutschen Hochschulstudentenschaft Prags*. Vienna: F. Tempsky; Leipzig: G. Freytag.

Winter, Zikmund. 1946. *Vzpomínky z mládi: K stému uýročí narozenin 27. prosince 1946* (Memoirs from youth: On the one-hundredth anniversary of his birth, 27 December 1946). Prague: Kvasnička & Hampl.

Wolf, Gerson. 1883. *Zur Geschichte der Wiener Universität*. Vienna: A. Hölder.

Wolmar, Wolfgang W. von. 1943. *Prag und das Reich: 600 Jahre Kampf deutscher Studenten*. Dresden: F. Müller.

Wotawa, August Ritter von. 1905. *Der deutsche Schulverein 1880–1905: Eine Gedenkschrift*. Vienna: Deutscher Schulverein.

______. 1918. *Das tschechische Schulwesen: 10. Flugschrift der* Deutschen Arbeit. Prague: Verlag Deutsche Arbeit.

Wrigley, E. A. 1969. *Population and History*. New York and Toronto: McGraw-Hill.

Wurzer, Rudolf. 1965–67. "Die Stellung der Technischen Hochschule Wien im Ablauf ihrer Geschichte." In *150 Jahre Technische Hochschule in Wien 1815–1965*, edited by Heinrich Sequenz, 1:11–157. 3 vols. Vienna: Technische Hochschule Wien.

Zenkl, F. D. 1892. *Slavnostní spis na pamět třicetiletého trvání cis. král. Reálného Gymnasia v Táboře 1862–1892* (Commemorative volume in honor of the thirty years of the imperial and royal *Real-Gymnasium* in Tábor, 1862–1892). Tábor: P. Frank.

Zöllner, Erich. 1965. "Formen und Wandlungen des Österreichsbegriffes." In *Historica: Studien zum geschichtlichen Denken und Forschen: Festschrift für Friedrich Engel-Janosi,* edited by Hugo Hantsch, Eric Voegelin, and Franco Valsecchi. Vienna: Herder.

______. 1980. "Perioden der österreichischen Geschichte und Wandlungen des Österreichbegriffes bis zum Ende der Habsburgermonarchie." In *Die Habsburgermonarchie, 1848–1918,* edited by Adam Wandruszka and Peter Urbanitsch, vol. 3, pt. 1:1–32. Vienna: Öster. Akademie der Wisssenschaften.

Zschokke, Hermann. 1894. *Die theologischen Studien und Anstalten der katholischen Kirche in Österreich*. Vienna and Leipzig: W. Braumüller.

Zweig, Stefan. 1970. *Die Welt von Gestern: Erinnerungen eines Europäers.* Frankfurt: Fischer Taschenbuch.

Zwitter, Fran. 1967. "The Slovenes and the Habsburg Monarchy." *Austrian History Yearbook,* vol. 3, pt. 2:159–88.

1868–1928: Šedesát Let Jirsíkova Gymnasia v Č. Budějovicích (1868–1928: Sixty years of the Jirsík Gymnasium in České Budějovice). 1928. České Budějovice: K. Fiala.

INDEX

Aachen, Rhenish-Westphalian Technical College, 206

Abitur examination in Prussia and other German states, 22

Academic Reading Society, Czech (Akademický čtenářský spolek, Prague), 235–36

Academy of Fine Arts (Vienna), 82

access to advanced education, ministerial policies during the 1850s, 30–31

Agriculture, College of (Vienna), 83

Akademischer Leseverein (Vienna), 235

Anderson, C. Arnold, 250

anti-Semitism, 135–36, 162, 166, 220, 233, 235, 236, 238

Association for School Reform, 121

Association of Friends of the Humanistic Gymnasium, 121

Association of German Students, 238

Austria, geographical definition, 8–9, 303n. 20

Austrian Republic, legacy of imperial Austrian education, 268–69

Austro-Hungarian Compromise (1867), 36

Bach, Alexander, 23, 36

Bahr, Hermann, 209

Beck, Max Vladimir, Freiherr von, 111

Berlin, university, 17

Billroth, Theodor, 166–68

Bismarck, Otto von, Prince, 1, 97

Blažek, Gabriel, 118

Bohemian lands, inhabitants' demand for higher education, 80

Bolzano (Bozen), Gymnasium, 104

Bonitz, Hermann, 27–29, 40, 125

Bourdieu, Pierre, 245

Boyer, John W., 2, 20, 110

Brno (Brünn): agitation for Czech university in, 113; Technical Institute/College, 32, 63; Czech Technical College, 118; German Technical College, 118

Broumov (Braunau), Gymnasium, 66

Bruck, Karl Ludwig, Freiherr von, 23

Bukovina, 48; inhabitants' demand for higher education, 81; secondary school enrollments, 72–73

Burschenschaften, 18, 236–37

cadet schools, 223, 296

Čáslav, communal secondary school, 105

Časopis českého studentstva (Magazine of Czech students), 242

Catholic church: influence in Austrian public education, 25, 33, 37, 49, 97, 110, 129–30; role of priests and religious orders in Austrian public education, 15, 16, 34, 37–38. *See also* Concordat of 1855

Catholic students. *See* students in Austrian higher education; students in Austrian secondary education

Catholic theological faculties: admissions requirements, 306n. 68; curricular reform (1873), 51; enrollment trends, 88–89. *See also individual cities with faculties*

Celje (Cilli), Gymnasium, 112

Český krumlov (Krumau), Real-Gymnasium, 67

Chernivtsi (Czernowitz): Francis Joseph University, 48, 63, 82, 161; Jewish residents, 138

Christian Social Party, 110

Chrudim, reálné gymnasium, 219

commercial academies, 223

Concordat of 1855, 33, 37

confidence intervals for sampled data, defined, 296–97

Conrad von Eybesfeld, Siegmund, Freiherr, 98–100
conservatives, Austrian, and educational policy, 97–100
Consular Academy (Academy of Oriental Languages, Vienna), 13
Corps, student organizations, 236
craft schools, 40, 70, 107, 223
Craig, John E., 204, 294
Cultural-Political Society, 121
Czech educators' political role, 243
Czech national movement, views on education, 95–96, 164–65, 240–43
Czech popular aspirations for advanced education, 195–98
Czech students. *See* students in Austrian higher education; students in Austrian secondary education
Czechoslovakia, legacy of imperial Austrian education, 267–68

doctors' colleges, 26, 49
dueling, among students in corporate fraternities, 236–37
Dumreicher, Armand, Freiherr von, 95, 101–2, 237
Dumreicher von Österreicher, Johann, Baron, 101

Ecole polytechnique (Paris), 14
economic trends and educational development, 61, 90–91, 250–53
educational expansion and development: general Austrian trends compared to European trends, 58, 60, 264–65; causes, 250–54
Ehrenfest, Paul, 233
Ehrlich, Eugen, 73, 224, 259, 263
Einstein, Albert, 233
Eisner, Pavel, 173, 220
Engelbrecht, Helmut, 30, 110
engineer, formal title, 53
enlightened absolutism and educational reform in eighteenth-century Austria, 15–16
ethnic and religious origins of students, methodology and problems in measuring, 134–40. *See also* students in Austrian higher education; students in Austrian secondary education
Exner, Franz Seraphin, 21, 25, 29, 40, 51, 125

Ferdinand I, Austrian emperor, 16, 20
foreign students in Austrian secondary and higher education, 138–39, 150, 153
Francis I, Austrian emperor, 16, 18, 20, 266
Francis Joseph I, Austrian emperor, 22–23, 36, 104, 233, 242
Frankl, Ludwig August, 18
freedom, academic, 18, 21, 25, 111–12

Galicia: inhabitants' demand for higher education, 80–81; secondary school enrollments, 72–73
Gautsch von Frankenthurn, Paul, Freiherr, 104–6, 109–10, 114, 225
German liberals, educational policies, 36–38, 47–49, 67, 97, 111
German literature, in Austrian Gymnasium curriculum, 19
German-speaking students. *See* students in Austrian higher education; students in Austrian secondary education
girls' *Lyzeen,* in Austria, 74; curriculum, 215–16
Gossler, Gustav von, 102
Graz: medical faculty, 82; Provincial Oberrealschule, 173; university, 12, 15, 178
Gymnasien, Austrian: conditions in the late eighteenth century, 15; conditions in the early nineteenth century, 12, 17, 19; curriculum, 42–44, 120–21, 215, 216; *Enquête* (1870), 42–44;

pedagogy, 216–17; reforms (1850s), 27–28; reforms (1860s–1870s), 41–42; reforms (1908–1910), 123–24. *See also* secondary education, Austrian; students in Austrian secondary education; *cities for individual institutions*

Habilitierung of docents: in Austrian higher education, 21; in technical colleges, 51
Hanka, Václav, alleged discovery of medieval Czech manuscripts, 243
Hanslick, Eduard, 19
Hartel, Wilhelm von, 119
Hartmann, Ludo M., 216
Hasner, Leopold, 18
higher education, Austrian: admission policies, 107–8; enrollment trends, 58–60, 62, 75–84, 273; enrollment trends compared with other European countries, 60; financial aid and stipends, 176–78; overall costs for students, 228–29; professors and instructors, 230–33; tuition and fees, 31, 176. *See also* students in Austrian higher education; mining and metallurgical schools, Austrian; technical institutes/colleges, Austrian; universities, Austrian; *the various university faculties; cities for individual institutions*
Hohenwart, Karl, Count, 47
Humboldtian reforms in Berlin and other German universities, 18, 22, 26
Hungary, students from, in Austrian higher education, 139, 155

inclusiveness of student recruitment: defined, 6; extent in late-nineteenth-century Austria, 202
industrial development, Austrian, 12
Innsbruck: Catholic theological faculty, 34, 79, 82; university, 15, 111, 112–13, 178
Italian-speaking students. *See* students in Austrian higher education; students in Austrian secondary education

Jarausch, Konrad H., 204, 245, 293
Jarcke, Karl Ernst, 24, 32, 33
Jesuit order, in Austrian education, 15, 34, 214
Jewish students. *See* students in Austrian higher education; students in Austrian secondary education
Jews, Austrian: assimilation and conversion, 135–36; demand for advanced education, 161–68, 195–202; employment as army doctors, 163; employment as teachers in Austrian public education, 99, 162–63, 220; employment in the state officialdom, 162–64; ethnic and national identification, 137–38; rights in advanced public education, 129; theological education, in Austria, 316n. 111
Jičín: as regional educational center, 219; Gymnasium, 66, 241, 242
Jireček, Josef, 47–48
Jodl, Friedrich, 120
Joseph II, Austrian emperor, 11, 14, 15, 128
Josephs-Akademie (Vienna), 14, 32, 50

Kaelble, Hartmut, 58, 60, 264
Karlsruhe, Technical College, 206
Klagenfurt, Gymnasium, 66
knights' academies (*Ritterakademien*), 13
Koerber, Ernest von, 112–13
Kořalka, Jiří, 263
Korb von Weidenheim, Karl, Baron, 103
Kotor, Gymnasium and Realschule, 104
Krakow, university, 47, 48, 315n. 76
Kranj, Gymnasium, 104

Krems an der Donau: as regional educational center, 219; Gymnasium, 66, 172
Kremsmünster, Benedictine Gymnasium, 66, 172, 214
Kudlich, Hans, 131–32
Kübeck, Carl Friedrich, 208

Landsmannschaften, Austrian, 236–38. *See also* students in Austrian higher education, sociability and organizations
language of instruction in Austrian public education, 34–35, 39, 45–47, 112–13, 129
law faculties, Austrian: enrollments in the 1840s, 19–20; enrollments in the 1850s, 32; curricular reform (1872), 49–50; curricular reform (1893), 113; growth during the second half of the nineteenth century, 85. *See also* students in Austrian law faculties
Leo XIII, Pope, condemnation of dueling, 237
Liechtenstein, Alois von, Prince, 98
Lienbacher, Georg, 98–99
Linz, Gymnasium, 66
literacy rates in nineteenth-century Austria, 64
Ljubljana (Laibach), Gymnasium, 66
Lundgreen, Peter, 5
L'viv (Lemberg, Lwów): medical faculty, 82, 116; university, 47–48, 129, 315n. 76

Mahler, Gustav, 10, 208
Marchet, Gustav, 74, 119, 123
Maria Theresa, Austrian empress, 11, 13, 14
Maribor (Marburg), Gymnasium, 66
Masaryk, Tomáš G., 10, 208, 209, 216–17, 263
Mattuš, Karel, 96
Matura examination (*Maturitätsprüfung, Reifeprüfung*), 22, 28; compared with French and Prussian examinations, 218; reform (1908), 123, 217–18
medical faculties, Austrian: conditions during the early nineteenth century, 13; curricular reform (1872), 50–51; curricular reforms (1899–1903), 113–17; *Enquête* of 1895, 115–16; enrollment trends during the second half of the nineteenth century, 85–87, 114. *See also* students in Austrian medical faculties
Melk, Benedictine Gymnasium, 66
Metternich, Prince Klemens von, 21, 266
middle class, Austrian, historiography on, 1–5
military academy (Wiener Neustadt), 14
military service, one-year volunteer, 40–41, 65, 223
Minerva, women's secondary school (Prague), 74
mining and metallurgical schools, Austrian, 14, 32, 82
Ministry of Religion and Instruction: created (1849), 24; dissolved (1860), 36; general administration of public education, 30, 89–91, 109–10, 124–26, 254–55; re-established (1867), 38
Mittelschul-Enquête (1898), 120–21; (1906–7), 121–22
mother tongue of students, as reported in registration records, 134, 136–37
Müller, Detlef K., 203

national identification, nation-building, and Austrian advanced education, 240–41, 243–46
nationalist agitation and politics, in Austrian higher education, 237–39
nationalist movements and Austrian educational development, 91–92
Nový bydžov, communal secondary school, 105

occupational categories: as reported in student registries, 170; class groupings, 180, 294–96
occupational stratification of the Austrian population (1910), 289
Oelwein, Artur, 120–21
Olomouc (Olmütz), university, 12, 32
Omladina affair, 343n. 120

Pan-German movement, among Austrian students, 238
Passeron, Jean-Claude, 245
pharmacy curriculum and degrees in Austrian universities, 226–27
philosophical faculties, Austrian: conditions during the early nineteenth century 13, 20; curricular reform (1848), 21; curricular reform (1850s), 32–33; curricular reform (1872), 49; curricular reform (1899), 113; enrollment trends during the second half of the nineteenth century, 87–88. *See also* students in Austrian higher education
Pichler, Adolf, 18
Plzeň (Pilsen), Gymnasium, 66
Poland, legacy of imperial Austrian education, 268
Polish students. *See* students in Austrian higher education; students in Austrian secondary education
politicization and advanced education, 243–45
polytechnic institutes. *See* technical institutes/colleges, Austrian
population growth: in early-nineteenth-century Austria, 11; in late-nineteenth-century Austria, 252
Prague: Akademické gymnasium, 214; Bohemian Polytechnic Institute, 14, 15, 46, 132; Charles-Ferdinand University, 12, 35, 46–47, 82, 131–32, 178, 188–89; Czech reálné gymnasium (Ječná Street), 173; Czech reálné gymnasium (Křemencová Street), 242; Czech reálné gymnasium (Malá strana), 67; Czech Technical College, 118, 179; German Technical College, 118, 179. *See also* Minerva
primary education, Austrian: *Bürgerschulen,* 22, 38–39; development and enrollment trends during the nineteenth century, 63–65; general primary school law (1869), 38, 99; state requirement for attendance, late eighteenth century, 15
Prinz, Friedrich, 92
professors. *See* higher education, Austrian, professors and instructors; secondary education, Austrian, professors and instructors
progressiveness of enrollment trends: in late-nineteenth-century Austria, 202–6; in Prussia and Germany, 202–6
"Proposal for the Organization of *Gymnasien* and *Realschulen* in Austria" (1849), 28
"Proposal of the Basic Features of Public Education in Austria" (1848), 21–22, 25, 31, 51
Protestants, development of rights in education, 129–30; theological faculty (Vienna), 33
Protestant students. *See* students in Austrian higher education; students in Austrian secondary education
"Provisional Law on the Organization of Academic Authorities" (1849), 25
Prussia: class origins of secondary school students, 171; debates over secondary school enrollments and curricular reforms (1890–1900), 102, 119–20; influence of Prussian models on Austrian educational reforms, 29–30, 41

Rauscher, Joseph Othmar, Ritter von, Cardinal, 35
Reading and Speech Hall of German Students (Prague), 235–36
Real-Gymnasien, Austrian, 41–42
Realgymnasien, Austrian, 123–24
Realschulen, Austrian: conditions in the early nineteenth century, 12; curriculum in the late nineteenth century, 215; enrollment decline in the 1880s, 70–71; reforms (1848), 22; reforms and policies (1850s), 27, 29; reforms and policies (late 1860s and 1870s), 36, 39–41, 95; reforms and policies (1906), 122; reforms and policies (1908–10), 123–24; status compared with *Gymnasien,* 127. *See also* students, Austrian secondary education; *cities for individual institutions*
Reform-Realgymnasium, 124
religious denomination of students: as recorded in school registries, 134–35. *See also* students in Austrian higher education; students in Austrian secondary education
Renner, Karl, 10, 270
Revolution of 1848 and educational reform in Austria, 21–23
Ringer, Fritz K., 6, 202, 204, 250–51
Romanian students. *See* students in Austrian higher education; students in Austrian secondary education
Roveredo, Gymnasium, 104
Rozenblit, Marsha L., 136, 172, 201
Ruthenian students. *See* students in Austrian higher education; students in Austrian secondary education

Salzburg, university, 32
sampling methods for student registration records, 293–94
Scheu, Robert, 120–22
Schnitzler, Arthur, 213
school boards, provincial, district, and local, in Austria, 38
Schorske, Carl E., 4
Schottengymnasium. *See* Vienna, Benedictine Schottengymnasium
Schramm, Heinrich, 101
Schwarzenberg, Felix zu, Prince, 23
secondary education, Austrian: admissions policies (1870), 42, 43, 45; admissions policies (1880), 99–104; admissions policies (1887), 104; admissions policies (1895), 109–10; certification of instructors, 113; discipline, 216; enrollment trends, 55–58, 62, 70–73, 106, 272; enrollment trends compared with other European countries, 58, 249; financial aid for students, 174–75; institutional growth, 66–70; ministerial conference on secondary education (1908), 122–23; pedagogy, 216–17; professors and instructors, 219–21; proposals for a unified secondary school, 121; public debate about curricula ca. 1900, 108–9, 119–26, 224; tuition costs, 16, 17, 31, 129, 174. *See also* girls' *Lyzeen; Gymnasien; Real-Gymnasien; Realgymnasien; Realschulen;* students in Austrian secondary education
Seipel, Ignaz, 10, 208
semiprofessional occupations, as goal of students, 246–47, 263, 269–70
Sereth, Untergymnasium, 104
Slovakia, development of advanced education after 1918, 267–68
Slovak students. *See* students in Austrian higher education
Slovene students. *See* students in Austrian higher education; students in Austrian secondary education
social classes, definition of groupings, 180, 294–96

Social Democratic Party, Austrian, 110–11
socialization of youth in schools and advanced education, 212–13
social mobility and education, 5–6, 194–211
Society for Expanded Women's Education (Vienna), 74
Society of Physicians in Vienna's First District, 86
Sommaruga, Franz, Freiherr von, 21, 22
South Slavic students. *See* students in Austrian higher education; students in Austrian secondary education
Stašek, Antal, 241–42
state bureaucracy, Austrian: growth trends and relationship with educational expansion, 32, 253–54; growth trends during the early nineteenth century, 133–34; ranks in Austrian state service, 295–96; recruitment of officials during the late nineteenth century, 209–10
Steyr, Realschule, 104
St. Paul, Gymnasium, 66
Stremayr, Karl von, 42, 48, 49, 98
students in Austrian Catholic theological faculties, occupational and class origins, 187
students in Austrian higher education: attendance of classes, 227–28; attrition, 105–6, 225–27, 262; average ages, 210–11; corporate fraternities, 236–38; economic conditions and part-time employment, 228–29; general ethnic and religious composition, 147–68, 255–59, 278–79; housing conditions, 229–30; migration and transfers between institutions, 226; nationalist politics and divisions, 237–39; occupational and class origins, 175–94, 260–62, 280–88, 290–92; political loyalties and agitation, 237–39; reading societies, 234–36; relations with instructors, 231–32; representation of Catholics, 152–53; rep. of Czech speakers, 150–51, 157, 164–65; rep. of Eastern Orthodox Christians, 155–56, 161; rep. of German speakers, 149–50, 157, 255; rep. of Jews, 146–47, 151, 153–55, 159–68; rep. of Magyar speakers, 159; rep. of Polish speakers, 151–52, 157–58; rep. of Protestants, 155, 159–61, 164–65; rep. of Romanians, 152; rep. of Slovaks, 151; rep. of South Slavs, 152; rep. of Ukrainians (Ruthenians), 152, 158–59; sociability and organizations, 233–40; social origins during the early nineteenth century, 131–34; social privileges, 213, 224–25. *See also* students in Austrian technical institutes/colleges; students in Austrian universities; *students in various university faculties*
students in Austrian law faculties, occupational and class origins, 186–87
students in Austrian medical faculties, occupational and class origins, 187–88
students in Austrian secondary education: attrition, 105, 175, 221–23, 262; general ethnic and religious composition, 140–47, 255–59, 274–77; housing conditions, 218–19; occupational and class origins, 170–75, 260; representation of Catholics, 145–46; rep. of Czech speakers, 142–43; rep. of Eastern Orthodox Christians, 145–46; rep. of German speakers, 140–42, 255; rep. of Italian speakers, 142; rep. of Jews, 145–47; rep. of Polish speakers, 143; rep. of Protestants, 145; rep. of Romanians, 144; rep. of Slovenes, 144–45; rep. of Ukrainians (Ruthenians), 143–44; rep. of Uniate Catholics, 143–44, 145–46; sociability, 219, 221; social origins during the

students (*continued*)
early nineteenth century, 128–31; social privileges, 127, 213; student journals, 219
students in Austrian technical institutes/colleges, occupational and class origins, 190–93, 290–92
students in Austrian universities: occupational and class origins, 181–93, 260–62, 280–88; social origins of women students, 189–90, 286–88
Studienhofkommission, 16, 20–21
Stürgkh, Karl, Count, 74, 119, 121, 126
surgeons' schools, 50, 86

Taaffe, Eduard, Count, 70, 91, 97–101, 126
Tábor, reálné gymnasium, 41
teacher training schools, 39
technical institutes/colleges, Austrian: 14, 26, 27, 51–53, 77; enrollment trends during the late nineteenth century, 83–84, 89, 117–18. *See also* higher education, Austrian; *cities for individual institutions*
Theresianum, Collegium (Vienna), 13, 14, 131, 214
Thun-Hohenstein, Franz von, Count, 241
Thun-Hohenstein, Leo von, Count, 23, 24, 30, 32, 34–36, 53
Titze, Hartmut, 250
trade schools, 107
Tržič, Gymnasium, 66

Ukrainians, assimilation with Poles in Galicia, 136, 137–38. *See also* students in Austrian higher education; students in Austrian secondary education
unidentified occupational origins, statistical problems in dealing with students from, 297–300
universities, Austrian: general conditions during the eighteenth century, 12; institutional growth during the second half of the nineteenth century, 81–84; reforms (1873), 49–51. *See also* higher education, Austrian; Catholic theological faculties; law faculties; medical faculties; philosophical faculties; *cities for individual universities*

Vienna: Akademisches Gymnasium, 214; Benedictine Schottengymnasium, 208, 213, 214; Gymnasium (Vienna IX, Wasagasse), 216; medical faculty, Jewish enrollments, 166–68; Oberrealschule (Vienna IV-Wieden), 173; Protestant theological faculty, 33; technical college, 118, 179; university, 12, 131–32, 178, 184, 188. *See also* Academy of Fine Arts; Agriculture, College of; Consular Academy; Josephs-Akademie; Protestants, theological faculty; Theresianum, Collegium
vocational education: government policies in the 1880s, 100–102; growth trends, 106–7

Wagner von Jauregg, Julius, Ritter, 121
Wahrmund, Ludwig, 111–12
Wiener Neustadt: Gymnasium, 66; Realschule, 67
women's advanced education in Austria, 73–75. *See also* girls' *Lyzeen;* students in Austrian universities
World War I, impact on Austrian secondary and higher education, 247
Wretschko, Mathias, 43

Yugoslavia, legacy of imperial Austrian education, 268